Teacher's book

von

Peter Bruck
Sabine Kranz
Petra Schmidt
Friedhold Schmidt
Anja Johannvordersielhorst
Thomas Tepe
T. Lothar Wullen

Ernst Klett Verlag
Stuttgart Düsseldorf Leipzig

Skyline, Advanced Level: Ausgabe C – Teacher's book

Herausgegeben von
Dr. Peter Bruck, Sabine Kranz, Petra Schmidt, Friedhold Schmidt, Anja Johannvordersielhorst,
Thomas Tepe, T. Lothar Wullen.

Die Werkteile von **Skyline, Advanced Level: Ausgabe C** im Überblick
- **Schülerbuch** 3-12-510470-x
- **Teacher's book** 3-12-510471-8
- Eine **CD** mit ausgewählten Texten und Liedern und den Hörverstehenstexten 3-12-510472-6
- Eine **Videokassette** 3-12-510473-4
- Eine **DVD** (inhaltsidentisch mit der Videokassette) 3-12-510474-2

1. Auflage   1 ⁶ 5 4 3 2 | 2009 08 07 06 05

Alle Drucke dieser Auflage können im Unterricht nebeneinander benutzt werden, sie sind untereinander
unverändert. Die letzte Zahl bezeichnet das Jahr dieses Druckes.
© Ernst Klett Verlag GmbH, Stuttgart 2004. Alle Rechte vorbehalten.
Das Werk und seine Teile sind urheberrechtlich geschützt. Jede Nutzung in anderen als den gesetzlich
zugelassenen Fällen bedarf der vorherigen schriftlichen Einwilligung des Verlages. Hinweis zu § 52 a UrhG:
Weder das Werk noch seine Teile dürfen ohne eine solche Einwilligung eingescannt und in ein Netzwerk
eingestellt werden. Dies gilt auch für Intranets von Schulen und sonstigen Bildungseinrichtungen.
Internetadresse: http://www.klett.de

Redaktion: Helen Smyth

Umschlaggestaltung: Nikolaus Keller, Stuttgart; Christian Dekelver, Weingarten
Reproduktion: Meyle + Müller Medien-Management, Pforzheim
Druck: Gutmann + Co. GmbH, Talheim
Printed in Germany.
ISBN 3-12-510471-8

Contents

Living the Dream

Didaktisches Inhaltsverzeichnis mit Einleitung 6
The immigrant story [collage] 7
An Amazing Journey [*US News & World Report*] 8
Being illegal in the US [film] 8
Mexico is memory [non-fiction] 9
Stuck in the middle [*TIME Asia*] 9
Making it Big in America [*Money*] 10
The United States of Anger [travelogue] 11
The dawning of a new millennium [speech] 12
The darkest day [speech] 13
A time to celebrate [*US News & World Report*] 14
The essence of the American Dream
[radio feature] 15
Los Vendidos [short play] 16
Using your skills: Forrest Gump 18
Tests – Suggested answers 18

Kopiervorlagen
Kernwortschatz 20
An immigrant on Ellis Island 21
The modern immigrant's story 22
Listening comprehension: The dawning of a new millennium 23
Listening comprehension: The essence of the American Dream 23
Using your skills: Forrest Gump – model scene profile 24
Test: Our rainbow underclass
[*US News & World Report*] 25
Test: Ambition and its enemies [*Newsweek*] 26
Mündliche Prüfung: A nation of immigrants
[novel] 27

Cultural mix and clash – UK

Didaktisches Inhaltsverzeichnis mit Einleitung 28
Britain as a multicultural society [collage] 29
England was a peculiar-tasting smoked fish [novel] 29
Listen Mr Oxford Don [poem] 31
Telephone conversation [poem] 32
Ghettos in the north [*The Guardian*] 33
The Indian who thought he was English [poem] 34
Multicultural Britain [fact file] 35
Do you think anybody is English?
Really English? [novel] 35
Using your skills: Reading a novel: *White Teeth* 36
A new understanding of Britishness [speech] 36
Multiculturalism – a recipe for racism [*The Guardian*] 39
Tests – Suggested answers 39
Selected bibliography 41

Kopiervorlagen
Mündliche Prüfung: Neighbours [poem] 42
Kernwortschatz 43
Role play 44
Talking about immigration 44
Listening comprehension: A new understanding of Britishness 45
Immigration in the UK – a timeline 46
Test: A Distant Shore [novel] 47
Test: Bogus friends of asylum seekers
[*The Guardian*] 48

First Peoples

Einleitung 49
Didaktisches Inhaltsverzeichnis – Aborigines 49
Images of Aborigines [collage] 50
The Songlines [travelogue] 50
Land [poem extract] 51
Please don't climb our rock [*The Guardian*] 51
Mourning closes Ayers Rock [*The Guardian*] 51
Child of the stolen generation [personal account] 52
Over to you: Australian reconciliation off the cards
[*The Guardian*] 52
Using your skills: *Angela:* Growing up in Australia 53
Tests – Suggested answers 54
Didaktisches Inhaltsverzeichnis – Maoris 55
Being Maori [collage] 55
The Treaty of Waitangi [historic document] 56
Ngati Kangaru [short story extract] 57
The Pakeha judge's antlers on the wall
[short story extract] 58
Waitangi Day with gritted teeth
[*New Zealand Herald*] 59
After all, we're one people, aren't we? from Waitangi Day
to New Zealand Day [*New Zealand Herald*] 59
**Didaktisches Inhaltsverzeichnis –
Native Americans** 60
Native American past and present [collage] 60
My country, 'tis of thy people you're dying [song] 60
Indian education [short story extract] 62
Voices of the Navajo [documentary] 63
Getting rich with the casino tribes [*The Independent*] 65
Over to you: Indians hear a high-tech drumbeat
[*The Christian Science Monitor*] 66
Over to you: First peoples 66

Kopiervorlagen
Kernwortschatz: Aborigines 67
Over to you: Australian reconciliation off the cards 68
Mündliche Prüfung: Living life on the edge
[*The Guardian*] 68
Test: Fenced out [*Guardian Unlimited*] 69
Test: Living life on the edge [*The Guardian*] 70
Climbing Uluru 71
Kernwortschatz: Maoris / Native Americans 73
The Treaty of Waitangi 74
Over to you: Indians hear a high-tech drumbeat 75
Listening comprehension: My country 'tis of
thy people you're dying 76

Focus on The Matrix

Didaktisches Inhaltsverzeichnis mit Einleitung 77
First impressions [photo] 78
Understanding the plot [plot puzzle] 78
The future world [screenplay] 78
How real is reality? [screenplay] 79
Characterization: Who am I? [screenplay] 79
Neo – a second Christ? [screenplay] 80
Cinematic devices [screenplay] 80

3

Contents

We love you, Keanu! [film review] 81
Over to you: The Matrix – our future
[commentary] 82
Tests – Suggested answers 83
Selected bibliography 84

🗐 Kopiervorlagen
Kernwortschatz 85
More on *The Matrix* 85
Over to you: The Matrix – our future 86
Test: Matrix films blamed for series of murders by obsessed fans [*The Guardian*] 86
Test: The Matrix Reloaded [*The Independent*] 87
Mündliche Prüfung: Neo meets the Architect
[film script] 88

Barriers and bridges

Didaktisches Inhaltsverzeichnis mit Einleitung 89
Pictures in our heads [photo] 90
🎞 If only we all played cricket [documentary] 91
Using your skills: The ambassadors' game 92
The Germans throw in the towel [*The Daily Mail*] 92
Auf wiedersehen, with great respect
[*Electronic Telegraph*] 93
Britain and Europe [speech] 95
Using your skills: Advertising a German product
abroad 96
Making fun of it all [screenplay] 96
Over to you: Culture shock Asia [travel guide] 97
Using your skills: Working abroad 98
Tests – Suggested answers 98

🗐 Kopiervorlagen
Adjectives for characterization 100
Kernwortschatz 101
Role cards for the ambassadors' game 102
Planning a chat show / panel discussion 103
Survival role card for a guest 104
Moderator role card 105
Reduced role card: guest 106
Evaluation sheet for adverts / commercials 107
Useful vocabulary to evaluate a presentation 108
Test: Why Germans love the British
[*Daily Telegraph*] 109
Test: Germans – the new Americans?
[travelogue] 110
Mündliche Abschlussprüfung zu
"Barriers and Bridges" 111
Mündliche Prüfung: Germans 'take too many
holidays' 112
On the phone 113
The world of work 114

Facing a global future

Didaktisches Inhaltsverzeichnis mit Einleitung 115
Building a dream [advert] 116
🎞 Robots [documentary] 117
Surefire predictions [non-fiction] 118
Professor Cyborg [salon.com] 119

Shopping for humans [*The Guardian*] 120
The brave new world of "Gattaca" [film review] 120
🎞 Forests for life [commercial] 121
The view from Ghana [commentary] 122
What happens if you drink GM coffee [advert] 123
🎞 The challenge of change [speech] 124
🔊 Globalization – the key issues [statement] 125
The other side of the global village [non-fiction] 127
Over to you: Globalization [*National Geographic*] 127
Tests – Suggested answers 129

🗐 Kopiervorlagen
Kernwortschatz: Genetic engineering 132
Kernwortschatz: Globalization 133
Test: (You)^2 – You Again [*Wired Magazine*] 134
Test: How would we feel if blind women claimed
the right to a blind baby? [*The Guardian*] 135
Mündliche Prüfung: The ever-growing presence of the
US culture industry [non-fiction] 136
Over to you: Globalization 136
🔊 Listening comprehension: Globalization –
the key issues 137
Global research 138
Presenting a company profile 139
Globalization: Work practices in
developing countries 140

Shakespeare & love

Didaktisches Inhaltsverzeichnis mit Einleitung 141
🔊 Shakespeare's words [quotes] 143
Shakespeare and his times [fact file] 143
🎞 Shakespeare's early years [documentary] 144
Elizabethan England [fact file] 144
All the world's a stage – Shakespeare's theatre
[fact file] 145
Shakespeare's love poetry 145
🔊 Sonnet 18 145
🔊 Sonnet 116 146
The world's most famous love story
[plot puzzle] 147
The Prologue 147
The first meeting of the lovers 147
The balcony scene 148
"Farewell, farewell" 149
Using your skills: Projects: Romeo and Juliet 150
Shakespeare in love [screenplay] 150
Shakespeare – man of the Millennium
[*The Telegraph*] 152
🎞 Shakespeare – a great author 153
Using your skills: *Romeo and Juliet* on film 154
The music of love:
🎞 Love is a stranger [music video clip] 154
🎞 All Woman [music video clip] 155
The poetry of modern love 156
🎞 Lessons in love [sketch] 157
The four stages of love [*The Telegraph*] 157
The way of the Wodaabe [non-fiction] 158
Using your skills: Love story: writing a
twenty-minute script 159
Tests – Suggested answers 160

Contents

📋 Kopiervorlagen
Kernwortschatz 162
Participating in a talk show 164
Test: "Shakespeare and love" 164
Shall I compare thee...? 165
Sonnet 116 – a model interpretation 166
Body language 167
Test: All the World's in Love with Shakespeare I
[*The New York Times*] 168
Test: Sonnet 73 169
Test: All the World's in Love with Shakespeare II
[*The New York Times*] 169

City lights

Didaktisches Inhaltsverzeichnis mit Einleitung 170
Aspects of the city [collage] 171
🎧 Out in the city [poem] 171
🎧 New York [song] 171
It's London vs. Britain [*The Observer*] 172
Using your skills: Project: A trip to London 173
🎧 Can you hear me at the back? [play] 173
Using your skills: Project: A talk on improving your town 174
The Language of the Streets [non-fiction] 174
The Cabbie from Calcutta [short play] 175
Using your skills: Projects 177
Power to the cities [*Newsweek*] 177
Los Angeles sprawl bumps angry neighbor
[*The New York Times*] 178
Why I live where I live [non-fiction] 179
Tests – Suggested answers 179
📼 A bad dream [sketch] 180

📋 Kopiervorlagen
Kernwortschatz 182
🎧 Listening comprehension: New York 183
Project: A week in New York City 183
Test: Why my plan for London will work
[*The Observer*] 184
Test: Big City Glissando [poem] 185
A bad dream 186
Viewing log assessment 187
Discussion: moderation rules 188
Discussion: feedback rules 189

Abkürzungen und Symbole in diesem Werk

cf.	compare, see
GA	Gruppenarbeit
KV	Kopiervorlage(n)
L	Lehrerin(-nen) und Lehrer
M	Moderatorin / Moderator
p. / pp.	page / pages
PA	Partnerarbeit
S	Schülerin(-nen) und Schüler
S.	Seite / Seiten
SB / TB	Student's / Teacher's book
s.o. / s.th.	someone, something
S-page	Strategy page

■ Symbol (auch im SB verwendet), um mögliche pre- / post-reading activities zu kennzeichnen.

👁 Informationen zum Bildmaterial

🎧 Symbol zeigt, dass der Text sich auf der Begleit-CD befindet.

📼 Symbol zeigt, dass die Sequenz sich auf der Begleit-DVD bzw. auf dem Begleit-Video befindet.

Living the dream

Didaktisches Inhaltsverzeichnis

	Titel	Textsorte (Wortzahl ca.)	Thema	Text- und Spracharbeit	Textproduktion (schriftlich / mündlich)
	The immigrant… SB S. 6, TB S. 7 TB S. 20, 21, 22	photo collage	immigration: myth and reality	collect ideas about the aspirations of immigrants	speculate about photos • collect vocabulary
	An Amazing… SB S. 7, TB S. 8	expository text (1,182 words)	immigration in 1900 and 2000	analyse pie / bar charts • describe signs of success • define being an American • describe expectations	comparative analysis of statistics • discuss an attitude
📺	Being illegal… SB S. 9, TB S. 8	feature film extract	illegal immigration	scene analysis: interpret script, characters, camera work	act out a scene
	Mexico is memory SB S. 10, TB S. 9	expository text (980 words)	effects of emigration on Mexico	assess the effects of mass emigration • characterize the US • personification • summarize an opinion	discuss the influence of American culture
	Stuck in the… SB S. 12, TB S. 9	human interest story (930 words)	identity of third-generation Amerasian	summarize facts • describe/analyse s.o.'s background	discuss problems of assimilation and integration • compare texts
	Making it Big… SB S. 14, TB S. 10	career profiles (965 words)	how to succeed in America	summarize • evaluate career profiles • assess the American success myth, compare with Europe, agree/disagree	give career advice • list factors leading to success • rank factors in order of importance • write an introduction
	The United States of Anger SB S. 16, TB S. 11	human interest story (945 words)	failure in America	interpret meaning of 'American Dream' • describe an individual • compare texts • agree/disagree • lexical fields: 'success', 'failure'	speculate about a book title • compare texts/situations in US and Europe • act out a conversation
🔊	The dawning… SB S. 17, TB S. 12 TB S. 23	speech (760 words)	America on the brink of a new millennium	listen for key words • summarize ideas • find rhetorical devices	predict key words • evaluate wording of speech
	The darkest day SB S. 18, TB S. 13	speech (905 words)	September 11 terrorist attack	speculate about a role • interpret and give one's opinion of the text • talk about rhetorical analysis	suggest a memorial • talking about a cartoon
	A time to celebrate SB S. 20, TB S. 14	editorial (780 words)	US self-image: celebration of American ideals	summarize ideas • analyse criticism/a quote	talk about a photo/national holiday, give an opinion • agree/disagree
🔊	The essence… SB S. 21, TB S. 15 TB S. 23	radio feature (600 words)	the re-invention of the American Dream	complete sentences • explain a quote	think of key words • compare the feature and a text
	Los Vendidos SB S. 22, TB S. 16	play (3,100 words)	stereotype views of Hispanic immigrants	discuss use of Spanish • analyse criticism, short plays, dialogue • identify key speeches	discuss stereotyping
Using your skills	Forrest Gump SB S. 30, TB S. 18 TB S. 24	film extracts	scene profile, key scenes, viewing log, trailer	analyse opening scene	write the director's commentary • identify key scenes, develop scene profiles • create a viewing log • develop a trailer

Living the Dream

Einleitung

Von jeher werden mit den Vereinigten Staaten Vorstellungen verknüpft, die um Begriffe wie Gleichheit, Freiheit, Glück und Erfolg kreisen. Diese Vorstellungskomplexe, die nicht nur Teil des amerikanischen Selbstverständnisses sind, sondern auch die stark klischeehaften Visionen prospektiver Einwanderer widerspiegeln, bilden eine wesentliche Grundlage dessen, was als 'American Dream' bezeichnet wird.

Eine weitere Bedeutungskomponente, die charakteristisches Merkmal des amerikanischen Selbstverständnisses ist, betrifft den Glauben an einen Messianismus, an den Auftrag der amerikanischen Nation, die Menschheit in politischer, sozialer und ökonomischer Hinsicht zu erlösen. Letzteres begründet zugleich den globalen Führungsanspruch der Weltmacht USA und rechtfertigt aus amerikanischer Sicht diesen Anspruch.

Die Attraktivität der USA als Einwanderungsland ist auch im 21. Jahrhundert ungebrochen. Auffällig ist in diesem Zusammenhang die ethnische Verschiebung der Einwanderungsströme. An der Spitze der Einwanderer stehen Latein-Amerikaner, gefolgt von Asiaten.

Der Text "An Amazing Journey" (SB S. 7–9) stellt Einwandererfahrung im New York von 1900 vor und vergleicht diese mit den heutigen Lebensbedingungen im gleichen East Side Viertel. Darüber hinaus verdeutlicht der Text, dass es immer eine hohe Rückwanderungsquote gegeben hat (die nicht in das gängige Klischee passt). Nicht jeder Einwanderer wurde ein Teil des American Dream.

Die Sogkraft der Vereinigten Staaten auf potentielle Einwanderer hat auch Schattenseiten für die Länder, die einen Teil der erwerbsfähigen Bevölkerung verlieren. So zeigt der Text "Mexico is memory" (SB S. 10–11) nicht nur die Entvölkerung mexikanischer Dörfern sondern beschreibt auch die vom Autor als negativ bewerteten kulturellen Einflüsse der USA auf Mexiko.

Eine eher parodistische Perspektive auf die Einwanderung stellt der Einakter "Los Vendidos" (SB S. 22–29) bereit, der mit amerikanischen Klischeevorstellungen von Mexikanern spielt und diese als rassistisch zu entlarven sucht.

Die Teilsequenz Immigration wird beschlossen durch den autobiographischen Bericht einer Chinese-American ("Stuck in the middle", SB S. 12–13). Die Autorin vergleicht die Migrationserfahrung des Urgroßvaters mit der eigenen Akkulturation und berichtet von der Notwendigkeit, einen Teil des chinesischen Erbes zu bewahren.

Die zweite Teilsequenz ist dem Thema 'success and failure' gewidmet. Der Text "Making it Big in America" (SB S. 14–15) steht in der Tradition des von Benjamin Franklin kreierten 'do-it-yourself'-Typus, der den Traum vom individuellen Glück verkörpert. Die zwei Lebensläufe, die beschrieben werden, machen deutlich, dass Lebenserfolg nicht nur von Leistungsbereitschaft abhängig ist, sondern dass Eigeninitiative, Risikobereitschaft sowie die Bereitschaft zur ständigen Veränderung der eigenen Berufsbiographie wesentliche Voraussetzungen dafür sind, in sozialer wie ökonomischer Hinsicht aufzusteigen.

Der Bericht des britischen Journalisten Gavin Esler "The United States of Anger", (SB S. 16–17), zeigt, dass Misserfolg auch ein Mittelklassephänomen ist; er zeigt überdies, dass es kein soziales Netz gibt, das einen Arbeitslosen auffängt, und er verdeutlicht die Ängste der Betroffenen, die befürchten (müssen), an der Wohlstandsentwicklung nicht teilhaben zu können.

Die dritte Teilsequenz lässt sich am ehesten unter dem Stichwort 'American self-images' zusammenfassen. Der frühere Bürgermeister von New York, Rudolph Giuliani, greift in seiner Gedenkrede zum Anschlag am 11. September 2001 ("The darkest day", SB S. 18–19) auf zahlreiche patriotische Topoi zurück und benutzt sie zur Beschwörung amerikanischer Werte und deren messianischer Verbreitung.

Der ungekürzte Leitartikel des Chefredakteurs der Zeitschrift *US News & World Report* ("A time to celebrate", SB S. 20–21) fasst abschließend das Fortwirken des American Dream im öffentlichen Raum beispielhaft zusammen. Mortimer Zuckerman betont die ungebrochene Attraktivität der USA für den Rest der Welt und führt diese Anziehungskraft auf die Strahlkraft des American Dream zurück, dessen unterschiedliche Bedeutungskomponenten er affirmativ diskutiert.

Der Hörverstehenstext "The essence of the American Dream" (SB S. 21) fasst noch einmal wesentliche Bedeutungskomponenten zusammen und eignet sich besonders zur Festigung und Vertiefung des im Verlauf der Unterrichtsarbeit erworbenen thementypischen Vokabulars.

Der Film *Forrest Gump*, der den Aufstiegs- und Erfolgsmythos verkörpert, beschließt die Unterrichtsreihe (SB S. 30–31). Die Arbeit mit dem Film ist als S aktivierendes Vorhaben angelegt, in dem es neben der Analyse der üblichen filmsprachlichen Elemente um die eigenständige Erarbeitung von Schlüsselszenen, der zentralen Figuren sowie der Bezüge zum American Dream geht.

The immigrant story   SB S. 6

Looking and thinking

■ **Speculate about photos**

Mögliche Antworten:
The top photo shows the fate of Hispanic migrant workers; when it is set against the second photo, it is clear that the immigrants' chances of success are slim; the top photo underlines the need for cheap, unskilled labour in the US and it also suggests that migrant workers have no choice but to accept menial work.

The bottom photo shows the view of the Manhattan skyline from Ellis Island. The immigrant family is probably longing to leave the island (incoming immigrants were processed on the island before being admitted into the US). Depending on their reasons for leaving their home country, their hopes and aspirations will have centred around the new political or religious freedom or the possibility of finding a job and making money.

■ **Collect vocabulary**
Siehe Kernwortschatz auf Seite 20 für Ideen.

Living the dream

Kopiervorlage: An immigrant on Ellis Island, TB S. 21

Das Worksheet (TB S. 21) dient als Raster zum Festhalten von Informationen. Die S sollten ihre Ergebnisse auf einem Extrablatt in ein 'eyewitness report' umschreiben.
Wichtig bei dieser kreativen Aufgabe ist es, dass die S nicht nur den Inhalt der Webseite prüfen und Informationen ausfiltern, sondern auch möglichst Eindrücke und Erfahrungen eines Immigranten anhand der vielen Fenster und Fotos beschreiben. Einige Informationen können in Form von 'reported speech' wiedergegeben werden.

Kopiervorlage: The modern immigrant's story, TB S. 22

Das Worksheet auf TB S. 22 bietet die Möglichkeit die Erfahrungen von drei Immigranten kennen zu lernen. Da die online präsentierten Beispiele sich zwangsläufig ändern, wird im Worksheet auf konkrete Namensnennungen, usw. verzichtet.

An Amazing Journey SB S. 7–9

Before you read

■ **Analyse pie charts**

1900: living alone, D; households headed by a married couple, C; people living in big households, A; share of income spent on food, B
2000: living alone, C; households headed by a married couple, B; people living in big households, A; share of income spent on food, D

Exploring the text

1 a) In 1900, making it in America meant firstly that all family members survived and the children found jobs to help the family get by. If the family did very well, the children did not need to work and attended school instead. Hence a family made it if it survived in the new country and was able to provide the children with a better future.
b) Julius Streicher is an example of s.o. who ultimately did not succeed. Within the space of 35 years he went from being a self-employed store owner to an unskilled factory worker. Nor did he manage to acquire American citizenship. The text also gives statistics about immigration in the early 20th century. Mention is made of a large percentage of Europeans who returned to their native countries.
2 First and foremost, being an American today means living in an urban area and possibly coming from a mixed racial background. It can also mean having access to social and economic opportunities such as a good education and a well-paying job. Many Americans live alone, and those living with partners often do not get married. People have fewer children and they normally have them later in life. As the example of Harvey Weissman shows, an American is defined as s.o. who is optimistic and flexible.
3 Harvey Weissman no longer aspires to middle-class values such as owning a house and having a family. The pursuit of his own aims, i.e. building an acting career and enjoying life on his own, are more important to him.

Close-up: statistics

■ **Analyse bar charts**

a) The chart shows a decisive shift in the origin of immigrants from European countries to Mexico and Asia, the Philippines and India in particular. Immigration from Russia is still quite significant.
b) –

Webseite: Germany immigration statistics

Contact the Federal Statistical Office of Germany:
www.destatis.de/e_home.htm or
Postal address: 65180 Wiesbaden, Germany.
Compare the data on the foreign population in Germany with the bar charts on SB page 9.

A step further

■ **Describe expectations**

Harvey Weissman clearly displays initiative as he is not afraid to change careers: he gave up a secure, well-paid job in order to become an actor. It should also be noted that he retrains on his own initiative without financial support from a public body. He is also self-reliant as he learns to enjoy life alone.

Being illegal in the US SB S. 9

Transkript

SAM: What's this? What is this?
MAYA: Don't you even remember?
SAM: No, I'll see in the morning.
MAYA: You left it in the basement and Peres found it. The supervisor.
SAM: Oh, no. Oh, no.
MAYA: Have you any idea what it's like to have this guy in our back? Can I ask you something? What do you risk? How much do you get paid?
SAM: $22,250. … So what happened? Are you fired?
MAYA: No, they fired Berta.
SAM: Shit!
MAYA: They wanted to know who organized the meeting but she wouldn't tell him so…
SAM: I feel really stupid, okay, I feel, I don't know … I fucked up.
MAYA: I know that. She has all her family in El Salvador and sending her money, all her money, for them, since seventeen years ago. She was saving the money for her daughter's wedding. She has not seen her for five years.
SAM: I'm sorry. Easy, easy. We're going to work it out, I'll work something out. You want a drink? I don't know what else to offer you. I'm sorry.
MAYA: Yes, thanks.
SAM: Okay, because I need one.

Living the Dream

Exploring the scene

1 Sam is a labour union representative, whose salary is paid by the union. He neither risks being fired nor does he risk being caught as an illegal immigrant by the police.

2 Berta is from San Salvador. She has been supporting her family back home for seventeen years so she is utterly dependent on her cleaning job. She was saving up for her daughter's wedding. Berta has not seen her for five years.

3 The camera moves from Sam to Maya and back again during the first half of the scene. We are mainly shown Sam's reactions from Maya's point of view in over-the-shoulder shots. In the second half of the scene, the focus is on Maya and we see her in a static, close-up, which clearly conveys her strong feelings. We only hear Sam in a voiceover.

4 The scene ends with Sam leaving the room, thus marking the end of the confrontation. The scene has come to a climax with Maya's outburst of feeling, and the natural break in the conversation, signalled by Sam's departure to the kitchen, opens the way for a possibly more harmonious scene as the two characters have a drink.

Zusätzliche Aufgabe

> ■ Watch the scene again. Make a note of the grammatical mistakes Maya makes and then try to correct them.
> E.g. Maya says of Berta, "She … sends her money, all her money, for them, since seventeen years ago." What she should have said was, "She has been sending them all of her money for seventeen years."

A step further

■ **Act out a scene**

Mögliche Hinweise an S: Berta has lost her job because of Sam's carelessness. She could be angry with Maya for going to see Sam and for inviting the union to meet the cleaners in the first place. Maya cannot really console her. She could say that the union might be able to help Berta in some way.
Die S sollten sich vor einer melodramatisch-kitschigen Annäherung hüten und die Tatsache berücksichtigen, dass es keine einfache Lösung für Bertas verzweifelte Situation gibt.

Mexico is memory
SB S. 10–11

Before you read

■ **Discuss the influence of American culture**

E.g. American TV series, Hollywood films and products such as Coca Cola, Levi's or McDonalds' hamburgers have become global phenomena. TV series, in particular, shape our understanding of many aspects of life in the US. Sometimes, some aspects such as courtroom situations are mistakenly applied to Germany.

Zusätzliche Aufgabe

> a) Check a TV guide to work out the percentage of American productions shown on German channels on any one day.
> b) What impression do the programmes give of life in America?

Exploring the text

1 Rodriguez basically mentions two types of effects. First he points out the attraction the US has for many Mexicans. The US is seen as a better place to live than Mexico as it offers job opportunities and a high standard of living ("Mexico has watched many more of her children … head north for work, for wages; north for life", ll. 32–34). This prosperous view of the US is primarily created by television and films and it is not necessarily correct: "Mexicans know very little of the United States, though they have seen America the TV show, and America, the movie" (ll. 18–19).
Secondly, the stereotyped images Mexicans have of the US have led to the exodus of the younger generation and the depopulation of Mexican villages. Hence, traditions are destroyed completely or replaced by American values.

2 The US is seen first and foremost as an economic haven that has cast a spell on Mexico with its promise of affluence. Thus, Mexican villages live with the rumour about America and the economic and social opportunities it supposedly offers. By extension, the US is seen in materialistic terms (cf. the reference to consumer goods in ll. 15–16).
On another level, the US is viewed as a destructive force. It is said to "imperil" (l. 4) the lives of Mexicans. It exposes them to conditions they are not prepared for ("an industry, an optimism, a solitude", ll. 22–23). The US ruthlessly exploits its attraction by using Mexicans as a source of cheap labour.
The destructive force exerted by the US is further emphasized by phrases such as "tide" (l. 48) and "polluted with gringo optimism" (l. 49), which indicate Mexico's powerlessness. This force is also seen in phrases such as "unclean enchantments of the gringo" (l. 71) which here refer to the different music, sexual standards and drug use; the enumeration signals the dominant nature of American culture and life style, which Mexicans have surrendered to.

3 The US and Mexico are personified in the text. By using this device, the writer achieves a twofold effect. Mexico is associated with a female and the exodus of Mexican males is seen as a kind of adultery: Mexico becomes the one who has been left behind ("so many left her for the gringo", l. 34).
Conversely, by associating the US with a male, the writer underlines the strength and power of that country.
On another level, the use of personification suggests that both countries are linked as closely as a married couple. However, it should be pointed out that each country is given a distinct role: while the Mexican is submissive, the American takes on the role of the dominant partner. This distribution of roles underlines the inequality of the countries' relationship.

4 The writer takes a very pessimistic view of Mexico's future. He conveys the impression that Mexico has no future as it is losing its identity and traditions (cf. "What influence shall she have? The village is international now", ll. 74–75). The young people who are left behind cannot remember what Mexico used to be like before mass migration began (l. 79).

Stuck in the middle
SB S. 12–13

Before you read

■ **Discuss problems of assimilation and integration**

a) Whereas the first generation faced problems such as finding a job, securing the family's livelihood in the US and

Living the dream

learning the language, their children often have identity problems. The young people tend to ignore the ethnic traditions their parents value and submerge themselves in American culture and morals.
b) Parents often have mixed feelings. On the one hand, they are proud of their children, particularly if they complete school successfully. On the other hand, they realize that their children are somehow alienated from them as they become more American and leave their parents' traditions and values behind.

Exploring the text

1 At the turn of the century, Chinese immigrants in the US faced discrimination and racism (cf. ll. 12–20). They were not allowed to marry whites or become American citizens. In California, they were not allowed to own property. Worst of all, they had no constitutional rights (cf. ll. 15–17) and were targeted for violent attacks by white people.
2 a) The writer has a truly mixed-raced background. She is only one-eighth Chinese, the remaining seven-eighths stem from various Caucasian ancestors from different European countries. In this respect, she embodies multi-racial America.
b) Lisa See wants to draw attention to the fact that even though she is a third-generation American she has retained a Chinese 'core' and is loyal to a particular cultural group, namely to the one she grew up in (ll. 31–32).
3 On the one hand, it could be said that she is assimilated into mainstream America. On the other hand, she is acutely aware of being different from Caucasian Americans and occasionally faces quite negative reactions or even latent racism (cf. ll. 45–52). She has intentionally held on to some Chinese traditions and cherishes them. Thus the title of the text, "Stuck in the middle", may be taken to mean that Lisa is caught between two identities: unlike her forefathers, she is both biologically and culturally assimilated into white America, and unlike her sons, she makes sure that she maintains her ethnic background and is not absorbed into mainstream (Caucasian/white) America.

A step further

■ Choosing a cultural identity

Mögliche Hinweise:
- 9% of the population of Germany is foreign born;
- the large majority of foreign-born nationals come from outside the EU.

Mögliche Diskussionsanlässe

> ■ To what extent should immigrants who are living in Germany try to retain their customs and traditions?
> ■ How would you define being a 'German'?

■ Compare texts

	Chinese immigrants	Mexican immigrants
Similarities	– were lured to the US with the promise of work	– were lured to the US with the promise of work
	– started at the bottom of the ladder with menial jobs, e.g. Lisa See's grandfather made underwear	– also started at the bottom of the ladder e.g. Mexicans work as gardeners, nannies or cooks
Differences	– were victims of racism and discrimination in the past	– racism is not mentioned in relation to Mexicans
	– China has not been subjected to cultural colonization by the US	– Mexico has been subjected to cultural colonization by the US
	– The main influx of immigrants to the US took place in the past: Chinese immigrants intermarried and assimilated with the Caucasian population.	– Mexicans influence the way of life, and particularly the language, in the Southwest US; they have strong ties to Mexico and intend to return there.

Making it Big in America SB S. 14–15

Before you read

■ Give career advice
E.g. He/she should think of hobbies that they enjoy, (training) courses they have completed or skills which could be useful in starting a new career, the job centre (Arbeitsamt) gives advice about career prospects in different areas. He or she should check websites such as www.monster.de for detailed careers advice as well as vacancies.
Hinweis an S: Job centres which advise unemployed people as well as providing them with financial support, such as unemployment benefit, do not exist in the US.

■ List factors leading to success
People: Arnold Schwarzenegger, Bill Gates, Jennifer Lopez, Madonna…
Factors: popularity with an audience, shows initiative, takes risks, has a good (public relations) manager…

Exploring the text

1 The first heading suggests that the text which follows will be about successful people. It is like a recipe for success.
- The second heading gives more detail about one aspect of the 'recipe'. It refers to the fact that one can overcome social disadvantages.
- The third heading suggests that showing initiative, and a willingness to take risks and switch careers are important steps towards professional success.

2 a) *Mögliches Tafelbild:*

	José Gaitán	Mike Hernacki
Background	– disadvantaged social background (father: illegal immigrant from San Salvador, mother: a heroin addict)	– son of Polish immigrants – is from a working-class background
Career	– good grades at school – scholarship to a private college – earns a law degree – works as a prosecutor – establishes his own law firm → relies on his ambition, resources and competence	– attains a bachelor's degree – goes on to get a law degree – works as a stock-broker – now works as a freelance writer → displays a high degree of mobility and adaptability
Characteristics in common	self-made men; both are upwardly mobile	

b) The texts are like personality profiles in a magazine or in a manual on how to be successful.

Background information

The self-help book was first championed by Benjamin Franklin (1706–1790), American writer, philosopher and scientist. He strongly believed in self-improvement and gave advice on how to lead a successful life.

3 The writer claims that access to higher education in Europe, and Germany in particular, is not easy and a distinct class consciousness prevents both career and upward social mobility in Europe. She seems to think that success is based mainly on one's ancestry or having inherited wealth.
Agree: The writer is correct in her observation that uncommon career changes are highly unusual in Germany. Normally people's careers follow established patterns.
Disagree: The writer's attitude towards Europe and/or Germany is both clichéd and dated.

A step further

■ **Rank factors in order of importance**
Equal educational opportunities, openness to immigrants, easy access to higher education, upward mobility as opposed to class consciousness and acceptance of frequent career changes.
Ranking: –

■ **Write an introduction**
Mögliche Hinweise: Mike Hernacki would probably use superlatives, an optimistic tone and a can-do-attitude to highlight his experiences. Use imperative (negative) forms, e.g. "Don't do …" and conditional clauses ("If you do …, you will …") to give advice and instructions.

The United States of Anger
SB S. 16–17

Before you read

■ **Speculate about a book title**
Book title: The writer is taking a very critical look at the US and the American Dream. He writes about people who are angry because they are not successful.
Mögliche Ideen: The promises of the American Dream often excluded/still exclude ethnic minorities; not everyone is making it in America, and there are millions of jobless people who are angry at their inability to find employment/support their families/break the cycle of poverty.

Exploring the text

1 a) Gavin Esler uses the term to describe the reality of the American Dream in the 1990s.
Mögliches Tafelbild:

Reality of the American Dream in the 1990s
– The writer personifies the term in an ironic way (Hinweis auf "My appointment with the American Dream", l. 1)
– It is losing its momentum as an ideal for the middle classes (Hinweis auf "nowhere is there such a sense that the Dream is fading as there is for the middle-class Americans", ll. 50–51)
– Optimism and a belief in the ability to improve one's situation have been replaced by pessimism and doubt (Hinweis auf "opinion polls … better off", ll. 48–49)
– Pioneer ideals take on a new meaning as people are being forced to uproot and start afresh (Hinweis auf ll. 44–45.)

b) The Morins' ideals include living in a house which they built themselves (cf. ll. 21–22) and succeeding through hard work (cf. ll. 47–48). Ideally, they should do better than their parents and their daughter should do even better again.
The idea of the American Dream provides the Morins with a feeling of security; it is almost like a religious dogma. They cling to the ideals they grew up with (ll. 25–26).
2 Gavin Esler shows Claude Morin to be a strong, rugged individual (ll. 4–5) and places him in the pioneer tradition (cf. "with the enthusiasm of a pioneer", l. 39). However this tradition is no longer valid and Claude is left trying to understand the world: he is portrayed as being angry and desperate (ll. 14–16). The writer's description shows Claude to be appealing and idealistic. He is prepared to "uproot … to pursue the American Dream" (ll. 65–66).
3 In contrast to the examples set out in the text, "Making it Big in America", the Morins have not shown that they are either mobile or willing to take the initiative to change their lives. The adaptability displayed by Mike Hernacki in the previous text emphasizes aspects such as the willingness to retrain and reinvent himself as well as the ability to rely on his own resources. Gavin Esler seems to suggest that this is precisely what the Morins lack: they hold onto their version of the American Dream even after all hope is gone.
4 *Mögliche Diskussionspunkte:*
Siehe Tabelle auf TB, S. 12.

Living the dream

Europe	Comments
– Europeans benefit from public health systems and do not understand American anxieties about becoming ill (l. 32).	– The state is responsible for its citizens' needs.
– Europeans are worried that the next generation will not be better off than the present one (ll. 49–50).	– People rely on the social welfare system when they are unemployed, i.e. they expect state intervention.
US	**Comments**
– Not everyone is covered by a health insurance system (ll. 35–37).	– The social welfare system does not automatically provide for s.o.'s needs.
– Not only do Americans worry about the future of the next generation, the present middle class is also worried about its own future as hard work does not automatically lead to financial security (ll. 50–51).	– Self-help: The unemployed are expected to help themselves to get back into full-time employment. (In the 1990s, states such as California and Wisconsin introduced "welfare-to-work" programmes aimed at making welfare recipients more employable.)

Close-up: vocabulary

Making it: the home the family built themselves (l. 22); we have lived the American Dream (l. 28); he chose the land, cleared the trees ... fathers and cousins (ll. 39–42); He and Ann Marie still dared to believe that they might do better than their parents and that three-year-old Mary could do even better still (ll. 46–47).
Not making it: much needed cash (l. 10); wife is the sole breadwinner (l. 15); panic, running out of options (l. 16); dead end, lose the log cabin (ll. 20–21); desperation (l. 22); the Dream ... crumbles (l. 24); to lose a job in the United States ... means to lose health insurance (l. 33); the Dream is fading ... for middle class Americans (ll. 50–51); problems with bill collectors (ll. 55–56); filing for personal bankruptcy (l. 57).

A step further

■ **Act out a conversation**
The discussion should centre around the painful decision whether to sell the log cabin, of which they are so proud, and to move south where job prospects are better.
Die S sollen Pro und Kontra Argumente im Text finden.
Mögliche Rollen:
– Claude Morin is desperate because he is afraid of losing the house and worried he will not find a job in the area.
– Ann Marie Morin thinks that there is still a chance for them if they just wait a while.

Projects

■ Read Benjamin Franklin's "Advice to a Young Tradesman" in *The American Dream: Past and Present*, (ISBN 3-12-513610-5) Stuttgart: Klett 15. Druck 2003, pp. 32–33.
Write a comment in which you outline Benjamin Franklin's attitude towards self-help and improvement and respond with your own point of view. (cf. Skills file, "Comments" on page 188 of your book.)
■ Write a summary of Arnold Schwarzenegger's career as an actor and politician in which you analyse his rise to success. You could use search machines such as www.google.de and read the interview with Arnold Schwarzenegger in Studs Terkel's, *American Dreams: Lost & Found*. New York: Pantheon Books, 1980, pp. 126–129. The book is available via interlibrary loan.
■ Watch the film *Death of a Salesman* and work out the reasons for the failure of Willy Loman, of his sons and the clichés they believed in.

Talking about the photo S. 17

E.g. Man in a suit: My dream would be to find a job as a manager again but it is difficult to enter a company at managerial level, especially if you were laid off by your last employer. I would settle for a job as a clerk and once I get back on my feet financially, I could go to college in the evening and maybe start my own small business some day...

The dawning of a new millennium SB S. 17

Eine mögliche Aufbereitung zu diesem Hörverstehenstext finden Sie auf einer Kopiervorlage auf S. 23. Die Trackpunkte geben den Anfang des Abschnitts auf der Begleit-CD (ISBN 3-12-510472-6) an.

Transkript

1 Ladies and gentlemen, tonight we celebrate. The change of centuries, the dawning of a new millennium are now just minutes away. We celebrate the past. We have honored America's remarkable achievements, struggles, and triumphs in the 20th century. We celebrate the future, imagining an even more remarkable 21st century.

As we marvel at the changes of the last hundred years, we dream of what changes the next hundred, and the next thousand, will bring. And as powerful as our memories are, our dreams must be even stronger. For when our memories outweigh our dreams we become old, and it is the eternal destiny of America to remain for ever young, always reaching beyond, always becoming, as our founders pledged, a more perfect union. So we Americans must not fear change. Instead, let us welcome it, embrace it, and create it.

The great story of the 20th century is the triumph of freedom and free people, a story told in the drama of new immigrants, the struggles for equal rights, the victories over totalitarianism, the stunning advances in economic well-being, in culture, in health, in space and telecommunications, and in building a world in which more than half the people live under governments of their own choosing, for the first time in all history. We must never forget the meaning of the 20th century, or the gifts of those who worked and marched, who fought and died, for the triumph of freedom.

So as we ring in this new year, in a new century, in a new millennium, we must, now and always, echo Dr. King, in the words of the old American hymn, "Let freedom ring."

2 If the story of the 20th century is the triumph of freedom, what will the story of the 21st century be? Let it be the triumph of freedom wisely used, to bring peace to a world in which we honor our differences, and even more, our common humanity. Such a triumph will require great efforts from us all. It will require us to stand against the forces of hatred and bigotry, terror and destruction. It will require us to continue to prosper, to alleviate poverty, to better balance the demands of work and family, and to serve each of us in our communities.

It will require us to take better care of our environment. It will require us to make further breakthroughs in science and technology, to cure dread diseases, heal broken bodies, lengthen life, and unlock secrets from global warming to the black holes in the universe. And, perhaps most important, it will require us to share – with our fellow Americans and, increasingly, with our fellow citizens of the world – the economic benefits of globalization; the political benefits of democracy and human rights; the educational and health benefits of all things modern, from the Internet to the genetic encyclopedia, to the mysteries beyond our solar system.

3 Now, we may not be able to eliminate all hateful intolerance, but we can develop a healthy intolerance of bigotry, oppression, and abject poverty. We may not be able to eliminate all the harsh consequences of globalization, but we can communicate more and travel more and trade more, in a way that lifts the lives of ordinary working families everywhere, and the quality of our global environment.

We may not be able to eliminate all the failures of government and international institutions, but we can certainly strengthen democracy so all children are prepared for the 21st century world and protected from its harshest side effects. And we can do so much more to work together, to cooperate among ourselves, to seize the problems and the opportunities of this ever small planet we all call home. In short, if we want the story of the 21st century to be the triumph of peace and harmony, we must embrace our common humanity and our shared destiny.

Now, we're just moments from that new millennium. Two centuries ago, as the framers were crafting our Constitution, Benjamin Franklin was often seen in Independence Hall looking at a painting of the sun low on the horizon. When, at long last, the Constitution finally was signed, Mr. Franklin said: "I have often wondered whether that sun was rising or setting. Today I have the happiness to know it is a rising sun."

Well, two centuries later, we know the sun will always rise on America, as long as each new generation lights the fire of freedom. Our children are ready. So, again, the torch is passed – to a new century of young Americans!

Before you listen

■ Predict key words

Stichwörter aus der Rede: Progress in science and technology and particularly in genetic engineering and space travel, greater equality for African Americans, the triumph of democracy, globalization, the internet...

Listening for gist

1 a)/b –
2 President Clinton calls the story of the 20th century "the triumph of freedom". This probably refers to the end of discrimination against African Americans. He also mentions great advances in economic well-being, science and technology, and the spread of democracy around the globe.
Talking about the future, the speaker says that our environment needs to be better taken care of and further breakthroughs in science are required to combat disease and alleviate poverty. He emphasizes the need to share the economic benefits of globalization with other countries.

Listening for detail

1 The speaker refers to three aspects of the American Dream:
– America is destined to be an open, continually changing society, in which everyone works for the benefit of the country;
– The US has always been a haven for the oppressed and political freedom is a major American concern;
– The idea of success should include all Americans.

2 E.g. – intensifying adjectives, e.g. "eternal", "more perfect", "stunning", emphasize his ideas.
– the use of enumeration and repetition (e.g. "the story of the 20th/21st century") underline the progress that has been made – according to the speaker – and also the tasks that still have to be tackled in the future.
– the Benjamin Franklin anecdote catches the audience's attention;
– the 'light' imagery finishes the speech on an upbeat note.

Hinweis: Die letzten Zeilen der Rede (ab "Now we're just moments …") können nochmal vorgespielt werden, damit S die letzten 2 Punkte herausbekommen können.

A step further

■ Evaluate wording of a speech

Die S sollten folgende Punkte überlegen:
– Does the speaker draw on verbal clichés?
– Is the speaker's tone and style suited to the occasion?
– To what extent does he use stock phrases, e.g. "the eternal destiny"?
– What use does he make of pathos (= quality that arouses feelings of pity or sympathy, e.g. "marvel", "triumph of freedom")?

The darkest day   SB S. 18–19

Before you read

■ Speculate about a role

Firefighters: They fought a long battle with the inferno, and many of them risked and lost their lives trying to rescue people in the debris; their bravery and dedication made them a symbol of America's strength and resourcefulness.

Exploring the text

1 Mayor Giuliani underlines the attraction of the freedom and constitutional rights of America to those people who live in dictatorships or who are persecuted for religious reasons.

Living the dream

Political freedom is referred to several times in the speech. For example, the speaker enumerates cases where America participated in wars that preserved or restored political freedom in other countries (cf. ll. 61–63).
Secondly, the mayor refers to "the promise of opportunity" (ll. 15–16), i.e. the image of America as an economic and social haven, that has attracted people from all over the world throughout the ages.

2 E.g. Mayor Giuliani calls for peace rather than revenge ("the olive branch of peace has been handed to us", l. 64); his rhetoric is neither jingoistic nor aggressive, on the contrary, he attempts to unify and strengthen his listeners.

Close-up: rhetorical devices

Mayor Giuliani begins with an antithetical contrast i.e. "darkest day" (l. 1) vs. "finest hour" (l. 2) that runs like a leitmotif through his speech. By contrasting the recent past ("no longer stand", l. 7) with the future ("will rise again", l. 8) he moves his listeners' attention to the tasks ahead. Instead of mourning, he invokes the notion of a better future: "our City ... will be better" (ll. 10–11). From this optimistic claim he moves on to enumerate the basic American beliefs that have made America attractive to people abroad.

Only in the second part of the speech (ll. 17–34) does the speaker speak about the victims of the attack. He praises them as heroes, thus seeking to attribute a meaning to their deaths. The use of the superlative ("best example", l. 28) and the religious phrase, "sacred" in l. 33, underline the speaker's efforts to glorify the victims.

The third part (ll. 35–55) is clearly dominated by the orator's pathos. Words like "darkest tragedy", "miracle(s)" and references to the inauguration of George Washington signal the speaker's attempt to extract a deeper, almost religious meaning from the terrorist attack. By referring to St. Paul's Chapel and the fact that it remained undamaged (ll. 51–52), Mayor Giuliani implies that America is indestructable.

In the fourth part (ll. 56–68), he links America's greatness to its ethnic diversity and reminds his listeners of America's obligation to defend freedom and democracy.

The speaker concludes his sermon-like speech (ll. 69–77) by asking for God's help.

Note: The use of anaphora (= repetition of a word/phrase at the beginning of successive clauses), enumeration and the inclusive "we" emphasize his attempts to create unity and solidarity at this difficult moment.

The structure and stylistic devices may be summarized as follows:

Sections 1–5/theme	Stylistic devices/function
1 (ll. 1–16): call for optimism and patriotism	– antithetical contrast, enumeration: instil hope and pride in his audience
2 (ll. 17–34): heroic deeds of victims	– use of superlatives, religious phrases and enumeration to glorify victims
3 (ll. 35–55): historical references	– pathos underlines America's greatness and indestructability
4 (ll. 56–68): America's global mission	– enumeration and metaphor of light emphasize America's mission
5 (ll. 69–77): asks for God's help	– religious phrase; use of anaphora, enumeration and inclusive "we" to create unity

A step further

■ **Suggest a memorial**

Hinweis auf den Entwurf von Daniel Libeskind, "Memory Foundation". Siehe beispielsweise www.google.de für aktuelle Informationen zum Projekt.

Talking about a cartoon SB S. 19

The cartoonist implies that the country, as symbolized by Uncle Sam's striped trouser legs, is still standing, i.e. it has not been destroyed completely by the terrrorist attacks. The attitude portrayed is one of defiance: The country will rise again out of the disaster.

Projects

The 9/11 attack has greatly traumatized America, and the after-effects are analysed at each anniversary. Prepare a presentation which examines how America has dealt with the attacks. (Siehe Skills file "Presentations", SB S. 182–183 und Ausgaben von amerikanischen Zeitungen zwischen dem 7. und 10. September.)
Wichtige Aspekte der Präsentation:
– how the attack is viewed in the media … years after;
– human interest stories: how people have coped with the loss of friends and loved ones;
– what Ground Zero looks like today and what stage the reconstruction is at. Siehe "A step further" oben.

A time to celebrate SB S. 20–21

Before you read

■ **Talk about a photo/national holiday, give an opinion**

a) He would probably say that he is proud to be an American; he wants to show solidarity with other Americans by wearing a T-shirt with the American flag on it; it is a special day and party and he wants to join in…

b) It celebrates the proclamation of the American Declaration of Independence in 1776; it commemorates the fact that the US is the first modern democracy with constitutional rights. Nowadays, the date signifies the celebration of American achievements: democratic freedom, equality and economic opportunities for all.

c) *Yes:* at a football match, for a joke, if s.th. funny/critical was printed on the T-shirt, too…
No: wearing the flag would be excessively nationalistic; could imagine wearing the flag of another country…

Living the Dream

Exploring the text

1 In his editorial, Mortimer Zuckerman describes America as a nation under God, dedicated to freedom, justice and equality. The idea of equality means equal opportunities for all, and political and social equality for all ethnic groups. This notion further stresses the multicultural nature of the US which is made obvious to the reader by the Italian phrase.
The writer also refers to the idea of upward mobility when he writes that "the American Dream … is … built on individual effort … and just plain hard work" (ll. 14–16). The Dream is possible because society is not static or hierarchical. Thus by showing initiative, persistence and ambition, anyone can go from rags to riches. The writer often takes a stereotyped view, which could be explained by the publication date: the editorial appeared in the issue following the 4th of July. Hence the patriotic rhetoric that runs through the whole text.

2 a) The writer refers to two aspects only. He concedes that there is economic inequality (l. 43) and that ambition as the major driving force in the pursuit of happiness may be seen critically ("Some may decry our ambitions in the pursuit of happiness", l. 46).
b) The writer's use of prolepsis (= anticipating criticism and answering it) disarms potential critics. His choice of words "inequality" and "inequity" (ll. 43–44) may be seen as hair-splitting; however, this choice serves a purpose, i.e. to refute criticism of the unequal distribution of wealth.
Similarly, those who "decry our ambitions" are countered with the argument that many more households want to buy luxury goods which are now regarded as essentials.

3 a) Mortimer Zuckerman's observation reflects a belief in upward mobility, i.e. that anyone can climb the social ladder, and America does not put obstacles in the way of those who truly want to go up in the world.
The second part of the term, "utopia", is misleading. By definition, as the ideal and perfect social or political system, a utopia is static. The writer seems to suggest that he views America as the ideal state: on the one hand, it allows, if not demands, constant change from its people, but on the other hand, it has a timeless, ideal quality (cf. quote in ll. 7–9).
b) The claim suggests that the American Dream is basically a never-ending story; it entails a continuous search for change and progress and makes for a dynamic social structure.

A step further

■ Agree/disagree
In GA die S sammeln Pro- und Kontra-Argumente für eine Diskussion. Siehe SB S. 193 für nützliche Redemittel.

The essence of the American Dream

 SB S. 21

Eine mögliche Aufbereitung zu diesem Hörverstehenstext finden Sie auf einer Kopiervorlage auf S. 23. Die Trackpunkte geben den Anfang des Abschnitts auf der Begleit-CD (ISBN 3-12-510472-6) an.

Transkript

4 Speaker: What is the essence of the American Dream? For many people it is personal material success – they seek primarily material well-being. But there is a great deal more to the American Dream than physical comfort – only it's not as tangible as money and it is difficult to define. While many books have been written on various aspects of the Dream, there are few precise explanations. And although, within the last few years the "American Dream" has become a household word, the term is not found in most reference books or in the indexes of American histories.

It was not until 1931 that the expression "American Dream" was defined specifically for the first time by James T. Adams and used consistently in his book the *Epic of America*:
Quotation (James Truslow Adams): The American Dream is that dream of a land in which life should be better, richer, and fuller for every man with opportunities for each according to his ability and achievement.

5 Speaker: Optimism is the mark of the American Dream. The American Dream is re-defined by every new generation. They decide what they consider a "better, richer, fuller" life. For some generations it meant exploiting the unlimited resources of a vast continent; now it means dealing with scarce sources of energy. Once the challenge was winning World War II, later it was ending Vietnam. At one time the challenge was to maintain the American Dream for those who had achieved it. More recently, it was to make the dream possible for those who had never known it. One woman interviewed in Washington, D.C. expressed it this way:
Woman: I think one of the problems is that Americans' concept of the American Dream is changing or perhaps has changed by now. The – when I was growing up in the 1950s, for example, I think the American Dream was: somehow every generation should be better off financially, educationally than their parents, than the previous generation. And we had this concept that you, I guess, could go on forever getting better and better; and I think Americans have lost their innocence a little bit about that.

6 I think the flight, the movement to the suburbs where everybody left the city was something that was part of the American Dream. Everyone would have their own piece of land, their own little house with the rose garden, and wonderful schools, and wonderful neighbours, and all the mothers would be home in their kitchens, cooking nice cookies, and daddies would be out in the office, working hard, and I think we've sort of perhaps found out that that didn't work so well, beginning in the '60s with the generation of children who were a product of that dream, who became hippies, who ran away, who turned off from American society, who turned off from the idea of always going out making money and getting better and better and better.

I think other things had happened like the energy crisis, which made us realize that we just can't keep spending and spending and spending and never running out of commodities. We are running out of space, we're running out of land, people are beginning to wonder now whether they can buy a new home, simply because it's something that Americans always do. So I'm beginning to wonder myself now what is the American Dream, what is the new American Dream, and I think there is a trend toward conserving, that is, looking backward a little bit, trying to decide what is the best and what isn't; looking for things – I don't think we've found anything yet, you know.

Living the dream

Before you listen

■ **Think of key words**

Mögliche Stichwörter: success, optimism, mobility, a willingness to change, unlimited opportunities, affluence, material well-being, carefree lifestyle…

Background information: James T. Adams

> The quote is taken from the epilogue of James Adams' work and can be placed in the following context: "If, as I have said, the things already listed [i.e. filling up the physical space of America] were all we had had to contribute, America would have made no distinctive and unique gift to mankind. But there has been also the American dream, *that dream of a land in which life should be better and richer and fuller for every man, with opportunity for each according to his ability or achievement.* … It is not a dream of motor cars and high wages merely, but a dream of a social order in which each man and each woman shall be able to attain to the fullest stature of which they are innately capable, and be recognized by others for what they are, regardless of the fortuitous circumstances of birth or position."
>
> *The Epic of America,* Boston: Little, Brown, 1931.

Listening for detail

1 a) … personal material success, they seek primarily material well-being.

b) "… life should be better, richer and fuller for every man with opportunities for each according to his ability and achievement".

c) Optimism is the mark of the American Dream. It is redefined by every generation: They decide what they consider a "better, richer, fuller life" to be like.

2 The female interviewee describes the essential openness of the American Dream and its underlying dynamism. Her statement may also be taken to mean that meeting new challenges and facing constant changes are a part of the American way of life.

A step further

■ **Compare the feature and the text**

E.g. The Morins have not enjoyed material success since Claude Morin was laid off his job. Their aims in life are echoed by the female interviewee: to have their own house in the country and be better off than their parents' generation.

Los Vendidos   SB S. 22–29

Background information

> In this one-act play, Luis Valdez (b. 1940) dramatizes tensions within the Chicano/Latino community and ridicules the stereotypical thinking of white American society. Luis Valdez has been a leading force in the establishment of Chicano theatre in the US, in particular through El Teatro Campesino, a company that emerged from his improvisations for migrant farm workers in the 1960s. Luis Valdez' best known plays are *Zoot Suit* (1978) and *I Don't Have to Show You No Stinking Badges* (1986). *Los Vendidos* was first produced in 1967.
>
> Find out more about El Teatro Campesino at: www.elteatrocampesino.com/campesin/campesin.html

Exploring the text

1 a) Diese Aufgabenstellung ist bewusst sehr offen gewählt. Sie ermöglicht durch die Aufforderung zur Fragestellung einen stärker schülerzentrierten Zugang. Über die Kontrolle der von den S angebotenen Antworten kann eine Überprüfung des Textverständnisses vorgenommen werden. Einige der möglichen Antworten nehmen u.U. Ergebnisse der nachfolgenden Aufgabenstellungen vorweg oder können zu diesen überleiten.
Mögliche Fragen und Antworten:

■ **What is the theme of the play? What is the play about?**
The play may be regarded as: a send-up of the way Mexicans are treated by American society;
– an illustration of the points of conflict in the Mexican-American relationship;
– an (ironic/satirical) analysis/portrait of the Mexican and the American characters.

■ **Who are the characters and what do they stand for?/ Who is Honest Sancho and what is his business?**
Honest Sancho runs the Used Mexican Lot and Mexican Curio Shop. He sells Mexican models like the four types on display: the Revolucionario, the farm-worker, Johnny Pachuco and the Mexican-American. Honest Sancho seems to be the protagonist in the play but, in the end, he turns out to be a puppet in the hands of the Mexican 'robots'. Thus, the attribute "honest" is shown to be a misnomer.
Armed to the teeth, the Revolucionario represents unrest and upheaval as well as the fight for freedom. As a bandit, he plays the virile macho and the Latin lover.
The farm worker is the underdog or slave who is kept in poor living conditions.
Johnny Pachuco, whom Sancho describes by using attributes which are usually applied to a new car, represents the partly Americanized, Mexican city dweller. He is characteristically associated with knife fights, crime and drugs.
In contrast, the Mexican-American plays the role of the educated, cultivated, middle-class businessman and ladies' man (satirically equipped with suction cups behind his lips to make him the perfect charmer). In a speech (ll. 248–254), he gives the impression of being a patriotic American, but when the deal with Ms Jimenez is complete, he turns back into the savage Mexican, calling loudly for Chicano Power.

■ **What is the function of the character of Ms Jimenez?**
As a secretary from the Governor's office Ms Jimenez speaks and acts on behalf of the administration. She also represents American society with all of its prejudices about Mexicans. In a way, she embodies capitalist attitudes, which encourage the belief that 'money-can-buy-everything'. In the end, her attitude makes her an easy prey to deception. It could also be argued that, as a Chicana, Ms Jimenez represents the Mexican-American careerist (note the "Ms" as a sign of emancipation) who has turned her back on her origins and gone over to the other side by becoming an aide in the administration.

■ **Whom or what does Luis Valdez attack/criticize in his play?**
On the whole, the dramatist attacks American society for the way it looks down on and treats Mexican immigrants. At first, Luis Valdez also seems to criticize the Chicanos for allowing

themselves to be treated in this way, and accepting American attitudes and the American way of life. After all, Honest Sancho seems to run his shop in answer to a demand created by the Americans. However, the play's conclusion implies that the dramatist sides with the Mexicans as they ultimately manage to outwit the 'dumb' Americans.

■ **What is the significance of the conclusion?**
The conclusion shows that both the audience and the American secretary have been fooled. It implies that the Mexicans are superior for organizing the whole set-up and tricking the superficial Americans. In this way, the dramatist scores a point for Chicano power.

2 a) Honest Sancho uses Spanish when he introduces himself in his monologue (ll. 11–13) and when he deliberately mistakes Ms Jimenez for a Chicana (l. 16). He also uses Spanish when he interprets Ms Jimenez' ideas in order to show that he understands (ll. 28–35), and he speaks Spanish when he does not seem to understand s.th. (l. 98), when he reacts spontaneously (ll. 121, 193) or tries to explain s.th. in more detail "yesca … mota … leños" (ll. 129–133).
The farm worker speaks Spanish only, which underlines the poor linguistic skills of many immigrant workers.
Johnny uses Spanish when he gets excited on Sancho's command (l. 116) and when he pretends to be a mugger in order to stress his mean streak (l. 159).
The Revolucionario uses Spanish on Sancho's command, in the role of a bandit (l. 181) or Latin lover (l. 194).
At first, the Mexican-American speaks perfect English but relapses into staccato Spanish (ll. 301–304) to suggest that he is capable of anything, even of starting a revolution. He causes the other characters to join in and conclude the scam.
b) *Reasons to include Spanish dialogues:*
– they make the characters seem more vivid and lively, e.g. ll. 191, 193;
– the use of Spanish and English indicates a polarity between the two cultures (ll. 18–20, 91–95), shows a greater contrast between the characters and creates humour (ll. 44–47, 194–195).

Possible effects on an English-speaking audience:
– It makes the situation seem authentic; linguistic abilities and accent are used as a means of characterization.
– Because the language is unintelligible the characters also seem unpredictable and unusual.
– It creates an awareness of the gap between the two languages and, consequently, the two cultures.

3 *Criticism of attitudes towards Mexicans in American society:*
Mexicans are looked down upon, treated as inferior/scapegoats/like slaves/as being easily exploited; they are stereotyped as being stupid and uneducated peasants/dangerous, volatile revolutionaries/slick criminals/smart machos.
Criticism of general American attitudes:
– The belief in one's own superiority; all others are inferior.
– The administration/governor uses minorities to get good publicity ("The Governor is having a luncheon … we need a brown face in the crowd", ll. 286–287).
– The belief that money can buy everything (ll. 268–269)
– The greedy, tight-fisted stance towards the workforce (saving money at the expense/taking advantage of the underdogs, "Is he economical … going all day", ll. 64–67)
Note: The play works to a large extent on hetero-stereotypes (= how a group is seen by others). The auto-stereotypes (= how we see ourselves as a group distinguished from others) of the Mexicans only become relevant at the end of the play.

Means used to voice criticism include:
– irony: "built close to the ground" (l. 40), "little holes on his arms that appear to be pores" (l. 60), "Suction cups behind his lips" (l. 237), "Fifteen thousand DOLLARS? For a MEXICAN!" (l. 274);
– parody: e.g. of a political speech in ll. 248–255;
– sarcasm/satire: "We can't have any more thieves in the State Administration" (l. 162);
– metaphorical language: "Honest Sancho" (telling name, later turns out to be a misnomer), "Ms Jimenez" (use of "Ms" in combination with a Spanish-sounding name implies that she is a naturalized American, "Used Mexican Lot" (l. 4) (ambiguity), "Cafecito con leche" (l. 35);
– puns: "Say the word 'acculturate' and he accelerates" (ll. 228–229), "political Machine" (l. 243);
– exaggeration/hyperbole:
  • the attitude that Mexican immigrants are machines/robots (with an inbuilt capacity to strike and be a scab);
  • the criminal tendencies of Mexican immigrants: "to liberate" = to steal (ll. 156–160); claim that a particular type of Mexican immigrant uses drugs (ll. 128–129);
  • the attitude that America is all-powerful: "the apex of American engineering" (l. 228);
  • the image of the "standard Revolutionary", "early Californian bandit type" and its association with film/TV presentation of Mexicans (ll. 174–178); the idea that the Mexican-American has hidden revolutionary tendencies (ll. 301–312);
  • the fear of the savage (l. 192);
– register: politeness and formality of the language (ll. 234, 248–255) contrast with underlying prejudices and superficiality, the formal register is in keeping with the patriotism expressed;
– characterisation: Sancho's salesmanship, his swift, sly changes in sales tactics show he is not a 'stupid Mexican';
– dénouement: the revelation of the set-up, in which the 'stupid' Mexicans turn out to be more clever (thus ironically bearing out the American stereotype of a Mexican tendency to commit crime).

Close-up: short plays

1 All of the features listed in the box can be found in the play: the play is short in length. The action happens in one place, Sancho's shop, and the morning/lunch time of one particular day. The focus is less on plot (the plot could be summarized in one sentence) than on situation. The situations change in accordance with the characters involved. The number of characters is limited as is their participation in the dialogue. At any one time, a maximum of three characters is involved in the action (the secretary + Sancho + a model). The only exception is the conclusion where four of the characters are involved.

2 Examples of key speeches which:
– add to character development (Ms JIM-enez in ll. 18–20; model of Mexican wanted: ll. 26–35; about Johnny: "he's economical … yesca", ll. 126–129), and plot development (ll. 22–23), the introductions to each new model, e.g. "Over here in this corner … JOHNNY PACHUCO model" (ll. 100–102);
– show the relationships between characters, e.g. how the men work (ll. 318–323); reveal the truth about Sancho and the 'models' (l. 335);

Living the dream

- set the tone: indicate a particular tone, e.g. demonstrate how absurd the situation is as in ll. 24–43; use an ironic tone as in ll. 38–40;
- provoke a particular reaction among the audience: e.g. "And here's an added feature … he also scabs" (ll. 79–88) remind the audience of their image of the immigrant worker who traditionally goes home at the end of the season. In the year the play was first produced, Mexican immigrant workers were on strike; "You think you're better…" the image of the aggressive, criminal Mexican may be familiar to the audience, cf. ll. 121–124, 152–153.

Zusätzliche Aufgabe

Ein Vergleich zwischen *Los Vendidos* und *The Cabbie from Calcutta*, SB S. 175 ("Using your skills", SB S. 175). Diese Aufgabe wäre auch im Rahmen einer Facharbeit leistbar.

A step further

■ Discuss stereotyping

Zur Vorbereitung können Vorlagen aus SB S. 94–95 oder der Cartoon, SB S. 98 bzw. der Comicstrip auf SB S. 39 hinzugezogen werden. Denkbar wäre auch ein vorbereitender Auftrag an die S, nach Materialien zu suchen, die das Thema ‚national stereotypes' ansprechen.

Forest Gump   Using your skills   SB S. 30–31

Getting started

■ Scene profile

a)–d) Siehe Kopiervorlage "Model scene profile" auf S. 24.

Watching and thinking

■ Key scenes

Die Auswahl ist variabel je nach thematischen Schwerpunkten; mögliche Schlüsselszenen aus der 'scene selection' der *Forest Gump* DVD:
1. I'm Forrest … Forrest Gump (Introducing the protagonist);
4. Run Forrest Run! (Forrest as a runner and a witness of history; vgl. "Filmanalyse – Vorschläge für Klausuren und Klassenarbeiten" ISBN 3-12-577463-2);
8. Wounded In The Buttocks (Forrest as a Vietnam hero);
16. A Little Run (Forrest runs across America);
18. Beloved Mother, Wife And Friend (Forrest looks back on his life).

■ Viewing log

Bestandteile siehe detaillierte Aufgabenstellung (ggf. Auswahl treffen/obligatorische Elemente festlegen/individuelle Schwerpunktsetzungen zulassen); zur Motivation sollte dieses "Dossier" nach Abschluss der Reihe vom L gesichtet und benotet werden (Anteil an "Sonstiger Mitarbeit" vorab mitteilen; vgl. auch Kopiervorlage "Viewing log assessment" auf TB S. 187); bei einer entsprechenden Klausur zur Reihe könnte auch die Verwendung des Dossiers bei der Klausur erwogen werden.

A step further

■ Trailer

a) A possible definition: A short sequence of shots from a film which is used as one form of advertisement.
A trailer usu. has the following characteristics:
- between 30 and 120 seconds long;
- quick sequence of extracts from particularly amusing/ appealing/dramatic scenes;
- a voice-over links the scenes into a narrative structure;
- the problem/conflict is presented in a nutshell to evoke curiosity;
- memorable soundbites from the film;
- short visual introduction of the main characters;
- a focus on essential information: usually the film title, the names of the main actors and the release date of the film (sometimes printed on the screen).

b) Anwendungs- und produktionsorientierte Aufgabe, gut auch für PA oder GA geeignet.

Zusätzliche Aufgabe

Develop a shooting script for a *Forrest Gump* trailer in the form of a grid. Present your ideas in class and then compare your trailers.
Materials: definition of "trailer" (see above); viewing log
Your grid could have two columns in which you briefly describe: What is seen? (e.g. a shot or scene from the film, text on screen), What is heard? (e.g. film dialogue, voice-over, music).
Hinweis: Auf der „Special Collector's Edition" von *Forrest Gump* finden sich weitere unterrichtsgeeignete audio-visuelle Materialien:
Disc 1: „Commentary by director Robert Zemeckis" (einsetzbar zum Vergleich nach „Getting started," Task d)
Disc 2: Trailer (als Modell des Textformats und zur Herleitung der Definition, vgl. Trailer, Task a))
Disc 2: „Seeing Is Believing – Visual Effects" (zur Veranschaulichung des ‚computer-generated imaging')

Test: Our rainbow underclass   TB S. 25

Klausur für den Grundkurs
Textformat: editorial, 477 words
Vorschlag/Klausurtyp NRW: Tasks 1–3, A2
Zentraler Bezugstext des Kapitels: "A time to celebrate", SB S. 20. Es handelt sich nicht nur um denselben Leitartikelverfasser, sondern auch um dieselbe Textsorte. Der Autor revidiert z.T. seinen Optimismus und Patriotismus, so dass sich eine sinnvolle Vergleichsmöglichkeit zwischen den Texten ergibt.

Der Klausurtest und die entsprechenden Fragen befinden sich auf einer Kopiervorlage auf S. 25.

Comprehension

1 The writer uses the 9/11 ceremonies as a starting point to prove the necessity for a broad national dialogue on immigration. He then compares the "swift assimilation" and "middle class lifestyle" of immigrants in the past to the "subnation" in which present-day Latino immigrants live.
Another central aspect is the fate of second generation Hispanic immigrants, whom the writer calls the "rainbow under-

Living the Dream

class". He describes in detail what he calls "a cycle of downward assimilation", in which young Latinos who fail to acculterate remain at the bottom of society.

Mortimer Zuckerman sketches a scenario for the future development of the US population. Based on the prediction that the population will be doubled by 2050 – half will be immigrants and their descendants – he fortells major environmental and social problems.

In his concluding paragraph, the writer mentions three ways of dealing with problems caused by large-scale immigration: schools should be better equipped to deal with second-generation children, the issuing of visas to family members from abroad should be restricted and skilled immigrants should be given priority, and the process of immigration should be slowed down.

Analysis

2 The writer uses several stylistic devices. He uses *antithetical contrasts* to compare immigration, then and now. He underlines the fact that immigrants in the past were successfully absorbed into the American mainstream. According to the writer, Latino immigrants today do not integrate into society. An antithetical contrast may also be observed in the depiction of immigrants. Earlier immigrants took pains to learn English and secure schooling for their children, whereas today's Latinos keep their ethnicity and as a result, are segregated from the rest of society. The negative effects of this voluntary segregation are *enumerated* and support the writer's view. The scenario which he outlines almost has a xenophobic ring to it, particularly since he does not specify what the "incalculable social tensions" (l. 49) are.

The writer follows a clear line of argumentation: he describes the situation in the past and then outlines present problems before giving predictions for the future, and concluding with suggestions as to how to deal with the problems.

Comment/re-creation of text

3 The editorial differs markedly from Mr Zuckerman's text, "A time to celebrate" (SB page 20), which was written two years earlier: Patriotism has given way to concern, and pride in America's history as a nation of immigrants has been replaced by worries about America's future.

Mögliche Kritikpunkte: The US is a never-ending source of attraction to Mexicans. As long as US firms do not invest in job creation in Mexico, Mexicans will continue to cross the border illegally. The American Dream has taken on a global dimension in so far as it has become the dream of economic success for immigrants from Third World countries.

Test: Ambition and its enemies   TB S. 26

Klausur für den Leistungskurs
Textformat: magazine article, 603 words
Vorschlag/Klausurtyp NRW: Tasks 1–3, A2
Zentrale Bezugstexte des Kapitels: "Mexico is memory" (SB S. 10), "Making it Big in America" (SB S. 14) und "The United States of Anger" (SB S. 16).

Der Klausurtest und die entsprechenden Fragen befinden sich auf einer Kopiervorlage auf S. 26.

Comprehension

1 The writer discusses the two sides of ambition. The negative side is seen as being self-destructive because it promotes status-seeking, self-exploitation and excessive consumption; people compete with one another in an endless game in which they acquire status symbols.

The positive side of ambition is its social and economic functions. It is also part of the ideal of unlimited opportunity.

Analysis

2 The writer uses antitheses (= use of opposites for effect), e.g. "excesses of striving and craving that are self-destructive" (ll. 8–9) and "anyone starting poor could become rich" (l. 58), and enumeration, e.g. "status symbols – a bigger house, … a faster computer" (ll. 14–15) to underline his view of ambition. Quotes from *The New York Times*, the Census Bureau, the writers Thorsten Veblen and Tocqueville support his views. The writer also uses short, declarative sentences which have more impact than long sentences. The oxymoron in the last line ("Ambition is bitter as often as sweet") indicates the ambivalent nature of ambition but also makes it clear that the writer sees it as the main driving force in American society.

Comment/re-creation of text

3 *Mögliche Ideen:* The writer is not an ideological advocate of the idea of success, as he mentions both positive and negative effects. The search for success is not only a national mania but also a sign of economic vitality. By viewing ambition as a prerequisite for economic growth, prosperity and innovation, the writer stresses its importance and endows it with a timeless quality. Comparisons with other texts, e.g.

- "Making it Big in America" (SB p. 14): Robert Samuelson's view that "people can write their own life stories" (cf. ll. 36–37) is reflected in the career profiles of the successful lawyer who came from poor beginnings and the writer who changed careers until he finally managed to achieve personal fulfilment.
- "Mexico is memory" (SB p. 10): An immigrant needs ambition to make it in the US. However, the desire to succeed is not enough to realize one's dreams. Viewed in this light, ambition may be seen as a destructive force as it drives Mexicans from their home into an uncertain future.
- "The United States of Anger" (SB p. 16): The extract illustrates how ambition will remain fruitless as long as social and economic circumstances prevent one putting one's ambition to use.

Test: A nation of immigrants   TB S. 27

Mündliche Prüfung
Textformat: novel extract, 384 words
Vorschlag/Klausurtyp NRW: Tasks 1–3, Mündliche Prüfung
Zentraler Bezugstext des Kapitels: "Mexico is memory" (SB S. 10). Der Text knüpft an die Teilsequenz "immigration" an.

Der Klausurtest und die entsprechenden Fragen befinden sich auf einer Kopiervorlage auf S. 27.
Siehe *The Tortilla Curtain*, Klett-Ausgabe (ISBN 3-12-573840-7).

Living the dream

Tasks: Suggested answers

1 Jack Jardine takes a xenophobic view. He speaks out against Latinos who enter the US to find work. He justifies his position on the grounds that the illegals have no skills and there is no work for them, as machines nowadays do the manual labour. He further justifies closing the borders by pointing out the enormous amounts of money the State of California spends on illegals. For him, it is a mathematical equation: the immigrants cost more than they pay into the system, so there is no room for them.
In contrast, Delaney represents a liberal position that is rooted in American history. For him, the US has always been a nation of immigrants and it must remain so.

2 Delaney clearly follows in the tradition of the American Dream, i.e. he is prepared to accept immigrants and his image of the US is that of a country that attracts people from all over the world and offers them a haven.

3 *Ideen:* Jack is xenophobic; his reference to crime, as caused by Hispanics, may be seen as racist in so far as it is completely unsubstantiated;
– He has forgotten his own roots: his ancestors probably found themselves in a similar situation to the present-day immigrants and were also forced to make a living by means of physical labour.
– Jack's claim that immigrants from Latin America are not needed is contradicted by examples in the text "Mexico is memory" (SB pp. 10–11), which outlines the extent to which the US depends on cheap immigrant labour to do jobs such as babysitting, and restaurant and hospital work.

Kernwortschatz

Immigration
views of America
land/promise of opportunity
abundance
equality
chance to start a new life
to begin afresh
to extend a welcome/hospitality to newcomers
migration
an influx of illegal immigrants
economic refugee
to leave one's home for economic reasons
to become a naturalized citizen

Finding one's place
assimilation, to assimilate
acculturation, to acculturate
to undergo a process of acculturation
to uproot
to adjust
to adapt to
to retain/keep one's ethnic identity
ethnic community
to stress the distinctness of ethnic groups
the concern with one's ethnicity
to promote cultural diversity
to lead to segregation
to be melted into a new race
melting pot
the salad bowl, the quilt

Dreams of success
common stock of beliefs
the idea of self-help
to have a can-do-attitude/mentality
to try one's hand at new tasks
optimism
to rise in life from poverty to riches
to climb the social ladder
to go from rags to riches
to be a self-made man
to overcome one's upbringing
to reinvent oneself
to offer scope for upward social mobility
a strong belief in unlimited opportunities
job mobility
personal initiative
resourcefulness
self-reliance
risk-taking
to have a strong streak of competitiveness
… ambition
competitive attitude
man as the master of his destiny
to show vigour,
… enterprise,
… an adventurous spirit,
… energy,
… forcefulness
to win a scholarship
to set up one's own business
to seek personal material success

… the nightmare of failure
all efforts end in failure
to be unable to get on in life
to lose faith in the American Dream
to be disillusioned
to be fooled by images of America
to reject one's parents' values

American self-images
freedom, egalitarianism, respect for human life
meritocratic society
American singularity and exceptionalism
haven/refuge for oppressed people
global attraction
belief in God's help
destiny to spread democracy
to find strength in diversity
to unite under the banner of *E Pluribus Unum*
to enjoy the political benefits of democracy and human rights

An immigrant on Ellis Island

Ellis Island

Immigrants arriving in the United States by steamship at the end of the 19th. and the beginning of the 20th. century were first processed in the immigration centre on Ellis Island. The lucky ones spent a few days on the island but many had to wait for weeks or even months before they were allowed onto the mainland. Others never made it and were sent home again.

Tasks

a) Find out more about the history of Ellis Island and what happened to the immigrants who went through processing there.
  - Use the worksheet below to organise your ideas.
  - You can collect relevant information on Ellis Island at the following website: http://teacher.scholastic.com/activities/immigration/index.htm. Here you should go to the link "Interactive tour of Ellis Island".

b) Present your findings in the form of an eyewitness report by one immigrant. Try to include as much detail about your impression of Ellis Island and the immigration procedure as possible. You can make up any biographical details.

Worksheet

Arrival: We were taken to Ellis Island _____

_____

The Baggage Room _____

_____

The stairways to the Great Hall _____

_____

In the medical exam _____

_____

The Great Hall _____

_____

Legal inspection _____

_____

Money Exchange _____

_____

The exit to Ellis Island _____

_____

_____

Living the Dream

The modern immigrant's story

■ Find out what happens to immigrants who enter the US today.
You could consult the following website:
http:teacher.scholastic.com/activities/immigration/index.htm
Follow the link featuring three recent immigrants.

1 Jot down notes about **one** of the immigrants under the following headings:

Why the person emigrated to the US _____

_____

_____

What he or she thinks of America _____

_____

_____

What he or she misses most about home _____

_____

_____

Which aspect(s) of American life surprise him/her the most _____

_____

_____

2 Assess the information you have gathered in the course of your research.

– What obvious clichés/stereotypes of the US are mentioned? _____

_____

_____

– What hopes and aspirations does each immigrant have? _____

_____

_____

3 Prepare a fifteen-minute TV feature entitled "Immigrant of the Year". You should work in teams of two to four students.
 – Deal with the aspects below.
   a) Write a brief introduction to the person you are featuring.
   b) Outline the environment(s) you want to present him/her in (for example: an American school).
   c) Imagine and hold a short interview with the immigrant you have chosen.
 – Present the feature in class.

4 When checking through the online biographies you will come across further information in the form of the immigrants' replies to questions posed by visitors to the website. You could mail your own questions to the website and report the answers you receive to fellow students.

Living the Dream

The dawning of a new millennium SB S. 17

Vocabulary
dawning *here fig.* beginning – 7 **to marvel** to look in admiration – 13 **to pledge** *(formal)* to promise in a serious way – 19 **stunning** amazing – 35 **bigotry** unreasonable, one-sided opinions – 36 **to alleviate** to make less painful – 51 **abject** extremely bad – 66 **framer** s.o. who writes a new law

Before you listen
- Make a list of key words that you would expect to hear in a presidential speech made at the turn of the millennium.

Listening for gist
1. a) As you listen to the recording the first time, tick any key words which the speaker mentions.
   b) Compare your results with a classmate's.
2. What does the speaker say about America's past and future?

Listening for detail
1. Which aspects of the American Dream are mentioned in the speech?
2. What rhetorical devices does the speaker use to emphasize his vision of the new millennium?

A step further
- Given the occasion on which the president delivered the speech, how effective do you find his wording?

The essence of the American Dream SB S. 21

Vocabulary
5 **tangible** which can be felt or touched – 8 **a household word** s.th. which is well known – 21 **to exploit** to use extensively – 23 **scarce** limited – 53 **commodity** resource

Before you listen
- Make a list of key words that you would expect to hear in a radio feature entitled "The essence of the American Dream".

Listening for detail
1. Look again at your list of key words. Which ones were mentioned and in what kind of context?

2. Complete the following sentences based on what you hear in the feature.

   a) For many people the essence of the American Dream is _____.

   b) James Truslow Adams defined the American Dream as that of "a land in which _____".

   c) _____ is the mark of the American Dream. It is _____.

3. The woman who is interviewed in the feature says, "There is a trend toward ... looking for things – I don't think we've found anything yet, you know." What do you think she means by this claim?

A step further
- Read the text "The United States of Anger" on pages 16–17 of your book. How does the picture of the American Dream relate to the essence of the American Dream as defined in the radio programme?

Living the Dream

Forrest Gump – model scene profile
Using your skills   SB S. 30–31

Narrative devices

Characters

appearance
white jacket, long trousers, check shirt buttoned to the top; neatly if not fashionably dressed, worn-out running shoes, short hair
→ *orderly, tidy, neat*

body language
uncertain glance; upright, stiff posture; twitching eyes; funny movements of the mouth
→ *nervous, insecure or not 'normal'*

at the end, frowns with eyes closed
→ *is concentrating to remember a childhood scene*

use of language/communication
funny intonation/monologue focuses on "Mom" and "shoes"/does not listen/tries to engage the woman in conversation (only gets short replies)/speaks with his mouth full
→ *lost in thought, acts strangely, seems slightly retarded*

Action

setting
time: a sunny summer's day in 1981 (see bus)
→ *peaceful atmosphere*

place: a bench at a bus stop
→ *waiting for a bus to visit s.o. or go somewhere*

plot
a feather flies downwards and lands next to the hero's shoes; hero picks it up and places it in a suitcase, then he chats to a woman; her shoes bring back memories…
→ *slow exposition*
suspense: Who is the hero? Why is he at the bus stop? …

→ *likeable, if mysterious, character (creates audience empathy*

Main function of the scene: Introduces the protagonist

Cinematic devices

Camera operations

two long shots (one cut before the bus arrives): camera follows the flight of the feather
→ *slow-paced start*,
then focuses on shoes (close-up), tilts upwards to show the hero who has picked up the feather; zooms out into a long, static shot of the hero in his immediate surroundings
→ *links the feather and the shoes with the protagonist (cf. visual symbols)*

Film music/sound effects

piano solo, then strings; slow, melodious, sad tune; at times the noise of the wind
→ *bitter-sweet memories; nostalgic/sad mood*

Visual symbols

feather → ~ in the wind
→ *irregular biography, hero driven by forces outside his control*

worn-out shoes → *he has travelled a long way*

contents of suitcase: picture book (acrobat on a high wire, tennis racket, baseball cap)
→ *interests, phases in his life*

box of chocolates → *link with his mother (close relationship: "Mom always said life is like a box…") and a simile for life*

Other effects

- computer-generated flight of the feather → *not used for effect (technically necessary to give a realistic impression)*
- symmetrical picture → *presents contrast between woman and hero in terms of sex, skin colour, footwear and communicativeness to underline the hero's appearance and personality*
- blurred screen at the end of the scene → *prepares flashback (evoked by the shoes) = childhood memory*

Living the Dream

Test: Our rainbow underclass

The roll of honor read at the 9/11 ceremonies was a tapestry of America, of native-born Americans of all ethnic origins and more recent immigrants. Of course, we know too well that some of the assassins and others plotting against America were immigrants who betrayed our ideals, so it is natural that many people feel we should now close the door altogether, beginning with immigrants from Muslim countries. Natural, and wrong. What is long overdue, however, is a sustained national dialogue on immigration. [...]

Traditionally, there were well-paid manufacturing jobs for immigrants, enabling them to join the ranks of blue-collar workers who secured a middle-class lifestyle without much formal education. Those days are gone. Schooling is today's ticket for a better future – with a high school diploma as the minimum. The original European newcomers could also send their children to high-quality urban schools. Assimilation was swift. The immigrants, however numerous, were from many different countries, so they took to English more rapidly. There was no linguistic minority to dominate any large city the way Spanish speakers now dominate Miami and Los Angeles. Today Latino immigrants live in a subnation with their own radio and TV stations, newspapers, films, and magazines, stunting assimilation and diminishing economic opportunity. [...]

A critical question that is almost never asked: What is the impact on children, the second generation? Some thrive, but the majority do not. They form a rainbow underclass, caught in a cycle of downward assimilation, poverty combined with racial segregation. Often separated for long periods from their parents, especially their fathers, during immigration process, they stop doing homework, reject their parents' values, and succumb to the dangers of an overcrowded inner-city culture. They face overwhelmed teachers, limited social resources, and a decaying infrastructure, and they often adopt the negative behavior pattern of their peer groups, such as academic indifference and substance abuse, leading to dropout rates three times as high as for native-born Americans. [...]

There is another disquieting conncection, the trifecta effect of rising immigrant fertility rates. Our population is projected to rise to over 500 million by 2050, roughly doubled what America is today – with post-1965 immigrants and their descendants making up about half. The effect of these numbers on myriad aspects of our environment, from rush-hour traffic to air and water pollution and social tensions, is incalculable.

How, then, should we proceed? No matter what, we must find more resources for the schools and other institutions that will support the development of second-generation children. Second, we must rebalance the number of visas provided for extended-family programs and add more to attract immigrants with skills transferable to the information economy. Third, we should slow down the process until we can thoroughly assess how the children of today's immigrants will fare as adults. Only through such measures can a national consensus on these issues begin to be forged. (477 words)

By Mortimer B. Zuckerman, *US News & World Report,* September 23, 2002.

---

25 **to stunt** *here:* to prevent s.th. – 39 **substance abuse** drug use – 42 **trifecta** *here:* threefold – 60 **to forge a consensus** *here:* to reach an agreement

Tasks

1 Outline the key issues Mortimer Zuckerman deals with in his editorial.

2 Analyse how the issue of immigration is dealt with in the text. Pay special attention to the writer's style and line of argumentation.

3 Discuss Mortimer Zuckerman's position by comparing it with your knowledge of problems faced by immigrants in the US.

Living the Dream

Test: Ambition and its enemies

We are a nation of ambitious people, and ambition is a quality that is hard to praise and easy to deplore. It's a great engine of American creativity, but it also can be an unrelenting oppressor, which robs us of time and peace of mind. Especially in highly prosperous periods – periods like the present – it becomes fashionable to question whether ambition has gotten out of hand and is driving us to excesses of striving and craving that are self-destructive. […]

One-upsmanship is a national mania. You see it every time a wide receiver prances into the end zone and raises his index finger in a triumphant "We're No. 1" salute, even if his team is mired in a losing season. More common is the search for status symbols – a bigger house, a more exotic vacation, a niftier bike, a faster computer – that separate us from the crowd. Money may not be the only way to satisfy this urge, but it's most common because it can so easily translate itself into some other badge of identity and standing.

For many people, the contest seems futile. *The New York Times* recently ran a long story on four families with roughly $50,000 of income who "wonder why they have to struggle so hard just to pay the bills." The answer isn't that their incomes are stagnating. Between 1992 and 1997, the median income of married couples rose from $48,008 to $51,681 in inflation-adjusted dollars, reports the Census Bureau. They are surely higher now. All families profiled by the *Times* owned homes. Their recent purchases included "double-door refrigerators, radiant-heat stoves … big-screen TVs, computers and elaborate outdoor grills."

The problem isn't that they're running in place but that they're running in the pack with everyone else. Consumer products morph from luxury to convenience to necessity. Cars, TVs and microwaves all followed the cycle; now it describes Internet connections and cell phones. If you don't buy by the final stage, you're considered a crank or pauper. There's nothing new here. In the *Theory of the Leisure Class* (1899), Thorstein Veblen argued that, once an item becomes widely owned, possessing it becomes a requisite for "self-respect. People try to consume just beyond [their] reach" so that they "can outdo" those with whom they compare themselves. […]

Let's rethink. Though unlovable, ambition is socially useful. It sustains economic vitality. It prods people to take risks and exert themselves. The Internet is the offspring of workaholics spending eight-day weeks to invent a new world and make a fortune. When the process works well, gains overwhelm losses – and not just in economic output. Today's hyperprosperity has improved the social climate. Almost all indicators of confidence have increased.

What people disdain as ambition they also venerate as opportunity. As Tocqueville long ago noted, America was built on the notion that – unlike Europe, with its hereditary aristocracy – people could write their own life stories. The ideal endures. A 1996 survey asked whether anyone starting poor could become rich; 78 percent of Americans thought so. But it's not just the economy or even politics. Social standing is fluid everywhere. Ambition and its creative powers permeate the arts, the professions, academia, science. Because everyone can be someone, the competition to rise above the crowd is unrelenting and often ruthless.

Few of us escape ambition's wounds. There are damaged dreams, abandoned projects and missed promotions. Most of us face the pressures of balancing competing demands between our inner selves and outer lives. A society that peddles so many extravagant promises sows much disappointment. Ambition is bitter as often as sweet; but without it, we'd be sunk.

(603 words)

By Robert J. Samuelson, *Newsweek,* August 23, 1999.

---

10 **one-upsmanship** *(informal)* when one makes a point of doing better than a rival – 11 **wide receiver** *(American football)* an offensive player used as a pass receiver – 11 **end zone** *(American football)* the area at either end of the field between the goal line and the end line – 54 **Tocqueville** (1805–1859), French statesman and writer who was an early interpreter of American life

Tasks

1 Outline the writer's attitude towards ambition and then explain how his attitude fits in with the American Dream.

2 Examine the stylistic devices the writer uses in order to convince the reader of his view of ambition in American life.

3 Briefly compare the writer's view to other views of the success mythology that you know.

Living the Dream

Test: A nation of immigrants

In the following extract from the novel The Tortilla Curtain *two residents of a wealthy settlement near Los Angeles, Delaney Mossbacher and Jack Jardine are standing in a supermarket discussing the issue of immigration. Jack Jardine speaks first.*

"Did you know that the US accepted more immigrants last year than all the other countries of the world *combined* – and that half of them settled in California? And that's *legal* immigrants, people with skills, money, education. The ones coming in through the Tortilla Curtain down there, those are the ones that are killing us. They're peasants, my friend. No education, no resources, no skills – all they've got to offer is a strong back, and the irony is we need fewer and fewer strong backs every day, because we've got robotics and computers and farm machinery that can do the labour of a hundred men at a fraction of the cost." He dropped his hand in dismissal. "It's old news". […]

"I can't believe you," he (Delaney) said and he couldn't seem to control his free arm, waving it in an expanding loop. "Do you realize what you're saying. Immigrants are the lifeblood of this country – we're a nation of immigrants – and neither of us would be standing here today if it wasn't."

"Clichés. There's a point of saturation. Besides which, the Jardines fought in the Revolutionary War – you could hardly call us immigrants."

"Everybody's an immigrant from somewhere. My grandfather came over from Bremen and my grandmother was Irish – does that make me any less a citizen than the Jardines?"

A woman with frosted hair and a face drawn tight as a drumskin ducked between them for a jar of olives. Jack worked a little grit into his voice. "That's not the point. Times have changed, my friend. Radically. Do you have any idea what these people are costing us, and not just in terms of crime, but in real tax dollars for social services? No? Well, you ought to. You must have seen that thing in the *Times* a couple weeks ago, about the San Diego study?" […]

"Look, Delaney," Jack went on, cool reasonable, his voice in full song now, "it's a simple equation, so much in, so much out. The illegals in San Diego County contributed seventy million in tax revenues and at the same time they used up two hundred and forty million in services – welfare, emergency care, schooling and the like. You want to pay for that? And for the crime that comes with it?"

(384 words)

From *The Tortilla Curtain* by T. C. Boyle, New York: Penguin Books, 1996, pp. 101–102.

---

5 **Tortilla Curtain** *(negative)* the Mexican-American border – 7 **resource** quality, ability – 19 **point of saturation** state when s.th. is so full that it is impossible to add any more – 20 **Revolutionary War** War of Independence of the American colonists against the British (1775–1783) – 38 **tax revenue** money which the state collects from its citizens

Tasks

1 What are Delaney's and Jack's positions on immigration as expressed in their conversation?

2 How does Delaney's position reflect the American Dream?

3 Delaney acccuses Jack of being a racist. Do you agree with him, or not? Give reasons for your answer.

Cultural mix and clash – UK

Didaktisches Inhaltsverzeichnis

	Titel	Textsorte (Wortzahl ca.)	Thema	Text- und Spracharbeit	Textproduktion (schriftlich / mündlich)
	Britain as … SB S. 32, TB S. 29	photo collage / statistics (52 words)	racial (dis-)harmony	analyse / interpret statistics • describe/comment on photos	mind map: benefits and problems of immigration
	England was a… SB S. 33, TB S. 29	novel extract (1,446 words)	Indian boy adjusts to life in Britain	describe feelings / images / allusions • describe text structure / point of view	comment on a quotation
🎧	Listen Mr Oxford… SB S. 37, TB S. 31	dub poem (195 words)	language differences	compare West Indian and Standard British English • characterize speaker • sum up message • humour	rewrite a poem as a prose text • web search: dub poetry / poets • analyse statistics
🎧	Telephone… SB S. 38, TB S. 32	poem (230 words)	racial discrimination	identify linguistic features of a poem • describe feelings • characterization	rewrite poem from a different point of view / as a dramatic scene
	Ghettos… SB S. 40, TB S. 33	newspaper article (733 words)	segregation / racial tension	identify features of a comment • define / give examples of 'ghettos'	write a text based on key words • discuss causes of ethnic tensions
🎧	The Indian who… SB S. 42, TB S. 34	poem (194 words)	the problem of belonging / identity	identify/interpret language difficulties • examine diction • structure • imagery	write a letter • a dialogue • a summary
	Do you think… SB S. 44, TB S. 35 TB S. 44	novel extract (1,294 words)	prejudice vs tolerance, defining one's culture	analyse statements • discuss language as a means of characterization • describe a relationship, attitudes • function of humour	express an opinion about the text • imagine / act out a scene
Using your skills	Reading a novel… SB S. 47, TB S. 36	novel	reading a novel	–	speculate about the novel • web search: reviews • group work • review-writing • present a novel • write a class paper
🎧	A new… SB S. 48, TB S. 36 TB S. 44, 45, 46	speech (700 words)	national identity / immigration	listening comprehension	write short articles
	Multiculturalism… SB S. 48, TB S. 39	newspaper article (610 words)	the negative aspects of multiculturalism	explain terms • brainstorm • express (dis-)agreement	write slogans for a poster • compare two texts, write a paragraph • debate

Einleitung

Dieses Kapitel entwirft ein Bild der multikulturellen Gesellschaft in Großbritannien und beschreibt einige der Begleiterscheinungen und Probleme. So werden die Erfahrungen und die daraus resultierende Befindlichkeit der Einwanderer anhand von Beispielen aus der post-kolonialen Literatur (Romanauszüge und Lyrik) dargestellt: Themen wie Entfremdung ("England is a peculiar-tasting smoked fish", SB S. 33, Salman Rushdie), Diskriminierung und Rassismus ("Listen Mr Oxford Don" von John Agard, SB S. 37 und "Telephone conversation" von Wole Soyinka, SB S. 38) und Schwierigkeiten der Identitätsfindung und Integration ("The Indian who thought he was English" von Khan Singh Kumar, SB S. 42) werden zunächst aufgegriffen. Im Romanauszug "Do you think anybody is English? Really English?", SB S. 44 (aus *White Teeth* von Zadie Smith) werden die Fragen der ethnischen und religiösen Zugehörigkeit am Beispiel der Verbrennung des Romans *The Satanic Verses* im englischen Oldham näher beleuchtet.

Die fiktionalen Darstellungen werden durch Artikel aus der britischen Presse ergänzt und vertieft, u.a. zu ethnischen Spannungen im heutigen Bradford, die sogar zu Krawallen geführt haben ("Ghettos in the North", SB S. 40). Ein weiteres Thema ist die Kontroverse über 'multiculturalism', der von vielen Beobachtern als "neuer Rassismus" abgelehnt wird ("Multiculturalism – a recipe for racism", SB S. 48). Dabei spielt die Frage nach Identität und der Definition von

Cultural mix and clash – UK

‚Britishness' bzw. ‚Englishness' eine wichtige Rolle, insbesondere beim Hörverstehenstext "A new understanding of Britishness", SB S. 48, einem Auszug aus einer Rede des früheren britischen Außenministers Robin Cook. Abgerundet wird das Bild durch Statistiken u.a. zur Einwanderung und multikulturellen Gesellschaft (Fact file: "Multicultural Britain", SB S. 43).
Die Aufgabenstellungen zielen neben der sachlichen Diskussion auf das Erkennen und Beurteilen sprachlicher und formaler Besonderheiten der Texte ab (Stil, Struktur, ‚point of view', Texttyp, usw.). Darüber hinaus wird die Lektüre und Analyse eines Romans (*White Teeth*) als GA oder Sonderaufgabe / Facharbeit für einzelne S angeregt (SB S. 47).

Kopiervorlage: Kernwortschatz TB S. 43

Bei der Bearbeitung eines Themas im Kapitel sollten S einen entsprechenden Wortschatz beispielsweise in Mind maps oder Topic webs zusammenstellen. Eine Zusammenstellung von relevanten Vokabeln finden Sie auf einer Kopiervorlage auf S. 43.

Britain as a multicultural society   SB S. 32

Looking and thinking

■ **Photos/statistics**
The photo on the left suggests that Britain is a colourful, multi-ethnic country where people live in harmony. The photo on the right shows a violent race riot during which youths have set a car alight.
The statistics relating to asylum applications in 2001 show that of the three countries listed, the UK was the most popular with asylum seekers with a total of 92,000 applications. The UK was closely followed by Germany with some 88,287 applications. However, applicants were more likely to be allowed to stay in the UK than Germany: The UK accepted about 43.5% of applicants and deported as few as 10%, whereas Germany only allowed 22.59% to remain and deported as many as 31.6%. France had about half as many applications as the UK, but only allowed 15.48% to remain.

■ **Factors**
- "43% of black Britons …": The quality of life in Britain for Afro-Caribbean immigrants has improved over the last 50 years and this group has become the most integrated, and possibly successful, of the ethnic minorities in Britain (cf. fact file, SB page 43).
- "47% of white Britons …": This section of the community may see a decline in social cohesion due to the presence of a variety of cultures and languages. They probably feel that immigrants place a burden on the welfare and educational systems, cause crime and unemployment levels to increase, and create social unrest and tension.

■ **Mind map**

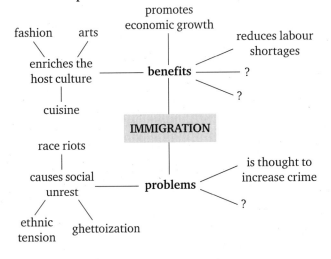

England was a peculiar-tasting smoked fish   SB S. 33–35

Background information

Salman Rushdie (b. 1947), novelist and short-story writer, was born to Muslim parents in Bombay, India. He came to England in 1961, where he was educated at Rugby School and Cambridge University. His many novels include *The Satanic Verses* (1988), *Midnight's Children* (1981) [Booker Prize], *The Moor's Last Sigh* (1996) and *Fury* (2001). He has also written short stories, non-fiction and a screenplay.
The Satanic Verses is a satire on politics and society. Its leitmotifs are emigration (problems adjusting to life in the host country, prejudice, institutionalized discrimination, police brutality, race riots) and the dichotomy of good and evil in the world. The novel interweaves three distinct narratives, one of which involves Salahuddin Chamcha, a stage and radio actor in London. The novel was perceived to be insulting to the Muslim faith. In 1989 Muslim leader Ayatollah Khomeini called on Muslims to kill Salman Rushdie and all those connected with the novel. On January 14, 1989, *The Satanic Verses* was burnt by an angry crowd of Muslims in Bradford, which has about 60,000 Muslim inhabitants (cf. "Do you think anybody is English? Really English?" SB pp. 44–46). The threat on Salman Rushdie's life was withdrawn in 1999.

Before you read

■ **Living in another country**
a) You might find it difficult to adjust because you do not speak the language fluently; you know very little about the culture of the country; you have problems finding employment and dealing with the authorities; you are confronted with prejudice; you cannot get used to the climate…
b) You could go to language classes; get information about the country and its culture; go on a short visit first to see whether you could live there; join clubs to make friends; try to find a job and accommodation before you go there…

■ **Reasons to emigrate**
Motivating factors: to do a degree at a foreign university or spend time working abroad in order to improve one's chances of promotion (both in the short term); in order to continue a relationship; to be reunited with one's family…
When s.o. is forced to emigrate: for political reasons if s.o. is being persecuted, for economic reasons (the host country offers the chance to earn enough money to live)…

Cultural mix and clash – UK

Exploring the text

1 a) *Reaction:* –
b) The text conveys various aspects of the 'immigrant experience'. Salahuddin is left very much on his own. He does not experience a warm welcome, and instead he has to cope with differences in basic customs, the unpleasant climate and bleak surroundings. His feeling of alienation in the hotel, and later at boarding school, make him defiant and defensive. Die S können überlegen, wie typisch seine Erfahrungen sind.

2 *Feelings:* In spite of his emotional state on leaving his home, Salahuddin does not cry (ll. 3–4). He has fantasies of flying to a brave new world. He is full of enthusiasm, high expectations and feels virile (ll. 16–17).
Thoughts: He has a childish attitude to the flight: he imagines that he is in a spaceship which is flying the chosen people to a new world (ll. 6–8). He feels a rush of love for his father – possibly because he is Salahuddin's only link to home (l. 12).
Worries: He does not have any real anxieties but seems slightly uneasy about the enormous distance (ll. 21–22).

3 Salahuddin remembers his first two weeks in England as a nightmare filled with worries about money, hunger, nervousness and embarrassment. He also remembers his growing rage, defiance and determination to become English.

4 What makes Salahuddin determined to become a "goodandproper Englishman" is his renewed alienation from his father who "was-not-could-never-be" (ll. 77–78) an Englishman, i.e. in this way he can distance himself from his father. The exclusion he experiences at the school, which is based on the fact that he is different, makes him defiant and want to succeed in becoming English.

5 a) The impression conveyed is one of a country with a cold, wet climate where the days are dark, and of a strange, scornful, unhelpful and racist people who have low standards of hygiene.
b) By implication, in India he was used to a more agreeable climate, higher standards of hygiene and being surrounded by his family who cared for him.

6 a) The text contains the following sense units:
– Journey to England, ll. 1–28: Salahuddin is elated and full of joyful expectation. He adores his father although the narrator mentions recent doubts and future bitterness.
– The first two weeks in England, ll. 29–91: ll. 29–62 are mainly concerned with Salahuddin's relationship with his father, who forces him to take on financial responsibility; ll. 63–78 are still mainly concerned with the father-son relationship, which slowly changes from adoration to rage; ll. 78–91: stress Salahuddin's initial experiences in England and how he deals with them.
– The kipper anecdote, ll. 92–104: This encounter with English unhelpfulness strengthens Salahuddin's determination to become English.

b) *Point of view:* The writer uses a 3rd person narrator. The unity of the passage is ensured by Salahuddin's experience, though the same point of view is not used consistently. There is a mixture of:
– narrator-focusing (i.e. Salahuddin is seen from the outside by the narrator, who reports his feelings and thoughts, and comments on them, though sometimes we seem to have a closer insight into Salahuddin's feelings (cf. ll. 79, 85–86);
– character-focusing (we have a direct insight into the boy's consciousness and see events from his point of view). This is especially the case when direct thought is used, e.g. "*I accuse ... faith*" (ll. 15–16), "*My father ... Time*" (ll. 19–20).

Close-up: language

■ **Images:**
– the aeroplane is a spaceship (ll. 6–10): The journey is made to seem more exciting, especially as it is probably Salahuddin's first flight.
– the aircraft is not a "womb" / it is a "phallus" (ll. 16–18): The reference implies that the thirteen-year-old boy is becoming a man.
– "as if a blunt knife were being pushed in" (ll. 51–52): The image shows Salahuddin's difficulties in getting used to England / wearing a uniform / being an adult.
– "winter-naked trees whose fingers clutched despairingly at the few pale hours of light" (ll. 81–82): The image conveys how cold and miserable life in Britain was for the Indian boy and arouses the reader's sympathy.
– "the way a sensitive human ... his mouth" (ll. 90–91): The comparison with a gorilla shows how stupid the English people were and conveys Salahuddin's scornful attitude towards them.
– "England was a peculiar-tasting smoked fish full of spikes and bones" (l. 100): The image characterizes English people in one phrase and conveys Salahuddin's problems in fitting in.
– "the eaten kipper was his first victory" (ll. 102–103): The image creates humour and depicts Salahuddin as a 'hero'.

Allusions:
– "Asimov's *Foundation*, Ray Bradbury's *Martian Chronicles* (l. 6): Salahuddin is going to a completely foreign world.
– "The Pure Hell of St. Trinians" (l. 55): The reference to the boarding school in a comedy film contrasts with the boy's experiences and shows that he had a naive expectation that boarding schools were funny places.
– The story of Chanakya (ll. 57–62): This includes colourful elements from Salahuddin's culture / gives an insight into how he experiences his first weeks in England.
– "condemned by the gods to have a boulder ... chest" (ll. 84–85) (derived originally from the torment imposed on the slave Bilal by his master, who tried to get him to renounce Islam): Salahuddin's difficulties weigh upon him like a heavy stone.
– William the Conqueror (l. 104): The allusion implies that William, too, came to Britain as a foreigner and still conquered the country after an unpromising start.

Cf. Rushdie's lyrical prose style, e.g. in ll. 80–82.

Background information

Isaac Asimov (1920–1992) science-fiction writer.
Foundation (1951) is the first in a trilogy which is regarded as one of the cornerstones of science-fiction writing.
Ray Bradbury (b. 1920) American novelist and short-story writer. *The Martian Chronicles* (1950) is one of his best known works and describes the first attempts to conquer and colonize Mars, and the unintended consequences.
The Pure Hell of St. Trinians (1957), one in a series of comedy films about an English all-girls boarding school.
Chanakya lived in India during the period 350–275 BC.
William the Conqueror won the Battle of Hastings and became king of England from 1066–1087.

Cultural mix and clash – UK

A step further

■ **Comment on a quotation**

Ideen: The culture and lifestyle in big cities around the world have become similar partly due to the presence of international restaurant and retail chains. Cities are also the meeting places of many cultures, which is why street scenes in Western cities often look similar. On the other hand, there is still a vast difference between city and rural dwellers, esp. in Asia and Africa as country areas are often very poor.

Listen Mister Oxford Don SB S. 36–37

Background information

Dub poetry, also known as oral or performance poetry, has its roots in popular Jamaican culture and more generally in reggae and Rastafarianism. As it makes use of languages spoken in the Caribbean, dub poetry was not taken seriously in the West at first. Indeed, it was considered to be too simple and uneducated. Gradually however, it was recognized as a creative source of new poetic forms.

Dub poetry is performed to music. The poet's relationship with the audience is most important as is the ability to communicate and deliver his message. The publication of the work does not have a high priority. "We put poetry into music, into plays. On television, radio, we perform like crazy people, we put poems on postcards and in micro chips, in fact we do anything to change the dead, white and boring image of poetry." (Benjamin Zephaniah) cf. background information on page 32.

Dub poetry has become a powerful means for West Indian immigrants to assert their identity in a multiracial, multilingual Britain. This type of poetry has been popularized in the UK by Afro-Caribbean poets such as John Agard, Linton Kwesi Johnson and Benjamin Zephaniah.

Before you read

■ **Reactions**

a) You might be amused, ironic, impatient, helpful, afraid of misunderstanding them and try to speak their language, pleased that s.o. makes an effort to speak your language…

b) You might feel embarrassed, out of your depth, amused, afraid of being misunderstood or laughed at; if you were abroad, you might be afraid that you would not understand the answer you got…

Close-up: language

■ **Features of West Indian English**

Pronunciation:
– [d] instead of [ð];
– [e] instead of [eɪ] (ent = ain't);
– [t] instead of final [ð] (wit = with);
– [ʌ] instead of [aɪ] ("muh" l. 30).

Vocabulary: the way words are spelt reflects how they are spoken, e.g.
– "imagin" (l. 24) is missing a final 'e',
– "I tekkin" (l. 27) instead of 'taking',
– "mek" (l. 33) instead of 'make'.

Grammar:
– "me" and "them" (i.e. "dem") are used as the subject forms (ll. 1, 2, 22, 25);
– double negation ("Me not no Oxford don", l. 1) instead of a single negative;
– omission of 'be' ("I warning you", l. 18);
– use of present tense to refer to the past ("I immigrate", l. 5);
– "ent" instead of 'am not' (l. 34) and 'don't' (ll. 10, 11);
– personal pronoun 'yu' instead of possessive determiner 'your' (ll. 15, 17) (possibly also a feature of pronunciation);
– adjectives instead of adverbs ("quiet", l. 27);
– omission of the article(s) ("I bashing future with present tense", l. 36);
– use of the bare infinitive instead of to-infinitive after 'want' ("dem want me serve time", l. 25).

Exploring the text

1 The speaker of the poem is an immigrant living in Clapham Common, London (ll. 2–3). He characterizes himself as being "simple" (l. 2) and "peaceful" (l. 24). He is conscious of his lack of education (l. 4) and inability to speak Standard English (ll. 12–13), but he is not embarrassed by this.

2 The message is that people are prejudiced against the immigrant and expect him to be violent simply because of the way he speaks English. He would like a peaceful life but is not prepared to give up his own dialect just to fit in (ll. 35–38).

3 *Humorous aspects:* His description of the way he murders the Queen's English, which makes him a criminal; the violent vocabulary (e.g. "mug", "mash up", "assault", "slash", "bash", "inciting to riot") are made to seem ridiculous because they are applied to a language, and the 'murder' of a language is as violent as the speaker can become.

Serious aspects: The speaker realizes that the way he speaks can provoke people and get him into trouble. He is probably not exaggerating people's reactions to him as an immigrant. However, he does not want to be considered a criminal, and he does not deserve punishment or to be discriminated against.

4 Probably not. However, because he uses a 'different' language the speaker may be regarded by some people as being inferior or threatening in some way. This may lead to discrimination in certain situations. Speaking a 'different language' may also give the immigrant an inferiority complex or feeling of otherness. A lack of understanding, caused by being different, may lead to fear, frustration, aggression and even violence.

A step further

■ **Rewrite the poem** –

■ **Dub poetry**

Background information

John Agard (b. 1949, Guyana) moved to England in 1977 and distinguished himself as a poet-performer. His use of language, inclusion of political themes and performance of his poems called conventional poetry into question. He uses irony and satire to expose common stereotypes of

Cultural mix and clash – UK

black people in the UK and to attack corruption and injustice. His major works are *Shoot me with Flowers* (1973) and *Lovelines for a Goat-Born Lady* (1990).

Linton Kwesi Johnson (b. 1952, Jamaica) emigrated to England in 1963. Much of his poetry deals with his rebellion against the racism he experienced there and the daily struggle of the black working class in the UK. His principal works are *Voices of the Living and the Dead* (1974), *Dread, Beat and Blood* (1975), *Inglan is a Bitch* (1980) and *Tings and Times* (1991).

Benjamin Zephaniah (b. 1958, Birmingham, UK) got into trouble and ended up in prison for burglary. After his release in 1979 he moved to London and turned from crime to music and performance poetry. He has frequently performed at festivals, appeared on television, published poetry and novels, and made recordings. He has also written for radio and television. According to the poet, he lives in two places, Britain and the world, and considers it his duty to explore and express the state of justice in both of them. Benjamin Zephaniah is the author of a number of novels: *Face* (1999), *Refugee Boy* (2001), poetry collections: *Pen Rhythm* (1980); *The Dread Affair* (1985); *Inna Liverpool* (1988); *Propa Propaganda* (1996); *Too Black, Too Strong* (2001); *We are Britain!* (2002) as well as prose and plays.

Websites

Siehe auch folgende Webseiten für mehr Informationen zu den Dichtern und ihren Werken:
http://www.contemporarywriters.com/
http://lister.ultrakohl.com/homepage/Lkj/lkj.htm
http://www.poetrysociety.org.uk/places/johnagar.htm
http://www.benjaminzephaniah.com/

■ Analyse statistics

a) *Comparison:* The statistics show that in four of the seven European countries listed more than half of the population thinks that immigrants are a threat to security. Only just over a third of the UK population feels that immigrants pose a threat in spite of a relatively high influx of immigrants in 2001. Compared with Germany, which has the highest percentage of immigrants in its population with a total of 9%, the UK shows a relatively high degree of scepticism towards immigrants. Compared with Portugal, which has the lowest percentage of immigrants and a relatively high degree of scepticism at 51%, the UK population is significantly more tolerant.

Among the countries listed, the UK holds the fifth place as regards the percentage of legal immigrants in its population but second place as regards the total number of immigrants in 2001.

Germany and the UK had by far the most immigrants in absolute numbers in 2001 even though Germany and Belgium had the highest percentage of legal immigrants.

b) *Patterns:*
– There is no evidence that immigration is actually related to unemployment levels: the UK has a high total number of immigrants yet a relatively low rate of unemployment, whereas Finland has a high unemployment rate and a relatively low number of legal immigrants.

– Apart from the UK, high levels of immigration seem to be accompanied by a marked level of scepticism towards immigrants as shown by the statistics for France and Germany.

Telephone conversation   SB S. 38–39

Background information

Wole Soyinka (b. 1934, Nigeria) was educated in the universities of Ibadan (1952–1954) and Leeds (1954–1957). He is a dramatist, novelist, poet and critic, and probably Africa's most distinguished writer. In the late 1950s, several of his plays were produced at the Royal Theatre in London. When he returned to Nigeria in 1960, he took a leading role in Nigerian theatre. As Nigeria underwent various political crises following independence in 1960, Wole Soyinka spoke out in defence of democracy and human rights with the result that he was repeatedly imprisoned. When the country became a dictatorship in 1993, he had to go into exile.

Wole Soyinka has become a dominant voice in anglophone African literature through his enormous creativity and versatility. He was awarded the Nobel Prize in 1986.

His works include plays such as *The Trials of Brother Jero* (1963), *The Lion and the Jewel* (1959) and *Death and the King's Horseman* (1975), poems such as *Idanre and Other Poems* (1968), *Ogun Abibiman* (1976), and the novels: *The Interpreters* (1965) and *Season of Anomy* (1973). Wole Soyinka has also written for radio, television and film.

Before you read

■ **Discrimination**

a) Discrimination may be defined as the act of treating one group differently, and usually more unfairly, than another. People may be discriminated against because of their race, sex, religion, appearance, way of speaking or a handicap. Discrimination may manifest itself in exclusion from certain social circles or jobs, from access to education or suitable housing, as well as in verbal and physical aggression.

b) –

c) *Measures:* anti-discrimination laws, cross-cultural education programmes, multi-ethnic (sports) clubs, intercultural festivals, mixed-ethnic housing, promotion of intermarriage…

Exploring the text

1 The speaker in the poem is trying to find accommodation. He has found that his West African origins are an obstacle and no less so in the telephone conversation in the poem. When he admits to being African, the landlady insists on knowing what colour he is. He is hurt and shamed, and the conversation probably ends when he responds with sarcasm and the landlady drops the phone.

2 The landlady may be characterized as being racist (cf. "How dark?" l. 10). Colour is obviously important to her in the choice of tenant. She is also insensitive towards people's feelings (she asks a personal question). She is "ill-mannered" (l. 15). Her voice suggests "good breeding" (l. 7) but she later shows that she is not so well educated when she admits to not knowing what colour "sepia" is (l. 25).

3 Initially, the speaker is resigned to the fact that landlords and landladies find his origins so important (l. 5). At first the speaker reacts with disbelief to her question "I had not misheard" (l. 10). Then he is so upset that he is temporarily unable to answer. When he realizes that she really wants to know what colour he is, he is "shamed" (ll. 14–15). His growing anger is conveyed by the repetition of "red … red … red" (l. 13). The speaker then defends himself by using irony ("Friction, caused … raven black", ll. 30–32). After this outburst, he becomes desperate again as he appeals to her to at least see him before she decides (ll. 34–35). This could also be ironic.

Close-up: structure and language

a) The text is arranged like a poem (in free verse); thus the reader expects formal, poetic elements:
- in the syntax, e.g. the sentence structure in ll. 5–9 is more typical of poetry than of prose;
- in the sound effects: onomatopoeia, e.g. "pipped" (l. 9), "squelching" (l. 14), "clanged" (l. 24); alliteration or near-alliteration, e.g. "lipstick … long", (l. 8), "silence, surrender" (l. 15); assonance, rhythm (ll. 12–35), unusual collocations e. g. "cigarette holder pipped" (l. 9), "crushing in its light impersonality" (ll. 20–21); pun "hide-and-speak" (l. 12), repetition "red … red … red" (l. 13), metaphor "voice (was) lipstick-coated, long gold-rolled" (l. 7–8), simile "like plain or milk chocolate" (l. 19).

b) *Structure:* The text is structured by the development of the speaker's emotions. He goes from being calm and matter-of-fact (ll. 1–5), as reflected by the short but complete factual sentences, to being confused and upset, a state conveyed by the incomplete, disjointed sentences in ll. 6–18. In the final stage he becomes fluent again and his sentences are more complete and logical, if somewhat ironic.
Language: The language in the poem is a powerful means of characterization. The speaker's creative and imaginative use of language distinguishes him as an articulate and educated person. This contrasts with the landlady's bluntness, poor vocabulary and simpler sentences. The fact that her part of the conversation is printed in capitals suggests that she uses a loud, arrogant tone.

A step further

■ **Rewrite the poem** –

■ **Dramatic scene**
Hinweis: Die S sollten Regieanweisungen sowohl für die zwei Standorte als auch für die Reaktionen und Körpersprache der zwei Rollen skizzieren.
- Write stage directions for both speakers in the scene before acting it out. Take the non-verbal behaviour of the two characters into consideration. Try to imagine the conversation before the caller's confession that he is African.

👁 Cartoon SB S. 39

Comparison: The cartoon deals with the same subject: discrimination because of skin colour/ethnic differences. The landlady is pleased to take a white lodger after refusing a black and an Asian candidate. She finds, however, that her new lodger's friends are the very people she rejected. The cartoon takes a more humorous view of discrimination – despite the landlady's best efforts, the very people she did not want in her home will be coming there as visitors. We do not find out whether the landlady in the poem agrees to meet the potential tenant, but her negative attitude implies that this is probably not the case.
Sketch: –

Ghettos in the north SB S. 40–41

Background information

In some North England towns, e.g. Bradford, Halifax, Oldham, Burnley and Rochdale, the white and Asian communities often live in different worlds with little contact. Discrimination and segregation are more clearly apparent there than in other parts of the country with Bangladeshis and Pakistanis being the two most disadvantaged groups. Indeed, these communities are by far the most deprived in the country with unemployment levels which are about three times as high as the national average.
Social exclusion, racism and alienation, as well as the concentration of immigrants in areas with low-quality housing have led to the present situation of 'ghettoization'. So far it has proved nearly impossible to encourage Asians to leave their traditional areas.
Despite being born in Britain, the younger generation of Asians often feels excluded from society. They are frustrated and distrustful of authority, and have shed the servile attitude of their elders. They demand radical change and rights, not tolerance. Just as the Asian communities live in fear of police brutality and attacks by the National Front, so too does the white community feel threatened by the Asian communities. Indeed, the split between the two communities seems to be widening.

Website

http://www.guardian.co.uk/ (*The Guardian*)
Diese Webseite bietet aktuelle Artikel zu Themen wie 'race riots', 'race relations' und 'ghettoisation in the UK'.

Before you read

■ **Ghettos**
a) *Mögliche Antworten:* A ghetto is a part of a city where people of a particular social class or ethnicity live separately from the main population. These ghetto inhabitants are not accepted as full citizens. A ghetto is usually slumlike and characterized by poverty, poor living conditions and derelict housing. It is usually crowded and isolated.
Causes: social / political discrimination, massive immigration.
b) *The Middle Ages:* the part of a city where Jews lived; 19th-century ghettos housed the poor in industrialized England; the 2nd World War: the Warsaw ghetto; the ghettos of the black underclass in the inner cities of the US; Asian ghettos in cities in Northern England.

Cultural mix and clash – UK

Exploring the text

1 Tension is caused by illegal discrimination against Asians who are offered lower-quality housing and have to wait longer for accommodation (ll. 10–11); ethnic segregation as estate agents restrict Asians to specific estates, so-called 'redlining'; the overall economic decline, which has led to unemployment and poverty among some Asian communities (l. 25).

2 The process of ghettoization in Northern England can be described as follows: the economic decline led to the decline of working-class areas and as a result the white community moved out. This was followed by the arrival of more Asian immigrants, attracted by low house prices; thus areas have become more racially specific, and Asians no longer have contact with the white community.

3 There is also tension between different Asian groups, such as the Pakistanis and Bangladeshis, dating from the separation of east and west Pakistan (ll. 52–53). Each group has kept its own identity and not been encouraged to integrate into society (ll. 47–49). Also, when grants are given to one community, other groups perceive this as preferential treatment and this has created ill-feeling (ll. 43–44).

4 The writer mentions putting emphasis on integration (ll. 49–50); bringing together young people from different backgrounds (ll. 57–59); taking a multi-ethnic approach to housing (ll. 59–60); having people live, work and play together (ll. 62–63). Die S können weitere Vorschläge bieten.

5 The text is characterized as a comment:
- It *focuses on a particular problem*, i.e. the northern towns suffer from ethnic tension and economic decline (ll. 4–8).
- It *states facts* e.g. "In 1990 an Oldham council report … centre" (ll. 9–15).
- It *expresses the writer's personal opinion*, e.g. "The recent report warning … is timely" (l. 8); "What has changed? Not a lot … show" (l. 16).
- It *suggests reasons for the problem*, cf. ll. 19, 25, 42–43.
- It *evaluates solutions* which have already been tried, cf. "We need to encourage … not reward them for becoming reclusive and defensive" (ll. 49–50).
- It *suggests how the problem could be tackled*, cf. ll. 62–63.

A step further

Social cohesion

Community cohesion or social cohesion are terms that have become more common in political debates on inclusion and exclusion, ethnic segregation, polarization of communities in British towns and cities and the resulting tensions.
The domains of social cohesion are as follows:
Empowerment: people feel that they are involved in processes that affect them, they can take action to initiate change.
Supporting networks: individuals and organizations cooperate and support one another; help is given when needed.
Participation: people take part in community activities.
Belonging: people feel connected to their co-residents and their area, they have a sense of belonging to the place and its people, thus giving a place a certain identity.
Trust: people feel they can trust their co-residents and the local organizations which govern or serve their area; bringing conflicting groups together.
Social order and control: there should be no general conflict or threats to the existing order; hostilities should be non-existent. Informal social control must promote tolerance, respect for differences and inter-group co-operation.
Common aims: people form groups that cooperate with one another in order to promote common interests; they develop common values and norms of behaviour and promote community interests to secure harmonious social relations.
Safety: people must feel safe in their neighbourhood and not be restricted in their use of public space by fear. Local crime prevention should be organized and there should be visible evidence of security measures.

Based on *Community Cohesion. A report of the Independent Review Team* chaired by Ted Cantle and published by the Home Office, January 1, 2003.

The Indian who thought he was English

SB S. 42–43

Before you read

■ **Belonging to a group**
Mögliche Ideen: A group is held together when its members have one or more of the following in common: language, customs, values, social background, political views, ethnicity, religion and education.

Exploring the text

1 The speaker feels physically close to them ("thick with their skin", l. 2); he speaks the same language (l. 3), he can go for a drink with his mates in the local pub and feel accepted because no one questions him about his origins (ll. 4–5); he feels included in the "us" as he supports the same side at sporting events ("our nation" l. 16); he feels no guilt, shame or sense of being different (ll. 17–18); race is not important to him (l. 21).

2 His wife rejects the drunken vandals, or possibly her husband's friends ("those shrubby people" l. 27). She is made aware of prejudice and xenophobia by the graffiti – probably racist slogans – on their wall) and is upset by it. She would like to return to her home country (l. 30).

3 The poem shows the identity crisis s.o. may undergo when they emigrate to another country. The use of the past tense in the title denies the possibility of assuming a new identity. The husband seems to have integrated better than his wife, he speaks good English and has English friends with whom he shares common interests such as the pub and football. His wife seems to have language difficulties and possibly does not have English friends. She sees their stay in England as being temporary.

Close-up: language

1 *Mögliche Antworten:*
- the image in l. 18: The Indian has succeeded in creating a new English identity. However, if something reminded him of home, "a guilt-word from a turban'd ghost", he would remember that he is still Indian and feel guilty for forgetting / ignoring his origins.
- the word "frame" in l. 25 could imply a different scene, as if his life is a film. In that scene, his wife is suffering. "Frame" could also refer to a frame of mind, i.e. his wife's unhappiness.

2 The last four lines of the poem are distinguished from the rest by being printed in italics. The wife's language is clearly marked as being different, i.e. non-standard English, which may signal a poor level of English, a lack of contact with the English population and her stronger ties with her origins. The italics and language signal a change of speakers. The section also contradicts the rest of the poem – the Indian is not English as long as people daub what are probably racist slogans on his wall.

3 *Diction* (= choice of words): There is an effective mixture of informal and more formal language, and of less common language, i.e. coinages (= the invention of new words in a language) e.g. "sojourner", "ends-of-the-earth nostalgia", "guilt-word", "estrangeness", "secret-self"). The coinages are unexpected and create an exotic, mysterious atmosphere, which contradicts the speaker's feeling of Englishness.

Structure: The poet uses free verse and divides the poem into two parts of unequal length. The second part is further divided by the use of italics for the last four lines. This use of italics creates a strong contrast with the rest of the poem; the first-person-singular pronoun "I", which is so prominent in the first part, is absent from the second part: the speaker was so carried away by his own new identity that his wife was not taken into consideration at all.

Images: e.g. "thick with their skin / with just their words" (ll. 2–3) but the following lines reveal that he is labouring under an illusion and refer to his true origin; "tucked my voice into theirs" (l. 17) shows how well he has integrated; "a childhood of bud-bud" (l. 7) sounds familiar yet exotic.

A step further

■ Letter –

■ Discussion

Siehe Fact file "Multicultural Britain", SB S. 43 für mögliche Argumente.

The Indian's wife: There is racial discrimination in many areas. Ethnic minorities are treated unfairly. They do not enjoy equal opportunities, and are often excluded from society and discriminated against. Better education has not necessarily eliminated job discrimination: ethnic minorities still suffer from higher unemployment and receive lower wages. I want to keep my Indian identity and return to India because I will never be really accepted here.

The husband: I do not think that the situation here is so bad. Not everyone is prejudiced. Most ethnic minorities do not live in segregated areas. The Indian middle class is relatively well-off, earning similar wages to white workers, or is even slightly better-off. Our children are able to get a good education and achieve above-average school results. We can be accepted in this country and make friends with the local people.

Hinweis: Es soll den S überlassen sein zu entscheiden, wie das Gespräch ausgeht.

Fact file: Multicultural Britain   SB S. 43

Die S sollten kurze Angaben im Fact file zu folgenden Gruppen zusammenfassen: black Britons / Afro-Caribbeans, British Asians, British Indians, people from Pakistan and Bangladesh.

Cultural mix and clash – UK

Do you think anybody is English? Really English?   SB S. 44–47

Background information

Zadie Smith (b. 1975) has a mixed-race background (Jamaican-English) and lives in North-West London. When her debut novel, *White Teeth* (2000), was published, critics hailed it as being "extraordinary", "stunning", "outstanding", and its author as a significant new talent, worthy to be compared with such established writers as Salman Rushdie. Zadie Smith has been awarded numerous prizes for her novel and has since published a second novel, *The Autograph Man* (2002).

White Teeth shows cultural collisions and absurdities in the multicultural environment of London. The events focus on two dysfunctional families: the Joneses have a mixed marriage (he is Anglo-Saxon and she is of Jamaican origin), and Samad and Alsana Iqbal are displaced Bangladeshis, who have twin sons, Millat and Magid.

Samad has problems with his identity, the tenets of his Muslim religion and his Hindu wife, with whom he is forever quarrelling. Their son Millat ultimately turns to fundamentalist terrorism.

The novel deals with the inevitability of the mixing of cultures in Britain in the past as well as in the present.

Before you read

■ **Quote**

"Do you think anyone is English?" The speaker might be referring to the fact that the English (Anglo-Saxons) are made up of different races. It is impossible for a nation to exclude mixed marriages and the mixing of races. Der Redeauszug von Robin Cook beschäftigt sich mit diesem Thema (cf. "A new understanding of Britishness", SB S. 48, TB S. 36).

■ **Statements**

a) / b) Die S können die Bezüge auf ‚culture' in Form einer Mind map sammeln und anschließend kommentieren. Siehe Ideen unten.

– Culture is not the same as race.
– Culture is on the inside.
– If you're black in Britain, you don't have the culture.
– Immigrants enrich a decaying white culture.
– Indian sweets, beautiful Asian women, wonderful clothes from another culture
– Cultural diversity vs. a shared national culture

Additional activities

■ Find a definition of 'culture' in your dictionary. (E.g. "the way of life, especially the general customs and belief of a particular group of people at a particular time" *Cambridge Advanced Learner's Dictionary* ISBN 3-12-517994).

■ To what extent are the things that people do or say determined by the culture they grow up in?

Cultural mix and clash – UK

Exploring the text

1 a) They are going to take part in the demonstration against a book because they think it is blasphemous (l. 29) and full of "nastiness" (l. 26).
b) They have not read the book, so their anger is based mainly on hearsay and prejudice. But it is also stems from the prejudice ethnic minorities experience daily in British society. The book gives them the publicity they would otherwise never have, cf. "suddenly people like Millat were on every channel and every radio and every newspaper" (ll. 19–20).
Hinweis: The events in the extract refer to a real event in Bradford, England, when Salman Rushdie's novel *The Satanic Verses* was burnt during a demonstration on January 14, 1989. (Cf. Salman Rushdie, TB p. 29.)

2 a) The couple's relationship seems to be based on conflict: both are prepared to defend their point of view. They resort to sarcasm ("Will someone remind my husband … bloody A–Z", ll. 34–35) and insults ("You don't know what you're talking about. You're out of your depth", l. 83). Husband and wife are obviously at loggerheads.
b) They hold distinctly different opinions on "the book", culture and tolerance. See table below.

	Iqbal	Alsana
book	prejudiced (l. 32), finds it offensive (ll. 30–31, 51), sees it as a way for his countrymen to get publicity (ll. 38–39)	tolerant (l. 59), feels that the author has a right to his own opinion (ll. 55–56)
culture	thinks one has to protect one's culture (religion, race) from attack (ll. 60–61)	is not sure what her own culture is (l. 66), thinks there is no pure culture (l. 81)
tolerance	thinks that one must fight to protect one's culture (ll. 60–61)	restraint, tolerance, a willingness to compromise and respect for others are essential (ll. 52–56)

3 The first two scenes are linked by the demonstration and book-burning in Bradford.
Parallels: While Millat takes an active part in the event, his parents watch it on television and suddenly see their son among the demonstrators. The prejudices which come to light in the boys' discussion on the train are brought into the argument between Samad and Alsana. Both father and son share the same prejudices and intolerance. Alsana's anger with her son leads to the final scene, in which she teaches him a lesson.

4 *Humour* is created by:
– the vulgar language which the teenagers use to justify the fact that they have never read the book. This fact makes their arguments less credible;
– the flippant, ironic tone which husband and wife take with one another and Alsana's comments about the "Hoover bag" (l. 81). This image conveys the reality of racial differences and tolerance much more effectively than a political speech.
Function: Because of the humour of the extract, the situations are presented in a lively, interesting and realistic way and thus contrast with the serious side of the issue.

Close-up: language

The vulgar language and taboo words in the first section of the text characterize Millat and his friends as being intolerant, aggressive, naive and wanting to fit in with the group. In their dispute, Alsana and Samad do not use slang, but they do use depreciatory words and expressions, and irony to put each other down. Both are characterized as being lively and quick at repartee, although Alsana obviously has better arguments. Samad uses idiomatic expressions in an amusing way ("tickle in the sneeze", "all grey cells in good condition", "hardly the same kettle with fish in it") which shows how he likes to play with a language which is not his own.

A step further

- Express an opinion about the text –

- Imagine / act out a scene
Siehe "Role play", TB S. 44 für mögliche Rollen.

Reading a novel: White Teeth *Using your skills* SB S. 47

Das "Using your skills" Projekt auf SB S. 47 ist als Anleitung zur EA oder GA, insbesondere für den Leistungskurs gedacht. Die S sollten bereits mit Lese- und Interpretationstechniken von fiktionalen Texten vertraut sein und auch ihren ersten englischsprachigen Roman im Kurs gelesen und besprochen haben.
Unter "Before you read" werden Anregungen gegeben, wie man sich einem Roman annähert. Anschließend werden die S aufgefordert sich im Internet darüber zu informieren. Die Ergebnisse sollten dann im Kurs mündlich oder auf einem Wandplakat vorgestellt werden.
Da der Umfang des Romans die S abschrecken könnte, ist in jedem Fall zu diskutieren, mit welchen Lesetechniken vorzugehen ist und wie arbeitsteilig verfahren werden kann. Dazu gibt "While reading: groupwork" einige Hinweise.
Wegen des Umfangs und zur Förderung der Selbständigkeit sollte der Roman über einen länger zu bemessenen Zeitraum in HA gelesen werden, wobei Notizen zu den einzelnen Aspekten anzufertigen sind. Für die anschließende GA sollten mindestens zwei Doppelstunden anberaumt werden, in denen die Gruppen ihre individuellen Ergebnisse vergleichen und abstimmen können. Für die Präsentation und Diskussion im Plenum sollten ebenfalls zwei Doppelstunden angesetzt werden.
Schließlich ist "A step further" produktorientiert. Die Gruppen können ihre Ergebnisse vorstellen und sich nach einer 'pyramid discussion' darauf einigen, wie die endgültige 'book review' aussehen soll. Schließlich kann der Roman auch zu einer Facharbeit genutzt werden, indem man ihn mit einer bestimmten Themensetzung untersuchen lässt.

A new understanding of Britishness   SB S. 48

Background information

Immigration has been, and still is, a highly controversial topic in the UK. In the extract from a speech by Robin

Cultural mix and clash – UK

Cook, former British Foreign Minister, the listener receives an altogether more positive view of immigration and definition of immigration laws than has been the case in reality.

The speech was made to the Social Market Foundation in London. This is a registered charity and an independent organization which publishes papers by academics and other experts on key topics in the economic and social fields.

Eine mögliche Bearbeitung des Hörverstehenstexts befindet sich auf einer Kopiervorlage im TB S. 45. Die Trackpunkte geben den Anfang des Abschnitts auf der Begleit-CD (ISBN 3-12-510472-6) an.

Transkript

10 The first element in the debate about the future of Britishness is the changing ethnic composition of the British people themselves. The British are not a race, but a gathering of countless different races and communities, the vast majority of which were not indigenous to these islands. In the pre-industrial era, when transport and communications were often easier by sea than by land, Britain was unusually open to external influence; first through foreign invasion, then, after Britain achieved naval supremacy, through commerce and imperial expansion. It is not their purity that makes the British unique, but the sheer pluralism of their ancestry.

London was first established as the capital of a Celtic Britain by Romans from Italy. They were in turn driven out by Saxons and Angles from Germany. The great cathedrals of this land were built mostly by Norman Bishops, but the religion practised in them was secured by the succession of a Dutch Prince. Outside our Parliament, Richard the Lionheart proudly sits astride his steed. A symbol of British courage and defiance. Yet he spoke French much of his life and depended on the Jewish community of England to put up the ransom that freed him from prison.

11 The idea that Britain was a 'pure' Anglo-Saxon society before the arrival of communities from the Caribbean, Asia and Africa is fantasy. But if this view of British identity is false to our past, it is false to our future, too. The global era has produced population movements of a breadth and richness without parallel in history.

Today's London is a perfect hub of the globe. It is home to over 30 ethnic communities of at least 10,000 residents each. In this city tonight, over 300 languages will be spoken by families over their evening meal at home.

This pluralism is not a burden we must reluctantly accept. It is an immense asset that contributes to the cultural and economic vitality of our nation.

Legitimate immigration is the necessary and unavoidable result of economic success, which generates a demand for labour faster than can be met by the birthrate of a modern developed country. Every country needs firm but fair immigration laws. There is no more evil business than trafficking in human beings and nothing corrodes social cohesion worse than a furtive underground of illegal migrants beyond legal protection against exploitation. But we must also create an open and inclusive society that welcomes incomers for their contribution to our growth and prosperity. Our measures to attract specialists in information technology is a good example.

12 Our cultural diversity is one of the reasons why Britain continues to be the preferred location for multinational companies setting up in Europe. The national airline of a major European country has recently relocated its booking operation to London precisely because of the linguistic variety of the staff whom it can recruit here.

And it isn't just our economy that has been enriched by the arrival of new communities. Our lifestyles and cultural horizons have also been broadened in the process. This point is perhaps more readily understood by young Britons, who are more open to new influences and more likely to have been educated in a multi-ethnic environment. But it reaches into every aspect of our national life.

Chicken Tikka Masala is now a true British national dish, not only because it is the most popular, but because it is a perfect illustration of the way Britain absorbs and adapts external influences. Chicken Tikka is an Indian dish. The Masala sauce was added to satisfy the desire of British people to have their meat served in gravy.

Coming to terms with multiculturalism as a positive force for our economy and society will have significant implications for our understanding of Britishness.

The modern notion of national identity cannot be based on race and ethnicity, but must be based on shared ideals and aspirations. Some of the most successful countries in the modern world, such as the United States and Canada, are immigrant societies. Their experience shows how cultural diversity, allied to a shared concept of equal citizenship, can be a source of enormous strength. We should draw inspiration from their experience.

Listening for gist

1 hub of the globe, cultural diversity, linguistic variety, lifestyles and cultural horizons have been broadened, open and inclusive society, multi-ethnic environment, immigrant societies

2 Upbeat: The speaker uses positive language such as "immense asset", "to be enriched", "positive force for our economy and society". He creates a positive picture of the future and encourages everyone to participate in creating an "open and inclusive society". In the last sentence, he asks his listeners to draw inspiration from the examples given by the US and Canada.

Listening for detail

1 From the beginning Britain has always been a mixture of different races and peoples, e.g. Romans, Angles, Saxons, Normans, Dutch and Jews to name but a few. The make-up of Britain's population has been influenced by invasions and expansion. A pure Anglo-Saxon society has never existed.

2 Many people think that Britain's population was just made up of Anglo-Saxons in the past where in fact it was characterized by pluralism and diversity. These features will continue into the future because of immigration and multiculturalism.

3 Britain's multiculturalism is an asset that creates cultural and economic vitality: legitimate immigration is a consequence of a demand for labour and it contributes to Britain's growth and prosperity. The diversity of its population makes

Cultural mix and clash – UK

Britain a favoured economic location. British society is open to diverse lifestyles, and ethnic and cultural differences.

4 Immigration laws are needed to prevent the trafficking of illegal immigrants. The presence of illegal immigrants, who can be easily exploited, can have a negative effect on social cohesion. It is also possible to attract qualified immigrants that the country needs for specialized work.

5 National identity is not a question of race or ethnicity but of shared ideals and goals, of diversity and a concept of equal citizenship.

6 Robin Cook uses this example to prove, in a simple way, what a good thing cultural diversity is and how much British culture may be enriched by immigration and contact with other cultures. The adaptation of the original Indian dish to suit British tastes illustrates Britain's ability to combine British and foreign influences.

A step further

■ Comment

Für Kritikpunkte siehe Fact file "Multicultural Britain", SB S. 43. Robin Cook does not mention the fact that immigration laws keep out thousands of potential immigrants, many of whom seek political asylum. He does not mention the problems young Pakistanis and Bangladeshis have in integrating and being accepted in British society. The US in particular has many difficulties maintaining harmony and order in its multicultural society. Illegal immigration is a big problem as is the exploitation of illegal workers.

■ News item

Siehe Skills file "Newspaper texts", SB S. 188 für Ideen.
E.g. In a speech last night at the Social Foundation, London, Robin Cook drew an upbeat picture of multicultural society in Britain. He began and ended with the statement that British identity/Britishness is not based on race or ethnicity but on its pluralism and cultural diversity. By means of references to Britain's past he underlined the fact that the idea of Britain as a pure Anglo-Saxon society before Caribbean, Asian and African immigrants arrived is nothing but a myth. From this he concluded that population movements would continue into the future. Indeed, London is already a global centre. He supplied convincing arguments that, far from being a burden, legitimate immigration was an asset for a number of reasons: it improved the labour situation, and led to economic growth, new lifestyles and an openness to cultural differences. He illustrated this with the example of Chicken Tikka Masala before taking up the initial idea of a national identity again with a reference to the immigrant societies of Canada and the USA, which might serve as an example to Britain. In conclusion, it can be said that Mr Cook's reasoning in this part of the speech was quite convincing.

■ Respond to the speech –

Project work –

Kopiervorlage: Immigration in the UK – a timeline

Die S können die Kopiervorlage auf TB S. 46 in Form einer Facharbeit aufbereiten.

Kopiervorlage: Talking about immigration

Die S können die Kopiervorlage im TB S. 44 auf zwei Arten und Weisen aufbereiten. Siehe auch "Background information" unten.

■ With a partner, read the statement you are given and decide whether it contains a positive or negative attitude towards immigration. Then comment on your statement in more detail.

■ Read the statement you are given and walk around the class. When you meet another student, read out your statement and try to make an additional comment explaining/justifying your attitude. The other student does the same. Then move on to the next person.

Background information

Enoch Powell (1912–1997), English Conservative politician, became well-known in the 1960s for his opposition to immigration. In 1968, he made what is now referred to as the "Rivers of Blood" speech, in which he claimed that if too many black immigrants were allowed to live in Britain, violence would result and "rivers of blood" would flow in the streets. The black comedian Lenny Henry makes fun of Enoch Powell by implying that he did not realise that many black people have their homes in Britain and are British citizens.

A Sivanadam justifies the presence of immigrants in Britain by referring to the British Empire. If Britain had not founded an empire, there would not have been such an influx of coloured immigrants into Britain. Thus, immigrants have a right to be in Britain.

Mark Collett: This is the attitude of the extreme rightwing parties, the British National Party and the National Front, who make no bones about their racism.

Margaret Thatcher (b. 1925): Her governments' policies focused on monetary and economic issues. The word "swamped" implies that she was not particularly happy about immigration: possibly the British people's fear was caused by the financial burden of immigration.

Newspaper headlines: At their 2002 annual conference, the National Association of Head Teachers urged the government to remove the requirement for children between the ages of 11 and 14 to study at least one European foreign language. The linguistic abilities of large numbers of ethnic minority and refugee children were being ignored because they had to master English as well as learn a further European language. The NAHT wants the government to promote the status of Asian and African languages "and encourage their study as a qualification in addition to or instead of languages of European origin".

David Blunkett: In his government white paper *Secure Borders, Safe Haven,* David Blunkett demands that immigrants who apply for British citizenship take a compulsory English language test as well as a citizenship test.

Gary Younger: The statement shows that 'immigration' is an emotionally loaded term. He claims that politicians are thought to have a racist attitude because they use the word to refer to people of colour, who are thought to pose a threat to the host country, i.e. Britain.

Cultural mix and clash – UK

Multiculturalism – a recipe for racism
SB S. 48–49

Before you read

■ **Assimilation / integration / multiculturalism**

a) *Assimilation:* one group becomes part of or like another group: assimilation makes for greater uniformity, there is less insistence on the rights of individual groups, less prejudice and intolerance, fewer cultural / political / religious conflicts, there is no positive discrimination in favour of a disadvantaged group…

Integration: The minority is encouraged to join society and change their way of life and customs to suit what already exists; the minority interacts with the majority and pursues common interests; integration prevents ethnic segregation while allowing people to keep their individuality…

Multiculturalism emphasizes the difference between ethnic groups and cultures; it aims at greater diversity, more religious / ethnic / political autonomy, tolerance and respect for different cultures. However, multiculturalism may breed intolerance by separating ethnic groups and putting emphasis on special rights for each group. It may lead to excesses of political correctness, as in the US, and ultimately cause ethnic and religious tensions and violence…

b) –

■ **Englishness**

Ideen: cricket, Do-It-Yourself, punk, Shakespeare, double-decker buses, Charles Dickens, country churches, gardening, Christopher Wren and Monty Python, the Beatles, fish and chips, Cambridge, politeness, Rolls Royce, Mini Coopers…

Hinweis: Englishness and Britishness are not identical. Britishness is more inclusive as s.o. can be British Indian or British Asian and so on, but not English and any of these nationalities. In a speech in October 1997, Prime Minister Tony Blair characterized the "New Britain" as: "a meritocracy where we break down barriers of class, religion, race and culture".

■ **Recipe for division**

In the US, the concept of multiculturalism upheld the idea that American society did not have a common culture but distinctly different ethnic, racial or cultural communities and that ignoring these differences would breed intolerance, discrimination and racism.

Multiculturalism claims to eradicate cultural dominance and racism and promote tolerance towards minorities and respect for diversity. According to this concept people see themselves as members of a specific group (racial, ethnic, national, religious, etc.) with which they identify. Hence the many 'hyphenated' Americans. This situation can lead to hostility and rivalry between groups. In this way, an insistence on diversity and a celebration of differences turn out to be divisive and may institutionalize segregation and – since groups are often defined racially – even racism.

Exploring the text

1 Minette Marrin is against multiculturalism because it emphasizes differences, divides society, causes racism, confuses people and prevents the development of a shared British identity (ll. 31–34). What Britain needs – and is moving towards – is a multiracial society with "a tolerant, over-arching host culture" (ll. 59–60).

2 a) People feel that if they favour a "host culture", they then reject multiculturalism and a group's right to its own identity. They are afraid of being considered racist if they do not declare all cultures to be equal (ll. 48–51). Indeed, multiculturalists regard the idea of a "host culture" as being "supremacist and racist" (l. 64).

b) –

3 a) The writer cites examples where Christmas festivities were abolished in some schools and replaced with a more inclusive cultural festival (ll. 87–90). She also mentions a book about multicultural Britain which completely excluded the word "English".

b) –

A step further

■ **What could be done to reduce racism**

E.g. Celebrate festivals with people of different cultures, show interest in and respect for their language / values / customs; explain your own lifestyle to them; invite people from a different culture into your home; act as a mediator when there are problems between members of your own group and s.o. from a different culture; speak out against prejudice and discrimination…

■ **Robin Cook**

Yes: Mr Cook takes a very optimistic view of race relations and completely ignores the fact that integration is a major problem for some ethnic minorities (cf. "Ghettos in the north", SB pp. 40–41). These problems are not only caused by the ethnic minorities themselves but also by attitudes within British society, and economic and social factors.

No: It is important to point out the positive aspects of multiculturalism as integration often does work and immigrants provide a valuable workforce and cultural diversity.

■ **Debate**

Siehe "Discussions", SB S. 193 und *Password to Skyline Plus* (ISBN 3-12-510460-2), S. 106, "How to conduct a debate" für Ideen und nützliche Redemittel.

Test: A Distant Shore
TB S. 47

Klausur für den Grundkurs
Textformat: novel extract, 595 words
Zentrale Bezugstexte des Kapitels: "A new understanding of Britishness" (SB S. 48, TB S. 36) und "Multiculturalism – a recipe for racism" (SB S. 48). Der Romanauszug bietet den S Gelegenheit, Methodenkenntnisse im Umgang mit fiktionalen Texten anzuwenden (Analyse von Sprache, Struktur, Charaktere).
Der Klausurtest und die entsprechenden Fragen befinden sich auf einer Kopiervorlage auf S. 47.

Comprehension

1 According to Mr Anderson, people's attitudes are caused by prejudice and upset. England is a relatively small country and people feel that it is being overrun by immigrants to the extent that it cannot absorb them any longer. People feel that

Cultural mix and clash – UK

they have done their share for refugees and now it is the turn of other countries to accommodate them. They also feel that they are being taken advantage of by those who are only seeking "an easy living".

Mike thinks that to some extent, the immigrants – and he has "the Indian types" (Pakistanis, Bangladeshis, Indians) in mind – are themselves the cause of their rejection by the indigenous, British population: because of their different religions and customs, and their lack of education they are unable and unwilling to adjust to British society and are therefore unable to integrate. As the immigrants are arriving in great numbers, people fear that the country is changing beyond recognition and is becoming "foreign". In this way, 'bad attitudes' are caused. Moreover, people lump together all the immigrant groups so that genuine political refugees, like Solomon, who have a right to asylum, meet with the same prejudice and hostile treatment as economic refugees.

2 Neither Mr Anderson nor Mike agree with the hostile attitude of their countrymen. They are both sincerely sorry about the situation. Mr Anderson is embarrassed and pained at having to explain something to Solomon that he does not understand himself but which affects him and leaves him at a loss. He has no overall solution to offer. ("Mr Anderson was clearly unsettled by what had happened to his house and he did not know what to do.") He only mentions the possibility that if an immigrant, like Solomon, perseveres and tries to overcome people's prejudice, he may have an undisturbed life in Britain. In other words, it is the immigrant who has to break through "the first line of defence" in order to be accepted.

Mike feels that the immigrants should choose between education/training and repatriation. Immigrants should either get "some training" or "they should go back". However, Mike seems to have a better understanding of the situation than his parents, maybe because he gets around a bit more "than what the old folks does". He is not prejudiced, let alone racist (or he would not have helped Solomon), but he definitely sees cultural differences as being the greatest obstacle to mutual acceptance and integration. His tolerance of immigrants seems to reach a limit when his life-long, cherished habits are threatened and his country becomes "foreign" to him. On the other hand, he accepts genuine asylum seekers and the procedures that grant them the right to stay legally in Britain.

Analysis

3 The language marks the situation as being informal (cf. use of short forms of the auxiliary, e.g. "There's", don't", "we've"; colloquial lexical choices, e.g. "get", "things", "folk", "the Indian types" and simple syntax. The informal language suggests that the two speakers have a relatively close relationship with Solomon. The simplicity of the language may also have to do with the fact that both Mr Anderson and Mike are anxious to make themselves understood. This impression is corroborated when the men ask Solomon whether he understands their explanations.

The limited narrative parts refer to the whereabouts of the characters (a car park is mentioned in the first section, so one can assume that Mr Anderson and Solomon are having their conversation in Mr Anderson's car; however, nothing is said about where Mike talks to Solomon) and to the characters' reactions and feelings.

Evaluation / (re)creation of a text

4 Die S können u.a. folgende Ideen entwickeln:
– agree with the views presented in the extracts (add reasons as to why immigration can increase prejudice and racism / explain why multiculturalism is not acceptable);
– disagree with the views presented in the extracts (explain why immigration is an advantage for the host society, make suggestions as to what could be done to improve the situation, and fight prejudice and racism);
– discuss the pros and cons of immigration;
– point out to what extent the situation is different in Germany;
– suggest the necessity for a common European policy on immigration;
– make use of the statistics and the ideas in the mind map at the beginning of the chapter (cf. SB page 32).

Test: Bogus friends of asylum seekers TB S. 48

Klausur für den Leistungskurs
Textformat: newspaper article, 626 words
Vorschlag/Klausurtyp NRW: Tasks 1–3, A2
Zentraler Bezugstext des Kapitels: "A new understanding of Britishness", SB S. 48. Formal handelt es sich um einen Kommentar, so wie er im SB durch "Ghettos in the North", SB S. 40–41 und "Multiculturalism – a recipe for racism", SB S. 48–49 (von derselben Journalistin) vertreten ist.
Der Klausurtest und die entsprechenden Fragen befinden sich auf einer Kopiervorlage auf S. 48.

Comprehension

1 The writer considers the British asylum system to be unsatisfactory, badly organized and abused, with few applicants being genuine asylum seekers. Those whose application is rejected can appeal. The appeal procedure then takes years, at great cost to the taxpayer, and ends in failure for the applicant. Few of those turned down are ever deported: instead many go underground and live illegally in Britain. In addition, many economic migrants succeed in beating the system.

2 For one thing, people easily get emotional and irrational about the subject. There is the discussion about who is a genuine and who is a bogus refugee. All genuine asylum seekers have the right to stay, but it is impossible to accommodate the hundreds of thousands who deserve protection from persecution. And what is more, they are not wanted in Britain.

Analysis

3 *Style:* The article is a comment, i.e. subjective/persuasive set of arguments. It is characterized by personal values and beliefs that are put forward in subjective assertions (short and relatively simple sentences) that are difficult to contradict. The reader notices a personal bias in the repeated use of intensifying and attitudinal adverbs or equivalent expressions (e.g. unfortunately, unmistakably genuine, truly unforgivable, quite impossible, grossly unfair, badly abused and badly run, without any doubt, the left ought to feel angry, surely, I am convinced that, I think).
Tone: The negative tone of the article also influences the reader, cf. expressions such as nasty, nastier, muddle, bogus, no big idea, a waste and a shame. The writer also uses rhetorical questions to make her arguments more convincing

e.g. "And who can really blame them for trying to beat it?" and "Why should it be so disgraceful and racist to say so?"

Re-creation of a text
4 Die S können u.a. folgende Punkte in ihrer Antwort berücksichtigen:
- agree or disagree with the writer;
- present the issue in the larger context of global migration;
- suggest how Britain and other European countries can tackle the problem on a joint European basis;
- consider the option of stemming the tide of immigrants, both legal and illegal, by providing economic aid to developing countries / promoting human rights to prevent political persecution.

Test: Neighbours   TB S. 42

Mündliche Prüfung
Textformat: poem, 137 words
Zentrale Bezugstexte des Kapitels: "Listen Mr Oxford Don", SB S. 37, "Telephone conversation" SB S. 38, "The Indian who thought he was English", SB S. 42.
Die Prüfung und die entsprechenden Fragen befinden sich auf einer Kopiervorlage auf S. 42.

Comprehension
1 The speaker represents black, Afro-Caribbean males who have emigrated to Britain; the addressee is the indigenous British community. Their relationship is characterized by ambiguous feelings of fear and love on the part of the whites whereas the speaker takes an assertive, self-confident and also possibly provocative stance. The speaker sees himself as being the more active partner in the relationship: he has approached the addressee now that they are neighbours and he expects a positive response.

2 *Fear:* The speaker appears to be different: he is "black", speaks differently "in tongues" and looks "foreign" (l. 2), all of which imply that he does not belong. His habits, i.e. "I sleep with lions" (l. 8) and a "grass eater" (l. 4) suggest that he is still half wild and lacks civilized manners. The speaker makes noise at night and disturbs people, "I chant at night" (l. 6). His lack of education may seem threatening and his tendency towards melancholy disturbing ("and when the moon gets me I am a Wailer", ll. 9–10).

Attraction: because of the speaker's impressive stature and beauty, his mysterious nature, his naturalness, i.e. he is uncorrupted by civilization, possibly abstains from alcohol (pun "tea total", l. 25). He is also active in education and the media, is attractive to beautiful women ("cool cats"), and is exuberant when happy "and when the sun is shining I go Carnival" (ll. 30–31).

Analysis
3 *Structure:* The poem consists of 31 short lines grouped into six units of varying length. On closer inspection, three distinct sense units are revealed: ll. 1–10, 11–21, 22–31. The first and third units contrast strongly with one another: the first unit outlines reasons to fear the speaker and the third gives reasons to find him attractive. The 'negative' aspects mentioned in ll. 1–10 are taken up again one by one and turned into their 'positive' opposites by connotation and collocation. Both units focus completely on the speaker, who characterizes himself with the first-person pronoun "I", placed conspicuously at the beginning of most of the lines.

The second unit (ll. 11–21) develops the idea of "neighbours" and their interaction / relationship, and juxtaposes the first-person and second-person pronouns. The unit suggests answers to the question, "How will you feel?" in ll. 20–21 which, however, seem to be meant ironically.

Language: The syntax is characterized by short, simple, i.e. non-complex, sentences. There are only two relative clauses (ll. 1, 22), two temporal clauses (ll. 9–10, 30–31) and one consecutive clause (l. 13). The lexis, too, is mainly characterized by simple choices though some words have distinct connotations, e.g. "talk in tongues" has religious connotations; "dreadlocks" are linked with Rastafarianism (belief in Ras Tafari i.e. Haile Selassie of Ethiopia as the Messiah, and that Africa (especially Ethiopia) is the Promised Land); "moon" is a cause of melancholy, "Wailer" may refer to s.o. who cries loudly at funerals or even the reggae band "The Wailers" associated with musician Bob Marley; "sun" is synonymous with 'happiness', "Carnival" probably refers to the Caribbean music festival held in Notting Hill, London.

Style: Only a few words are marked stylistically: "grass eater" may have a double meaning as grass is a slang term for 'marijuana', "cool cats" (slang) = attractive women, "I go Carnival" (informal), "tea total" (pun on teetotal; tea is also a slang term for marijuana).

Images that need interpretation: ll. 8, 9–10, 18, 30–31.
The poem makes repeated use of alliteration: cf. ll. 2–3, 5, 7, 8, 24–27, 29.

Evaluation / (re)creation of a text
4 Die S können u.a. folgende Ideen entwickeln:
- agree or disagree with the poet;
- explain what you would do to promote a good relationship between neighbours;
- point out how multicultural differences are dealt with in Germany.

Selected bibliography

Die folgenden Literaturempfehlungen sind für die Hand des Lehrers gedacht:

Ashcroft, Bill / Griffiths, Gareth / Tiffin, Helen: *The Empire Writes Back, Theory and Practice in Post-Colonial Literatures,* London: Routledge, 1989.

Benson, Eugene / Conolly, L.W. (ed.): *Encyclopedia of Post-Colonial Literatures in English.* London: Routledge, 1994, mit umfangreichen Informationen über Autoren, Themen, literarische Genres, Literaturkritik, Film und Journalistik sowie Inhaltsangaben, Interpretationsansätzen und weiteren bibliographischen Angaben.

Brown, Stewart et al. (eds.): *Voice Print. An Anthology of Oral and Related Poetry from the Caribbean.* Harlow, Essex: Longman 1989, mit einer sehr brauchbaren und ausführlichen Einleitung.

Caspari, Daniela, *Kreativität im Umgang mit literarischen Texten im Fremdsprachenunterricht.* Frankfurt / M.: P. Lang, 1994.

Themenheft: Postkoloniale Literatur und Kultur. *fsu Fremdsprachenunterricht,* 4 / 1999.

Cultural mix and clash – UK

Zu allen Themen können Informationen, Artikel, Auszüge usw. unter den entsprechenden Stichwörtern im Internet mit den gängigen Suchmaschinen abgerufen werden. Für politische und z. T. auch für literarische Themen und Buchbesprechungen erweist sich das Archiv von *The Guardian* www.guardian.co.uk als besonders brauchbar. Buchbesprechungen finden sich auf der Webseite von Amazon (www.amazon.com).

Zum Thema des Kapitels sind für den Unterricht folgende Romane als Ganzschriften oder in Auszügen empfehlenswert:
Monica Ali, *Brick Lane*. London: Double Day, 2003.

Maggie Gee, *The White Family*, London: Saqi Books, 2002.
Hanif Kureishi, *The Buddha of Suburbia*. London: Faber and Faber, 1990.
Caryl Phillips, *The Final Passage*. London: Faber and Faber, 1999 and *A Distant Shore*, London: Secker&Warburg, 2003.
Nigel Williams, *East of Wimbledon*, London: Faber and Faber, 1993.

Test: Neighbours

I am the type you are supposed to fear
Black and foreign
Big and dreadlocks
An uneducated grass eater.

5 I talk in tongues
I chant at night
I appear anywhere,
I sleep with lions
And when the moon gets me
10 I am a Wailer.

I am moving in
Next door to you
So you can get to know me,
You will see my shadow
15 In the bathroom window,
My aromas will occupy
Your space,
Our ball will be in your court.
How will you feel?

20 You should feel good
You have been chosen.

I am the type you are supposed to love
Dark and mysterious
Tall and natural
25 Thinking, tea total.
I talk in schools
I sing on TV
I am in the papers,
I keep cool cats

30 And when the sun is shining
I go Carnival. (137 words)

By Benjamin Zephaniah, *Propa Propaganda*, Tarset, Northumberland: Bloodaxe Books, 1996.

10 **Wailer** s.o. who is unhappy and makes long high-pitched cries – 25 **tea total** *pun on* teetotal, i.e. not drinking alcohol; **tea** *(slang)* marijuana – 29 **cool cats** *(slang)* attractive women – 31 **Carnival** reference to the annual Caribbean music festival in Notting Hill, London

Tasks

1 Who is the speaker in the poem and who does he address? How does the speaker characterize the relationship between himself and the addressee?
2 Why does the addressee both fear and feel attracted to the speaker at the same time?
3 Evaluate the text as a poem, examining its structure and language.
4 Write a letter to the poet in which you express your opinion about his self-portrait and idea of 'neighbourhood'. Make suggestions as to how he could improve his relationship with the indigenous population.

Cultural mix and clash – UK

Kernwortschatz

asylum = permission to stay in a country as a recognized refugee
asylum seeker = s.o. who seeks refuge (a safe place) from persecution in their own country
business status *(GB)* = the status s.o. is given if they have at least £200,000 to set up, join or take over a business
deportation = the act of sending s.o. out of the country
entry clearance *(GB)* = permission to enter the UK on a visa or entry certificate
illegal entrant = s.o. who has entered the country illegally by bypassing immigration control or by deception
indefinite leave = permission to enter or remain without time restrictions
limited leave = permission to enter or remain in a country for a specified period of time
migrant = s.o. who moves from one country to another to live
naturalisation = the process by which immigrant adults become citizens of a country
overstayer *(GB)* = s.o. who remains beyond the granted period of time
right of abode *(GB)* = the right to live in the UK indefinitely and to come and go free of immigration control
settled status *(GB)* = the status s.o. has after receiving permission to stay permanently in the country
visa national *(GB)* = s.o. who needs entry clearance before travelling to the UK

Asylum
a genuine/bogus ~ seeker
to apply/to submit an application for political
an ~ seeker is…
   allowed to remain in the country/granted a reprieve
   deported/denied sanctuary/turned down
   repatriated/expelled
a political refugee
a refugee camp
deportation figures
illegal/undocumented alien

Citizen
to become a fully-fledged ~ of…
to receive/to be granted citizenship
to be eligible for/to qualify for citizenship
to acquire citizenship through naturalisation
to be granted legal residency

Culture
a host ~/the native ~
an over-arching common ~
a shared national ~
to value the beliefs of a ~
to protect one's ~
cultures are of equal value/deserve equal respect
cultural diversity/values/background
cultural mix/clash
cultural and economic vitality
a multi-denominational group
lifestyles and cultural horizons are broadened

to come to terms with multiculturalism
cultural homogenisation

Discrimination
unlawful/racial ~
an act of ~
to practice/to endure ~
to discriminate against s.o. on the grounds of skin colour
to provide legal protection against exploitation

Ethnic
~ tension/separation/minority/group/monitoring
ethnically mixed
the dangers of ~ segregation
to adopt a multi-ethnic approach
multi-ethnic environment

Ghetto
ghettoisation
the ghetto has consolidated and grown
to live in overcrowded housing
deprived areas
to grow up deprived of contact with people unlike o.s.
to fall into a decline
economic depression has deepened
the collapse of manufacturing
an urban regeneration grant
Asian versus white community
inner city strife
to be segregated on specific estates
a riot hit town
people of different backgrounds
to corrode social cohesion

Identity
to lose one's ~/to develop a shared ~
the modern notion of national identity
the future of Britishness
to be indigenous to a country
to absorb/to adapt to external influences

Alienation
to be alienated (from)
to be excluded (from)/to be caught between two worlds/cultures
to adjust badly to…/to be an outsider
to fit into/blend in/merge into/adapt to the mainstream culture

Immigration/Emigration
to benefit from/be enriched by/be damaged by ~
~ policy/law
firm and fair immigration laws
legal/illegal immigrant
an immigrant society
a tide/surge/flood of immigrants
to regulate the influx of immigrants
to immigrate
to force s.o. to emigrate

Cultural mix and clash – UK

Migration
internal / international / seasonal / mass ~
an incentive to migrate
an obstacle to ~
an economic migrant
population movements
mass mobility

Race
~ relations
~ riots
to be burdened with anxieties about race
to cause racism
racial equality / discrimination / tension / issue
multiracial society
to advocate racist / supremacist theories
overt / subtle / institutionalized / deep-rooted ~
racially distinctive
mixed marriage

Role play

Alsana upbraids her son
- "How could you possibly…?"
- "How on earth could you…?"
- "How am I supposed to / going to…?"
- "I couldn't believe my eyes when…"
- "Who do you think you are to…?"

Millat tries to defend himself
- "I was only… / I only meant to …"
- "You had no right to…"
- "How am I going to replace …?"
- "There was no need for you to…"
- "I had no intention of…"

Samad defends his son
- "The boy was only …"
- "You can't blame him for …"
- "There's no need to be so hard on …"
- "You shouldn't have…"
- "What's the use of …?"

Talking about immigration

"Enoch Powell wants to give us £1,000 to go home. Suits me. It only costs me 50p to go to Dudley."
Lenny Henry, black comedian

"We are here because you were there."
A Sivanandan, editor of *Race and Class*

"I'm drawn to a racially white society. Because I'm proud of being British and English."
Mark Collett, British National Party member

"People are really rather afraid that this country might be swamped by people with a different culture…"
Margaret Thatcher, former Conservative Prime Minister (1979–1990)

"Ditch French for Punjabi, say school heads."
Drop French, say heads, and teach Urdu instead.
Newspaper headlines, June 2002

"We have norms of acceptability. And those who come into our home – for that is what it is – should accept these norms just as we would have to do if we went elsewhere."
David Blunkett, Home Secretary

"When they (British politicians) refer to immigrants they do not mean Australians or Americans, they mean Caribbeans and Asians."
Gary Younger, "A Land fit for Racists", *The Guardian*, May 4, 2002.

Cultural mix and clash – UK

A new understanding of Britishness   SB S. 48

Vocabulary

5 **indigenous** [ɪnˈdɪdʒɪnəs] native – 11 **sheer** *here:* complete – **pluralism** presence of different groups in a society – 16 **Dutch Prince** reference to William of Orange who was crowned king of England (William III) in 1689 – 17 **Richard the Lionheart** (1157–1199) King of England from 1189 until his death – 18 **steed** *(poetic)* horse – 20 **ransom** money paid to free s.o. who is a prisoner – 28 **hub** *(here fig.)* the centre of activity – 32 **burden** responsibility – **reluctantly** unwillingly – 33 **asset** *here:* advantage, resource – 35 **legitimate** [lɪˈdʒɪtəmət] lawful – 40 **to traffic** *here:* to smuggle illegal immigrants into the country – 41 **furtive** *(negative)* secret

Listening for gist

1 What phrases does the speaker use to describe the multicultural nature of British society? List the key words you hear.
2 Which of the following adjectives would you use to describe the speaker's attitude towards multiculturalism: negative – upbeat – naive – warning – critical?
Give reasons for your answer.

Listening for detail

1 How does Robin Cook understand Britain's past with regard to 'Britishness'?
2 Explain the following quote from the speech: "But if this view of British identity is false to the past, it is false to our future, too".
3 What positive aspects of a multicultural Britain does the speaker mention?
4 What does the speaker see as the purpose of immigration laws?
5 What is Robin Cook's notion of national identity?
6 What is the significance of the reference to Chicken Tikka Masala?

A step further

- Write a comment giving your personal opinion of the speech extract. You could check skills file, "Comments" on page 188 of your book. How convincing do you find the speaker's arguments?
- Imagine you are a journalist reporting on Robin Cook's speech. Write a short news item giving readers a summary of his ideas.
- Read the extract "Do you think anyone is English? Really English?" on pages 44–46 of your book. How do you think Samad would respond to Robin Cook's speech?
With a partner, choose at least five key sentences from the speech. Then try to imagine how Samad would respond to them.

Project work

- a) In groups, find out more about ethnic communities in Britain. Each group could concentrate on one ethnic community and use the Internet to find information.
  b) Present the results of your research in a short report and collect the class's work on a wall chart.

Cultural mix and clash – UK

Immigration in the UK – a timeline

Tasks

- The following timeline shows landmarks in immigration policy in Britain since the middle of the 20th century. Find out more about the events in British history which may have led to the changes in British immigration and asylum policy. Summarize your findings in a class paper.
  You could refer to http://www.ind.homeoffice.gov.uk/

Prior to 1949 everyone living in the British Empire was a British subject. All others were aliens.

Aliens Act 1905 marked the beginning of immigration control. The Act tried to stop refugees (mainly Jews) from Eastern Europe coming to Britain.

British Nationality Act of 1948 (1949) established a "citizenship of the UK and Colonies" (CUKC). This Act excluded the dominions (from 1949 called "Independent Commonwealth Countries") which enacted their own nationality laws. As more and more colonies became independent Commonwealth countries, their citizens lost CUKC status.

1962 Commonwealth Immigration Act imposed the first major restrictions on immigration, clearly marking ethnic minorities from whites.

1971 Immigration Act (1973) regulated what is called the "right of abode in the UK", which allowed some CUKCs free access to the UK while subjecting others to strict immigration control. People from the former colonies, i.e. Indians, Pakistanis, Bangladeshis, and those from the Caribbean and Africa, found it very hard to get into the UK.

1981 British Nationality Act (1983) did away with CUKC status, replacing it with three new citizenships: British Citizenship, British Dependent Territories Citizenship, and British Overseas Citizenship. All those who had been CUKCs with a right of abode in the UK now became British citizens. The others could get this right only by acquiring British citizenship either:
- by birth (anyone born in the UK if either parent is a British citizen or settled in the UK);
- by descent (anyone born abroad if either parent is a British citizen other than by descent);
- by registration (= an entitlement to citizenship used mostly for minors);
- by naturalisation (citizenship which may be granted to adults, but only if the applicant meets a number of requirements).

1988 Immigration Act introduced further restrictions on non-white immigrants and their families.

1999 Immigration and Asylum Act was mainly concerned with the removal of persons residing unlawfully in the UK as well as asylum procedure and support for asylum seekers.

2002 Immigration and Asylum Act aims at reforming nationality, immigration, and asylum policy. It is based on the government white paper "Secure Borders, Safe Haven: Integration with Diversity in Modern Britain". It proposes citizenship ceremonies, a citizenship pledge and a requirement of knowledge about life in the UK, and sufficient knowledge of the English language.

Conclusion: British immigration and citizenship laws have not escaped harsh criticism and are seen by some as institutional racism. The 1971 Act has even drawn criticism from the European Human Rights Commission as being racially motivated and degrading. The 2002 Act, however, adjusts the laws to the standards of the 1997 European Convention on Nationality.

Cultural mix and clash – UK

Test: A Distant Shore

Solomon has fled from his war-torn African home, where his family was persecuted and murdered, and entered England illegally. On his way north, he is picked up by Mike Anderson, a friendly and understanding lorry-driver, who takes him to his parents' house. They help him in every possible way until he is finally granted political asylum and can legally stay in Britain. One night, the Andersons' house is smeared with racist slogans. Mr Anderson and Mike each have a talk with Solomon.

"Solomon, the first line of defence is prejudice. Once you get past that, there'll always be a little corner where you can live and be who or what you want to be. But you've got to get past that first line, and things are not getting any easier. There's an awful lot of you, and the system's already creaking to breaking point. I mean, things are particularly bad if you want to get into one of our hospitals. People are upset." He looked closely at me now, as though trying to read my thoughts. "You do understand what I'm trying to say to you, don't you, Solomon?"

I nodded, although I was unsure of what exactly Mr Anderson was trying to say.

"You see, Solomon, it's just that this isn't a very big island and we don't have that much room. People think that other countries should take you first because we've done our bit." He paused and looked away. "I'm sorry, Solomon, but some folk think these things. That you just want an easy living, or that you have too many children. They think that you don't really want to work. It's in their heads and it makes them mad."

"Who put it there?"

Mr Anderson turned to look at me, and I could see that he was surprised that I had asked this question. And then his face softened.

"I don't know, Solomon. I really don't know."

We sat together in the car park for many more minutes, but neither of us said anything further, nor did we make eye contact. Mr Anderson was clearly unsettled by what had happened to his house and he did not know what to do. I now understood that explaining these things to me was a way of explaining them to himself, but the puzzled look on Mr Anderson's face suggested that he remained troubled by many questions. [...]

"Look, Mum told me what happened, but you've got to understand that some people bring things on themselves, you know. I mean, these days particularly the Indian types." Mike stopped and sighed, and then he looked at me. "I'm an old traditionalist, Solomon. I want fish and chips, not curry and chips. I'm not prejudiced, but we'll soon be living in a foreign country unless somebody puts an end to all this immigration. These Indians, they still make their women trail after them, and they have their mosques and temples, and their butcher shops where they kill animals in the basement and do whatever they do with the blood. I mean, they're peasants. They come from the countryside and most of them have never seen a flush toilet or a light switch. It's too much for them. And for us. There ought to be some training or they should go back. It's these kinds of people that cause others to have bad attitudes and to do things like they've done to Mum's wall. I'm not saying they're right, because they're not. But I drive around a lot, and I see how people feel, more than what the old folks does. It's everywhere." Mike stopped talking and stared at me, but with a worried look on his face. "You see, you're in a different situation, Solomon. You're escaping oppression and that's different. We've got procedures for that. I mean, you're working. You're no scrounger. But they don't know that, and so that's what happens." Mike paused. "You do know what I'm saying, don't you, Solomon?" I looked at Mike and nodded. I knew what he was saying. I understood him.

(595 words)

From Caryl Philips, *A Distant Shore*, London: Secker & Warburg, 2003, pp. 289–291.

1 **line of defence** a way of defending o.s. – 34 **Mum told me ...** reference to the racist slogans that were painted on the Andersons' house – 53 **the old folks** *here:* Mr and Mrs Anderson

Tasks

1 a) How do Mr Anderson and Mike explain British people's attitudes towards immigrants?
b) How do the two men's approaches to the problem differ?

2 What are Mr Anderson's and Mike's personal attitudes towards immigrants? What ways do they suggest of dealing with prejudice?

3 Discuss how the extract is structured by argumentative and narrative elements and explain their respective functions.

4 Write a letter to Caryl Phillips in which you explain your view of the novel extract. You should evaluate opinions about immigration in Britain and compare them to the situation in your own country.

Cultural mix and clash – UK

Test: Bogus friends of asylum seekers

The subject of race, like sex, makes people lose their heads. It makes them emotional and irrational; […] This has made political debate on asylum seekers nasty […].

I am convinced that the left has been much nastier than the right. The accusations of racism constantly heaped on the right are truly unforgivable. […] I've come to suspect that the explanation for this undue nastiness is that the left feels much more guilt and confusion about asylum than the right.

Whether or not that's so, there is a great deal of confusion around. Take the idea of the genuine asylum seeker. There are endless arguments about who might be bogus, or whether the word should be breathed at all. But most people seem to agree that all genuine asylum seekers ought to be granted a safe haven here. That at least, in all the political muddle, is not problematic – all genuine asylum seekers have the right to stay.

Unfortunately it is nonsense. It would be quite impossible. The world is awash with people in desperate need of political asylum; there are millions of people who suffer prison, torture, violation and civil war, and millions in mortal fear of them. All they lack is transport; if they had it, they would be here on our doorstep and unmistakably genuine.

And if we really wanted asylum seekers, we know where to find them; we could go for a start to the vast refugee camps and gather them up in hundreds of thousands. Of course we don't, partly because we couldn't take them all, and partly – surely – because we don't want them.

There is nothing new about this. We tell ourselves, and in particular the left is given to saying, that this country has a proud tradition of accepting asylum seekers. Well, up to a point. We may have taken a few Kosovans, after a lot of soul searching, but Britain's doors were closed to the Hong Kong Chinese, just as they were to some of the Jewish refugees fleeing Nazism.

There is a lot of hypocrisy in all this, and I think it is a hypocrisy which troubles the internationalist left much more than the internationalist right – I mean the genuine left, as opposed to the bogus New Labour left.

Traditionally the left has felt responsible for the wretched of the Earth, at least in theory. In practice there is no big idea, no sense of what to do, no coherent policy. Those on the left ought to feel angry with New Labour, but seem to find it easier to rant at the Tories.

What we have, meanwhile, is an asylum system which is without any doubt badly abused and badly run. Fewer than one in five of the people who claim asylum here are found to be genuine. The rest can, and do, appeal through the courts for years, at huge public expense, but without success, even though British judges have the loosest definition in Europe of "fear of persecution".

In practice they stay anyway. Very few of those denied asylum are ever deported, and many of them – about 300,000 – have disappeared into the shadowy world of the illegals, discrediting the others. It is a waste and a shame.

Economic migrants are in need too, I admit. They are fleeing misery and deprivation too and, according to Refugee Council figures, published in the *Guardian* on Monday, many of them are highly employable and highly qualified – rather embarrassingly more so than the British; perhaps that's why they're so good at figuring out the system. And who can really blame them for trying to beat it? But it is grossly unfair to others in much more urgent need. Why should it be so disgraceful and racist to say so?

(626 words)

By Minette Marrin, "Bogus friends of asylum seekers", *The Guardian*, May 22, 2001.

bogus *here:* not having a genuine reason to be given asylum – 62 **to figure out the system** to understand how to get welfare benefits, etc.

Tasks

1 According to the writer what is wrong with Britain's asylum system?

2 Why does the writer think that there is a lot of confusion and hypocrisy as regards asylum seekers?

3 Analyse the style and tone of the article to determine whether it is objective or biased.

4 Write a letter to the editor of the *Guardian,* in which you evaluate Minette Marrin's position on asylum seekers in Britain and suggest what should be done to make immigration policy more efficient.

First peoples

Einleitung

Die Themen des dritten Kapitels gründen sich im Wesentlichen auf die im Lehrplan geforderte Auseinandersetzung mit gesellschaftlichen und historischen Aspekten aus englischsprachigen Ländern auch außerhalb des anglo-amerikanischen Raums. Die Beschäftigung mit zentralen Fragen und Problemen der australischen Aborigines, der neuseeländischen Maori und der nordamerikanischen Indianer soll den S ermöglichen, bereits in der Sekundarstufe I erworbenes Wissen zu reaktivieren, zu erweitern und – z. B. durch die historische Perspektive – zu differenzieren. Im Sinne des interkulturellen Lernens wird angestrebt, Offenheit für möglicherweise zunächst fremdartige kulturelle Besonderheiten und Traditionen zu fördern, ein kritisches Bewusstsein für die Rolle und Verantwortung weißer Kolonisatoren anzuregen und die gewonnenen Erkenntnisse und Einsichten für die eigene Lebenswelt der S nutzbar zu machen.

Mit der Auswahl unterschiedlicher Textsorten wird der im Lehrplan aufgestellten Forderung nach der Schulung der S in den Bereichen der Rezeption und angemessenen Analyse fiktionaler und nicht-fiktionaler Texte Rechnung getragen. Der die Texte begleitende Aufgabenapparat fördert die Fähigkeiten und Fertigkeiten der S sowohl im Bereich der formalen Textanalyse wie der produktiv-kreativen Auseinandersetzung mit den jeweiligen Problemstellungen. Hinweise zu weiterführenden Internet-Links ermutigen zur eigenen themenorientierten Recherche durch die S. Der Teilbereich zu den Aborigines schließt mit einem Vorschlag für ein Referat, eine Facharbeit oder eine Arbeit im Rahmen der "besonderen Lernleistung" ab.

Die zielsprachliche Förderung der S ist durch die Aufbereitung der Texte und die Vielfalt der Aufgaben gewährleistet. Insbesondere die Möglichkeiten zum Sprechen in unterschiedlichen kommunikativen Situationen sollten im Unterricht umgesetzt werden. Die Sammlung und Gliederung von themenrelevantem Wortschatz wird von Beginn an gefördert (vgl. beispielsweise "Looking and thinking", Task 2, SB S. 50).

Didaktisches Inhaltsverzeichnis – Aborigines

	Titel	Textsorte (Wortzahl ca.)	Thema	Text- und Spracharbeit	Textproduktion (schriftlich / mündlich)
◎	Images of... SB S. 50, TB S. 50 TB S. 67	photo collage	Aboriginal cultural and social circumstances	collect impressions conveyed by photos and music	collect key words
	The Songlines SB S. 51, TB S. 50	novel extract (1,254 words)	Aboriginal paintings • cultural clash	analyse tone and mode of narration • act out a dialogue	letter-writing (ordering) • script-writing
◎	Land / Please don't... / Mourning closes... SB S. 55, TB S. 51 TB S. 67	poem extract (45 words) newspaper articles (326 / 258 words)	sacred nature of the land • Aboriginal beliefs and taboos • interests of the tourism industry	interpret a photo and poem • collect facts • explain ideas • analyse text for objectivity	letter-writing • write a newspaper article (tabloid)
◎	Child of the... SB S. 57, TB S. 52	personal testimony (546 words)	conditions and effects of assimilation policies	imagine effects of a policy • talk about a photo • describe experiences • analyse the effect of a text	letter-writing • write a script / play • write a plot outline (film)
Over to you	Australian... SB S. 59, TB S. 52 TB S. 68	newspaper article (769 words)	the Australian government's position on a reconciliation treaty	collect / order information • outline a position • analyse text for objectivity	write an e-mail • write a comment • present an interview • hold a debate • write / act out a script
Using your skills	Angela... SB S. 61, TB S. 53 TB S. 69	independent work with a novel	friendship between an Aboriginal and a white girl against the background of the Stolen Generation	reading for gist / detail	reading log • talk or term paper • book review • change point of view • diary entry • personal letter

First peoples

Images of Aborigines SB S. 50

Looking and listening

■ **Collect impressions conveyed by photos and music**

Mögliche Antworten:
- Photo on left: Aboriginal culture and traditions: dance, music (*didgeridoo, *clapsticks) (*dot) painting, body painting, an *ancient / strange / 'primitive' culture, close links to nature (indicated by the branches held by dancers, bird sounds on the recording)
- Photo on right: living conditions today: poverty, poor housing, health problems
- Contrast between ancient culture and present living conditions
- Open questions: meaning of dances, music, body painting and dot painting; reasons for present social situation of Aboriginals…

■ **Collect key words**

Eine Liste mit themenrelevantem Wortschatz befindet sich auf einer Kopiervorlage im TB S. 67.

The Songlines SB S. 51–54

Exploring the text

1 a) *Colours:* *ochre, blue, *scarlet, pink; shapes: dots, circles, lines as in abstract paintings (ll. 1–4); meaning: representation of *totems / *Dreamings (= creation stories), they show the journeys of the *Spirit Ancestors (ll. 8–9, 22–23); highly important in Aboriginal culture (the only visual representation of the Dreamtime stories) (ll. 20–22, 96–100); an artist may not paint his / her own totem (*taboo) (ll. 52–53).
b) The painting shows no recognizable shapes (plant, animal, human). You need to know the story to understand the meaning of the painting, i.e. you have to be *initiated (ll. 20–25, 103–109).

2 Life in the bush: Aboriginals survive on what nature offers in the way of food (e.g. honey-ants) (ll. 13–17).
- Beliefs: every Aboriginal has his / her own totem (e.g. emu, honey-ant) and is not allowed to paint or eat it; it would be a sacrilege to do so and might even kill him / her (ll. 32–33, 52–53); ritual managers ensure that the laws are upheld (ll. 63–64); Aboriginals recognize the tracks of their Spirit Ancestors in their surroundings (these tracks are invisible to white people) (ll. 103–107); every track has a song that goes along with it; Songlines are like route maps all over Australia and help Aboriginals to find their way and survive in the bush; the land, songs and history cannot be separated (ll. 24, 101–109).
- Art: Aboriginals paint their creation stories (no written culture) (ll. 22–23).

3 a) *Behaviour:* They are interested in Aboriginal culture, yet in a *superficial way (ll. 88–89): they cannot appreciate the painting's deeper meaning (ll. 11, 18–19, 26–27); the painting is seen as an exotic souvenir (ll. 50–51).
Way of talking: lacks *genuine understanding (ll. 12, 20–21, 42, 71–74); implies that money can buy everything (ll. 46–51, 73–74).

b) American tourists and Stan: Tourists have money, but no cultural awareness; old Stan: seems inferior (lives in the desert, old, does not speak much), profits from them;
- American tourists and Mrs Lacey: they are business for her; she is a mediator: she complies with their request (answers their questions);
- Mrs Lacey and Stan: she takes care of her own business interests, she helps old Stan to get a good price; he is dependent on her for business, too.

4 a) amused, e.g. when Stan and Mrs Lacey gang up on the Americans (ll. 77–79), *ridicules the tourists' superficial attitude (ll. 18–19, 26–27, 45–46, 65–66, 88–89, 111)
b) First-person narrator as eye-witness: narrator knows old Stan and Mrs Lacey and sees through their behaviour (ll. 75–80) (Siehe "Kernwortschatz", "culture and traditions" / "beliefs", TB S. 67.)

A step further

■ **Letter-writing (ordering)**

> (name)
> (address)
> USA
>
> Date
>
> Desert Bookstore and Art Gallery
> c / o Mrs Lacey
> Alice Springs
> NT 0870
> Australia
>
> **Ref. Order for an Aboriginal dot painting**
>
> Dear Mrs Lacey,
> A couple of weeks ago my wife (/ my husband) and I visited your bookstore and gallery and bought a dot-painting by Mr Stan Tjakamarra representing the honey-ant dreaming. We would like to order a second painting to match the one by Mr Tjakamarra.
>
> The painting should be about four foot by three. The colours should correspond to the ones in Mr Tjakamarra's (ochre dots, blue and scarlet circles, and pink lines). We should like the painting to represent another dreaming to complement our first purchase. If possible, we should like the painting to be delivered within the next eight weeks. Our upper price limit is Aus$500, including commission, P&P and any other expenses.
>
> We look forward to hearing from you soon.
>
> Yours sincerely,
>
> XXXXX

■ **Script-writing**

Mögliche Inhalte:
- The narrator asks questions about Aboriginal beliefs (Dreamtime, Dreamings, Songlines, totems, taboos) and the Aboriginal way of life (nomadic life-style, bush tucker, bush medicine; social problems they experience today: low income and dependence on welfare, health problems); he may raise the question whether old Stan was paid adequately.

First peoples

- Arkady explains Aboriginal beliefs to the narrator. (Cf. introduction to text and photos, SB p. 55, internet);
- Stage directions: tone of voice, facial expressions, gestures (The men are possibly annoyed by the Americans' attitude, may feel sorry for Old Stan, question Mrs Lacey's role…)

■ **Aboriginal culture**

Die Ergebnisse der Internetrecherche können z. B. als Referat (zur Vorbereitung vgl. SB, Skills file, S. 182–183), als Poster oder Wandzeitung, als Powerpoint Präsentation oder als Beitrag für die Website der Schule präsentiert werden.

Land / Please don't climb our rock / Mourning closes Ayers Rock SB S. 55–56

Before you read

■ **Interpret a photo and poem**

Mögliche Antworten: Uluru: a special place, the only mountain in the desert (besides Kata Tjuta); a sacred place, must be treated with respect, should not be climbed; Aboriginals must take care of and preserve sacred places for themselves and the next generation (Aboriginal law); the white people should respect Aboriginal law…

Exploring the texts

(N.B. I = "Please don't climb …"; II = "Mourning closes …")
1 Name: Uluru (Aboriginal, i.e. *Anangu: traditional owners), Ayers Rock (white colonists) (I: ll. 13–15)
- General information: world's (second-) largest *monolith, red sandstone rock, 348 metres high, situated in Central Australia (280 miles south-west of Alice Springs) in Uluru-Kata Tjuta National Park, sometimes dangerous weather conditions (extreme heat or winds), six-mile walk around its base (I: ll. 1, 3, 22; II: ll. 1, 7–8, 11–15)
- History: a sacred site to the Anangu, named after a white and long-forgotten state governor and claimed by white colonists; returned to its traditional Aboriginal owners in 1985 (I: ll. 13–15; II: ll. 4–6, 9–10, 20–22)
- Tourism: about 400,000 visitors per year, about 200,000 tourists climb the rock (I: ll. 4, 16–17, 24–25; II: ll. 11–12)
2 Tourism: an important tourist attraction, climbing the rock is an essential part of any tourist's programme; a source of income for the Aboriginals; closing it would mean fewer tourists and a drop in income (I: ll. 4, 17, 22–23; II: ll. 11–12, 15–16).
- Anangu: a sacred place (part of the Anangu's creation story), it should be preserved as it is and it should not be climbed; white tourists should respect Aboriginal law and beliefs; tourists should be content to just walk around it (I: ll. 5–6, 8–9; II: 13, 20–22)
3 Presentation of arguments in a neutral way: factual information (I: e.g. ll. 4–6, 13–15; II: e.g. ll. 7–9); quotations from both sides give reasons for both positions (I: ll. 10, 24–26; II: e.g. ll. 4–6); yet there are some indications of bias in favour of the Aboriginals' position: headline "Please don't climb our rock" appeals to the reader, emotional choice of words, e.g. I: "a matter of manners" (l. 9), "a rite of passage" (l. 18); II: "to clamber all over their site" (l. 13) 'clamber' is somewhat negative and implies a lack of respect. (Cf. "Kernwortschatz", beliefs / Aboriginal lands, TB p. 67.)

A step further

■ **Letter-writing**

Beim Verfassen eines der Briefe sollten die S auf ihre bisherigen Kenntnisse über Kultur, Traditionen und gegenwärtige Lebenssituation der Aborigines zurückgreifen, um ihre Position zu untermauern. Vor dem Verfassen der Reinschrift sollten Techniken der Stoffsammlung, Gliederung und Überarbeitung des ersten Entwurfs geübt werden. Ein Beispiel für die formale Gestaltung eines Briefes befindet sich im SB auf S. 111. Die Briefe können an das Ayers Rock Resort adressiert werden: Yulara, NT 0872.

■ **Write a newspaper article (tabloid)**

Beim Verfassen und der Gestaltung des Zeitungsartikels sollen die S die Informationen aus den beiden Texten im SB sowie ihre bisherigen Kenntnisse verwenden. Zur Gestaltung des Arbeitsprozesses vgl. SB, Skills file, S. 188.
Ideen: An Australian tabloid would probably support white interests and argue against the closing of the rock.
- Headline: eye-catching, sensational, outraged, in the form of a question or an exclamation
- Content: probably highlights the negative consequences (less attractive to visit, a tourists' 'right' denied)
- Structure: headline, sub-heading, introduction; short paragraphs, crossheads such as "Closed", "Outrage"; possibly include a photo
- Language: simple sentence structure (main clauses), colloquial English or slang, quotations from tourists and/or tour operators

Kopiervorlage: Role play, Climbing Uluru, TB S. 71

■ In groups, prepare and have a discussion in roles about the pros and cons of closing Uluru (cf. TB pp. 71–72).
Hinweise zur Durchführung: Je nach Größe des Kurses können die einzelnen Rollen mit mehreren S besetzt werden, die die jeweilige Rolle entweder gemeinsam oder individuell vorbereiten. Die S werden aufgefordert, ihre Rolle gemäß ihres Vorwissens auszugestalten und eine kurze Erläuterung ihrer jeweiligen Position zur Eröffnung der Debatte vorzubereiten. Wenn vor der Debatte bekannt ist, welche unterschiedlichen Positionen vertreten werden, können die S gebeten werden, bei ihrer Vorbereitung auch schon Gegenargumente hinsichtlich der anderen Standpunkte zu entwerfen. Der Anspruch an die S zur spontanen Reaktion auf Gegenargumente ist natürlich höher, wenn vor Beginn der Debatte die unterschiedlichen Positionen nicht bekannt sind.
In schwächeren Lerngruppen kann der L die Rolle des Moderators übernehmen. Eine weitere Variante ist es, den Moderator mit zusätzlichen Informationen zu versorgen oder seine eigentlich neutrale Position zugunsten der Unterstützung einer der beiden Seiten zu verändern, was von den S während der Debatte eine größere Wachsamkeit und Reaktionsfähigkeit verlangt, die Diskussion aber in starken Lerngruppen umso interessanter machen kann.

First peoples

Child of the stolen generation SB S. 57–58

Before you read

■ **Imagine the effects of a policy**

In the past: isolated, abandoned, lonely, lost, frightened, did not understand what was happening to them, helpless, in a hopeless situation, mistreated, exploited…
Today: uprooted, helpless, discriminated against, frustrated, angry… (Cf. "Kernwortschatz", "recent history" / "social situation", TB p. 67.)

👁 **Talk about a photo** SB S. 57

Mögliche Antworten: close, harmonious, caring; children are being well looked after; different generations share activities; the family / clan offers protection… (N.B. The weaving of string into intricate patterns is an essential part of telling and visualising Dreamtime stories.)

Exploring the text

1 At Nowra: no idea about their true origins or families (l. 3), no notion of the meaning of 'parents' (ll. 7–8), no visits from Aboriginal family members (ll. 19–20), brainwashed into thinking they are white (ll. 10–14)
– At Kinchela: deprived of all possessions, individuality and their identity (ll. 30–33), humiliated, severely punished, suffered corporal punishment (ll. 34–35), isolated from the outside world (l. 45); Kinchela was like a prison (l. 44), life = hard work (ll. 45–46); a show was put on for visiting officials to conceal the true situation in the home and the abuse of the children (ll. 46–48).
2 Aboriginal parents were thought to be unfit to raise their children, the children were taught that they were white (l. 10); they had no names, just numbers; personal possessions and individuality (hair style, clothes) were not allowed (ll. 31–33); excessive corporal punishment was designed to break family ties and friendships (ll. 35–36); the Aboriginal children were considered to be animals (ll. 42–43).
3 Content: brutal / inhumane treatment of the Aboriginal children by white authorities (separated from their families at a very young age and placed in orphanages and boarding schools, brainwashed, severely punished, looked down upon, deprived of any individuality) (ll. 28–44).
– Language: choice of words, e.g. "drummed into our heads" (ll. 10, 12–13), "treasured" (l. 24) shows how important the ports were and how serious their loss was;
– Comparisons: "kick us like a dog" (l. 44), "It was just like a prison" (l. 44);
– Repetition: "white" (ll. 11–16), "visits" (ll. 19–20), "work" (ll. 45–46), "prisoners" (ll. 49–51);
– Colloquial language (cf. e.g. l. 46) and simple sentence structure make the statements more authentic.
N.B. The text is a transcript of an oral testimony.
(Cf. "Kernwortschatz", "recent history", TB p. 67.)

A step further

■ **Letter-writing**

Wie beim Verfassen der Briefe zum vorherigen Themenbereich sollten die S auf ihre Kenntnisse über die Konsequenzen der Zwangsassimilierung australischer Aborigines, aber auch auf ihr weiteres Wissen über Kultur, Traditionen und die gegenwärtige Lebenssituation der Aborigines zurückgreifen, um ihre Position zu untermauern. Vor dem Verfassen der Reinschrift sollten wiederum Techniken der Stoffsammlung, Gliederung und Überarbeitung des ersten Entwurfs geübt werden. Ein Beispiel für die formale Gestaltung eines Briefes befindet sich im SB auf S. III. Die Briefe können adressiert werden an: The Department of Indigenous Affairs, Canberra, ACT 2600.

■ **Write a script / play**

Zur Vorbereitung sollten folgende Aspekte unter Zuhilfenahme der bisher gelesenen Texte und der Abbildungen im SB mit den S erarbeitet bzw. wiederholt werden:
Characters and lines of argument:
– Aboriginal men and women recall life before the policy of forced assimilation (e.g. life in the bush, hunting and gathering, using 'bush knowledge' to survive, observing traditions and laws, living in harmony with nature, close family ties); life during and after the implementation of assimilation policies (broken families, loss of parents / children, despair, feeling isolated / humiliated / uprooted, suffering in the children's homes and afterwards, no sense of personal value or a future worth living);
– Supervisor feels shame at treating the Aboriginal children "like prisoners", wishes to improve their lives;
– Welfare officer sees the policy as an opportunity to integrate Aborigines into society; inferiority of Aboriginal way of life / traditions / laws compared to white society; may even be prejudiced against non-whites in general.
Place and time: possible settings, e.g. an Aboriginal bush camp, an office, a children's home.
Stage directions: Think of suitable gestures, actions, facial expressions and tone of voice to convey emotion;
Structure: short exposition, rising action with climax, turning point (optional), short falling action, ending: open, surprise, happy;
Language (if possible): Use different registers, e.g. simple and colloquial language for Aborigines, formal language for the supervisor and welfare officer.

■ **Write a plot outline (film)**

Möglicher Handlungsverlauf: happy life with family in the bush, shock of being taken away to Bomaderry Children's Home, feelings of loneliness and alienation, treatment at Nowra, central experience: transfer to Kinchela, experiences there, e.g. relationships between the boys, and the boys and their supervisors, humiliation, mistreatment, effect of being uprooted), a visit by the welfare officers, later life, e.g. as a stockman, escape to find his family, fight against alcoholism and delinquency, fight for recognition and an apology from the authorities, suffers discrimination in white society…

Australian reconciliation off the cards ⟨over to you⟩ SB S. 59–60

Before you read

Hopes:
– a united Australia on the basis of the promise to accept apology and forgive past injustices (ll. 8–9)

- recognition for the Aboriginal heritage (l. 9)
- justice and equal rights for all (l. 10)

Demands:
- recognition of Aborigines as the traditional and thus lawful owners of Australian lands and waters (ll. 2–3)
- recognition as equal citizens of Australia (ll. 3–4)
- acknowledgement of past injustices by the Australian government (l. 5)
- apology / expression of sincere regret by the Australian government (l. 7)

Over to you

Die Arbeitsaufträge auf der Kopiervorlage, TB S. 68 können von den S bearbeitet werden, wenn ihnen der Text nicht zur eigenständigen Auseinandersetzung vorgelegt wird.

Two flags   SB S. 59
Background information

The upper flag was designed by Harold Thomas, an Aboriginal artist in 1971, in the hopes of making the Aboriginal cause more visible. The black represents the Aboriginal people, the red the earth and their spiritual relationship to the land, and the yellow symbolizes the sun, the giver of life. The flag has been in use since 1972.
The lower flag symbolizes the unity of all Torres Strait Islanders. The white Dari (headdress) is a symbol of Torres Strait Islanders and the white, five-pointed star represents the five major island groups and the navigational importance of stars to these seafaring people. The green stripes represent the land, the black stripes the people, and the blue the sea. It has been in use since 1992.
Both flags were adopted in 1995 and are being flown more widely as indigenous issues become more important in Australia.

Exploring the text

1   1991: calls for a treaty between the government and the Aborigines, creation of the "Council for Aboriginal Reconciliation"
- 1991 onwards: emergence of a clear acknowledgement of the existence of the "stolen generation". Mr Howard's attitude has softened.
- 2000: march of one million Australians calling for reconciliation.
"Council for Aboriginal Reconciliation" delivers its final recommendations and is disbanded; calls for a treaty are rejected by Mr Howard.
- 2001: establishment of "Reconciliation Australia", a private organisation to continue the reconciliation process

2 Inequalities between Aboriginals and white Australians still exist. Aboriginals usually live 20 years less than white Australians and infant mortality is significantly higher because of insufficient health care. Despite an 18% increase in Aboriginal students enrolled in tertiary education programmes, the unemployment rate among Aboriginals is more than three times higher than among white Australians. A high number of Aboriginals depend on government welfare. Aboriginal men are 15 times more likely to go to prison. Aborigines still suffer from the consequences of being driven from their land and cut off from their traditional, cultural background.

3 In the early 1990s, the government seemed open to reconciliation when it founded the Council. The present government feels that the reconciliation process is not finished. It has however moved responsibility to a private organisation. Mr Howard refuses to give legislative guarantees or an apology as he feels that a treaty is not necessary. He is more in favour of a practical approach which would concentrate on dealing with the Aborigines' health and employment difficulties. Mr Howard does not realize the importance of a symbolic gesture such as a formal apology.

4 Mr Howard is criticized for not considering the possibility of a treaty. According to one critic a treaty could settle issues such as the dispossession of Aborigines of their lands. Mr Howard fears that a treaty could divide society, yet critics point out that Aborigines are already outside society due to their social problems (ll. 38–40). Mr Howard favours a practical approach but so far the government's efforts have not been effective, as the Aborigines' health problems appear to be worsening (l. 44) and unemployment is also significantly higher among this group than in the rest of Australian society (ll. 47–48).

5 The article seems to be biased towards the government's critics. For every argument the government gives against signing a treaty or making an apology the writer comes up with examples, statistics or expert opinions to contradict it. The first lines of the article lay the blame for the failure to achieve reconciliation at the government's door (ll. 1–5). Mr Howard is portrayed as someone who is inflexible (ll. 30–31, 33–34) and misguided in his attitude towards the Aborigine issue (ll. 38–42, 50–52). Indeed, the last line of the article reinforces this image.

A step further

■ **Write a letter**
Siehe Layoutbeispiel im SB S. 111.

■ **Write a comment**
Siehe Skills file, "Comment" im SB S. 188.

■ **Present an interview** –

■ **Hold a debate** –

■ **Write / act out a script** –

Angela: Growing up in Australia   *Using your skills*   SB S. 61–62

Das folgende Projekt soll die S zum eigenständigen Arbeiten anleiten, z. B. im Rahmen einer Facharbeit oder der sogenannten "Besonderen Lernleistung". Es gelten dabei für die S die Rahmenbedingungen, die im Lehrplan für das Fach Englisch in der Sekundarstufe II, in den jeweiligen hausinternen Curricula und in den Vorschriften und Hinweisen zur Anfertigung einer Facharbeit bzw. zur Erbringung der sogenannten "Besonderen Lernleistung" erläutert werden.

First peoples

Alternative Bearbeitung

Die S können in Anlehnung an die Ideen und Arbeitsaufträge zu *Angela* Aspekte des Romans von Doris Pilkington/Nugi Garimara. *Follow the Rabbit-Proof Fence* (1996) oder des Films *Rabbit-Proof Fence* (2002) (bei Lingua Video Medien GmbH, www.lingua-video.com erhältlich) eigenständig bearbeiten oder unter einem selbst gewählten Schwerpunkt eine vergleichende Analyse erstellen (z. B. characters, *The Stolen Generation*, cinematic devices in selected scenes). Hinzugenommen werden können Buch- oder Filmkritiken wie z. B. der Klausurtext "Fenced out" auf TB S. 69.

Test: Fenced out   TB S. 69

Klausur für den Grundkurs
Textformat: newspaper article, 502 words
Vorschlag/Klausurtyp NRW: Tasks 1–3, Sach- und Gebrauchstext, Aufgabenart A 1 (Textaufgabe mit analytisch-interpretierendem Schwerpunkt)
Zentrale Bezugstexte des Kapitels: "Child of the stolen generation", SB S. 57–58); zur Bearbeitung der dritten Teilaufgabe, aber auch die Inhalte der Texte auf S. 51–56 im SB. Eine mögliche Aufbereitung zu diesem Test finden Sie auf einer Kopiervorlage auf S. 69.

Comprehension

1 *Content:* true story about three Aboriginal girls who manage to escape from a white settlement and return to their family. They walk 1,200 miles across the desert along the rabbit-proof fence without being caught by the Aboriginal tracker, police or welfare officials who are chasing them.
Qualities: appealing story, excellent and convincing actors, indigenous music, beautiful shots of the desert landscape; a mainstream film that appeals to a large audience...

Analysis

2 *Presentation of information:* the contrast in the introduction arouses interest – normally people are not interested in films about Aborigines but this time they are (ll. 1–8.), detailed information about the director (ll. 9–13), the film and its historical background (ll. 14–17, 23–31), and the actors (ll. 43–56)
Choice of words: emotive use of nouns and adjectives ("blaze of publicity", ll. 6–7, "solid box office takings", l. 63, "stark beauty", l. 41, "extraordinary", l. 19, "dramatic", l. 38) emphasizes the quality and success of the film; verbs ("snatched", l. 17; "dragged", l. 24, "forced", l. 25) and adjectives ("traumatic", l. 30) increase the drama of the plot and stress the white government's brutality, adjectives ("vast", l. 21; "huge", l. 34) convey the enormous challenge met by the girls to find their way home; nouns, adverbs and adjectives underline the qualities demonstrated by the actors ("utterly convincing", l. 43, "crossover appeal", l. 52, "genuine", l. 52, "beauty and charm", ll. 54–55).

Evaluation: comment

3 *Pros:* film is based on a true story; gives information about the Aboriginals' living conditions/the policy of forced assimilation; features attractive/interesting/Aboriginal actors, images of the landscape, an interesting/unusual score...
Cons: a mainstream film which probably sticks to a particular formula with a happy ending, possibly influenced by a Hollywood style of filmmaking, music by a white composer (Peter Gabriel) is not particularly authentic...

Test: Living life on the edge   TB S. 70

Klausur für den Leistungskurs
Textformat: newspaper article, 701 words
Vorschlag/Klausurtyp NRW: Tasks 1–3, Sach- und Gebrauchstext, Aufgabenart A 1 (Textaufgabe mit analytisch-interpretierendem Schwerpunkt bzw. mit anwendungs-/produktionsorientierter Aufgabenstellung)
Zentrale Bezugstexte des Kapitels: "Please don't climb our rock", SB S. 55, "Mourning closes Ayers Rock", SB S. 56
Eine mögliche Aufbereitung zu diesem Test finden Sie auf einer Kopiervorlage auf S. 70.

Comprehension

1 *WMC:* needs water for the mining of copper and uranium; is licensed by the Australian government; carries out thorough environmental research; tries to include the Aborigines and farmers; claims that cattle farming wastes more water than mining...
Protesters: mining for uranium; taking the water and planning an international nuclear waste dump all equal genocide; their task is to preserve the delicate ecological balance/to defend the underground water reserves, which are essential to the desert people and feed the pockets of wetland life...

Analysis

2 Introduction arouses interest by the use of what seems to be direct speech and proceeds to set the scene; balanced presentation of both sides of the conflict (ll. 40–48, 50–60); vivid, detailed descriptions using colourful adjectives and comparisons (ll. 3–5, 27–28), includes quotes (ll. 20, 38–39), mixes facts/observations with personal comments (ll. 9–11, 12–16); personal reaction/feelings and open questions at the end of the article make readers think (ll. 70–75).

Evaluation: comment

3 *Explanation:* Land is sacred/a link to history/ancestors (Dreamtime, Songlines); the destruction of the land means the destruction of the basis for the physical and spiritual survival of the Aboriginals; is sacrilege...
Letter: Within the frame of a personal letter, students may share the writer's doubts about the impact of the protesters' actions or support their aim to draw attention to the dangerous exploitation of Australia's fragile ecosystem and the destruction of the country's cultural heritage (see above).

Test: Living life on the edge   TB S. 68

Mündliche Prüfung
Textformat: newspaper article, 320 words
Vorschlag/Klausurtyp NRW: Tasks 1–3, Sach- und Gebrauchstext, Aufgabenart A 1 (Textaufgabe mit analytisch-interpretierendem Schwerpunkt)

First peoples

Zentrale Bezugstexte des Kapitels: Land rights Texte (siehe SB S. 55–56)

Comprehension
1 Siehe TB S. 54, "Living life on the edge", Task 1.

Analysis
2 The writer presents both sides of the conflict (ll. 16–23 and 26–35), includes quotes from both parties (ll. 4, 14–15), gives facts (ll. 8–13), uses adjectives and adverbs to make the report more vivid ("flyblown", l. 21; "vociferously", l. 46).

Evaluation: comment
3 Siehe Task 3 im TB S. 54.

Didaktisches Inhaltsverzeichnis – Maoris

	Titel	Textsorte (Wortzahl ca.)	Thema	Text- und Spracharbeit	Textproduktion (schriftlich / mündlich)
	Being Maori SB S. 63, TB S. 55, TB S. 73	definitions, photos	Maori values and images	interpret photos and texts	collect ideas in a mind map
	The Treaty of Waitangi SB S. 64, TB S. 56, TB S. 74	historical document (183 words)	treaty between Maori chiefs and the British government	speculate • interpret fact file: Maori land rights… • explain key ideas • interpret text	evaluate statements • hold a role play / discussion
	Ngati Kangaru SB S. 66, TB S. 57	short story extract (1,404 words)	reclaiming Maori land from the white population	compare statement / fact file • evaluate fact file • summarize text • work with adjectives • describe tone	define the target group • analyse use of English and Maori • write an ending • write a news report or story, record a radio interview • plan a TV newscast
	The Pakeha judge's… SB S. 70, TB S. 58	short story extract (1,284 words)	culture clash: white law enforcement vs. Maori values	analyse definitions • speculate about the story • talk about emotions • examine point of view / narrator	write and act out a scene • collect arguments, act out a meeting
	Waitangi Day… / After all, we're one people… SB S. 73–74, TB S. 59	newspaper article (318 words) comment (204 words)	symbolic meaning of Waitangi Day	describe the significance of Waitangi Day • characterize attitudes • find reasons / problems in texts • compare tone	act out a discussion • analyse a statement • look at statistics from particular points of view

Being Maori SB S. 63

Looking and thinking
■ Describe the photos, collect information

Kernwortschatz

Im Rahmen der Bearbeitung dieser Aufgabenstellung können S einen Kernwortschatz zum Thema 'Maoris' in Form von 'word fields' zusammenstellen. Eine Auflistung der wichtigsten Begriffe finden Sie auf S. 73 dieses Heftes.

a) *Waka:* The Maori are believed to have come to New Zealand from the Polynesian islands in seven canoes about 1,000 years ago. Every Maori dates his / her ancestry back to one of the tribes who came. The carvings on their boats symbolize their genealogy.

Hongi: gesture of greeting, in which people share the air they breathe; a sign of mutual acceptance and trust.

Haka: generic term for Maori traditional dance; it is a very disciplined and ritualized way of expressing challenge, welcome, pleasure, defiance or contempt.

Moko: a (mainly facial) tattoo, it was originally chiselled into the skin. 'Te moko' symbolizes s.o.'s ancestry, social standing, function within the 'iwi' (= tribe) and personal experiences. As it is a very painful procedure, it signifies courage and strength as well as pride.

Texts: respect elders, importance of unity, social disadvantage makes people help one another, demonstration of strength, reject the British colonisers, modest expectations in life…

b) Die S kennen wahrscheinlich 'haka' von sportlichen Ereignissen, insbesondere wenn die Neuseeländische Rugby Mannschaft (the All Blacks) spielt; 'tattoos', weil sie gerade modern sind, und können auf diesen Assoziationen aufbauen.

First peoples

Kurzreferate, Internetrecherche

Es bieten sich Kurzreferate auf der Basis von gezielten Internet-Recherchen zu folgenden Themen an: tattoos, haka, carvings, waka, marae (= tribal meeting house; ceremonial and social center of the iwi/tribe), maoritanga (language, oral tradition). Siehe folgende Webseiten:
www.maori.org.nz
www.geocities.com/TheTropics/Shores/9338/culture.htm

c) Stichwörter für ein Mind map zu **Maori tradition:**
- display of strength, courage, aggression, pride, ability to suffer
- family values: strong family ties (extended family, clan) – mutual respect – altruism, charity, sense of responsibility towards other Maoris
- pride in Maori history, art, culture
- sense of loss due to colonization
- negative attitude towards 'Pakeha', (Whites, Europeans, New Zealanders of British origin)
- rejection of British influence…

Hinweis: Es wäre sinnvoll, einige sich aufwerfende Fragen hier schon anzureißen bzw. – u. U. auf der Grundlage der Auseinandersetzung mit Australian Aborigines (siehe "Before you read", SB S. 55) – Erwartungen an das Kapitel zu formulieren:
- the differences between tradition and folklore;
- the reasons why people keep up traditions;
- the integration/assimilation of the modern Maori.

The Treaty of Waitangi   SB S. 64–65

Before you read

■ **Compare Maoris and Aborigines**
Diese Aufgabe baut auf den Ergebnissen der SB S. 63 auf:
The Maoris
- had a higher degree of pride/aggression;
- were more ready to fight; they were not overrun as easily;
- their stationary lifestyle (agriculture, fishing) meant that they were more difficult to disperse;
- it was not possible to define the country as "terra nullius";
- geography (island): little possibility of driving the Maoris inland;
- clear hierarchical social/political structure within the tribes made it necessary to negotiate.

■ **Fact file**
a) Importance of the Treaty for the British Crown:
- It prevented the French colonising the islands (l. 11).
- It legalised colonial privileges, i.e. they had a governor representing the monarch's interests (l. 15)
- It gave control over land acquisition and the lawless settlers (ll. 12–13);
- It gave control over private companies dealing in New Zealand land (ll. 16–17).

Importance for missionaries:
- The treaty provided protection.
- It provided the possibility to convert Maori to Church of England tenets.

b) Reasons for the Maori chiefs to sign:
- It proved their acceptance as equal partners (government-to-government contracts/treaties).
- It promised to provide protection against lawless settlers and exploitation.

Exploring the text

1

The Maori		The British Crown	
get	give	gains	grants
– full and exclusive possession of land and sea (ll. 7–9) – rights and privileges of British citizens (ll. 16–17)	– sovereignty over their territories (ll. 2–3) – sole right to negotiate sale of land (ll. 10–12)	– new colony, edge over other European powers attempting to colonise the Pacific area (ll. 2–4) – right to control land sales (ll. 11–12)	– chiefs and tribes power over their own territory (ll. 6–10) – protection of individuals (l. 17)

2 *E.g.* The British monarch cannot really control unauthorised land acquisition;
- Those "persons appointed by her Majesty" need not negotiate fairly in terms of Maori law.
- Not all British settlers acquiring land are "appointed by her Majesty"; individual settlers will try to acquire land regardless of the treaty, as happened in the 1840s;
- British interest in a strong colony grants the New Zealand Company powers the treaty had been meant to control;
- Disagreement among Maori as to whether to sell land or not;
- Disagreement on whether ownership is tribal or individual, i.e. whether a chief can sell land without the consent of the whole *iwi* or an individual can sell part of the tribe's land.

3 *Hinweis:* Die Frage bezieht sich auf "Article the third".
a) protection from infringements by some settlers, land exploitation; b) acceptance as equal partners.

Internetrecherche

Hintergrundmaterial zum Treaty of Waitangi und dessen Folgen (für Schülerrecherchen: GA, Kurzreferate, learning by teaching) findet sich unter:
http://www.nzhistory.net.nz/index.html
http://www.govt.nz/
http://aotearoa.wellington.net.nz (Maori Independence)

A step further

■ **Evaluate statements**
1: assumes the good will but inability of the British Crown to enforce the concept of Maori "sovereignty" as long as the settlers did not recognize this right.
2: implies the unilateral self-interest of the colonial power (imperialism); The term "sovereignty" is interpreted as 'power sharing', a promise that was not kept.

3: qualifies the treaty as a comparatively sound basis for the recognition of the Maori people. The writer assumes that without the treaty the consequences of colonialism would have been much worse.

■ **Hold a role play**

Kopiervorlage, The Treaty of Waitangi, TB S. 74
Für eine Ausarbeitung der Rollen siehe TB S. 74.

■ **Hold a discussion**
Siehe auch Kernwortschatz: Maoris "History", TB S. 73.

a) Improvements	b) Implementation…
– a clear definition of all passages / terms which are open to interpretation such as "sovereignty"	– was impossible, as misunderstandings / different interpretations could not have been anticipated.
– a definition of the "rights and privileges of British subjects"	– was not feasible, as a treaty is, by definition, a general agreement not a law.
– a clear definition of the authority of the British Crown and legal consequences if settlers infringe on Maoris' rights	– of the treaty probably was not seriously intended to protect the Maori tribes' rights, considering the aims and rules of colonialism.

Ngati Kangaru SB S. 66–69

Before you read

■ **Compare a statement / fact file**
The statement confirms the supposition that the Maori were cheated by the Treaty of Waitangi and lost their rights to use their land.

New Zealand Land Wars

> Within two decades of the signing of the Treaty of Waitangi, the growing number of European settlers, the introduction of muskets, diseases and trading led to disputes over land sales and the New Zealand Land Wars, in the North Island. The Wars were fought approximately between 1860 and 1872. By the time the Wars ended both sides were exhausted, the Maori had lost huge areas of land and their society was permanently disrupted.

■ **Evaluate the fact file**
Yes: redress the Maoris' loss in terms of money…
No: cannot return land which is now owned by government, industry or private individuals; 100 years of development cannot be undone; the Maoris' traditional lifestyle has been greatly damaged

■ **Outline expectations**
E.g. Billy may see his being made redundant as one of the long-term consequences of colonization and decide to put his case for compensation to the Waitangi Tribunal…

Exploring the text

1 Billy plans to draw up documents which transfer the rights for the land and buildings at Claire Vista, a luxury holiday resort, to a group of returning Maoris. He arranges for the documents to be signed by some homeless people in return for food, whiskey and clothing.

2 The land Billy chooses belonged to his clan in the previous century, which gives him some entitlement to use it. According to the book he is reading on the Wakefield's plan, New Zealand is classed as a 'wasteland' (l. 36) and the holiday homes are also wasted during the winter as they lie idle. Billy simulates the original methods used to buy Maori territories – one chose s.o. who had no right to the land, had them sign a contract and gave them a few commodities in return which in no way corresponded to the value of the property. He compares his actions to those of the Wakefields' "high and holy work" (l. 66).

3 a)/b) *Maoris:* resourceful, vengeful, endearing, daring, colourful, hard-working, unconventional…
The reader's sympathies lie immediately with the wily, but likeable Billy. One hopes that his scheme works because it is so daring and selfless (Billy is doing something for a whole group of people).
Non-Maoris: bewildered, powerless, ridiculous, conventional, comfortable, unattractive, prosperous…
The reader gets to know very little about the non-Maoris apart from the fact that they can afford holiday homes but cannot even defend them against the Maoris. They are not described in very attractive terms (cf. ll. 83–85) and the reader is not allowed to feel any sympathy for them.

4 Tone: *humorous:* cf. the descriptions of the holidaymakers (ll. 78–85) and reactions to them (ll. 103–104);
absurd: Billy's unbelievably daring scheme actually seems to work, the returning Maoris seem to get away with squatting in the holiday homes and there is nothing the owners can do about it;
realistic: the references to the Wakefield plan show the single-minded way in which the country was colonized (cf. ll. 40–42, 48–50); Billy uses those in need for his own ends (ll. 55–57); the holiday home owners do not really need the houses, not like the returning Maori do (l. 63);
satirical: Billy criticizes the methods used originally by the Wakefield's to get control of the land (ll. 8–10, 48–50);
wishful: –
bitter: Billy calls what he is doing "high and holy work" (l. 66), which was originally given as justification for cheating Maori tribes of their lands. He feels that he can do anything as long as it is a "worthy cause" (l. 11);
ironic: Billy suggests that the holidaymakers can learn from their experience ("they might have a 'peculiar aptitude for being improved'" (ll. 65–66); he realizes only too well that the holidaymakers will not recognize his right to the land which is why he arranges for the Maoris to return when the houses are unoccupied.

A step further

■ **Define the target group**
Both the Maori and white New Zealanders could be the target of the story. On the one hand the writer encourages the Maori to be daring and reclaim what belongs to them as the white New Zealanders have no right to the land. The story might

First peoples

also be a warning to white New Zealanders that some day the Maoris will be unified and claim what was taken from them. In the story they are shown to be unable to utilise the land whereas the Maori need the homes.

- **Analyse use of English and Maori**

a) It reminds the reader that the writer is Maori, too, and she is probably giving the Maori side of the story; it makes the story more interesting as it subtly incorporates information about the Maori culture while still being understandable; the use of Maori will also make her stories appeal to that people, even if they do not speak maoritanga anymore, they will recognize some terms…
b) –

- **Write an ending**

Ngati Kangaru – the ending

> In the course of the resettlement programme, Billy and his cousin bring thousands of Maoris to Claire Vista. This has a very positive effect on the town which begins to boom all year round. The court cases brought by the holiday home owners have little media impact unlike the petition put together by local businesses supporting the Maoris. Billy and his family turn their efforts to other areas where they successfully resettle more Maoris. The family is employed full time in the resettlement business and becomes well off. At the end, Billy plans to reclaim huge areas of New Zealand which belonged to the Maori clans.

- **Creative tasks**

Siehe Kernwortschatz: Maoris, TB S. 73.

The Pakeha judge's antlers on the wall   SB S. 70–72

Before you read

- **Statements**

a) Relations are characterized by conflict: the Maori are regarded as being inferior, "dumb", and the only way that they can react is with aggression; the Maori feel no solidarity with white New Zealanders despite being born in the same country.
b) *Situations:* Young Maori who have difficulties in schools run by the state where no consideration is given to their needs and interests; as in the short story "The judge's antlers…", young Maori are considered to be criminals in the eyes of a set of laws which are not recognized within the tribe.

- **Speculation**

a) E.g. A hunter would hang antlers on the wall as a trophy/prize to show how good a shot he/she is…
b) –

- **Photo of a judge**   SB S. 72

The initial description of Judge Forbes as being "higher than anybody else" (ll. 20–21) implies that he is superior. Later, he speaks severely to one of the defendants and accuses him of committing a serious crime (ll. 41–44). He seems to be convinced that his judgement is correct. Simeon also refers to the fact that the judge is wearing a ridiculous wig (ll. 64–65). Later, he shows a more human side (ll. 86–97). The judge in the photo may or may not correspond to these ideas.

Exploring the text

1 *humiliation:* when he is expected to make a speech of thanks to the judge (ll. 53–54); *guilt:* he feels as if he is on the wrong side by being with a group of non-Maori students rather than in the gallery with the Maoris (l. 28); *embarrassment:* He knows most of the people in the gallery. They have come to see their family members be sentenced and he knows that it is embarrassing for them, too. He does not want them to see him (ll. 25–27, 60). He is also "lost and bewildered" (l. 64).

2 *Narrator:* Simeon describes events at the courthouse in the role of a first-person, limited narrator; he only gives us an insight into his own feelings, (e.g. l. 71) and reactions (e.g. ll. 60–61), and not into those of the judge or Miss Dalrymple.
Active main character: The action is centered around Simeon in the second half of the story as he speaks to the judge. Because we the readers know how he feels by line 65 we are not surprised that he turns his speech into a plea for understanding and mercy for the young plaintiffs.
Detached observer: In this role Simeon gives us details about the courthouse, the people in it and the cases almost as if he were a court reporter, e.g. ll. 18–23. Even here though, Simeon interrupts the report with short comments as a first-person narrator, e.g. "A pair of antlers on the wall", ll. 34, 38, 45. The mixture of points of view increases the tension in the story.

A step further

- **Write and act out a scene**

Der Charakter von Miss Dalrymple wird mit höchster Wahrscheinlichkeit sehr höfliche Floskeln anwenden. Judge Forbes wird einerseits Simeon verteidigen wollen und andererseits Miss Dalrymple beruhigen, dass er sich nicht beleidigt fühlt. Der Dialog könnte folgendermaßen anfangen:

Miss Dalrymple: Your honour, could I possibly have a word with you in private / I can only apologise for what just happened / I had no idea that that boy was capable of insulting someone like yourself who deserves every respect / I will make sure that he is punished accordingly / his behaviour does not go unpunished…
Judge Forbes: There is no need to apologise / I appreciate the fact that you did not expect such a reaction / I can only repeat that he is entitled to his opinion…

- **Collect arguments, act out a meeting**

Mögliche Ideen: Miss Dalrymple will not want to condone such behaviour by allowing Simeon to go unpunished and allowing visits to the court to continue; she will probably refuse to take further groups of students there…
The non-Maori teachers at the meeting might sympathise with Miss Dalrymple and understand that she was embarrassed by Simeon's speech or they might say that it had been insensitive to send a young, impressionable boy to the courthouse where many of his relatives are being sentenced – this would be a good reason to stop visits there…

First peoples

The Maori teachers might praise Simeon's actions but suggest that visits to the courthouse might be stopped because of the embarrassment caused to Maori students…

Waitangi Day with gritted teeth / After all we're one people, aren't we? from Waitangi Day to New Zealand Day SB S. 73–74

Before you read

■ **Significance of Waitangi Day**
a) Cf. Fact file, "Maori land rights …", SB S. 64 and Kernwortschatz: Maoris, TB S. 73.
b) *Photo top right:* The situation is very civilised and downbeat; the couple seem to be enjoying listening to the pipe band, mainly because it gives them a chance to sit in the sunshine. Celebrations are not very enthusiastic if we compare them, for example, to 4th of July parades in the US.
Photo bottom left: A group of Maoris is demonstrating as a sign of protest against the Treaty of Waitangi; the message on one of the banners calls for the fulfilment of the Treaty of Waitangi; the demonstration seems to be relatively peaceful as the police are dressed normally – not in riot gear – and some of the protestors seem to be smiling…

Exploring the text

1 Carroll du Chateau emphasizes the fact that both the Maori and non-Maori communities share a common past. Both came to New Zealand in a boat of some kind and risked building a new life in a new country. They also share the same unterprising spirit and love for their country.

2 Diane Wichtel feels that the holiday only underlines previous conflicts and present divisions between the Maori and non-Maori communities. The celebrations seem very forced and artificial (cf. the laying of an egg on the place where the treaty was signed). No one, including politicians present at the ceremonies on the day, seems to enjoy the occasion.

3 Tone of Diane Wichtel's article:
- critical: The holiday only seems to make differences more pronounced (ll. 2–4);
- realistic: The writer recognizes the failure of the holiday;
- slightly hopeful: Waitangi Day in 2002 seemed to be trying to fulfil its original purpose to unify (ll. 18–20) and it "felt like a step forward" (ll. 34–35);
- sarcastic: The writer expects little of the Prime Minister, Helen Clark, the most one can expect from her is to keep her feelings under control and not be upset by criticism (ll. 24–28), the writer implies that those who are involved in Waitangi Day are like "adolescents" (l. 36) who are just beginning to grow up.

Tone of Carroll du Chateau's comment:
- romantic: In ll. 2–3, she quotes English writer, Rudyard Kipling (1865–1936), who referred to New Zealand as the "last loveliest loneliest land apart"; she writes that most New Zealanders who emigrate do so because they are driven by "that restless spirit" to "search the world for fresh and better opportunities" (ll. 18–19);
- sentimental: She suggests that most emigrants return to New Zealand because they love it there (ll. 19–21);
- idealistic: She suggests that the original settlers were "pushed by a thirst for adventure" (ll. 6–7) when in fact they probably had little choice; she also calls them the "self-selected bravest people around" (ll. 11–12);
- conciliatory: The writer refers to the "common core" (l. 22) and love of New Zealand which link the Maori and Pakeha communities (ll. 25–28).

A step further

■ **Imagine and act out a discussion**
Cf. "Exploring the text", Task 3 and "Discussions", SB S. 193 für nützliche Ausdrücke.

■ **Analyse a statement**
a) Relations between the two groups seem to be hindered by misunderstandings and unintended rudeness. The Maori culture is governed by particular rules of etiquette which are unintelligible to the non-Maoris. As a result, neither side seems to be able to communicate with the other.
b) A Maori activist might agree with Diane Wichtel's more down-to-earth assessment of the holiday as being a tense occasion on which the divide between the Maori and Pakeha communities becomes more obvious. The activist might also agree with Ms. Wichtel's description of the Prime Minister as being chilly and reserved. He / she might not feel that the Day is worth saving as Ms. Wichtel implies in ll. 29–30 as it can only have painful associations for the Maoris.
The activist is likely to disagree with Carroll du Chateau's assessment as he / she is unlikely to feel a common cause with the first settlers. The Maori suffered at the settlers' hands in that they lost their lands, contracted diseases and ultimately lost their culture and way of life. The activist might point out that he / she is a Maori not a New Zealander, a term which was introduced by the Europeans.
Siehe Briefvorlage auf SB S. 111.

■ **Look at statistics from particular points of view**
a) A Maori activist would probably point out that the percentage of speakers of Maori has remained consistently low over the last thirty-five years. He / she might see this development as an indication that the training programmes since the 1960s have not been effective in promoting the language. He / she might suggest that more money has to be invested in teaching the language, in particular to under 30-year-olds who cannot hold a conversation in Maori. The pie chart which shows "Parents' preference for Maori language education" implies that very few children are initially educated through Maori and over half of parents choose a mixture of English and Maori for their children, which prevents total immersion in the language.
b) A government representative might say that it is important for young Maori to receive a balanced education which does not neglect their English skills. These skills will enable them to find a place and a job in modern New Zealand society. He / she might point out that the government has done its best to accommodate the Maori community since the 1960s by providing training programmes which also take the Maori culture into account. Over 800 schools which teach Maori have been established. This is also an indication of the government's willingness to promote that culture. It is the parents' decision whether to send their children to an all-Maori school or not. (Cf. Kernwortschatz: Maoris, TB S. 73.)

First peoples

Didaktisches Inhaltsverzeichnis – Native Americans

	Titel	Textsorte (Wortzahl ca.)	Thema	Text- und Spracharbeit	Textproduktion (schriftlich / mündlich)
	Native American… SB S. 75, TB S. 60 TB S. 73	photo collage, lyrics	images of Native American past and present	describe photos • interpret images in lyrics	collect key words in a mind map
🎵	My country 'tis… SB S. 75, TB S. 60 TB S. 76	song (567 words)	treatment of Native Americans by white Americans	listening comprehension • discuss images • describe emotions • explain chorus	collect and present information
🎵	Indian education SB S. 76, TB S. 62 TB S. 113	short story extract (811 words)	education on a reservation, Native American vs. white American values	collect / examine memories of primary school • discuss integration • examine stereotypes, point of view	speculate based on the text • write a letter of application, CV • prepare a storyboard, write a dialogue • Meet the media: write an e-mail
📺	Voices of the Navajo SB S. 79, TB S. 63	documentary (965 words)	life on a reservation, land rights	collect information from sequences • isolate film material, voiceover • make notes about interviews	talk about photos • plan a documentary • have a discussion in roles
	Getting rich… SB S. 80, TB S. 65 TB S. 104, 106	feature (934 words)	controversy surrounding casinos on reservations	describe the atmosphere in a photo • find pros and cons • describe the writer's opinion • analyse text type: feature	turn the feature into a comment • write a letter to the editor
Over to you	Indians hear… SB S. 82, TB S. 66 TB S. 75	newspaper report (516 words)	integration of modern technology into traditional lifestyles, political commitment	comprehension • define point of the article	prepare and give a talk • associate ideas with the title • brainstorm ideas
Over to you	First peoples SB S. 83, TB S. 66	creative activities related to the chapter	present-day situation of first peoples	compare texts	discuss the impression the text made • analyse photo • examine Western interest in first peoples • make a mind map • write an essay

Native American past and present   SB S. 75

Looking and thinking

1 a) Photo of Seminole chiefs: The Seminole chiefs have been bound at the wrist in an undignified way by the soldiers. The soldiers are heavily armed with rifles and bayonets and it is unlikely that the chiefs could escape. The picture conveys the powerlessness of the Native Americans.
The main photo shows a little Navajo girl who is a kind of tourist attraction. For two dollars, tourists can take her photo against the background of the desert. This shows how Native Americans are forced to sell their culture in order to make a living.
b) *Collage:* Siehe Sequenzen 2 und 3 auf dem Begleit-Video / der DVD (ISBN 3-12-510473-4 / 510474-2) für mögliche Ideen.
Lyrics: Film scenes where Indian warriors are chased by a platoon of soldiers; old black-and-white photo of a chief with feather headdress and ceremonial pipe…

2 The singer possibly wanted to catch listeners' attention by using a line that is familiar to them, and then to make them think by changing the lyrics that follow. She manages to show that there are two sides to the story of the settlement of America. As far as the Native American population was concerned, the settlers took away their "liberty" and had nothing to be proud about.
3 Siehe Kernwortschatz, TB S. 73 für Ideen.

My country 'tis of thy people you're dying 🎵   SB S. 75

Eine Aufbereitung des Hörverstehenstext befindet sich auf einer Kopiervorlage auf TB S. 76. Die Trackpunkte geben den Anfang des Abschnitts auf der Begleit-CD (ISBN 3-12-510472-6) an.

First peoples

Transkript

18 Now that your big eyes have finally opened,
Now that you're wondering how must they feel,
Meaning them that you've chased across America's movie screens.
5 Now that you're wondering how can it be real
That the ones you've called colorful, noble and proud
In your school propaganda
They starved in their splendor?
You've asked for my comment I simply will render:
10 My country 'tis of thy people you're dying.

Now that the longhouses breed superstition
You force us to send our toddlers away
To your schools where they're taught to despise their traditions.
15 You forbid them their languages, then further say
That American history really began
When Columbus set sail out of Europe, and stress
That the nation of leeches that conquered this land
Are the biggest and bravest and boldest and best.
20 And yet where in your history books is the tale
Of the genocide basic to this country's birth,
Of the preachers who lied, how the Bill of Rights failed,
How a nation of patriots returned to their earth?
And where will it tell of the Liberty Bell
25 As it rang with a thud
O'er Kinzua mud,
And of brave Uncle Sam in Alaska this year?
My country 'tis of thy people you're dying.

Hear how the bargain was made for the West:
30 With her shivering children in zero degrees,
Blankets for your land, so the treaties attest,
Oh well, blankets for land is a bargain indeed,
And the blankets were those Uncle Sam had collected
From smallpox-diseased dying soldiers that day.
35 And the tribes were wiped out and the history books censored,
A hundred years of your statesmen have felt it's better this way.
And yet a few of the conquered have somehow survived,
Their blood runs the redder though genes have been paled.
40 From the Grand Canyon's caverns to craven sad hills
The wounded, the losers, the robbed sing their tale.
From Los Angeles County to upstate New York
The white nation fattens while others grow lean;
Oh the tricked and evicted they know what I mean.
45 My country 'tis of thy people you're dying.

The past it just crumbled, the future just threatens;
Our life blood shut up in your chemical tanks.
And now here you come, bill of sale in your hands
And surprise in your eyes that we're lacking in thanks
50 For the blessings of civilization you've brought us,
The lessons you've taught us, the ruin you've wrought us –
Oh see what our trust in America's brought us.
My country 'tis of thy people you're dying.

Now that the pride of the sires receives charity,
55 Now that we're harmless and safe behind laws,
Now that my life's to be known as your "heritage,"
Now that even the graves have been robbed,
Now that our own chosen way is a novelty –
Hands on our hearts we salute you your victory,
60 Choke on your blue white and scarlet hypocrisy
Pitying the blindness that you've never seen
That the eagles of war whose wings lent you glory
They were never no more than carrion crows,
Pushed the wrens from their nest, stole their eggs, changed their story;
65 The mockingbird sings it, it's all that she knows.
"Ah what can I do?" say a powerless few
With a lump in your throat and a tear in your eye –
Can't you see that their poverty's profiting you.
My country 'tis of thy people you're dying. 70

Words and music by Buffy Sainte-Marie, © Copyright 1968 by Gypsy Boy Music Incorporated/Rondor Music (London) Limited. Used by permission of Music Sales Ltd. All Rights Reserved. International Copyright Secured.

Background information: Buffy Sainte-Marie

Buffy Sainte-Marie was born on a Cree reservation in Saskatchewan and raised in Maine and Massachusetts. She became famous in the 1960s as a folk singer who brought the cause of the Native Americans to the attention of the world. She has also written songs which have been performed by other artists and even done a five-year appearance on the American children's programme *Sesame Street*. Since 1984, she has also been a digital artist. Cf. www.creative-native.com for more information.

Before you listen

■ **Images**
a)/b) The singer refers to the 'film Indian' who is always the 'bad guy' and is chased by soldiers, for example. She suggests that people have never considered the situation from the Indians' point of view. Also, people have an image of the proud, feather-clad Indian chief when in reality they were often starving.
c) E.g. Confiscation of the Indians' lands, the killing of thousands of Indians in wars, the loss of cultural identity…

Listening for gist

1 a) *Mögliches Vokabeltraining:* Die S erhalten ein Blatt mit passenden und unzutreffenden Stimmungs-Adjektiven (bzw. -Nomina) oder erstellen dieses selber – ggfs. auch erst bei "Listening for detail" einsetzen. Im Folgenden sind unzutreffende Zuordnungen kursiv gedruckt:
euphoric – dejected (dejection) – desperate (despair) – *arrogant (arrogance)* – sad (sadness) – committed (commitment) – *condoning* – enthusiastic (enthusiasm) – angry (anger) – sarcastic (sarcasm) – *polite (politeness)* – aggressive (aggression) – *elated (elation)* – bitter (bitterness) – indignant (indignation) – outraged (outrage) – disheartened – incensed – *condescending (condescension)* – despondent (despondence) – *conciliatory (reconciliation)* – despising (spite) – condemning (condemnation) – *forgiving (forgiveness)*
b) *Voice:* expressive; can sound pathetic/hard/accusing; seems to quiver when the singer is moved by the theme.
Tune: it does not seem to have a regular beat, which means that the listeners' attention is held by the changing rhythm.
Instrumentation: the singer is accompanied by a guitar which seems to follow her moods; the guitar accompaniment

First peoples

neither distracts from the lyrics nor overrides the singer's voice.

2 a) *Mögliche Ergebnisse am Ende der Globalbesprechung:*
1st stanza, chorus: relationship between white and Native Americans in the 60s;
- speaker/singer addresses white audience; refers to their naive, belated concern about Native Americans: she will confront them with reality;
- sets mood: white American listeners will not be spared; despite an improvement in their attitude towards Native Americans, they will be held responsible for the consequences of history.

2nd stanza, chorus: trauma of Native American experiences in history contrast with milestones in US history;
- Part 1: flashlights (not in chronological order) on ideology of 'white supremacy'; the destruction of cultural identity through mission schools and the negation of the Native American past as independent nations and cultures;
- Part 2: mocking flashlights on eurocentric history and its symbols (European conquest, Declaration of Independence, Bill of Rights, Liberty Bell), and the devastating consequences of hegemony for Native Americans (events of the recent past, e.g. Kinzua, Alaska where they are still being denied their rights).

3rd stanza, chorus; wiping out of the tribes, Native Americans are still badly treated;
- Part 1: more flashlights on historical acts of white hegemony: treacherous treaties, expulsion from native territories, deliberate extinction of tribes, distortion of reality in history books;
- Part 2: survival against all odds, renewed strength through suffering (ll. 41–42) despite the fact that white hegemony still prevails (l. 43).

4th stanza, chorus; current situation (60s)
- reference to problems with industrial pollution on reservations; continuing tension in relations between two sides; white Americans naively expect thanks for helping Native Americans; implicit reproach for being hypocritical.

5th stanza, chorus; accusation of hypocrisy;
- Part 1: Native Americans are seen as a charity, the white American's heritage, a novelty;
- Part 2: most bitter attack on white America's claim of being noble, points out that society benefits from the poverty of the Native Americans.

Listening for detail

1 E.g. nation of leeches (accuses the white settlers of sucking all of the goodness out of the nation), brave Uncle Sam (irony, given the context the singer means the opposite, cf. l. 27), blue, white and scarlet hypocrisy (often the flag is regarded as a symbol of freedom, but the reference to scarlet has a negative effect as one thinks of blood), the white nation fattens (image of cattle which feed on the Native Americans' territory), eagles of war (traditional image of the American soldier as the noble liberator; in the context the eagle is really a carrion crow which feeds on dead matter, i.e. becomes rich from wiping out the Native American tribes).

2 The chorus "My country 'tis of thy people you're dying" may be explained as follows: "country" refers to the Native American people and their lands which are being abused by "thy people", i.e. white American society.

A step further

■ **Do research / a presentation in groups**
Siehe Skills file "Presentations", SB S. 182–183 für Ideen.

Indian education SB S. 76–78

Before you read

■ **Collect / examine memories of primary school**
a) –
b) E.g. affects a child's attitude to school, he/she sees it as an enjoyable learning experience, or not; it should provide a solid basis for later schooling; it establishes friendships which last through school years…

■ **Discuss integration**
Schools could organise special language programmes, mentoring programmes (students are assigned as mentors to help with homework, help out with difficulties), offer classes in intercultural awareness where (groups of) non-national students present their country…

👁 Talking about a cartoon SB S. 77

Possible responses: "Well, your national heritage actually…"
– "Neither. Guess again…"

Exploring the text

1 a) *Mögliche Ideen:*
reservation school experiences
- *positive:* Junior has his parents' support; it becomes obvious that he is a very bright child;
- *negative:* He is a target for bullying by other Indian boys; he is discriminated against by one of the teachers because he is a Native American.

state high school experiences
- *positive:* he is able to use his talents as a basketball player; he makes friends with white people, who help him when he is ill; he does well academically at high school.
- *negative:* he is again made conscious of the discrimination against Native Americans; he is given the impression that society expects Native Americans to be drunk, violent and anti-social; he discovers that he has diabetes; he realises that most of the people that he went to school with on the reservation have little chance of finding employment.

2 In his first year, Junior does not seem to fit in with the other boys as they bully him. Later, he probably does not fit in because he is brighter than the other students (cf. ll. 23–25), a fact which seems to make Miss Towle dislike him; he even retaliates in a different way to the other children probably would, i.e. he draws an uncomplimentary picture rather than becoming aggressive.
At the high school in the farm town, he is again isolated but this time because he seems to be the only Native American there. Here he has white friends (l. 52) but he is still conscious of prejudices about Native Americans.

3 *Mögliche Beispiele:* Stereotype views of Native Americans as being the ones who caused all of the trouble with the settlers (ll. 15–17); they cause trouble on the reservations (ll. 35–37); they become alcoholics at a young age (ll. 54–55); they make good team mascots (ll. 60–63).

4 Point of view (first-person narration): is appropriate for the diary format of the short story; illustrates how inappropriate and distorting prejudices can be (ll. 38–39), and how quickly they arise (ll. 52–55); brings home to the reader how hurtful prejudices can be as shown by Junior's comments on the discrimination he experiences (ll. 19–20, 66–67).

A step further

■ Speculate based on the text
Popular with Native Americans: readers can identify with the (discriminatory) situations, attitudes and settings in his stories; they feel taken seriously – Sherman Alexie represents them in some way; his stories are not pathetic and his heroes deal positively with any setbacks they encounter…
Popular with non-Native Americans: Sherman Alexie does not portray the Native Americans as suffering – yet again – at the hands of white society; he pokes fun at himself, but at the same time he manages to get across what it is like to be a Native American, both on and off the reservation…

■ Write a letter of application / CV
Cf. Kopiervorlage, TB S. 114 "The world of work".

■ Prepare a storyboard, write a dialogue –

Meet the media: Dances with Wolves, Smoke signals

■ Write e-mails
Compensates for images of blood-thirsty savages: The Native Americans are dealt with very sensitively, and the audience is bound to sympathise with characters such as Kicking Bird and Black Shawl. The stereotypes of killer Indians are undermined by the fact that Stands with a Fist is taken in by the Indian tribe after losing her family. Later, when Dunbar fights as Dances with Wolves, he realises that he is fighting for food, survival and, in particular, for the children and women of the tribe.
Sentimental fantasy: The film might be perceived as too little, too late. The contact between John Dunbar and the Sioux is highly romanticised: at the time the film was set, Native Americans were seldom dealt with respectfully by the white settlers, who were not interested in their culture; the Native Americans were the natural rivals, if not enemies, of the settlers. At worst, they would have been regarded as killers and criminals (cf. the Westerns dealing with attacks by Indians).

■ Web search
a) Siehe http://www.imdb.com für Links zu Rezensionen (siehe Rubrik "Awards and reviews").
b) *Plot:* Two young Native American men travel together to Phoenix to collect the ashes of one of the men's father. During the road movie they learn a lot about themselves.
Characters: Victor is tall and silent. He resents the father who left him and his mother twenty years before. Thomas Builds-the-Fire is talkative and, according to Victor, has learned everything he knows about Indians from the film *Dances with Wolves*. Victor, however, has to take Thomas along because he has enough money to fund the trip.
c) –

Voices of the Navajo SB S. 79

Before you watch

■ Talk about photos
E.g. Nellie Martin: life is hard but it has always been so; content to have a few sheep and live on a farm even if it is isolated; does not understand why people have to buy so many things – we should make the things we need because then we value them more…
Shayna Lynn: It is not much fun / boring sitting in the sun after school every day; sometimes tourists give a few extra coins so I can buy some sweets; we need the money as there is little money on the reservation and no jobs, so the money from the photos makes a difference…

■ Plan a documentary
a) Aspects to include: unemployment / social problems on the reservations, specific problems faced by young people who have little to do on the reservation (cf. special case of Shayna Lynn), passing on one's culture and traditions to the younger generation, loss of the old lifestyles as more people move away to the cities to find work (cf. Nellie Martin who is left behind)…
b) / c) –

Hinweis: Sequence 1 entspricht Sequenz 2 und Sequence 2 entspricht Sequenz 3 auf dem Begleit-Video (ISBN 3-12-510473-4) und der DVD (ISBN 3-12-510474-2).

Transkript: Growing up on the reservation

Voice-over (VO): The office of the "Community action for children and youth" in Tuba. This is where volunteer work is organised. For a long time Vanessa Brown has been dedicated to improving the range of activities for the reservation's children. There are not enough playgrounds or youth activities and of course not enough money. The volunteer workers have not seen one cent from Washington. But Vanessa doesn't let that discourage her. The main thing is the children. The future of the Navajo in Tuba City.
Vanessa Brown: With nothing to do and just a lot of idle time, they can find a place where drugs are sold, there's plenty of bootleggers although alcohol is illegal on the reservation. There's places they can go and find fun, you know in a negative way because of nothing to do.
VO: Boredom creates crime. Gang wars and drugs have also come to the dreary reservation settlement. The government provides the people with homes, schools and a hospital. But what's missing in Tuba City, and the other towns on the Navajo reservation, are jobs, especially for young people. The unemployment rate is fifty percent and welfare is the main source of income. For many Native American children Navajo country offers no future perspective.
VO: Carved rocks somewhere in the desert near Tuba City. Vanessa Brown brings children here from the town to explain the meaning of the symbols. In this way the Navajo culture can stay alive as a part of their identity. Vanessa passes on what she heard about the mysterious signs on the rocks from her mother and grandmother. Storytelling has a long tradition with the Navajo. In winter the children often hear stories all night long about the magical kachina doll or about the adventurous coyote who loves to play tricks. For Vanessa this is as much a part of education as physics classes in college.

First peoples

Vanessa: Our greatest challenge with our children is trying to stay afloat in two worlds like one foot in one canoe the modern world, your education, getting a job, you know survival yet the other foot in another canoe carrying your traditions and your roots, your language. If you stand too far on one side you'll fall, same visa versa. If you lose your identity and only go in a modern world then again you will fall, so they have a great challenge to carry these two parts as one.

12 **bootlegger** s.o. who makes and sells alcohol illegally

Transkript: Navajo land rights

Voice-over (VO): The issues at stake here are water, land and this woman. Maxine Keskaly lives in the middle of the Black Mesa and she's in the way of the coalmine. The road to Maxine's place goes right through the Black Mesa and is known only to her friends. Leroy is one of them.
Maxine's family has been living on this land for generations. They still live in the traditional style and are opposed to the coalmine. Leroy and a few friends support them in their battle with the companies that have been active here for thirty years. Their goal is to stop North America's largest coal mining enterprise and prevent resettlement of the Mesa's remaining inhabitants. Since Maxine speaks only Dineh, Leroy acts as translator, in court for instance. Maxine refuses to get out of the steam shovel's path.
Maxine / Translator: The mine people said to me that I should go away from here, but as a Dineh I cannot leave this land. I pray to the land, the trees, the sheep fodder. My prayers make this land sacred and I pray to be able to stay here.
VO: 33 million gallons of ground water a day are pumped out of the Mesa in order to transport pulverised coal 250 miles through a pipeline to the Mohave power station. "Water that my sheep need", as Maxine says. But this conflict is not just about water and environmental protection. This is about modern civilization invading the life of the Navajo. Along with bulldozers, the values of the white society came to stay in the land of the Native Americans. They brought to the reservation not only modern machines but also jobs, training, schools and money. Because of this, many Navajos take a more differentiated stand on the 'sacred' Black Mesa issue.
Teddy Magay, who is Navajo and works as an engineer for the coal company, explains his viewpoint.
Teddy: I was not born in a hospital, I was born in a hogan. And my mother's teaching was that … she said, you know, the holy spirit put a lot of things into this earth meant to be utilized to the best way that it can to help mankind. We go back into our old silversmithing. We took the precious turquoise stones out of the earth, we have taken the metal of the silver out of the earth.
VO: Today they take valuable hard coal out of the earth. The Navajo government have leased the land to the company, a legally complicated matter. The black gold of the Navajo has been the topic of a year-long court battle. For Leroy the issue is clear…
Leroy: And the suggestion of coal mining is, you know … you're raping it or stabbing it. And you're just doing it daily. And if you are like a Mother Earth – I don't know what it's feeling like to be a Mother Earth – it's like someone is going after your liver, wants it for money and it's not in a good standard doing that.
VO: Leroy's compromise with white values works like this. For good dollars, he allows inexperienced palefaces to ride his horses across the sacred land in order to earn money, in order to survive. Leroy has no choice but to surrender the land. He speaks of gentle tourism. Clearly earning a living this way leaves fewer marks on Mother Earth than the steam shovels do.

Background information: Tuba City, Black Mesa

Tuba City is at the junction of state Highway 264 and U.S. 160, about 80 miles northeast of Flagstaff, Arizona. It is an urban centre in the western part of the Navajo Reservation. The town has a population of 9,244 (Source: Arizona Department of Economic Security, 1999) and an unemployment rate of 17.4%. The largest employers are services, mining and public administration.
Black Mesa is part of the Colorado Plateau and is located in northeastern Arizona. Since the mid-1990s, the aquifer beneath the Mesa has been lowering resulting in the reduced flow or elimination of springs. It is unclear if this results from the activities of the coal mining companies located in the Mesa. (Source: Colorado Plateau – Land Use History of North America,
www.cpluhna.nau.edu/Places/black_mesa.htm)

Sequence 1: Growing up on the reservation

1 Young people are very vulnerable because there is very little for them to do on the reservation. As a result, they are tempted by the attractions of alcohol and drugs, which are sold illegally on the reservation.
The children in the sequence are lucky to be told about their culture and traditions, yet one day they may have to balance this knowledge with the demands of modern day life.
2 a) The film material shows how little Tuba City offers. The houses seem to be located in the middle of a desert. A car passes now and then but the place seems to be practically deserted. Only a few children wander around aimlessly looking for a bit of fun. There is wild grass growing beside the pavement and there is no colour or attempt to make the town look more attractive.
The scenes in the desert, with the carvings on the rocks, show that there is a lot to learn there, and the desert holds a link to the Navajos' past.
b) The voiceover confirms much of what the images already suggest about the disadvantaged nature of the town. It tries to address questions which might occur to viewers, e.g. why little has been done to the town (there has been no funding from the government).
The voiceover also conveys information, which may not have been obvious from the images, e.g. Vanessa Brown's enthusiasm for passing on Navajo traditions, and adds details, e.g. the importance of storytelling to the Navajo.
The voiceover also links the scenes to the interviews.

Sequence 2: Navajo land rights

1 *Maxine:* The land is her home and her people have lived there for generations. She is linked to the land and she prays to it. She does not wish to leave it.
Teddy: The land can be put to use for mining purposes as this is beneficial to man. There is a long mining tradition – in the

First peoples

past, turquoise and silver were extracted from the ground and now it happens to be coal.
Leroy: The land is under attack by the coalmine as all its resources are being taken out of it every day. He finds this inacceptable as this activity harms the earth. He favours a more gentle approach to using the earth. He feels that "gentle tourism", such as horseback rides across the land, does far less harm.

2 The issue of land rights is a complicated one. On the one hand, engineers like Teddy are dependent on the coalmine for their livelihood. On the other hand, so is Maxine and the question is whether her right is stronger as she has lived and worked on the Mesa for longer than Teddy. The coalmine seems to want to get rid of the Mesa's inhabitants in order to expand its production, which is difficult to justify.

A step further

■ **Have a discussion in roles**
Diese Aufgabe leitet die Bearbeitung des Texts auf SB S. 80–81 ein. (Siehe Kernwortschatz, TB S. 73) Mögliche Ideen:

	pros	cons
relationship	development would bring tourists from other states to the reservation and show how many Native Americans live in poverty	reservation will be heavily dependent on incoming tourists; the latter might have a negative influence on the young people and make them forget their traditions completely
employment	more jobs on building sites, in hotels, casinos, cafés, tourist information centres…	these jobs require few skills; more specialized work will probably be done by people from outside the reservation
effect	development can be limited so that builders do not have to encroach on sacred land	large areas of land are necessary to provide hotels, roads and other facilities for visitors
social consequences	there will be more money to invest in facilities for young people and schools	the young are more likely to leave, attracted by the big cities
traditional way of life:	more money will be available for tribal education programmes, etc.	outsiders will reduce the influence of tribal elders, especially on the young who are more likely to forget their traditions

Getting rich with the casino tribes SB S. 80–81

👁 **Talk about the photo** SB S. 80

E.g. desolate, rundown, abandoned, empty of all life, unhospitable, unwelcoming…

Exploring the text

1 *Pros:* Reservations can build other facilities such as shopping malls, museums, cultural centres (l. 4), which also provide income/tourist attractions; casinos bring people of all nations and creeds together under one roof (ll. 11–13); the reservations make millions in profits from the casinos (l. 15) and as a result banks are more willing to give them loans for development (ll. 16–17); unemployment is reduced, the reservations can afford better facilities for young and old, they can promote education and training, and finance programmes to teach the tribal language and crafts (ll. 23–26); reservations can have their own police force (ll. 27–28); people's dignity has been restored, they can expect s.th. of life, as a result they take better care of themselves (ll. 40–43).
Cons: There is speculation that the profits from the casinos are spent by individual chiefs on their personal needs rather than being put back into the reservation (ll. 34–36); the state may try to force the reservations to pay tax on their profits, which would mean a serious loss in income (ll. 48–50); the profits from the casinos endanger the reservations' claim on government subsidies for education and social benefits (ll. 57–59); the rich tribes are being divided from the poor (ll. 69–70); developers take little notice of environment issues or the beauty of the reservations where they build (ll. 70–72).

2 The writer mentions her impressions, feelings and opinions, using the first person "I", e.g. "the most racially integrated scene I have witnessed" (ll. 12–13), "If I were an Indian, I would be…" (ll. 73–74); she includes information about her research in the same way, e.g. "That, says Rivera, is a MYTH – and he makes sure that I write this in my notebook …" (ll. 37–38); the writer also uses a rhetorical question to convey her opinion, cf. "After centuries of indigence, what have they to lose?" (ll. 74–75); she also paraphrases quotes from other sources, e.g. "In other words …" (ll. 41–42).

3 a) Siehe Tabelle unten.

Features	Getting rich…	Mourning closes…
Composition/line of argument	– arguments given for and against; writer comes down on one side in the last line	– is more objective; gives arguments for both sides
Background information	– is well researched, includes details about legal changes/social impact on the reservation	– outlines issues briefly in short paragraphs
Human interest	– the writer reports what she sees on the reservation first hand	– impersonal; details could have been taken from another article/a press agency report
Use of quotations	– quotes both directly and indirectly	– quotes indirectly
Form one's own opinion	– writer is in favour of the casinos; this comes across strongly	– writer states facts in a way which allows readers to make up their minds

b) Good feature: –

A step further

■ **Turn the feature into a comment**
Siehe Kernwortschatz: Native Americans, TB S. 73.

First peoples

- **Write a letter to the editor**

Hinweis: Diese Aufgabe läßt sich auch mündlich in Gruppen als *talk show* bearbeiten. Die Teilnehmer sollten ihre Rollenkarten ausarbeiten (siehe TB S. 104) und dem Moderator eine "Reduced survival role card" geben (siehe TB S. 106).

Indians hear a high-tech drumbeat ⟨over to you⟩ SB S. 82

Eine Aufbereitung dieses Texts befindet sich auf einer Kopiervorlage auf Seite 75.

Before you read

- **Speculate about the title**

The writer is referring to high-tech / electronic methods of communication; drums are often considered to be a method of communication between tribes by non-Native Americans although, in reality, drums have a greater significance for Native Americans, simply as a musical instrument which expresses the earth's spirit.

- **Brainstorm ideas**

E.g. collect names on a petition which you submit; write e-mails to various representatives of government and persuade your class / family / friends to do likewise; write a letter to the editor of the local newspaper expressing your ideas, hang up posters in a public place and hand out leaflets which call on others to support your protest…

Exploring the text

1 Since the 1980s, the US government has been using Native American reservations as waste disposal sites for nuclear and other matter. The government offers hundreds of millions of dollars to tribes to allow waste to be dumped. This puts a lot of pressure on poor tribes who could badly do with the money.
2 In the past, the reservations were more isolated and unable to support one another in a protest situation. Nowadays, modern technologies allow them to communicate with and support one another. They can also use e-mail and other modes of communication to write official protests to the authorities and to organize themselves. The internet is also a useful tool to find out what is going on and to increase the public's awareness of Native American problems.
3 The writer seems to be saying that the tribes are finally working together to protest against the dumping of waste on their reservations. This co-operation seems to be effective.
The writer is also interested in the function of infomation technology in making this co-operation between tribes possible. This aspect is explored almost as extensively as the coalition itself. This makes the issue somewhat unclear. The title also emphasizes the importance of technology.

A step further

- **Think of slogans**

E.g. We were here first – so go away!; Together we can beat the paleface!; Don't dump your waste on us – we have enough problems!

- **Design a pamphlet** –

- **Interview**

Für weitere Informationen zum "Indigenous Environmental Network", das von Tom Goldtooth gegründet wurde, siehe folgende Webseite:
www.ienearth.org.
Siehe auch Kernwortschatz: Native Americans, "Present trends" und "Life on the reservation", TB S. 73.

- **Write a verse or verses**

E.g. Now that you have given us mobiles and e-mail,
Now that you're wondering what your next move will be,
Against those you have poisoned all of these years.
Now we're going to put up a real fight,
We'll all stand together both noble and proud
From Florida to California, from Arizona to New York
We won't let you pollute our deserts and hovels,
You've asked for my land but I simply will tell you
My country 'tis my people will never betray you.

First peoples ⟨over to you⟩ SB S. 83

- **"Indian education", "The Pakeha judge…"**

Similarities: Both boys experience discrimination first hand, although in Simeon's case, it probably was not intentional on Miss Dalrymple's part; both boys respond to this discrimination in their own way without resorting to violence.
Characteristics: Both boys seem intelligent, sensitive, able to express themselves well and make 'white' friends. Junior has a more fatalistic attitude and seems to observe more, whereas Simeon speaks up against what he sees as injustice.
In the short story extract, Junior seems to be constantly confronted by discrimination whereas Simeon only mentions one case. The example is still serious as it suggests that something is terribly wrong with the legal system in New Zealand.
Common aims: Both wanted to raise consciousness of discrimination against their people; they suggest peaceful ways of dealing with discriminatory behaviour, e.g. one has to speak out like Simeon, one has to make a silent protest like Junior's parents, who drag their braids across Betty Towle's desk.

- **"Indian education", "The Pakeha…", "Child…"** –

- **Analyse the photo**

Mögliche Argumente für: The primary school pupils are more likely to identify with the little boys than the big issues affecting Aborigines; it conveys a positive image of young Aborigines being willing to learn and use new technology…
… *gegen:* probably unrealistic, posed photo, other issues are more pressing for the Aborigine people, e.g. social issues such as alcoholism, drug abuse and unemployment…

- **Examine Western interest in first peoples**

a) E.g. (Maori) tattoos, clothing such as mocassins and suede boots, turquoise jewellery, dreamcatchers to wear and to hang up, Hollywood films such as *Dances with Wolves* (1990), *Thunderheart* (1992), *The Missing* (2003), *Rabbit-Proof Fence* (2002).
b) / c) / d): –

Kernwortschatz: Aborigines

General terms
Aboriginal (n/adj)
Aborigine (n)
Torres Strait Islander
indigenous (adj)
tribe, clan
nomad
(semi-)desert
red earth
shelter
hunter
gatherer
survival, to survive

Culture and traditions
body painting
clapsticks
didgeridoo
dot painting
boomerang
bush tucker
bush medicine
kangaroo, wallaby, emu
honey-ant

Beliefs
Spirit Ancestors
the Rainbow Serpent
Dreamtime
Dreamings
creation stories
legend
myth
to respect the law
to follow the law
to break the law
totem
Songlines
Dreaming-tracks
an oral culture
an ancient culture
sacred site
ceremonial centre
Uluru (Ayers Rock)
Kata Tjuta (The Olgas)
ceremony
initiation, to be initiated
taboo
sacrilege, sacrilegious

Recent history
the Stolen Generation
to be put in…
    an orphanage
    a children's home
    a foster home
mission station
(forced) assimilation
to be assimilated (into white society)
to be uprooted
to be discriminated against
to be exploited
to be mistreated
to be humiliated
to be stigmatised
to be traumatised
to be dispossessed
injustice
to be unjust
discrimination
racism, racist (n/adj)
genocide
reconciliation, to reconcile
apology, to apologise to
to acknowledge responsibility
to pay compensation to s.o.
to sign a treaty

Social situation
welfare dependency
to depend on welfare
inequality
bad housing
health problems
inadequate health care
to be more likely…
    to suffer from alcohol/drug abuse
    to sniff glue
    to be unemployed/without a job
    to be incarcerated/imprisoned
    to commit suicide
suicide rate
psychological damage
counselling

Aboriginal lands
self-administration
to have/gain political representation
joint management
bilingual schools
to take part in job schemes
to gain the respect of …/justice/equity

First peoples

Australian reconciliation off the cards SB S. 59

Exploring the text

1 Collect all the information in the text about the historical process of reconciliation with the Aboriginal population and put it in chronological order.
2 Collect all references in the text to the present situation of the Aboriginal population.
3 Outline the Australian government's and prime minister's position on reconciliation.
4 What points of criticism are directed at Mr Howard's position on reconciliation?
5 Would you consider the article to be neutral, or biased towards either the government or its critics? Find evidence in the article to support your point of view. Consider in particular the structure of the text and the writer's choice of words.

A step further

- Write a letter to the Australian government stating your position on reconciliation and suggesting how it should continue with this process.
- Write a comment on the pros and cons of a formal reconciliation treaty between the Aboriginal population and the Australian government/people (for ideas see SB, p. 188).
- Prepare questions and answers for an interview between a journalist and one of the following:
  – a representative of the Australian government who is against reconciliation;
  – a supporter of formal reconciliation such as Aden Ridgeway (l. 26).
  Present the interview live in class or record it as part of a radio programme.
- Prepare and hold a debate between supporters and critics of the government reconciliation policy.
- Write a script for a discussion between a representative of the Australian government defending Mr Howard's position and a supporter of a formal reconciliation treaty. Act out the discussion in class.

Mündliche Prüfung: Living life on the edge

"Aboriginal embassy, all welcome" the sign read, diverting travellers a short distance off the Oodnadatta Track, near Lake Eyre, in outback South Australia. [...]
"We're here to protect the water," the first man said, and offered us a drink and some flyblown bread. The Keepers of Lake Eyre, they called themselves. [...]
It is not the waters of the vast Eyre salt lake system that concern them so much. The waters they are campaigning for are largely unseen: the Great Artesian Basin, which underpins 1.7m square kilometres of this parched continent. Before the arrival of Europeans this water surfaced only in springs that were oases for desert people, and which remain microcosms of wetland life. Now the basin is being threatened by one of the world's largest mining companies. "They're sucking the nation dry," the protesters said, "and we're here to stop them."
Their target is the Western Mining Corporation (WMC), which operates the giant Olympic Dam copper mine 100km to the south. Licensed to use 30m litres of groundwater a day, the mine will also produce 1m tonnes of uranium. Citing a shameful history of nuclear testing and dumping in the South Australian desert, the protesters vociferously oppose the mine. There are also plans for an international nuclear waste dump in this most geologically stable of territories. "These are acts of genocide against this land's original people," one protester said.
WMC begs to differ. Environmental impact research and consultation with Aborigines and pastoralists have been thorough, it says. Four times the water it uses is wasted each day at bores for livestock. The protesters are illegal squatters, says WMC – "terrorists", even. In the year since the camp was set up there have been many incidents at the mines: road blockades, vandalising of pumping equipment, assaults on security personnel. The protesters, with their matted hair, tattered clothes and piercings, also intimidate people in the mine township supermarket, the company complains. [...]
(320 words)

By Gabi Mocatta, *The Guardian*, December 7, 2000.

2 **Oodnadatta Track** name of a dirt road in the Australian bush – 26 **to beg to differ** to see things differently – **environmental impact research** research into the effects industry has on the environment – 27 **pastoralist** cattle or sheep farmer – 29 **bore** a man-made waterhole

Tasks

1 Point out and explain the different positions expressed by the WMC and the protesters regarding the use of groundwater in the mining of uranium.

2 How does the writer try to get her readers interested in the conflict between the mining company and the protesters?

3 Explain why preserving nature is such an important issue for Australian Aboriginals. You could draw on your knowledge of Aboriginal culture, traditions and laws in your answer.

First peoples

Test: Fenced out

The received wisdom in Australia is that no one really wants to watch films about Aborigines. At best, such subject matter is confined to art house cinemas, and in recent years hardly any films about Australia's indigenous
5 people have dented the public's consciousness.

That has changed in the last month with the blaze of publicity surrounding the release of Philip Noyce's *Rabbit-Proof Fence*, starring Kenneth Branagh.

Although Noyce began his directorial career with a
10 groundbreaking film about Aborigines in the 1970s, he is now better known as the Hollywood-based master of muscular blockbusters such as *Dead Calm* and *Patriot Games*.

Last year he returned to the Australian outback to film
15 the true story of three young Aboriginal girls who walked 1,200 miles across the desert back to the mother they were snatched from by the white authorities in 1931.

Branagh plays AO Neville, an English administrator given the extraordinary title of chief protector of the
20 Aborigines. From 1915 to 1940 Neville was the legal guardian of all Aboriginal people in the vast deserts of Western Australia.

In 1931, 14-year-old Molly Craig and her two young sisters were dragged from their mother and taken to the
25 Moore River settlement, where they were forced to learn domestic skills and forget their culture.

They were just three of thousands of Aborigines who are now called the "stolen generation", forcibly taken by the authorities or given up by their mothers to be brought
30 up in white society – a traumatic practice that continued until the 1970s.

But, unlike others, they escaped. Molly outwitted the Aboriginal tracker sent to find them and found her way home by following the rabbit-proof fence – a huge barrier stretching across the whole of Western Australia which 35 was designed to halt the spread of rabbits across Australia (it failed).

Noyce has turned such naturally dramatic material into an unabashedly mainstream film – with an epic easy listening indigenous soundtrack by Peter Gabriel and 40 sweeping aerial shots of the stark beauty of the Australian outback.

Branagh is utterly convincing, with earnest preachy mannerisms that could almost come from Tony Blair, and David Gulpilil, who once starred as Crocodile Dundee's 45 good-natured Aboriginal sidekick, impassively conveys a sense of torn loyalties as he is dispatched to track the girls down.

The rest of the cast is less well known. Noyce trawled the wilds of Western Australia to find his young stars 50 but admitted he cast Everlyn Sampi as Molly for her "crossover appeal". She was a genuine outback girl, who had not only never acted but never been to the movies before, but Noyce says he calculated that her beauty and charm would appeal to white and black cinema audiences 55 in America.

With political reconciliation stalled between white and black Australia while the current government refuses to issue a formal apology for the stolen generations, Noyce hopes white Australian audiences are more ready for a 60 mainstream film with Aboriginal heroes – and white villains.

The film's solid box office takings suggest they may be.

(500 words)

By Patrick Barkham, *Guardian Unlimited*, March 6, 2002.

---

1 **received wisdom** what everybody thinks – 3 **art house cinema** cinema showing films that are only of interest to special groups of people –
5 **to dent s.th.** to leave an impression on s.th. – 33 **tracker** s.o. who can read human or animal tracks on the ground and follow them –
43 **preachy mannerism** exaggerated way of behaving as if one knows everything – 46 **sidekick** *(in films)* an unimportant friend of one of the main characters – 52 **crossover appeal** *here:* being attractive to Aborigines and white Australians – 63 **takings** money earned

Tasks

1 What does the article tell you about the content and the qualities of the film *Rabbit-Proof Fence*?

2 How does the writer try to get his readers interested in watching the film? Look closely at the way the information is presented and at his choice of words.

3 After reading the review decide whether you would like to watch the film *Rabbit-Proof Fence*, or not. Support your position by referring back to what you have learnt about the culture, history and present situation of Australian Aboriginals, especially the 'Stolen Generation'.

First peoples

Test: Living life on the edge

"Aboriginal embassy, all welcome" the sign read, diverting travellers a short distance off the Oodnadatta Track, near Lake Eyre, in outback South Australia. In the distance a black, red and yellow Aboriginal flag flapped frantically, and rangy, orange dogs barked themselves hoarse.

Up close the compound was made of corrugated iron that swayed and clattered in the gale. At one end green plastic sheeting and hessian cloth provided shade from the desert sun. The outer walls were daubed with slogans. "Stop the Genocide," read one, and the menacing nuclear hazard symbol was everywhere.

But the man who came out to meet us was not an Aboriginal Australian. He had a pale face under a shock of dusty hair, and a winding scar across his forehead as if something had burrowed a ponderous path between his skin and his skull. Nor did the five or six others in the shadows claim to be Aboriginal. They were what Australians call "feral"; people who have abandoned mainstream values.

"We're here to protect the water," the first man said, and offered us a drink and some flyblown bread. The Keepers of Lake Eyre, they called themselves, this band of full-time, itinerant protesters, veterans of direct environmental action in this country of such delicate ecological balance. The title seemed spiritual, incongruous. Perched on a sand dune with the salt-encrusted expanse of the lake in the background, their camp of twisted metal was like something out of *Mad Max*. Strange that they should be champions of water.

It is not the waters of the vast Eyre salt lake system that concern them so much. The waters they are campaigning for are largely unseen: the Great Artesian Basin, which underpins 1.7m square kilometres of this parched continent. Before the arrival of Europeans this water surfaced only in springs that were oases for desert people, and which remain microcosms of wetland life. Now the basin is being threatened by one of the world's largest mining companies. "They're sucking the nation dry," the protesters said, "and we're here to stop them."

Their target is the Western Mining Corporation (WMC), which operates the giant Olympic Dam copper mine 100km to the south. Licensed to use 30m litres of groundwater a day, the mine will also produce 1m tonnes of uranium. Citing a shameful history of nuclear testing and dumping in the South Australian desert, the protesters vociferously oppose the mine. There are also plans for an international nuclear waste dump in this most geologically stable of territories. "These are acts of genocide against this land's original people," one protester said.

WMC begs to differ. Environmental impact research and consultation with Aborigines and pastoralists have been thorough, it says. Four times the water it uses is wasted each day at bores for livestock. The protesters are illegal squatters, says WMC – "terrorists", even. In the year since the camp was set up there have been many incidents at the mines: road blockades, vandalising of pumping equipment, assaults on security personnel. The protesters, with their matted hair, tattered clothes and piercings, also intimidate people in the mine township supermarket, the company complains.

Repeated court action to evict the protesters has failed: they refuse to give their names and origins. Thirty Aborigines and anti-uranium, pro-water protesters made a 1,800km "peace walk" from the camp to Sydney this year, keen for their campaign to be taken up by the international media there for the Olympics. The media proved more interested in the sport.

As we talked, I watched a young boy with a wide leather collar studded with 7.5cm metal spikes, lying listlessly in the half-dark. What could this boy do? Was his being here making a difference? And what did the protesters do all day? Their acts of blockade and sabotage had been only sporadic: their chief action was simply to be there. What did they live off? Surely they didn't collect dole cheques from the society they so obviously rejected?

As we left we felt uneasy. These people were dedicated, but hopelessly marginal. Yet they were doing what they believed in. They were doing more than I was, more than most. When we parted I promised I'd write about them. So I have.

(701 words)

By Gabi Mocatta, *The Guardian*, December 7, 2000.

---

2 **Oodnadatta Track** name of a dirt road in the Australian bush – 5 **rangy** ['reɪndʒɪ] thin, long-legged – 6 **up close** when one is near to s.th. – **compound** *here:* building – **corrugated iron** Wellblech – 8 **hessian cloth** a rough type of cloth, usu. used for making sacks – 28 **Mad Max** title of a film set after the near-total destruction of the earth – 50 **to beg to differ** to see things differently – **environmental impact research** research into the effects industry has on the environment – 51 **pastoralist** cattle or sheep farmer – 53 **bore** a man-made waterhole

Tasks

1. Point out and explain the different positions expressed by the WMC and the protesters regarding the use of groundwater in the mining of uranium.

2. How does the writer try to get her readers interested in the conflict between the mining company and the protesters?

3. Explain why preserving nature is such an important issue for Australian Aboriginals. You could draw on your knowledge of Aboriginal culture, traditions and laws in your answer.

   or

   Write a letter to Gabi Mocatta in which you try to answer the questions at the end of her article (ll. 70 –75). Draw on what you know about the importance of nature for Australian Aborigines.

Climbing Uluru

Role: You are the chairperson.
Position: You should remain neutral during the debate.
Task: Open the debate and invite participants to make a short statement outlining their position. During the debate, make sure that everybody gets the chance to put forward his or her arguments. If necessary, sum up what has been said or invite participants to enlarge on a specific point. At the end of the debate, ask participants to vote for or against a ban on climbing the rock.
(Cf. page 193 of your book for suitable phrases which you can use.)

Role: You are an overseas tourist.
Position: You want to climb Uluru. You have seen pictures of the rock and heard stories about it, and it will be the highlight of your trip to Australia. You have paid a lot of money for your trip. Besides, climbing the rock has been possible up to now, so why ban it? ...
Task: Insist on your right to climb Uluru as you have paid for it.
(Cf. page 193 of your book for ideas on how to present and defend your position in a discussion.)

Role: You are a tourist, possibly from overseas
Position: You want to visit Uluru, but you respect the Aborigines' wish that people would not climb the rock. You are very interested in Aboriginal culture and history and you would like to know more ...
Task: Support the rights of the Anangu people and try to persuade other tourists not to climb the rock.
(Cf. page 193 of your book for ideas on how to present and defend your position in a discussion.)

Role: You are a white tour operator.
Position: Your programme includes the chance for tourists to climb Uluru. You are afraid of losing money if you cannot offer this climb any longer. The climb is the highlight of the tour you offer in Central Australia and fewer tourists will book your tours as a result of the ban...
Task: Fight for your right to offer the climb to your customers.
(Cf. page 193 of your book for ideas on how to present and defend your position in a discussion.)

Role: You are an Aboriginal tour guide and you belong to the Anangu people.
Position: You want to tell tourists about the traditions, religious beliefs and cultural background of Aborigines. You think that walking around the rock and learning about its meaning is enough...
Task: Try to make tourists understand why they should not climb the rock.
(Cf. page 193 of your book for ideas on how to present and defend your position in a discussion.)

Role: You are a hotel/restaurant owner/manager at Yulara, the tourist resort near Uluru-Kata Tjuta National Park.
Position: You are afraid of losing money/your job if fewer tourists come to Uluru because they can no longer climb the rock. Lots of your friends work at the resort (e.g. in the hotels, shops and restaurants, at the camping site, for the bus service, at the airport, etc.) and they may lose their jobs...
Task: Try to make your opponents understand the economic importance of keeping the rock open to tourists.
(Cf. page 193 of your book for ideas on how to present and defend your position in a discussion.)

---

continued on page 72

First peoples

Role: You are an environmental activist.
Position: You are very concerned about the mass tourism at Uluru-Kata Tjuta National Park which threatens the environment in a number of ways (pollution, waste disposal problems, pressure on scarce water supplies, erosion, damage to flora and fauna). You would be only too glad to see fewer tourists coming to the area…
Task: Try to make your opponents understand that in order to preserve the delicate ecological balance of the desert, mass tourism has to be curbed.
(Cf. page 193 of your book for ideas on how to present and defend your position in a discussion.)

Role: You are an Anangu elder.
Position: You are not happy about tourists climbing the sacred rock, but you realise that your people badly need the money the tourists spend on entry fees, guided tours, Aboriginal arts and crafts, souvenirs, meals, etc. You think that a compromise should be found between the demands of the modern tourist industry and the needs of your people…
Task: Try to find a compromise between the supporters and the opponents of the proposal to close Uluru to tourists.
(Cf. page 193 of your book for ideas on how to present and defend your position in a discussion.)

Role: You are an Anangu elder.
Position: For you, climbing Uluru is sacrilege, as the rock is one of your people's most sacred sites. You want an immediate ban. You think that tourists who come to your land should respect your laws, culture and traditions. You are strongly opposed to the idea of making money from something that is sacred. If you could, you would close the whole area to tourism…
Task: Fight for the immediate closure of Uluru to tourists.
(Cf. page 193 of your book for ideas on how to present and defend your position in a discussion.)

Role: You are an Anangu artist.
Position: You are not happy about tourists climbing the sacred rock, but you also see it as a chance to create interest in Aboriginal culture and traditions. You and your people are also dependent on the money you make from selling paintings and wooden sculptures to tourists. You are afraid that fewer tourists will come if the rock is closed and that will mean less money for you and your people…
Task: Try to find a compromise between the supporters and the opponents of the proposition to close Uluru to tourists.
(Cf. page 193 of your book for ideas on how to present and defend your position in a discussion.)

Role: You are a white political activist.
Position: You support the position of Uluru's traditional owners. You think that the white man did enough damage to the Aborigines and their culture in the past, so it is high time that their rights were respected. A ban on climbing Uluru would be a highly symbolic gesture, which would show a desire for reconciliation with the Anangu people and Aborigines in general. A ban would also give official recognition to the great spiritual significance of the rock…
Task: Fight for the immediate closure of Uluru to tourists.
(Cf. page 193 of your book for ideas on how to present and defend your position in a discussion.)

First peoples

Kernwortschatz: Maoris

Culture and traditions
sea-faring tradition
haka, hongi
ta moko (= tattoos)
Maori chiefs
marae (meeting house) as a focus for the iwi (= clan)
to have strong family ties
to have a sense of responsibility
  towards other Maoris
to pass on one's traditions

History
Treaty of Waitangi
the New Zealand Company
loss of sovereignty
to sign away one's rights to…
to yield one's rights to…
to seize Maori land for public use
Maori morale was shaken
population numbers were reduced by disease
to keep one's side of the bargain
to recognize the rights of the Maoris
to grant … the exclusive right to purchase land
to put up resistance
to become a British subject
to ban the teaching of the Maori language
  in schools
to encourage the assimilation of
  the Maori population

Recent history
to demonstrate against the Treaty
to force the government to fulfil their part of…
to fight for the recognition of one's identity
to make land claims
to settle land claims
to receive compensation for confiscated land
to be subjected to an all-white administration
to be conscious of a cultural,
  political and social divide
to watch one's traditional way of life disappear
to commemorate the Treaty of Waitangi
to take part in celebrations on…
to maintain one's cultural identity apart
  from the rest of society
to revive/regain one's language through
… schools teaching in Maori
… university courses in the Maori language
… a separate court to handle Maori affairs

Kernwortschatz: Native Americans

History
arrival of the first white settlers
loss of territories and hunting grounds
removal of tribes to reservations
to be deprived of almost all their land
starvation, epidemics
extinction of large Native American populations
to wipe out tribes/to drastically reduce
    the Native American population
to be conquered/suppressed
to be confined to the reservations
land dispossession makes traditional
    self-sufficiency through farming and ranching impossible

Present trends
greater unity among Native American nations
to be the victim of stereotypes
to propagate stereotypical images
to be represented/portrayed as
… a mascot
… a chief with a feather headdress
to seek compensation for the loss of tribal lands
to conduct law suits over…
to gain recognition as Indian nations/
    an increasing degree of self-determination/
    economic self-sufficiency

Life on the reservation
welfare is the main source of income
to be characterized by a high rate of unemployment
problems with pollution caused by coal-mining, industry, the
    dumping of nuclear waste
to eliminate springs/to lower water levels
industrial developments
… have serious consequences for the environment
… cause health problems
to claim government subsidies for education
    and social benefits
to take advantage of federal legislation
to establish a casino on the reservation
the so-called 'casino tribes'
to finance
… youth activities
… programmes to teach the tribal language and crafts
… education and training programmes
to overcome social and economic problems
to restore people's dignity
to practise gentle tourism
to do as little harm/be as uninvasive as possible
internet as a tool
… to inform the public regarding Native American issues
… to arouse the public's conscience
… to create a forum for discussion
… to create a network among the tribes

First peoples

The Treaty of Waitangi SB S. 65

You are one of the chiefs who is willing to sign the Treaty. In your role you should:

- attempt to convince the other chiefs that they have to negotiate with the British "chiefs" to make them control the lawless settlers;
- argue that the clan will profit from organized and controlled Pakeha settlements.

You are one of the more sceptical chiefs. In your role you should:

- challenge the British Crown;
- ask for guarantees for your people;
- challenge the New Zealand Company.

You are one of the representatives of the British Crown. In your role you should:

- assure the chiefs of their position within their iwi, their sovereignty as iwis and their cultural self-determination;
- assure the sceptical chiefs of your support against the usurpation of land. You will deal severely with settlers who infringe on Maori land rights.

You are one of the members of the New Zealand Company. You fear restrictions on your land acquisition activities through the treaty. In your role you should:

- Try to convince the Maori chiefs that:
  - accepting British sovereignty will mean giving up their own power. It will also put an end to Maori self-determination;
  - direct negotiations with the Company's representatives over land rights will be more profitable.
- Try to convince the representatives of the British Crown that:
  - the new colony can only be firmly established by quick and organized land acquisition, which you can guarantee;
  - you will ensure legal acquisition of the land and share profits with the Crown;
  - French attempts to gain control of New Zealand will be curbed if the Company buys up as much land as possible.

First peoples

Indians hear a high-tech drumbeat SB S. 82

Before you read

- What do you think the writer is referring to with the phrase "high-tech drumbeat" in the title of the article?
- With a partner, brainstorm ideas about ways of putting pressure on your local government/politicians in order to change laws you disagree with.

Exploring the text

1 What events have led to the protests described in the article?
2 a) How have new techologies helped the Native American protesters in their cause?
  b) What other factors have made protests by Native Americans more effective?
3 What point is the writer trying to make in the article? In your opinion, does he get his point across clearly, or not?

A step further

- With a partner, think of at least five other slogans which the Native American demonstrators could use (cf. ll. 3–4 of the article).
- Using the following key words from the article, put together a brief pamphlet which calls on the tribes to: "communicate, educate, mobilize and stand up for themselves" (ll. 19–20).
- Prepare and act out an interview with Tom Goldtooth in which he explains his aims and activities on behalf of the Native American cause.
- Write a further verse for Buffy Sainte-Marie's song "My country 'tis of thy people you're dying", in which you take the developments in the text "Indians hear…" (SB page 82) into consideration.

First peoples

My country 'tis of thy people you're dying SB S. 74

Annotations

12 **toddler** small child which has just learned to walk – 13 **to despise** [dɪˈspaɪz] to regard s.th. as being worthless – 18 **leech** blood-sucking worm; *(fig.)* s.o. who takes all of the energy out of s.th. else – 21 **genocide** deliberate killing of a nation or ethnic group – 22 **Bill of Rights** amendments (= changes) to the US constitution – 24 **Liberty Bell** bell made to commemorate the original constitution of Pennsylvania; it was sounded at the adoption of the Declaration of Independence (1776) – 26 **Kinzua** the US government built a dam across the Allegheny River at Kinzua (1962), this led to the flooding of Indian country and the displacement of 130 families – 27 **Alaska** reference to the land claims situation in that US state in 1966, a situation which was made more controversial by the discovery of huge oil reserves – 39 **paled** weakened – 46 **craven** cowardly – 44 **evicted** forced off one's land – 51 **wrought** [rɔːt] caused – 54 **sire** *here:* historical chief, ancestor – 60 **scarlet** bright red (associated with violence, blood) – 60 **hypocrisy** [hɪˈpɒkrəsɪ] pretending to be better than one is – 63 **carrion crow** black bird which feeds on dead and rotting meat – 64 **wren** tiny brown songbird *(Zaunkönig)* – 66 **mockingbird** American songbird that can copy the songs of other birds

Before you listen

■ Read the first lines from the song "My country 'tis of thy people you'e dying" in your book on page 75.
  a) What images of Native Americans does the singer refer to?
  b) How realistic are these images?
  c) The singer is obviously going to deal critically with the treatment of the Native American population. What aspects would you expect her to mention in the song?

Listening for gist

1 a) Close your eyes and listen to the song without paying too much attention to the words. Then write down your first impression of the emotions conveyed by the song.
   b) Discuss your impressions in class. Try to work out how the singer's voice, the tune and the instrumentation contribute to this effect.
2 a) Listen to the song again. This time you should try to get the gist of each stanza. Find key words for each of the topics the singer deals with.
   b) Make a grid like the one below and fill in details about each stanza as you listen.
   c) If necessary, listen to the whole song again and make additions to your notes.

Stanza	Topic	Details
1st stanza chorus	relationship between white and Native Americans in the 1960s	…
2nd stanza	…	

Listening for detail

1 What images does the singer use to refer to white Americans? What effect do these images have?
2 Explain the ambivalence of the chorus on the basis of your understanding of the whole song.

A step further

■ Form expert groups. Collect information about one of the following and present it in class.
  – the historical and political facts Buffy Sainte-Marie mentions in the song.
  – Buffy Sainte-Marie's role in the civil rights movement. Then, discuss the function of protest songs for the political cause of the Native Americans in the sixties.
  – the aims of Native American civil rights activities in the 60s and 70s and their effects.

Focus on The Matrix

Didaktisches Inhaltsverzeichnis

	Titel	Textsorte (Wortzahl ca.)	Thema	Spracharbeit	Textproduktion (schriftlich / mündlich)
	First impressions SB S. 84, TB S. 78	photo	film genres	interpret a photo • choose a film genre to go with a photo	describe appeal of film
	Understanding… SB S. 85, TB S. 78	summary (ca. 265 words)	plot	dictionary work • special effects: fast shots	interpret a quote
	The future world SB S. 86, TB S. 78	film script (ca. 290 words)	setting of the film	explain images	collect references to the future • identify elements of a 'dystopia'
	How real is reality? SB S. 87, TB S. 79	film script (ca. 142 words)	levels of reality	describe the function of the levels of reality • do dictionary work	identify levels of reality • link levels of reality to special effects
	Characterization: Who am I SB S. 87, TB S. 79	film script (ca. 197 words)	characterization	interpret a scene • assess importance of events for the plot	scene analysis: characters • compare Neo and Cypher
	Neo – a second Christ? SB S. 88, TB S. 80	film script (ca. 154 words)	parallels with the life of Christ	interpret the film ending • explain images • describe character development	work out parallels between Neo and Christ • scene analysis: Neo is killed
	Cinematic devices SB S. 89, TB S. 80	tasks	effect of cinematic devices	–	scene analysis • discuss: 'fast motion' • analyse camera angles, sound effects • analyse function of 'violence'
	We love you, Keanu! SB S. 90, TB S. 81	film review (ca. 535 words)	text type: film review	find plot details • analyse text structure • characterization • describe the writer's attitude	think of a title • list words / phrases • write a letter • web search: film reviews • list pulp classics • think of a plot • act out a dialogue • work with prequel / sequels
over to you	**The Matrix – our future** SB S. 92, TB S. 82 TB S. 86	commentary (ca. 1,081 words)	relationship between humans, intelligent robots	outline train of thought • divide into sections / find headings • summarise	speculate about a reaction • write an e-mail • hold a discussion • write a diary entry

Einleitung

Angesichts des Kultstatus des Films *The Matrix* und des damit einhergehenden hohen Bekanntheitsgrades wird davon ausgegangen, dass zumindest der Handlungskern den S vertraut ist, so dass auf Verständnis sichernde Maßnahmen verzichtet werden kann. Ferner wird davon ausgegangen, dass die Lerngruppe mit dem Fachvokabular und den Methoden der Filmanalyse hinlänglich vertraut ist, so dass die filmbezogene Spracharbeit im Wesentlichen der Festigung und Vertiefung dient. Dementsprechend liegt das Schwergewicht der Arbeit auf der themenbezogenen Filmanalyse.

The Matrix ist ein außergewöhnlich komplexer Film, dessen Action-Spektakel und Spezialeffekte nur zu leicht den Blick auf differenziertere Verstehensebenen verstellen. Die Einteilung im Kapitel in fünf Themenbereiche (future world, reality, characterization, Neo as Christ, cinematic devices, siehe "Film analysis" SB S. 86–89) ist aus heuristischen Gründen vorgenommen worden. Sie eröffnet unterschiedliche Interpretationsmöglichkeiten und stellt sicher, dass verschiedene Zugänge gefunden werden können.

Auf der **dystopischen** Ebene des Films werden wir mit einer Zukunftswelt konfrontiert, in der Maschinen die Herrschaft über die Menschen angetreten haben. Eine kleine Gruppe von Kräften versucht, diese Herrschaft nachhaltig zu stören. Die Menschen sind zu Energielieferanten für die künstlichen Intelligenzsysteme geworden, sie existieren ohne eigenes Bewusstsein auf riesigen Batterienfeldern. Ein Computersimulationsprogramm – die Matrix – sorgt dafür, dass die Menschen nichts von ihrem Zustand wissen. Außerhalb

Focus on The Matrix

dieser simulierten Computerwelt leben Morpheus und seine Mannschaft, die sich in die simulierte Welt der Matrix 'einhacken' und mittels mentaler, neurointeraktiver Projektion Zugang zur simulierten Welt der Matrix finden.

The Matrix entwirft nicht nur ein düsteres Zukunftsszenario, es wirft gleichfalls fundamentale **epistemologische** Fragen sowie Fragen nach der menschlichen Identität auf. Dabei wird deutlich, dass es weder eine absolute Erkenntnis noch eine objektive Wirklichkeit gibt. Der Film spielt mit konstruierten Wirklichkeiten und erzeugten Illusionen. Vor diesem Hintergrund ist auch die Frage nach der Identität zu beantworten. Das Besatzungsmitglied Cypher zieht das Getäuscht-Werden und die damit verbundene Illusion eines guten Lebens dem entbehrungsreichen Leben an Bord der Hovercraft vor. Der Film führt also unterschiedliche Existenzmöglichkeiten – illusionäre vs. authentische – vor und zeigt, wie der Mensch dazu neigt, seine Selbstbestimmung zugunsten vordergründiger Glückseligkeit aufzugeben.

Die Logik der Fabel verlangt nach einer **Retter- oder Erlöserfigur**. Morpheus glaubt, in dem Hacker Thomas "Neo" Anderson diese Figur gefunden zu haben. Zahlreiche biblische Verweise sowie Parallelen zum Lebensweg Jesu legen es nahe, Neo als Erretter der Menschheit zu begreifen, der diese aus dem Zustand der Knechtschaft erlösen wird. Einschränkend ist hier allerdings anzumerken, dass die weiteren Teile der Trilogie – *The Matrix Reloaded*, *The Matrix Revolutions* – eine derartige Deutung nur als eine Möglichkeit erscheinen lassen. Die Trilogie ist nämlich darauf abgestellt, in postmoderner Manie Deutungsschlüssel anzubieten und gleichzeitig mit ihnen zu spielen. Illusion und Wirklichkeit, Wahrheit und Schein sind austauschbar geworden.

Die Rezeption des Films *The Matrix* ("We love you Keanu!", SB S. 90–91) war durchweg positiv, die Kritik lobte vor allem die zahlreichen Spezialeffekte sowie die computergestützte Kameraführung, die ungewöhnliche Aufnahmen ermöglichte. Interessanterweise blieben dabei die komplexen inhaltlichen Aspekte weitgehend unberücksichtigt.

Der Kommentar des britischen Kybernetikers Kevin Warwick (SB S. 92–93) stellt abschließend eine alternative Sicht dar. Dr. Warwick diskutiert das Verhältnis Mensch–künstliche Intelligenzsysteme und beschreibt die aus seiner Sicht positiven Auswirkungen von Mikrochip-Iimplantaten, die den Menschen zu einem Cyborg machen. Die S werden aufgefordert den Text in eigener Regie zu bearbeiten.

Kopiervorlage: Kernwortschatz TB S. 85

Bei der Bearbeitung eines Themas im Kapitel sollten S einen entsprechenden Wortschatz beispielsweise in Mind maps oder Topic webs zusammenstellen. Eine Zusammenstellung von relevanten Vokabeln finden Sie auf einer Kopiervorlage auf S. 85.

First impressions SB S. 84

Looking and thinking

a) The four characters seem to be ready to fight. Their faces convey an impression of fierce determination, which is further underscored by their dark clothing and the weapons they are carrying. The letters in the background imply that a computer might be involved in the plot.
b) The photo illustrates the eclectic nature of the film. The weapons and the characters' clothing suggest an action film. The posture of the character in the foreground could also be associated with a showdown in a Western.
c) The characters' unusual clothing, weapons and facial expressions seem to suggest an action-packed thriller with some futuristic elements.

Understanding the plot SB S. 85

Looking and thinking

1 *Antwort:* 5, 8, 3, 1, 7, 9, 2, 4, 6.
2 a)/b) Die relevantesten Bedeutungen für *The Matrix* sind folgende: a situation or environment in which s.th. takes form; a network; (in computing) a group of electronic circuit elements arranged in rows and columns.

3 We see a sequence of spectacular fight scenes, which promise an action-packed plot; the speed of the action suggests that the story will be fast-moving; the special effects (characters run up walls and jump incredible distances) indicate a new and innovative use of the camera.
4 If this quote is set against the array of meanings of the word 'matrix' (cf. Task 2), Morpheus is referring to the world outside the network of electronic circuit elements, hence to the world as we know it.

The future world SB S. 86

Watching and thinking

1 The grid may be filled in as follows:

Physical features	Human aspects	Machines
Ruined cities, eternal darkness wasteland; fields of humans in pods; dark, stormy sky	mankind is bred as an energy source; humans exist in a digital, neuro-interactive state; their lives are an illusion generated by a computer; they exist in a state of bondage/ have lost free will	robots equipped with artificial intelligence, rulers of the earth; like monstrous insects; they service the fields of pods

2 The world has a twofold structure: there is a barren wasteland which is supplemented by the computer-generated world; the hovercraft and its crew exist and operate outside the Matrix.
3 The future world in *The Matrix* is made up of familiar characteristics: a negative picture of the future – robots as rulers;

Focus on The Matrix

mankind is enslaved – fields of humans in pods; some form of rebellion / opposition – Morpheus and his crew fight the Matrix.

Exploring the text

1 The central images are of a "map" and "territory" (l. 8). The map (= s.th. which gives a two-dimensional picture of a place) refers to the computer-generated world, which Neo has lived in until now and which is nothing but a virtual construct. Territory refers to the empirical, genuine world.
2 Morpheus does not say anything about his own background or that of his crew; neither do we learn anything about how they manage to exist outside the Matrix. He also fails to explain why the Matrix exists at all.

How real is reality? SB S. 87

Watching and thinking

a) The first level may be called 'life inside the Matrix'. It is an artificially created world which people are plugged into by means of implants in their brains. The humans are unaware of these implants.
The second level may be called 'the real world'. It exists outside of the Matrix and is real in the sense that it is not an artificial construct. This 'real world' is set under the earth on board the hovercraft. It is only possible for the crew to enter the Matrix by hacking into its computer.
b) There are several indications of which level is being presented. For example, all of the scenes in which the laws of gravity are broken point to the simulated world. Whenever special effects are used, the action is taking place inside the Matrix. Conversely, whenever the setting is on the hovercraft, the action is taking place in the real world. The transition from one world to the other happens via phone lines.
Another indication of the level of reality the characters are in is their clothing. When the crew of the Nebuchadnezzar hack into the system and become virtual, they wear mirrored sunglasses and black clothing. When they are 'real', i.e. on the hovercraft, they are dressed more simply.
The grid may look like this:

Level of reality	Characteristics	Special effects
simulated, digital world, cyberspace	urban life in the twentieth century; computer programmes are downloaded into people's brains; inhabitants of the cyberworld have brain implants	break all laws of physics; characters have superhuman powers, they can instantly acquire skills, (use of bullet-time technology*)
real world: characterized by a radioactive wilderness, ruins and deserts	hovercraft: refuge for last humans; life is reduced to existence on the hovercraft	–

* An action is frozen while the camera appears to turn around in a circle.

Exploring the text

a) Morpheus claims that reality is made up of sensory experiences, which in turn means that taste, smell, touch, vision and hearing are merely perceptions. Put differently: what exists is to be perceived (*esse est percipi*). This view refers to the humans who are captive in the Matrix and whose sensory experiences are only provided by the computer they are hooked up to. Hence, only electrical impulses provide us with stimulation.
b) Morpheus refers to the world of illusions created by computers and, ultimately, by the Matrix. In chapter 12 of the DVD he calls this a "prison for your mind".
c) The function of the scene is to show that sensations are more than just interpretations of brain stimuli: they are also indicators of an external reality. Just as Morpheus urges Neo to see beyond illusion, the viewer is led to distinguish between appearance and reality.

Characterization: Who am I? SB S. 87–88

Watching and thinking

1 a) Siehe Szenen 19, 20 und 25 auf der DVD.
Tired of life on board the ship and the ongoing war with the machines, and plagued by doubts about Neo's role as saviour, Cypher betrays his companions. All he wants is to forget his past and live within a programme that provides him with the comforts that are not available on the ship. Cypher's sensuous tendencies are portrayed best in the restaurant scene. The use of the color 'red' underlines his temptation.
b) The word 'cypher' means the number 'O' (zero) / 's.o. of no importance'. Within the constellation of characters, Cypher (zero) becomes Neo's (the One) opposite number. When Cypher betrays Morpheus, he assumes the role of Judas. Hence the name fits his role.
2 Siehe grid unten.

	Cypher	Neo
Characterization	selfish, hedonistic	has doubts about the role he has been given; a heroic figure; eager to learn; deeply humane
Self-image	disbeliever, sceptic	initially unsure about his role, he comes to accept it when he realizes that he must rescue Morpheus
Attitude to reality / the Matrix	favours a reality that provides the most vivid and pleasurable experiences	he takes the red pill; he wants to make the moral choice
Who am I?	Judas figure	Messiah

Focus on The Matrix

Exploring the text

1 The scene contrasts markedly with the spartan life on board the hovercraft. Cypher finds the plush atmosphere in the restaurant so attractive that he opts for a carefree life in the Matrix. He has come to believe that the world of the Matrix is more real than the one outside. It does not matter where his sensory experiences come from as long as they provide pleasure. Hence, he settles for illusion rather than reality.

2 Cypher plays a crucial role in Neo's development. It is only after he betrays Morpheus to the Agents of the Matrix that Neo begins to accept his mission as a saviour. As Neo says to Trinity in scene 27: "Morpheus believed in something and he was ready to give his life for what he believed. […] That's why I have to go. […] I believe I can bring him back."

Neo – a second Christ? SB S. 88–89

Watching and thinking

1 Neo's experiences have many elements of the story of Jesus. When Neo is rescued from the Matrix (cf. DVD, Scene 10), he finds himself in a womb-like vat. He is unplugged from umbilical-cord-like cables and slides down a tube which symbolizes the birth canal. Jesus was baptized in the River Jordan as a grown man by John the Baptist and similarly, Neo is 'baptized' in the human battery refuse tank by Morpheus. Just as Jesus was tempted by the devil in the desert (Luke 3:1–13), Neo is tempted by Agent Smith to betray Morpheus. In the Gospels, Jesus gave his life as "a ransom for many" (Mark 10:45). In the film, Neo knowingly sacrifices his life to save Morpheus. Further parallels include Neo's being brought back to life, and his upward flight in the final scene, which is reminiscent of Jesus' ascension into heaven.
The grid may be filled in as follows:

	Christ	**Neo**
Birth	virgin birth	virgin birth (humans are grown in the Matrix, not born)
Role	Messiah, redeemer	saviour, the One
Disciples	12 followers	crew of the hovercraft
John the Baptist	baptized the adult Jesus	Morpheus symbolically baptizes Neo
Predicted coming	e.g. Luke 7:19	Oracle
Death and resurrection	raised to life after three days	restored to life by Trinity's kiss; cf. Oracle's prediction: "You're waiting for something […] your next life maybe." (DVD, Scene 22)

2 Trinity's belief in Neo brings him back to life. The Oracle told her that the man she would fall in love with would be the One and she has fallen in love with Neo. She literally breathes life back into him with her life-giving kiss.

Exploring the text

1 *Final scene:* Neo ascends towards heaven in a Superman style, i.e. he has truly become the One, in what is an obvious biblical parallel. The final scene can also be read differently as Neo's overvoice suggests that he is not a Superman but a universal teacher. When he speaks to the Matrix, he announces his task of universal liberation: "I'm going to show these people what you don't want them to see. I'm going to show them a world without you. A world without rules and controls, without borders or boundaries, a world where anything is possible." (DVD, Scene 37).
Change in script: Set against the lines of the original filmscript on SB page 89, the words in the film clearly emphasize Neo's view of himself as a redeemer. He envisages a world in which everyone has the power to shape reality outside the Matrix. The original script is more philosophical as Neo describes his vision of the future world "A world of hope. Of peace." (l. 14). The original text is also more reflective as Neo compares the Matrix to a cage and a chrysalis. The script which is used in the film is more active and challenging as Neo declares how he is going to open people's eyes to reality (cf. above).
Significance: The script used in the film opens the way for the sequel in which Neo once again fights the Matrix. At the end of the film he issues a challenge to the Matrix and says what he plans to do.

2 The central images Neo uses are "cage" and "chrysalis" (l. 11), both of which are not used in the final film script. The image of the cage echoes an earlier image used by Morpheus when he spoke of the Matrix as "a prison for the mind". Leaving the cage involves making choices: Neo left the Matrix when he chose the red pill and he later chooses between saving himself or Morpheus. The biological image of the chrysalis is a more positive one in that it is only a temporary form of captivity. One can escape from a chrysalis and be a better, more mature person. For Neo, this development signals mental growth: he has accepted that he is the One.

3 The development of Neo's character may be observed on two main levels. As he accepts his role, Neo undergoes the following changes:
– his body and mind come together, cf. his symbolic birth;
– he acquires the freedom of choice;
– he faces and accepts the possibility of his own death.
The second level refers to Neo's second lifetime in which he will fulfil the Oracle's prophecy that the One will destroy the Matrix.

Cinematic devices SB S. 89

Watching and thinking

1 a) A variety of camera operations are used in the filming of the first scene with Trinity and the policemen. There is a rapid succession of various types of shots (medium-long shots, medium shots, close-ups) and camera angles (overhead, high angle, eye-level and low angle), all of which create tension and underline the dramatic impact of this scene.

Focus on The Matrix

E.g. The grid may be filled out like the example below. [Note: It is not necessary to examine every single scene!]

scene	location	characters	cinematic devices	effect
Trinity fights the police	inside an abandoned hotel	Trinity, policemen	rapid succession of shots and angles; three-dimensional shots*	tension, high drama
Trinity seeks to escape	various rooftops, inside a house	Trinity, Agent Smith	bullet time; stunts; change from slow to fast motion	see above
Trinity escapes the truck via the phone box	in the street	Trinity, agents	zoom-in on truck	emphasizes danger, increases tension

*Another innovative aspect of *The Matrix* is the use of three-dimensional stills as in the fight between Trinity and the policemen. The effect is achieved by a series of single cameras that are grouped in a circle around the actor(s). A single shot is put together so that you get the impression of both a stationary and a moving camera.

b) *Special effects:* Trinity tumbles and seems to float in midair for a moment or she achieves a corkscrew flight off of a rooftop and into a tiny window which is some distance away; bullet time, a time-distorting effect, is also used (cf. TB S. 79). Für weitere Informationen siehe "The Making of the Matrix", Title 21 (Minuten 12–18) auf der *Matrix* DVD.
The use of fast motion again increases dramatic tension as the action is obviously taking place in a world where the rules of gravity no longer apply and anything can happen.

2 *Camera angles:* the use of a high-angle shot of Neo underlines his helplessness as he is questioned by the agents. Agent Smith is filmed using a slightly low-angle shot to emphasize his dominant position. The interrogation is mostly filmed in over-the-shoulder shots, which seem to include the viewer in the dialogue.

3 The sound effects of the attack are faded out when Trinity starts to speak to Neo, thus increasing the intimacy of the scene. The music is initially soft, almost seductive, when Trinity declares her love. It rises to a crescendo when Neo re-awakens and goes on to eliminate Agent Smith.

A step further

■ **Analyse the function of violence**
Most of the violence and combat scenes occur within the Matrix and involve stunts which are not possible in reality, e.g. Neo cartwheels across the floor while firing a machine gun. The combat scenes are often played in slow motion and the main characters – Neo and the agents – can dodge bullets, which further adds to the unreality of the situation. In addition, Neo and Trinity are never hit by flying debris or injured as a normal person would be. It is clear that they are the heroes and the end justifies the means as regards their actions, i.e. violence is necessary to rescue mankind.

We love you, Keanu!   SB S. 90–92

Before you read

■ **Think of a title for a review**
Neo Superman; Jesus the Cyber star…

■ **Make a list of words / phrases**
E.g. Spectacular stunts, extraordinary special effects, innovative filming, dystopian future world; rule of machines, humans as energy sources for machines; saviour figure…

Exploring the text

1 a) A computer hacker called Neo is contacted by a young woman, Trinity. She brings him to Morpheus (ll. 5, 11–13) and it is from him that Neo learns about the Matrix and the true nature of his own existence (ll. 14–15). Humans lost a nuclear war with the machines and since then they have existed in battery fields which supply energy to the new rulers of the world, the machines (ll. 17–19). The humans are not aware that they are plugged in to a computer, instead they are under the illusion that they are leading normal lives (ll. 19–20).
b) introduction (ll. 1–4): positive assessment of the film and main character ("wonderfully enjoyable", "unalloyed pleasure", "spiffy effects");
– plot summary (ll. 5–20): "Keanu plays", "alternative reality system", "Neo is contacted", "truth about The Matrix", "virtual reality illusion");
– evaluation of acting performances (ll. 21–31): ("tough, stoic alertness", "pale wussy Keanu");
– favourable comparison of *The Matrix* ("surmounts these obstacles", l. 38) with other virtual reality movies ("tend to be bad", "no brainer stuff", ll. 32–41);
– conclusion / recommendation (ll. 42–44): "fantastically enjoyable" (l. 42), "check it out this weekend" (l. 43).

2 a) Neo: unconvincing facial expression (ll. 21–23), "impassivity", "tough stoic alertness" (l. 23), he does not look the part as he appears too weak ("pale wussy", l. 30); he has "stylish combat scenes" (ll. 30–31);
– Trinity: "devastatingly sexy cyber-warrior" (l. 11); dressed in a seductive way (l. 12);
– Morpheus: "big, bald, powerful" (l. 14).
The writer only mentions the characters' physical appearances. Apart from Keanu Reeves, he says nothing about how they play their roles.
b) Agent Smith: sinister, arrogant, superior, condescending;
– Cypher: sceptical, narrow-minded, selfish;
– Tank: committed, concerned, cooperative, unselfish.

3 The writer is extremely positive about the film and finds it very enjoyable. He mentions the huge appeal of the main actor Keanu Reeves whose acting he finds weak but who still delivers stylish fight scenes. Furthermore, the writer stresses the fact that *The Matrix* does not fall prey to the usual shortcomings of films about virtual reality. He mentions the fact that the special effects are not overdone, they are "worn lightly" (l. 39), and the scenes which take place in 'reality' seem plausible, "sweaty" (l. 41).

Focus on The Matrix

A step further

■ Write a letter to the editor
E.g. Peter Bradshaw does not say anything substantial about the actors' performances and he disregards the excessive displays of violence. He praises the "spiffy effects" (l. 2). Die S können ebenfalls Beispiele solcher "special effects" beschreiben und kommentieren.

■ Find reviews
Siehe folgende Webseiten:
http://enjoyment.independent.co.uk/film/reviews
http://us.imdb.com/ (Internet Movie Database)
http://www.suntimes.com/index/ebert.html (Rober Ebert, *Chicago-Sun Times* film critic)

■ List pulp classics
a) Factors which make films become pulp classics are, e.g. the popularity of the main actors, or even the discovery of a new star, innovative special effects, melodramatic elements such as a particularly moving / memorable scene…
b) *Plot:* Setting: cyber space or a love story and write a treatment accordingly. Die S sollen ihre Wahl der Schauspieler begründen.

■ Hold a conversation
Director: Neo is a character who is initially full of doubt about his role but he hardens with experience and finally has an air of decisiveness, energy and resourcefulness. He is lean, physically fit and a martial arts expert.
Mögliche Redemittel: So I suggest / I would advise you / I think you should / It might be a good idea if you … lost weight / had your hair cut / got a shave / adopted a body language that signals the above characteristics.

Project

■ Work with the prequel and sequels
a) Die S sollten sich auf folgende Aspekte konzentrieren: development of plot, performance / importance of the main characters, use of stunts and violence.
Als Alternative können die S den Artikel aus *The Independent* (cf. TB S. 87) im Unterricht bearbeiten und besprechen.
b) *The Matrix Reloaded* introduces Zion, a huge underground cavern, complete with stalactites. Neo consults the Oracle again from whom he learns that he has to find a mysterious Keymaker who will provide him with the key to the heart of the Matrix computer.
After he has overcome the now familiar obstacles of the agents, he meets the Architect, who claims to be the inventor of the Matrix. As in the first sequel, Neo is given a choice: This time he must choose between two doors – one will enable him to save Zion, but lead to Trinity's death, the other will bring him back to the dying Trinity but will cause the complete destruction of Zion. Neo, of course, opts for the second door.
c) The sequence from *The Animatrix* portrays machines with artificial intelligence as second-class citizens without any rights. Their attempts to win rights by means of lawsuits fail. In the riots which follow, most of the machines are destroyed. The surviving machines retreat to "the cradle of mankind" (an obvious biblical allusion) and set up their own state. This soon prospers and becomes economically stronger than all of the human states combined.

However, the humans refuse to negotiate with the machines and attack them instead. The result is the nuclear wasteland that we know from *The Matrix*.

The Matrix – our future SB S. 92–93

Before you start

■ Speculate about a reaction
Mögliche Ideen: The scientist might dismiss the concept of the film and the machine-domination of the world as being nothing more than science fiction, which bears no relation to the empirical world. The professor might give information about progress in the field of artificial intelligence.
Während der Lektüre sollten S sich auf die ethischen Aspekte von Implantaten konzentrieren und überlegen, welche Vor- und Nachteile solche Eingriffe ins Menschsein haben könnten.

Der Text soll von S selbst bearbeitet werden. Ein möglicher Aufgabenapparat befindet sich im TB S. 86.

Exploring the text

1 The writer points out that increasing numbers of scientists believe the future will bring intelligent machines (ll. 2–4). Considering the fact that computers improve their performance by 100% every 18 months, it is possible that they could develop a level of intelligence which would allow them to rule the world.

2 The article may be structured as follows:
ll. 1–8: the rapid development of artificial intelligence;
ll. 9–14: the plot of the *Matrix:* humans vs. Cyborgs;
ll. 15–24: the Matrix as the embodiment of evil; the unclear status of Cyborgs;
ll. 25–33: evil as propagated by one person vs. a network;
ll. 34–47: the internet is as uncontrollable as the Matrix;
ll. 48–55: the Matrix as a modern Big Brother;
ll. 56–66: Professor Warwick's own positive experiences with a computer-linked implant;
ll. 67–73: the Matrix as a humane supporter of life;
ll. 74–80: a Matrix-style society as an improvement on modern, backward society.

3 *Advantages:* one could have doors opened, lights switched on and other things done for one (ll. 58–59); life would be easier as the computer could make decisions (ll. 64–65)…
Disadvantages: one is monitored at all times (l. 58); one gives up some freedom (ll. 62–63)…

A step further

■ Write an e-mail
Siehe Skills file, "Comments", SB S. 188 für Ideen.

■ Hold a discussion
Die Rolle des Moderators soll von einem S übernommen werden. Siehe Skills file, "Discussions", SB S. 193 für nützliche Ausdrücke.

■ Write a diary entry –

Focus on The Matrix

Weiterführende Aufgaben: Kopiervorlage TB S. 85

Siehe Kopiervorlage "More on the Matrix" im TB S. 85 für weitere Ideen zur Aufbereitung der Film-Trilogie.
Erwartungshorizonte:
1 Morpheus believes that a saviour will come to end the slavery of the inhabitants of Zion. He believes that person to be Neo.
In the first part of the trilogy, Neo's role is established gradually. He comes to accept this role, fights the agents of the Matrix and resists Agent Smith's offer to change sides. His Superman-like flight at the end of the film as well as his final words echo the ascension of Christ as well as His teachings.
In *The Matrix Reloaded,* Neo continues to fight the agents of the Matrix; he is on a crusade against it and seeks to invade "Machine City" where the central computer is said to be stored. His aim is to destroy it and free mankind.
The Matrix Revolutions: Neo finally destroys Agent Smith, who as it turns out, is no longer under the control of the Matrix. After the defeat of Agent Smith, as a quid pro quo, the computer mastermind ("the voice") orders the retreat of the robot forces that have been invading Zion. Thus, mankind's refuge and its people are saved. Neo's role as redeemer is underscored by the extensive use of light imagery in the final scenes of the film.
2 On tracing the scenes in which the Oracle appears, it becomes obvious that the existence of this character has a threefold function, which is only revealed slowly.
Initially, the Oracle seeks to dispel Neo's doubts about his role as redeemer; thus she confirms her role as a prophet, which Morpheus, above all, strongly believes in. Secondly, the Oracle is a central part of the complex structure of the films, as most of her remarks are cryptic and do not make sense immediately.
Thirdly, the final scene of *Matrix Revolutions* shows that the Oracle is also part of the computer programme. Within that system she serves as a counterpart to the Architect. His purpose is to balance the equation or system, called the Matrix, whilst it is the Oracle's purpose to unbalance it.
3 If we set Neo's choices against the Architect's comments in *Matrix Reloaded* and the final scene of *Matrix Revolutions,* we realize that he is continually faced with pseudo choices. He, too, is part of the ever-continuing attempts to keep the equation in balance; thus without his realizing it, his choices are pre-determined.
4 *Hinweis:* Smith's clones may not think identically.

Test: Matrix films blamed for series of murders by obsessed fans   TB S. 86

Klausur für den Grundkurs
Textformat: newspaper article, 339 words
Vorschlag / Klausurtyp NRW: Tasks 1–3, A2
Bezugstext des Kapitels: "Cinematic devices" (SB S. 89)
Eine mögliche Aufbereitung zu diesem Test finden Sie auf einer Kopiervorlage im TB S. 86. Anders als in Leistungskursklausuren geht es nicht um die Analyse filmsprachlicher Elemente, vielmehr kann der Text als traditionelle Klausurform eingesetzt werden.

Comprehension
1 Duncan Campbell begins his article with an initial thesis, i.e. the blend of fantasy and reality in the film confused some people to such an extent that it led them to commit murder. In the first murder case, the perpetrator dressed like Neo and was "obsessed with" the film. He purchased a gun like Neo's and used it to kill his parents. The young man said that he was living inside the Matrix. The second person, who shot her landlord, also referred to being in a dream-like state which involved the film. Similarly, the third killer also claimed to have been under the influence of the Matrix. In the final case, a sniper seems to have felt as if he was living in the Matrix as he wrote that people should free themselves of the computer network.

Analysis
2 First of all, it should be pointed out that the writer does not establish a direct causal link between the cases and the film. His choice of words, i.e. "suggests" (l. 4), "seems to have spawned" (l. 23), shows that he is not presenting hard facts but is instead pointing out a potential connection. This leads the reader to believe that a connection does indeed exist.
This impression is supported by the positioning of the only contradictory quote in the middle of the article, where it could be overlooked. The writer precedes the prosecutor's comment in ll. 19–21 with a statement by a defence attorney ("He's just obsessed with it", ll. 16–17) and juxtaposes it with his own observation ("*The Matrix* seems to have spawned..." l. 23). The writer clearly wants the reader to dismiss the prosecutor's opinion as being of minor importance.
When the cases are examined closely, it becomes clear that the evidence presented is flimsy and, at best, circumstantial. At no point does Duncan Campbell prove that the murderers were clinically disturbed because of the film or unable to distinguish between reality and fantasy after watching it.

Comment / re-creation of text
3 *Mögliche Argumente:* Films and TV programmes certainly influence the viewers' perception of the world and some people have difficulties distinguishing between fact and fiction. The numerous special effects and stunts in *The Matrix* break all laws of physics and some viewers may be tempted to attempt similar stunts. However, trying to imitate Neo or Trinity's looks and incredible feats is far from becoming a murderer. Hence Duncan Campbell's case should be rejected as being suggestive.
Möglicher Wortschatz: to reproach s.o., to make unfounded allegations, to attempt to manipulate the reader, his biased view is unfounded / detrimental to impartial news reporting.

Test: The Matrix Reloaded   TB S. 87

Klausur für den Leistungskurs
Textformat: newspaper article, 608 words
Vorschlag / Klausurtyp NRW: Tasks 1–3, A2
Bezugstexte des Kapitels: "We love you, Keanu!", SB S. 90.
Der Test ist für Leistungskurse konzipiert, da die Analyse eines 'feature films' in der Regel nicht im Grundkursbereich stattfindet.
Eine mögliche Aufbereitung zu diesem Test finden Sie auf einer Kopiervorlage auf S. 87.

Focus on The Matrix

Comprehension
1 The writer's criticism of *The Matrix Reloaded* may be summarized as follows: the directors assume that filmgoers have a detailed recollection of *The Matrix*, and particularly of the "evils of the system". *The Matrix Reloaded* is first and foremost a "sensory experience" and the plot seems to be of minor importance. The emphasis on the sensory aspects of the film makes for the inclusion of numerous stunts and action scenes. Quinn feels that this emphasis was a mistake as many of the special effects from the first film are repeated. Another point that he criticizes is that the directors have overdone the action scenes, which is counterproductive: "you turn on, you plug in, you drop out" (ll. 21–22) and "when anything can happen, nothing matters" (ll. 53–54). The critic attributes the film's weaknesses to the fact that it is the second part of a trilogy and its function is to pave the way for the third part, rather than provide fresh insights.

Analysis
2 *Structure*: The writer starts on a personal note ("I found myself trying", l. 2, "I recalled", l. 4), which catches the reader's attention. He admits to having problems remembering certain aspects of *The Matrix* (which is something the reader can probably identify with).
– There is a widening of perspective as the writer voices criticism and characterizes the film as "a sensory experience" (l. 20).
– In the following paragraph, the critic specifies the individual faults of the film: it has many lengthy, illogical scenes that serve no particular function other than to stimulate our nervous systems.
– He concludes his criticism with a structural observation: as the second part of a trilogy, the film has an obvious bridging function which, however, it does not fulfil well.
Anthoy Quinn's assessment is an excellent example of what may be called a 'slating review'.
Style: The appeal of the article derives from the comparatively simple diction and syntax as well as from the varied register. Enumerative sentences such as "You turn on…" stay in the reader's mind. The rhetorical questions ("why do it again?" ll. 24–25, "So why doesn't … scrapping?" ll. 43–45) seek the reader's agreement.
The writer frequently changes register. Formal expressions such as "anointed" (l. 6), "attired" (l. 30) and "reprise" (l. 60) contrast with informal expressions such as "doing his Superman thing" (ll. 41–42), "scrapping" (l. 45) and "goons" (l. 47). This makes for varied reading.
The writer is categorical in his criticism of the film. He uses expressions such as "classic pitfall" (l. 53), "disease of sequelitis" (l. 63) or "going in circles" (l. 67), which leaves the reader in no doubt about his attitude to the film.

Re-creation of text
3 *Letter to the editor: Mögliche Ideen:*
– The critic disregards two important, new figures in *The Matrix Reloaded*, namely the Keymaker and the Architect. By introducing these two characters the directors did more than just provide a bridge to the final film in the trilogy.
– The critic claims that the action scenes are repetitive and *The Matrix Reloaded* is basically a sensory experience. In diesem Fall sollen S Beispiele aus dem Film nennen um diesen Standpunkt zu belegen. Außerdem sollten sie auf die Kritik in Zeilen 66–67 eingehen ("going in circles").

Test: Neo meets the Architect TB S. 88

Mündliche Prüfung
Textformat: film transcript, 376 words
Bezugstexte des Kapitels: "Film analysis" (SB S. 86–89)
Der Klausurtest und die entsprechenden Fragen befinden sich auf einer Kopiervorlage auf S. 88.

Comprehension
1 Neo learns that his existence is nothing but a flaw in the programming of the Matrix. He is an "anomaly" that cannot be corrected. He also learns that he is the sixth person who was believed to be the One. Zion has been destroyed five times and is about to be destroyed again. Neo's task, as outlined by the Architect, is to select a number of individuals to rebuild Zion. If he does not do this, both Zion and the Matrix will be destroyed and the human race with them.

Analysis
2 What the Architect says changes Neo's role in a number of ways and makes us see *The Matrix* in a different light. Neo's role as a 'saviour' was predetermined and he has no control over it. Secondly, he is the saviour only because that is his role, not because of some messianic quality that he possesses. The Architect changes our understanding of the first film: everything appears to be a game and each player has a fixed role. Viewed in this light, Neo did not make a conscious choice when he took the red pill because whatever he did was part of a design.

Comment
3 Z.B. The Architect sits at a giant computer. To underline his role and his superiority over Neo, the characters might be at different levels: Neo has to look up to the Architect (high-angle shots of the Architect and low-angle shots of Neo would convey this). The predominant shots could include full shots to show the character's positions and medium shots or close-ups to convey facial expressions. Neo's face should express incredulity, and the Architect's self-assurance.

Selected bibliography

Bronfen, Elisabeth: *Heimweh. Illusionsspiele in Hollywood.* Berlin: Volk & Welt, 1999.
Bruck, Peter: *Endzeitphantasien und Illusionsspiele: "The Matrix" im Englischunterricht der Sekundarstufe II.* Fremdsprachenunterricht 2004.
Hegemann, Carl: "Ist digitale Erlösung möglich? Matrix". Von den Brüdern Wachowski. Ein Film als Paradigma. *Ästhetik und Kommunikation.* 31. Jg. 2000.
Irwin, William Hrsg.: *The Matrix and Philosophy. Welcome to the Desert of the Real.* Chicago: Open Court, 2002.
Matrix. Arbeitshilfen. Frankfurt: Katholisches Filmwerk, 2000.

Focus on The Matrix

Kernwortschatz

Plot
action-packed plot
computer-generated world
fake reality
machine-made deceptions
to unravel reality
neuro-interactive state / process
brain implants
human battery fields
to be under the illusion that…
nuclear wasteland
mankind is powerless
 – enslaved
 – a slave to the machines
 – reduced to the level of a Cyborg

Characters
Neo:
to learn the truth
to be unplugged
to take a leap of faith
to undergo a re-awakening / restoration to life
rebirth, ascension, to ascend
to sacrifice his life for s.o. else

Cypher:
to desire a carefree life
a hedonistic, pleasurable existence
to turn out to be a traitor
to become disillusioned with s.th.

Special effects
bullet-time technology
spectacular stunts / fight scenes
emphasis on martial arts
three-dimensional shots
slow / fast motion
to suspend belief
the rules of gravity do not apply
to create dramatic tension
violence as a means to an end

Philosophical elements
Biblical allusions
to be a messiah, redeemer, saviour figure
to make a conscious choice
to play a pre-determined role / to have no choice
 in the matter
to go on a crusade
to seek guidance from s.o.

More on *The Matrix*

1 Development of plot

■ Trace Neo's role as a redeemer or saviour throughout the trilogy: *The Matrix – The Matrix Reloaded – The Matrix Revolutions* (concentrate on Neo's encounter with the "voice" after Trinity's death and his deal with that power; the shining figure of a crucified Christ in the last but one scene).

2 The role of the Oracle

■ Examine the scenes in which the Oracle appears in the trilogy (cf. *The Matrix*, Chapter 22, *Matrix Reloaded*, Chapter 13, *Matrix Revolutions*, the final scene).
 a) Apart from giving advice to Neo, what other functions does the Oracle have? Consider in particular their encounter in *The Matrix Revolutions* and also the final scene of that film.
 b) In your opinion, is the Oracle also a part of the programme called the Matrix, or not? Give reasons for your answer.

3 Freedom of choice?

■ In the first two films of the trilogy Neo is faced with a crucial choice.
 In *The Matrix* (Chapter 9) Morpheus offers Neo a choice between the red and the blue pill.
 In *The Matrix Reloaded* (Chapter 31) Neo must choose between two doors in his encounter with the Architect.
 Examine these scenes again and work out whether Neo's choices are genuine or simply part of the programme.
 You might also consider Neo's encounter with the Oracle in Chapter 13 of *The Matrix Reloaded*.

4 Creative writing

■ Look again at Chapter 28 of *The Matrix Reloaded*. Neo is on his way to the mysterious room where the master computer is said to be. Agent Smith and his clones are lying in wait for him. Devise a dialogue between Smith and some of his clones. You could begin as follows:
Agent Smith knew it was a perfect plan. And his clones knew it was a perfect plan as well. Although they were him as well, they would already think it was a perfect plan, because his thoughts were their thoughts and if they thought different then he … Smith decided to forget that line of thought and go on to another.
The key issue would soon be whether or not that goal would ever occur.
"How long have we been waiting?" Smith 34 asked…

Focus on The Matrix

The Matrix – our future   SB S. 92

Exploring the text

1 Outline the writer's train of thought with regard to future developments in artificial intelligence.
2 Divide the commentary into sections and think of a heading for each part.
3 Summarize the advantages and disadvantages of being linked to a computer as outlined in the text.

A step further

- Share your point of view of the implants described in the text with Kevin Warwick in an e-mail. The provocative last line of the commentary could form the basis for your e-mail.
- Prepare and hold a classroom discussion on the ethical implications of cyborgs. Will man/cyborg lose his free will and individuality? Can a cyborg be held responsible for his/her actions?
- Write a diary entry for Kevin Warwick for the day before he had the transponder removed from his arm. Try to imagine his feelings and thoughts on that day.

Test: Matrix films blamed for series of murders by obsessed fans

One of the attractions of *The Matrix*, the film whose sequel, *The Matrix Reloaded*, opens in Britain next week, was its blending of fantasy and reality. A series of murders in the United States suggests some people have been
5 unable to distinguish between the two.

Jos Cooke, a 19-year-old in Oakton, Virginia, owned a trenchcoat like the one worn by Neo, the character played by Keanu Reeves in the movie, kept a poster of his hero on his bedroom wall. Then he bought a gun similar to the one
10 used by Neo to fight evil.

In February, he shot his father and mother in the basement of their home and then called the police. His lawyers say he believed that he was living inside the Matrix.

The theme of the films is that computers have taken
15 over the earth, although humans exist in a computer-simulated world, battling to save humanity. "He's just obsessed with it," Cooke's defence attorney, Rachel Fierro, told the *Washington Post*.

The local prosecutor, Robert Horan said: "I don't think
20 the movie causes violence. Millions and millions of people have seen it and not killed anybody." Cooke will now be examined by a psychiatrist.

The Matrix seems to have spawned other imitators. Last week in Ohio, a woman was found not guilty of killing the
25 professor whose house she rented, on the grounds of insanity. Tonda Lynn Ansley, 37, said she had dreams which turned out not to be dreams. The local prosecutor said that, "in her warped perception", the film played a part in the killing.

30 In San Francisco in 2000, Vadim Mieseges, 27, killed his landlady, Ella Wong, and pleaded not guilty on grounds of insanity. The police who interviewed him said he had made "reference to being sucked into the Matrix".

The young man accused of taking part in last year's
35 sniper attacks in the Washington area has also cited the film. "Free yourself of the Matrix," wrote Lee Boyd Malvo, 18, one of the two defendants, in his jail cell.

(337 words)

By Duncan Campbell, *The Guardian*, May 19, 2003.

23 **to spawn** to produce – 28 **warped** disturbed – 33 **to be sucked into s.th.** to be pulled into s.th. with great force

Tasks

1 How is the film *The Matrix* said to have contributed to a series of murders in the US?
2 How does the writer try to convince the reader that the films influenced the murderers?
3 Write a letter to the editor of the *Guardian* in which you critically discuss the idea that *The Matrix* makes people violent.

Focus on The Matrix

Test: The Matrix Reloaded

Four years from *The Matrix*, the Wachowski brothers' hugely influential sci-fi-fantasia, I found myself trying, and failing, to remember exactly why "The Matrix" is a bad place to live. Yes, I recalled that it was a malignant
5 construct designed by machines to keep humankind in thrall; that Keanu Reeves was anointed as The One who would somehow liberate the world from this slavery; and that the guerilla warfare involved a great deal of balletic chopsocky performed at high speed. But I still couldn't
10 put my finger on why the "reality" of a dingy space module where the good guys live could be preferable to the chimera of the Matrix, where you could at least get a decent steak if the fancy took you.

Surely *The Matrix Reloaded* would provide a quick
15 refresher course for slackers on the evils of the system. This is, after all, the first of two longish sequels to be released this year – *The Matrix Revolutions* is to follow in November – so the brothers W had plenty of room to be expansive, to help clue us in. Not a chance. [...]
20 *The Matrix Reloaded* is a sensory experience rather than an intellectual one: you turn on, you plug in, you drop out. [...]

Neo's messianic destiny requires him to go and consult the Oracle (he did this in the first movie – why do it
25 again?), which means being strapped into his virtual-reality recliner and relocated inside the Matrix. Once there he's straight into dark glasses and a priestly soutane, ready to exchange short-arm jabs and blocks – the favoured Matrix fighting style – with his old adversary,
30 Agent Smith, attired in his familiar G-men suit and skinny black tie.

Actually there are now a hundred or so replicas of Agent Smith, and in the first big set piece they swarm over Neo like ants on a scorpion. Not that Neo is in the least put out
35 – he casually dispatches these myriad Smiths without even breaking a sweat. Later he fights on an ornamental staircase with thugs wielding pikes and axes, and once again emerges with barely a scratch. The problem is that when there is no possibility of being harmed, there is no
40 tension. When ground control in Zion checks Neo's whereabouts he is reported to be "doing his Superman thing", and we cut to a shot of Keanu whizzing through the air as if on jet-propelled heels. So why doesn't he just do this straight away and waste everybody's time with the
45 scrapping? The same thought occurs during a long chase down a freeway as Morpheus and Trinity slalom through traffic, fiercely pursued by Smith's goons and a pair of albino dreadlocked twins. Given that the latter can car-hop by morphing through the air, why do they use their
50 own car from which to fire some frankly passé machine-guns? Even fantasy must obey its own logic, but the Wachowskis seem unwilling to acknowledge the parameters they set themselves. It's a classic pitfall: when anything can happen, nothing matters.

55 Fans will say that this is too literal-minded an approach. Never mind the logic, feel the effects. I loved the shot from the first film of bullets slowing down as they reached Neo's protective force-field, so that he plucked them from mid-air as if inspecting gems from a jeweller's drawer.
60 There is a slight reprise of this in *Reloaded* when a hail of bullets aimed at Neo clatter to the floor at the raising of his hand. It's the same idea, only less surprising, which is the disease of sequelitis in a nutshell. [...]

For the rest, one feels the uncertainty of *The Matrix
65 Reloaded* as a bridge, a holding operation before the big showdown. For all its bravura effects, *The Matrix Reloaded* seems to be going in circles. (627 words)

By Anthony Quinn for *The Independent*,
from *enjoyment.independent.co.uk/film/reviews*,
May 23, 2003.

---

8 **balletic chopsocky** *(writer's own)* martial arts which include elements of ballet – 12 **chimera** [kaɪˈmɪərə] an impossible idea – 19 **to clue s.o. in** to give s.o. information to help them understand s.th. – 49 **to morph** to transform by computer – 63 **sequelitis** dangers which accompany the making of a sequel to a popular film

---

Tasks

1 What aspects of *The Matrix Reloaded* does the writer criticize?

2 Explain how the writer makes his review more appealing to readers. You should consider the structural and stylistic features of the text.

3 Write a letter to the editor of *The Independent* in which you critically discuss the writer's assessment of *The Matrix Reloaded*.

Focus on The Matrix

Test: Neo meets the Architect

The following text is a transcript of a scene in The Matrix Reloaded *(Chapter 19). In the film, Neo visits the Oracle again. He is told that he must find the Keymaker who will give him a key to the room where the central computer of the Matrix is kept. After many difficulties, Neo finally reaches this room in which he meets the Architect.*

Neo: Who are you?
The Architect: I am the Architect. I created the Matrix. I've been waiting for you. You have many questions and although the process has altered your conciousness you remain irrevocably human. [...]
Neo: Why am I here?
The Architect: [...] You are the eventuality of an anomaly which despite my sincerest efforts I have been unable to eliminate. [...]
Neo: You haven't answered my question.
The Architect: Quite right. Interesting. That was quicker than the others. The Matrix is older than you know. [...] This is the sixth version. ... The anomaly is systemic.
Neo: Choice. The problem is choice. [...]
The Architect: The first Matrix I designed was quite naturally perfect. It was a work of art, flawless, sublime, a triumph equivalent only to its monumental figure. The inevitability of its doom is apparent to me now as a consequence of the imperfection inherent in every human being as I re-designed it. [...]
You are here because Zion is about to be destroyed. [...] This will be the sixth time that we will have destroyed it. The function of the One is now to return to the source allowing a temporary dissemination of the code you carry, re-inserting the prime program after which you will be required to select from the Matrix twenty-three individuals, sixteen females, seven males, to rebuild Zion. Failure to comply with the process will result in a cataclysmic system crash killing everyone connected to the Matrix, which, coupled with the extermination of Zion, will ultimately result in the extinction of the entire human race.
Neo: You won't let it happen. You need human beings to survive.
The Architect: There are levels of survival we are prepared to accept. However, the relevant issue is whether or not you are ready to accept the responsibility of the death of every human being in this world. [...]
Which brings us at last to the moment of truth wherein the fundamental flaw is ultimately expressed and the anomaly revealed as both beginning and end. There are two doors. The door to the right leads to the source and salvation of Zion. The door to the left leads back to the Matrix, to her (=Trinity) and to the end of your species. As you adequately put it, the problem is choice. But we already know what you are going to do, don't we?

(376 words)

© 2003, Warner Brothers Entertainment Inc.

7 **anomaly** s.th. unusual – 13 **systemic** *here:* which affects the whole network

Tasks

1 Briefly summarize what the dialogue is about.

2 What light does the Architect throw on Neo's role as a 'saviour'? Consider in particular Neo's understanding of his role in the first part of *The Matrix*.

3 How would you as the director film this encounter? Think of an appropriate setting, camera angles and shots and be prepared to explain your choices.

Barriers and bridges

Didaktisches Inhaltsverzeichnis

	Titel	Textsorte (Wortzahl ca.)	Thema	Text- und Spracharbeit	Textproduktion (schriftlich / mündlich)
	Pictures in … SB S. 94, TB S. 90 TB S. 100	photo	national character, stereotyping	check adjectives for characterization	compare pictures and reality • talk about stereotypes • write an interview • make a speech
📺	**If only…** SB S. 95, TB S. 91	documentary (295 words)	mutual images	viewing comprehension	talk about images • discuss: national character
Using your skills	**The ambassadors…** SB S. 96, TB S. 92 TB S. 102	instructions for a simulation (295 words)	politeness	polite small talk	write a report • evaluate the method • write a letter
	The Germans throw… SB S. 98, TB S. 92	cartoon, article (452 words)	humour	describe a cartoon • explain images	write a letter, sketch, anecdote
	Auf wiedersehen… SB S. 100, TB S. 93 TB S. 103–106, 188, 189	newspaper article (763 words)	German stereotypes and reality	close reading • describe feelings • examine style / language / tone	hold a chat show • make a speech
	Britain and Europe SB S. 102, TB S. 95	speech (661 words)	Britain's future role in the world	interpret statistics • visualise line of argument • give an oral summary	fill in gaps • evaluate the method • develop a teaching plan • hold an interview • write a speech
Using your skills	**Advertising a German …** SB S. 104, TB S. 96 TB S. 107, 108	project suggestion	develop an advert, presentation	the language of advertising	develop an advert • prepare and conduct a group presentation • discuss the effectiveness of the project
	Making fun… SB S. 105, TB S. 96	screenplay (849 words)	the Germans on holiday	talking about humour	add stage directions • write a script • make comments
over to you	**Culture shock…** SB S. 108, TB S. 97	travel guide (706 words)	culture clash – cultural differences	explain rules of behaviour • guess meaning from context	act out a sketch • write a diary entry, a parallel text, a love story • analyse a film scene
Using your skills	**Working abroad** SB S. 110, TB S. 98	skills workshop	finding a job	the rules and registers of formal letters and job interviews	write a job application (covering letter, resumé / CV) • conduct role plays • write a follow-up letter

Einleitung

Das Kapitel "Barriers and bridges" widmet sich in besonderer Weise dem neuen Leitziel der interkulturellen Handlungsfähigkeit. Neuere wissenschaftliche Erkenntnisse des Konstruktivismus finden Eingang in die Auftaktseiten "Pictures in our heads" (SB S. 94), auf denen eigene Bilder von anderen Nationen bewusst gemacht und unter Berücksichtigung der Entstehung von Stereotypen diskutiert werden. Die Statements des Dokumentarfilms "If only we all played cricket" (SB S. 95) konkretisieren exemplarisch unterschiedliche Sichtweisen der Deutschen und der Engländer auf die jeweils andere Nation.
"The ambassadors' game" (SB S. 96–97) ist ein Simulationsspiel, das mit Hilfe von Rollenkarten die Interessengegensätze von Industrie- und Entwicklungsländern verdeutlicht.

Die Rollenübernahme und deren inhaltliche Ausgestaltung erfordert einen Perspektivenwechsel und, durch die offen arrangierte Begegnung der Akteure, eine hohe sprachlich-situative Flexibilität. Auf sprachlicher Ebene steht die Übung eines formalen Small Talk unter Akzentuierung von vorgegebenen Höflichkeitsregeln im Mittelpunkt.
Der *Daily Mail* Artikel "The Germans throw in the towel" (SB S. 98–99) und der Cartoon von Bill Caldwell zeichnen ein Bild des deutschen Touristen, das sich in den britischen Boulevard Zeitungen seit Jahren großer Beliebtheit erfreut. Die Aufdeckung humoristischer journalistischer Techniken sowie der angemessene Umgang mit der stereotypen Darstellung erlauben die Kombination des textanalytischen Arbeitens mit einem produktionsorientierten Verfahren.

Barriers and bridges

Der Electronic *Telegraph* Artikel ("Auf wiedersehen, with great respect", SB S. 100–101) ist in Ton, Sprache und Inhalt ein idealer Kontrast zum vorhergehenden Text und bietet sich für die (ggf. auch wiederholende) Gegenüberstellung von 'popular' und 'quality newspapers' an. Die thematisch und argumentativ anspruchsvollen "post-reading activities" "Conducting a chat show" und "Giving a speech" fordern die S zu einer vertieften Auseinandersetzung mit dem Bild Deutschlands im Ausland sowie der eigenen nationalen Geschichte und Zukunft auf.

In der Rede des früheren britischen Außenministers Robin Cook ("Britain and Europe", SB S. 102–103) wird der britische Blick auf Europa und Großbritanniens Rolle in der EU deutlich. Der Umgang mit dem Text erfolgt über neuere schüleraktivierende Verfahren: die Kugellagermethode in Verbindung mit der Komprimierung des Inhalts mittels einer 'crib card', oder als Alternative der "Schüler als Lehrer"-Ansatz Teach yourselves!

Das Mini-Projekt "Advertising a German product abroad" (SB S. 104) bietet die Möglichkeit, Erfahrungen mit Werbeformaten zu reaktivieren und auf ein selbst gewähltes deutsches Produkt umzusetzen. Über Werbestrategien hinaus ist der zielorientierte Umgang mit dem Deutschlandbild im Ausland gefordert. Besondere Schwerpunkte dieser komplexen Lernsituation sind die Förderung längerfristiger selbst gesteuerter GA sowie die Durchführung und Evaluation von Gruppenpräsentationen.

Das Fernsehskript "Making fun of it all" (SB S. 105–107) aus "The Germans", eine in Großbritannien sehr populäre Folge der Fernsehserie *Fawlty Towers* zeigt exemplarisch, wie das Fernsehen Nationalstereotypen zur Unterhaltung nutzt. Dieser Text erlaubt außerdem die Einbeziehung audiovisuellen Materials.

Die Auszüge aus einem Reiseführer "Culture shock Asia" (SB S. 108–109) konfrontieren die S mit fremden Sitten und Gebräuchen und geben Anregungen für ein angemessenes Verhalten im Ausland. Im Gegenzug werden die S aufgefordert einen Perspektivenwechsel vorzunehmen, sowie deutsche Verhaltensstandards zu thematisieren und in Paralleltexte "Culture shock Germany" umzusetzen. Die sprachlich-inhaltliche Verarbeitung der Informationen erfolgt darüber hinaus über den Transfer in andere Textformate wie Sketch, Tagebuch und Kurzgeschichte. Das Aufeinandertreffen sehr unterschiedlicher Kulturen lässt sich an Hand ausgewählter Schlüsselszenen aus dem Film *Dances with Wolves* (SB S. 109) anschaulich darstellen.

Im Abschlussbaustein des Kapitels ("Using your skills", "Working abroad", SB S. 110–111) werden konkrete Anwendungen der interkulturellen Handlungsfähigkeit praxisnah aufbereitet. Die notwendigen Fertigkeiten, um z. B. eine Bewerbung und einen Lebenslauf zu schreiben und ein Vorstellungsgespräch zu führen, werden formal und sprachlich vorbereitet und geübt.

Folgende Schwerpunkte können anhand unten aufgeführter Textsequenzen gesetzt werden:
- The German image abroad (combined with a revision of popular vs. quality press): Pictures in our heads – The Germans throw in the towel – Auf wiedersehen, with great respect – Advertising a German product abroad
- Stereotypes and humour: Pictures in our heads – The Germans throw in the towel – Making fun of it all (siehe auch Kapitel "Cultural mix and clash – UK")
- Political barriers / bridges (globalization): The ambassadors' game – Britain and Europe (siehe auch Kapitel "Facing a global future")
- Travelling and working abroad: Culture shock Asia – Working abroad.

Kernwortschatz: Kopiervorlage TB S. 101

Während der Lektüre der Texte können die S einen Kernwortschatz zum Thema 'intercultural experiences' in der Form von 'word fields' zusammen stellen, z. B.
Images: a controversial / vague / inaccurate image…
Stereotypes: to debunk / to break down a stereotype, to develop a critical attitude to stereotyping…
Ein Kernwortschatz befindet sich auf einer Kopiervorlage auf Seite 101.

Pictures in our heads SB S. 94–96

Before you look

■ **Adjectives**

a) Möglich als vorbereitende HA oder in EA. Überprüfung der Kenntnis der Adjektive mit Hilfe der Kopiervorlage "Adjectives for characterization", TB S. 100. Die Weiterverarbeitung könnte in Form einer 'pyramid discussion' erfolgen.
Step 1: In pairs, agree on reduced lists of 7 adjectives for each of the national characters. Argue your case but be prepared to make compromises. (Zeitlimit angeben, z. B. 8 Min.)
Step 2: Two pairs get together and work out their 'top five' list of adjectives for the two nations. (Zeitlimit, z. B. 12 Min.)
Step 3: Put your lists on the board and compare with the other groups. Then, discuss the following questions in class:
- Which adjectives have been chosen most frequently? Why was this the case?
- How many adjectives are positive/negative?
- What might s.o. who personifies most of these characteristics look like?

b) Nahe liegend: the Americans, the French…

Additional activities: focus on vocabulary

■ Complete the crossword on TB S. 100.
Lösungen: 1. straightforward, 2. communicative, 3. modest, 4. bureaucratic, 5. superstitious, 6. trustworthy, 7. hospitable, 8. civilised, 9. superficial, 10. imaginative, 11. ambitious, 12. mobile, 13. insular, 14. generous, 15. patriotic, 16. confident, 17. restless, 18. obedient, 19. selfish, 20. organized, 21. boastful

■ Work with the adjectives on page 94 of your book. Find synonyms / antonyms or arrange a selection of words on a scale from very positive to very negative.

Looking and thinking

1 *The traditional English businessman:* appearance – looks distinguished in a pin-striped suit with a white shirt, a tie and

a bowler hat; the smart, leather briefcase and the copy of *The Financial Times* indicate the figure's profession and interests; the umbrella not only serves as protection against the rain but is also part of a threatening pose which is supposed to keep Europe at a distance.
Adjectives: civilized, patriotic, insular, narrow-minded, conservative, old-fashioned, money-minded… (Vergleich mit zuvor erstellten Listen.)
The modern German tourist: Bavarian outfit which includes lederhosen and a hat with a goat's beard (obviously German = Bavarian!); Lufthansa bag (keen traveller); fat, almost obese (does little exercise, enjoys the good life); big smile, "Ich liebe dich" badge, British flag, peace sign (peace-loving, longs to be liked, uses flattery to make friends, unthreatening pose); wallet full of British banknotes (prosperous, has come to spend a lot of money in Britain)… (Vergleich mit zuvor erstellten Listen.)

2 Die Diskussion der "Pictures in our heads" und 'in the media' sollte diese Bilder als 'popular and widely-held', aber auch als 'simplified and generalized' charakterisieren. Auch den Wahrheitsgehalt erörtern: Do these images contain at least some truth? (E.g. figures who look similar to the businessman may be found in the City = the area of London which is still not only Britain's financial centre but also an international economic centre, or the Germans as Anglophiles and the world's keenest travellers)

If only we all played cricket… SB S. 95

Transkript

Speaker 1: The Germans seem … I don't know … more, not … they don't seem to want to have fun, I don't know and more serious and want to discuss politics and things and the Brits just want to have fun…

Speaker 2: And they're always the first people to get up in the morning and climb up a mountain before breakfast.

Speaker 3: They're always on the go, getting things organized whereas in England it'd be pretty much laid back.

Speaker 4: The English need a bit longer to thaw out and warm to people.

Speaker 5: I found it hard to deal with the fact that they have about five dustbins for different sorts of waste.

Speaker 6: I was unlucky with my first host family. It was just a woman on her own and she had a dog and it stank terribly.

Speaker 7: They're a lot more direct whereas the English always beat about the bush and you have to hide behind euphemisms.

Speaker 8: I was in Brighton once and met some young people there. They really had something against the Germans and seemed to think all young Germans were as extreme right-wing as in the past, although that really isn't true.

Speaker 9: I actually came to Germany with quite a few prejudices but to be honest they are some of the most wonderful people I have ever met. They have a great sense of humour and they are very sharp and witty.

Speaker 10: I find them a bit puzzling especially the English because they're a mixture of real eccentrics and total conformists.

Sigurd Hauff, Mayor of Spandau: If I may generalize, I would say that I like the English character because it is very aware, full of humour and self-reflection. Very often it finds a way of solving interpersonal problems without great conflict. 'Fair play' is after all an English expression.

a) Mutual images in key words: The Germans have no fun; are serious; discuss everything; on holiday they are the first to get up in the morning to climb a mountain; organized; have five dustbins; are direct; (Speaker 9) have a sense of humour, are sharp and witty.
The British have fun; are laid-back; need time to thaw out; have stinking dogs; beat about the bush; hide behind euphemisms; think all Germans are right-wing and stuck in the past; are a puzzling mixture of eccentrics and conformists; solve interpersonal conflicts fairly (fair play).
b) Factors that determine / influence / shape our perception of other nations: school, the media (TV, newspapers, magazines) parents, one's peer group…
c) –

A step further

■ The psychology of stereotypes

a) Die in den sechs Punkten formulierte "konstruktivistische" Sehweise von Stereotypen zwingt die S zur kritischen Auseinandersetzung mit der ihnen näher liegenden Pauschalablehnung von Stereotypen.
b) Mögliche HA oder in PA mit szenischer Präsentation: Schriftliche Vertiefung der vorherigen Diskussion unter Erarbeitung / Anwendung eines angemessenen formalen 'psychologischen' Registers.

Additional task: How the Americans see the Germans

Input: Surveys usually produce this hit list: proud of their country, intelligent, hard-working, strong-willed, fond of children, quick-tempered, home-loving, duty-conscious, technically advanced, cultured, musical, organized, brave … Die Konfrontation mit dem 'Fremdbild' (Perspektivenwechsel) erlaubt den Transfer eines nunmehr hoffentlich differenzierter verwendeten Stereotyp-Begriffs.

■ Make a speech

Vorab im Unterrichtsgespräch mögliche Sprecherprofile entwickeln, die die Vorgaben "provocative / humorous / one-sided" umsetzen, z. B. a confused, retired professor of psychology (who uses the ideas from the preceding activity but mixes everything up), a resident of London who is angered by the annual invasion of German tourists, a British car lover who looks back on the high-quality German cars he / she has owned, a British football fan, a German tourist in London. Jede / r der S sollte eine kurze Rede mit Hilfe einer 'prompt card' vorbereitet und geübt haben. Requisiten sind erwünscht (boxes to stand on, appropriate hats, etc.)

■ Postcard: stereotypes

a) Die Postkarte verdreht bekannte Stereotype in ihr Gegenteil, die so gut herausgearbeitet werden können: unavailable, inflexible, drunk, reserved…
Hinweis: Nicht alle Stereotype dieser in London bei Touristen beliebten Postkarte sind den S vertraut.
b) Die europäischen Stereotype der S werden aufgedeckt.

Barriers and bridges

Additional activity: Telling jokes

- Model joke: "In my idea of a European heaven, the police are British, the cooks French, the lovers Italian, the mechanics German and everything is organized by the Swiss." Write a definition of what a European hell might be like: "In my idea of a European hell…"

The ambassadors' game Using your skills SB S. 96–97

Diese unterhaltsame interkulturelle Simulation ist eine komplexe Lernsituation, in der die S in der Rolle von Diplomaten ziel- und interessenorientiert interagieren. Die deutschen Landesvertreter haben eine gemeinsame Handlungsvorgabe (vgl. SB S. 96–97), die ausländischen Botschafter der Dritte-Welt-Länder erhalten über eine Rollenkarte den Namen ihres fiktiven Landes und eine zentrale kommunikative Höflichkeitsregel (siehe Kopiervorlage, TB S. 102). Das zentrale Ziel ist die Übung von höflichem Sprachgebrauch in einer formalen Begegnungssituation.

In der zweiten Phase geht es dann für die ausländischen Diplomaten darum, ihr Land und dessen Probleme und Bedürfnisse angemessen dringlich darzustellen.

Die Simulation lässt sich so strukturieren:

1. Hinführung durch den L
- Vorstellung der Simulation "How to play…" (SB S. 96): necessary skills, students' / teacher's roles, useful phrases
- Sensibilisieren / Organisieren: "Before you play" (SB S. 96)

a) Notwendig ist in einer ersten Phase die Beherrschung des 'small talk', u.a. die Begrüßung, der Einstieg in das Gespräch über unverbindliche Themen und die Ausbalancierung der Redeanteile über geschicktes 'turn-taking'. Ideen können als 'pre-simulation activity' gesammelt werden (siehe unten):

How to survive a formal situation

- Ask questions and use question tags to get a response.
- Express gratitude for the invitation.
- Comment on the weather.
- Compliment your partner's country.
- Give positive signals (e.g. smile, establish eye contact).
- Be friendly.
- Tell an anecdote or a surprising fact.
- Speak slowly and not too loudly, make pauses to allow your partner to speak.

b) Rollenzuweisung nach Zufallsprinzip, die ausländischen Vertreter erhalten je eine Rollenkarte (vgl. Kopiervorlage, TB S. 102).
Möglicher Zeitrahmen:
Schritte 1 und 2 (Einführung und Organisation): 1 Stunde
Step 1 "Preparation": HA und 1 Stunde
Steps 2 und 3 "The diplomatic reception", "After the reception": 1 Doppelstunde
Step 4: HA.
c) Der L sollte situativ eingebunden sein: sie / er könnte den Empfang durch ein kurzes Statement eröffnen (auch durch S leistbar) und / oder als Kellner / -in fungieren und so in verschiedene Gespräche hineinhören.
d) Leitfrage für die Sichtung der "Discussion phrases", SB S. 193: Assess the phrases in terms of politeness. Note down seven to ten phrases on a prompt card which you might find useful for the reception.

2. Vorbereitung des Empfangs gemäß Step 1 (SB S. 96–97). GA für die deutschen Diplomaten; erst EA, dann evtl. 'rehearsal' in PA für die ausländischen Botschafter; Empfehlung: Namensschilder erleichtern die Identifizierung.

3. Durchführung des Empfangs gemäß Step 2 (SB S. 97).

4. Verarbeitung der Eindrücke und Informationen gemäß Step 3: für die Deutschen in einer Großgruppe mit Chairperson, die systematisch die Botschafter durchgeht und die Informationen schriftlich notiert; die Diplomaten tauschen sich in kleinen Gruppen aus (3–4 Mitglieder).

5. Mögliche HA gemäß Step 4.

A step further

- **Evaluate the method**

Im Plenum zuerst Positiva, dann Verbesserungsvorschläge.

- **Give a speech on politeness**

Vgl. Skills file "Presentations", SB S. 182–183.

- **Write a letter in role**

Ggf. vorab Wiederholung der wichtigsten formalen Konventionen der Textsorte formaler Brief hinsichtlich Adressen, Themanennung, Anrede und Abschluss (vgl. *Password to Skyline Plus Workbook*, S. 41, ISBN 3-12-510462-9); auf Vokabelbox zu dieser Teilaufgabe explizit hinweisen.

The Germans throw in the towel SB S. 98–99

Looking and laughing

1 *Setting:* a Mediterranean holiday resort (palm trees, sunbeds, swimming pool, sunshades / umbrellas); seven of the eight destinations on the sign are popular resorts: Mallorca, Menorca, Ibiza, Capri, Palma, Benidorm, Crete; the last destination – Dunkirk (coastal city in Normandy, France) – does not fit in: it symbolizes the evacuation of British and other Allied troops following the fall of France. A group of tourists (naked or in beachwear) are marching in a military goosestep along the beach towards the pool, the sunbeds are arranged in orderly rows – a clear allusion to the new, (allegedly) systematic and efficient German way of running the old travel firm (Note: In this case, the positive adjectives are connected with Germany's Nazi past, and thus take on a negative connotation.) The takeover of the English company, Thomas Cook, is reflected in the new name "Herr Thomas Kook" (Note the German spelling, and the formality which looks ridiculous in this setting.)

2 The Germans supervise the procession (two figures in uniform keep an eye on the group of tourists; one of them is pointing the way to the sunbeds); the tourists are British (as indicated by the Union Jack hats and shirts worn by members of the group).

3 Caption = resigned statement by one tourist, probably made to a fellow tourist and unnoticed by the Germans; it expresses dissatisfaction at the situation / suppressed anger / resignation, and alludes to the shortage of sunbeds in Mediterranean holiday resorts. British tabloids usu. blame German tourists for taking all of the sunbeds by rising early in the morning to reserve ("occupy") sunbeds with their towels.

4 The German guide (bottom right): "Turn right at the pool, then form an orderly queue. Sunbeds will be allocated in due course." – "Eyes ahead, keep in line…"
– A British tourist: "We should seriously consider travelling with another agent next year…"

Exploring the text

1 Die Überschrift des Artikels ist metaphorisch ("throw in the towel" = sign of defeat in a boxing match) als deutsches Eingeständnis einer deutschen Niederlage zu verstehen. Die 'sub-headline' benennt die Briten als Sieger (für S wohl nicht erkennbar: die Anspielung "wine army" – Rhine army) und den Konflikt als Kampf um die Sonnenliegen am Urlaubsort. Die Überschrift spielt auf ein in Großbritannien weit verbreitetes Bild des deutschen Urlaubers an, dem es mit System, Geschick und einer guten Portion Unverfrorenheit gelingt, bereits früh am Morgen die für die Urlauber verfügbaren Liegen für sich zu reklamieren.

2 Das Stereotyp des "sunbed-grabbers" spiegelt im Kern altbekannte vermeintlich urdeutsche Charakteristika wie 'efficiency' und 'impoliteness'. Der Artikel ergänzt dieses Bild noch in negativer Verschärfung um die Aspekte impudence (Col 1: ll. 15–17), bad losers (Col. 2: ll. 10–11), corruption and dishonesty (Col. 3: ll. 8–10), bossiness/arrogance/bad manners (Col. 3: ll. 12–18), selfishness (Col. 3: ll. 20–21) and delight at s.o.'s bad luck/Schadenfreude (Col. 3: ll. 29–31).

3 Die Beschreibung des 'Anglo-German conflict over sunbeds' erfolgt durch eine extensive und einfach zu erschließende Bildlichkeit mit Bezug auf die Bereiche ,war' (victory, battle, army, defeat, strike back, attack at the crack of dawn, hoisting the white flag,…) und ,boxing' (throw in the towel, the first round).

4 Humour is created by:
– stereotyping the nationalities involved, i.e. the sunbed-grabbing, arrogant Germans (cf. above) and the British 'lager louts' (Col 2: ll. 16–19: "huge and tattooed", heavy drinkers, boastful);
– dramatizing the events, cf. the extensive use of emotive language (e.g. Col. 1, ll. 1–2: "a victory to savour", l. 4: "humiliating defeat", ll. 8–9: "left fuming") and hyperbole (e.g. "another summer of international tension" Col. 3, ll. 26–28);
– personalizing the 'injuries' suffered by losers in the war such as Christa Konermann and creating the impression of authenticity through her informal language (e.g. Col. 2, ll. 3–5; "bagged", "didn't get a look in");
– pretending to be objective by including numerous quotations (German press, eye-witnesses from both sides).

A step further

■ Write a formal letter

Die formalen, inhaltlichen und sprachlichen Kennzeichen des Textformats 'letter to the editor' sind zu beachten (vgl. *Password to Skyline Plus Workbook*, ISBN 3-12-510462-9, S. 42). Der vorgegebene Schreibanlass erfordert die explizite kommentierende Bezugnahme auf die Kernaussagen des Ausgangstextes aus der vorgegebenen Perspektive. Für die Multiperspektivität ist es wichtig, Textbeispiele für alle vier Positionen miteinander zu vergleichen.

■ Write a sketch or anecdote

Zuerst das Textformat in Stichpunkten definieren (die auch anschließend in eine 'definition for a glossary of literary terms' umgesetzt werden können, z. B.
Sketch: A dramatic text which is short and self-contained; consists of one scene only (with a beginning, middle and end); usually has one setting only; has a limited number of characters; aims to entertain.
A sketch is usually humorous; as a rule, it is based on a quick exchange of remarks; it ends with a punch line (surprise ending).
Typical features: Sketches often include outsiders, cases of mistaken identity, strange/extreme behaviour, exaggeration, absurdities, confusion, slapstick, incompetence, cruelty…

■ Turn your notes into a dictionary definition.
Present an anecdote: Für dieses mündliche Textformat typische Redemittel sammeln lassen: You won't believe what happened to me last… – I couldn't believe my eyes… Auch nützliche (u.a. informelle) Phrasen aus dem Text aktivieren: to claim the best seats, to rise at the crack of dawn, to grab a sunlounger, not to get a look-in, to tie the sunbeds together with towels…
Mehrere szenisch-monologische Präsentationen; Bewertungskriterien: Sprache, Humor, Stimme, Inhalt.

Auf wiedersehen, with great respect   SB S. 100–101

Before you read

■ Quote

a)/b) Provokanter Vorabdruck der Z. 12–13 des folgenden Textes: inhaltliche Vorbereitung auf negative Sichtweisen des eigenen Landes. L führt im spekulativen Gespräch passende zentrale Begriffe des Textes ein: regulations – bureaucrats – intolerance – wartime past – envy of economic success – ruthless competition – fear of a united Germany.
Danach Überleitung zum Text: Quelle des Zitats, Autor und Zeitpunkt der Veröffentlichung.

Additional task

■ Divide the text into sections. Think of headings to describe its structure. Mögliche Aufteilung:
– a personal experience (anecdote) (ll. 3–5),
– the German image abroad (ll. 6–14),
– putting things into perspective (ll. 15–20),
– the cartoonist's exaggerated view of Germans (ll. 20–29),
– political factors (ll. 30–35),
– Germany – a country of contradictions and divisions (ll. 36–44),
– modern German reality (ll. 45–60),
– Germany within Europe – a look to the future (ll. 61–64).

Exploring the text

1 a) According to the writer, Germany's image in the world is mainly negative (l. 14). It is marked by overregulation, bureaucracy (ll. 9–10), a climate of intolerance (l. 10), stereotypical figures e.g. the beer-drinking Bavarian (ll. 21–22), the flashy drivers of fast cars (ll. 23–24), the former-Nazi officer

Barriers and bridges

(ll. 25–26), a ruthless/threatening economy (l. 28) and an ever-present wartime past (l. 13). However, there is also some respect for how Germany re-built itself from the ruins of World War II (ll. 18–19).
b) *Factors:* personal experiences of visitors (ll. 3–9), an awareness of Germany's wartime past, envy due to present success (l. 13), cartoons (and the media) (ll. 21–26), the views of major politicians (ll. 30–32) and Germany's guilt-ridden, over-cautious performance in international politics (ll. 34–35).
2 Put key words from page 101 into categories.
E.g. *Psychology:* contradictory attitudes – aware of their past – anxious for normality – search for a new identity
Economy: wealthy nation – high production costs – money floods abroad – trade union co-determination – rigid working practices – economically divided
Private and social life: long holidays – high income – short working hours – welfare state – free education – most people rent accommodation – a structured society – formal relationships – no yobs – controlled emotions – self-discipline
3 *Robin Gedye's feelings about Germany:*
– initial feeling of alienation caused by the encounter with the man in the black leather coat (ll. 3–7, associations with the Nazi Secret Service);
– fear of a persisting Nazi influence (ll. 28–29);
– admiration, particularly for Germany's post-war achievements (e.g. ll. 37, 49–50);
– hope for a positive future (ll. 61–63).
4 Der *Daily Telegraph* zeigt sich in diesem Artikel als 'quality newspaper' (broadsheet). Die Merkmale in den Kategorien primary aim, tone, language, structure, layout treffen hier uneingeschränkt zu. Robin Gedyes autobiographical report zeigt in der Kategorie 'presentation' jedoch zwangsläufig auch punktuell ansatzweise Merkmale einer 'popular paper' ("personalization through highlighting individual experiences, feelings and perspectives", siehe unten).
Die folgende Tabelle kann auch als Input in Form einer Kopiervorlage genutzt oder wiederholend erarbeitet werden.

category	popular paper (tabloid)	quality paper (broadsheet)
main aim	entertainment	information
presen-tation	visually attractive; events are: – **dramatized** by exaggeration, sensationalism, speculation – **personalized** by highlighting individual experiences, feelings, attitudes (focus on human interest)	verbally challenging; events are presented: – **objectively** (facts and figures) – **comprehensively** (i.e. placed in context, observe principles of balanced/detached reporting, include a variety of observations and comments)
tone	emotional	sober, down-to-earth
language	easy, everyday, colloquial, informal: – emotive diction to stir up feelings – easily accessible imagery describes events graphically	difficult, complex, abstract, formal: – neutral diction, sophisticated, specific vocabulary (e.g. to deteriorate), emotions are not
	– simple syntax: short sentences, incomplete sentences possible, phrasal verbs (e.g. to put off)	expressed directly – little imagery – complex syntax: long sentences with subordinate clauses
structure/layout	– text plus pictures – large print, different print sizes – short paragraphs (often one sentence only) – sub-headings	– focus on text – small print, little variation in print size – long paragraphs (two or more sentences) – no sub-headings

Additional task

■ Re-write the *Telegraph* article for a popular paper. The journalistic style of the *Daily Mail* (a middle-market newspaper with features of both popular and quality papers; siehe SB S. 99) may indicate the changes you will have to make (siehe http://www.dailymail.co.uk/).

A step further

■ **Hold a chat show**
Vorbereitung: Formulierung des Themas (z.B. "What is Germany's image and role in the world?") und Zusammenstellung der Gästeliste im Plenum (Kriterien für die Auswahl transparent machen!), dann Ausgestaltung der Rollen in arbeitsteiliger GA (je Gast – eine Gruppe von 3–5 S, eine Moderatoren-Gruppe); in der GA Erarbeitung einer "Survival role card for a guest" (siehe TB S. 104) bzw. einer "Moderator role card" (siehe TB S. 105); zur Optimierung der Koordination zwischen Moderator und Gast reichen die Gäste-Gruppen möglichst bald eine "Reduced role card: guest" (siehe TB S. 106) zur Information an die Moderatorengruppe weiter.
Mögliche Variationen bei der Moderatorenrolle: Statt einem S als Moderator Tandemmoderation durch zwei S oder der L übernimmt diese Rolle; sprachlich-strategische Hilfestellung durch Kopiervorlage, "Discussion: moderation rules", TB S. 188.
Erprobung der Show: Zur Vorbereitung führen neu gemischte Gruppen mit je einem Vertreter aus jeder Gäste-/Moderatorengruppe parallel im Klassenraum ein rehearsal durch. Eine Gruppe wird dann für die "öffentliche" Präsentation ausgewählt. Oder bei Zeitmangel: Auswahl des Gruppenrepräsentanten in der "öffentlichen" Diskussion am Ende der Vorbereitung nach Zufallsprinzip.
Während der Show machen sich die Zuschauer gezielt und arbeitsteilig Notizen zu den Argumenten und Positionen; zum kommunikativen Verhalten einzelner Gäste, zum Geschick des Moderators.
Der L notiert auf je einer kleinen 'hot card' pro S höchstens drei auffällige Fehler; die Karten werden zur persönlichen Information am Ende der Stunde den betreffenden S mit auf den Weg gegeben (die Fehler könnten auch ggf. zu Beginn der Folgestunde von ihnen vor der Klasse reflektiert werden).
Evaluation: mögliche Bausteine der lehrermoderierten Auswertungsphase:
– Eigenstatements der Teilnehmer: How did you feel …?/ How did you cope with the role?
– Rückmeldung der Gäste für die Teilnehmer

– Rückmeldung zur Methode an den L: What was effective / can be improved? Vereinbarungen für die nächste chat show bzw. panel discussion schriftlich auf Poster fixieren; vor Beginn der Evaluationsphase "Discussion: feedback rules" ins Gedächtnis rufen. (Siehe TB S. 189.)

Zur transparenten Information und zur Steuerung des komplexen Arbeitsprozesses ist eine Verlaufsübersicht hilfreich, die vom L nach der Festlegung des Themas und der Gäste per Folie den S vorgestellt wird (vgl. "Planning a chat show", TB S. 103).

■ Make a speech

Die Ideen des Textes gilt es hier zu reaktivieren und zu aktualisieren: Ideen und Wortschatz zur Beschreibung der aktuellen Situation Deutschlands und seiner Rolle in der Welt sollten vorab im Unterrichtsgespräch erarbeitet werden und z. B. in Form einer Mind map gesichert werden. Die Vokabelbox liefert hilfreiches Sprachmaterial und auch eine Strukturierungshilfe. Die besondere Bedeutung des Einstiegs und des Abschlusses sollte hervorgehoben werden. Hilfen zur Planung und Strukturierung finden sich im SB S. 182 ("Presentations"), für die 'performance' selbst ist der Abschnitt "While speaking" (SB S. 183) nützlich.

Britain and Europe   SB S. 102–104

Before you read

■ Statistics

a) The statements are fully or partly supported by the figures in the bar chart:
- Statement 1 is only true if the survey focused on young Europeans;
- In Statement 2 only the first sentence is borne out by the statistics: seeing o.s. as European cannot be directly equated with enthusiasm for political integration;
- Statement 3 is also borne out by the statistics;
- Statement 4 clearly over-interprets the implications of the figures for Britain's political future ("political union", "shifting power back to Britain").

To avoid over-interpretation, the evaluation of the figures should be closely related to the question: "To what extent do you see yourself as a European"?

Additional activity

■ Improve and extend the survey by adding questions which explore enthusiasm about political unity and the need for a greater centralization of power in Brussels. (e.g. Which powers should be transferred there?)
■ Conduct the improved survey in your English class and in other classes, too. Visualize and evaluate the results.

b) Oder: Write a paragraph which answers the question.

Over to you!

■ Analyse the text in pairs

Ggf. noch kleinschrittigere Vorbereitung der inhaltlichen Erarbeitung: Identify 22 key words in Robin Cook's speech which could serve as cues to help you memorize its content. Siehe Beispiel oben rechts:

My cues	Related ideas from the text in note form
…	…

Auswertung in PA:
1. Swap grids with a partner and compare the cues you chose. Give each other a cue and let your partner memorize related ideas from the text.
2. Explain to your partner how selected cues in your grid are logically connected. Try to visualize connections by means of lines, arrows, question marks, etc.

Lehrerinput: A crib sheet contains information written concisely on a small sheet of paper. It is sometimes used dishonestly by students in tests.

Hinweis an S: Turn your 22 cues into a crib sheet for Robin Cook's speech. Visualize logical connections. First make a draft, then write / draw the final version.

Das folgende Beispiel kann über eine Folie als Beispiel dienen.

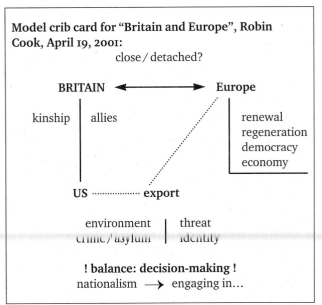

Die Verarbeitung der 'crib cards' erfolgt schrittweise gemäß Steps 2 bis 6.

Mögliche Variation: **Step 5:** The new pairs think of questions which they could ask Robin Cook in the role of TV interviewers. (The answers should be in the text.)

Step 6: The students in the outer circle move on again two places to the right. The new pairs turn their lists of questions into two interviews (swap interviewer / interviewee roles in the middle).

Diese Variation führt zu "A step further", Task 1, SB S. 104: One or two pairs might stage their TV interview live in class (cf. "Hard Talk" on CNN).

Step 7 ist eine abschließende Methodenreflexion zur Evaluation dieser Kugellagermethode. Mögliche Anregungen: Consider the advantages of the method – Suggest improvements – Decide what kind of texts it is suitable for.

■ Teach yourselves!

Mögliche Sequenz:
Introductory activity

"Statistics", SB S. 102 oder Unterrichtsgespräch: What are Germany's interests in the EU? Think of historical, economic and political aspects. What anti-European arguments might critics put forward? How justified are these arguments?

Barriers and bridges

Reading and understanding
Methode 1: Mit inner circle / outer circle (Kugellager SB S. 103), anschließend in groups 'a tour of a gallery'. Display the crib cards on the blackboard / on posters. Then discuss the visualization techniques used with a partner.
Methode 2: Divide the text into sections, give headings and explain Robin Cook's line of argument.
Methode 3: List the anti-European arguments referred to in the speech. How does Robin Cook deal with them?
Methode 4: In what tone do you think Robin Cook gave the speech? At which points do you expect his tone changed, and how? Reduce the speech to half its length and perform it in class.

Post-reading activities
TV interview or opposing speech (cf. SB S. 104, "A step further", Task 2).
Oder: Mr Cook answers journalists' questions in the 'hot seat' at a press conference. A moderator chairs the conference.

A step further

■ Hold an interview
a) / b) Hinweise für den Interviewer:
– Make sure that critical or provocative questions are introduced by two or three preceding sentences which establish a context.
– Never comment on the quality of an answer, but feel free to ask a question again if the interviewee ignores it.
Ergänzend: Discuss the quality of the live interviews in class. Agree on criteria for a successful interview before you start, e.g. liveliness, entertainment and information value, spontaneity and observation of the given roles.

■ Write a speech
Critical ideas from the text: "alternative future available to Britain" (ll. 4–5), i.e. a comfortable existence loosely linked to Brussels (ll. 6–7), "Britain's destiny lies outside Europe" (ll. 10–11), special relationship with the US more important than European ties (ll. 25–27), EU membership diminishes the British identity (ll. 29–31)…
Hinweis an S: Cf. "Skills file", "Presentations", SB pp. 182–183 for ideas on how to prepare and give a speech.

Advertising a German product abroad *Using your skills*   SB S. 104

a) Mögliches Beispiel im SB: "What happens if you drink GM coffee", S. 126).
b) Zeitrahmen: 3 Einzelstunden plus HA zur Entwicklung der Produktidee und Vorbereitung der Präsentation. Möglichst nur zwei Präsentationen pro Einzelstunde um Zeit für angemessenes Feedback zu haben. Situative Einbettung: Der L moderiert die Präsentationsphase in der Rolle des Managers einer Werbeagentur; die Gruppen treten mit ihren Vorschlägen in eine fiktive Konkurrenzsituation ein.

Task
– Zufallsgruppen stellen hier eine höhere Anforderung an kooperatives Arbeiten.
– German products, e.g. fitted kitchens, sausages, Moselle wine; German companies, e.g. BMW, Daimler-Chrysler, Lufthansa, Siemens; tourist attractions, e.g. Heidelberg, Berlin, Munich, the Brandenburg Gate, Neuschwanstein Castle, the Munich beer festival. Interessante Anzeigen sollten in *Newsweek* oder *Time Magazine* zu finden sein. Mögliche Schwachpunkte einer authentischen Anzeige könnte ein Ausgangspunkt für eine überzeugendere Werbeidee sein und die eigene Präsentation einleiten.
– Der L sollte 5 Minuten vor Stundenende die S erinnern: Do not forget to set your own tasks for work at home. Distribute different tasks so that everyone can contribute her / his skills and talents.

Ein Kurzbericht zum Arbeitsstand könnte beispielsweise zu Stundenbeginn von allen Gruppen wieder von einem nach Zufallsprinzip ausgewählten Sprecher erfolgen: Briefly report back to the manager what you have done so far, and what you are going to do next.
Die Werbeseite sollte obligatorisch sein, wünschenswert ist ebenso die Radiowerbung, beim TV commercial genügt eine 'key selling idea' (ambitionierter: szenische Darstellung): Beispiele fürs Letztere sind folgende: slice-of-life (people in everyday situations) – lifestyle (product epitomizes an attractive way of life) – dreamworld (product is presented in a futuristic setting) – scientific proof (an expert presents evidence proving the superiority of the product) – testimonial (a trustworthy / likeable person, e.g. a celebrity or a typical consumer, recommends the product).
Die Tipps zu Gruppenpräsentationen im SB S. 183 könnten als Kriterien der Präsentationsbewertung genommen werden. Eine mögliches Beobachtungsraster liefert die Kopiervorlage "Evaluation sheet for adverts / commercials" (TB S. 107), nützliches Evaluationsvokabular findet sich im TB S. 108 ("Useful vocabulary to evaluate a presentation").

Evaluation
– Vergleichende Bewertung der Produkte und der Präsentation auf der Grundlage der Notizen des Beobachtungsrasters (siehe TB S. 108, "Useful vocabulary to evaluate a presentation").
– Evaluation des Gesamtprojekts – Strukturierung durch Leitfragen: 1. What aspects of the project did you enjoy? 2. What improvements would you suggest?

Making fun of it all   SB S. 105–107

Before you read

■ Types of humour
a) *Situational humour* is produced by the actions of a set of characters in an amusing situation; humour is usu. created by stock characters who embody / personify a particular idea and lack the roundness of a real person (compare: flat / round characters in fiction); stock characters are based on stereotypes, i.e. fixed and generally accepted ideas of what a particular type of person is like (e.g. sexual, ethnic, or professional stereotypes). Another device is to parody s.o. / s.th., i.e. to copy or imitate s.o. / s.th. in an exaggerated way.
Verbal humour is produced through language. Popular verbal devices which create humour are:
– euphemisms: a more gentle expression is used to express unpleasant, frightening or embarrassing facts, e.g. comfort station / rest room in AE for public toilet;
– irony: saying one thing but meaning the opposite;

- hyperbole: a statement which is exaggerated;
- puns: when a word has two meanings, the sentence it is in can be understood in two different ways;
- sarcasm: irony which is cutting and meant to hurt;
- understatement: opposite of hyperbole, s.th. is presented as being less important than it really is.

Black humour focuses on the unpleasant parts of life such as murder and death.
Slapstick is based on physical actions such as hitting, kicking, throwing things at one another and falling down.

Additional question

■ How are the types of humour related?
Lösung: Humour may be divided into two main categories: situational humour and verbal humour; black humour may be found in both categories and slapstick is a situational device.

b) Vorbereitung als HA oder im Unterricht (EA, PA oder GA) unter Beachtung der vier vorgegebenen Beschreibungskategorien.

Additional activities

■ In pairs, compare what you and your partner find amusing. Think of programmes, film and TV characters, and books you both know.
■ Divide the comedy scene into sections. What criterion would you apply? (E.g. new character constellations as in ll. 1–7, 8–31, 32–56, 57–72, 73–92).

Talking about the photos — SB S. 105

Foto links: The character seems to be eccentric and unpredictable, his attention seems to be fixed on some point in the distance. His tongue is poking out of his mouth with the concentration required. His body language is out of character with his formal clothing.
Foto rechts: The character's raised eyebrows and open mouth suggest that he is surprised by s.th. or does not understand s.th. He seems to be carrying a tray with a glass jug and glasses, and his expression would lead you to believe that he might drop them…

Exploring the text

1 a) *The (elderly) Germans:* militaristic body language ("clicks his heels", l. 2), civilised/reserved/formal/polite in an old-fashioned way (ll. 2–4, 6), mostly poor command of English (ll. 3–4, 33–35) but with exceptions (ll. 79, 89); Basil expects them to be sensitive about their wartime past (ll. 59–60, 77: note the phrase "Don't mention the war" which has become part of common BE usage).
The Spanish (Manuel as a caricature of 'the Spanish waiter'): very poor command of English despite working in England, not very intelligent (ll. 16, 27), attentive/caring (ll. 21, 29), obedient/conscientious (l. 30).
The English: Basil Fawlty (note the pun on 'faulty'): eager to please the guests but obsessed with his prejudices against the Germans, condescending towards the Spanish waiter (ll. 10, 14–15), English 'stiff upper lip' i.e. one does not admit to having a problem (l. 18); Polly: businesslike, professional, in control; Misses Tibbs and Gatsby: concerned in a polite way (ll. 66, 68), tolerant of Basil's eccentric behaviour (l. 70).
b) E.g. slapstick (ll. 2, 19, 56, 59, 86, 90); hyperbole (l. 18); (unintentional) pun (l. 30); (unintentional) irony (ll. 31, 91–92); verbal humour caused by a series of synonyms (l. 48); situational humour caused by flimsy excuses (l. 57); strange or extreme behaviour (ll. 83–88) and confusion/incompetence (ll. 40–56); verbal humour due to misunderstandings (Basil and Manuel, Basil and the elderly Germans) and Basil's incorrect version of proverbs (ll. 63, 69).
2 Further causes of complication and misunderstanding: interpreting the menu, taking orders, table manners…
3 Vergleich der Unterrichtsergebnisse (the presentation of the different nationalities, humour and the predictions for the dining room) mit der audiovisuellen Umsetzung; weitere Aspekte: 'body language, use of voice, the characters' appearances'. Individuelle Kommentierung des Humorgehalts unter Beachtung der Tatsache, dass deutsche Zuschauer nicht die Zielgruppe sind.

A step further

■ **Add stage directions**
Typographisch im Text gekennzeichnet durch Klammern und Kursivschrift. Vorab Funktion wiederholen: stage directions (short or extensive) provide information about entrances/exits, the setting, body language, voice, moods, silences. Und an Textbeispielen belegen. Ergänzungen werden sich vornehmlich auf body language, voice und moods beziehen.

■ **Write a script**
Ggf. Ergebnisse von "Postcard: stereotypes", SB S. 96 reaktivieren. Wünschenswert: szenische Präsentation, die Zuschauer achten arbeitsteilig auf das Bild der jeweils beschriebenen Nation und auf Techniken der Humorerzeugung.

■ **Make comments**
Diskussion im Plenum unter Bezugnahme "Expressing opinions", "Presenting an argument" (SB S. 193).

Erweiterung

■ Do you think that different nationalities find different things funny? If so, think of examples based on what you have read or seen in the media or experienced in real life?

Culture shock Asia ‹over to you› SB S. 108–109

Before you read

■ **Preparing a trip**
E.g. collect information about sights, means of transport, accommodation, customs…
Sources: the Internet, travel guides, travel agents…

■ **German rules of behaviour**
a) Explain rules regarding:
- how to address people ('du'/'Sie', the use of first names and academic titles);
- how to greet people, e.g. with eye contact, a bow, a handshake, a hug, a kiss…;

Barriers and bridges

- how to give and receive gifts;
- how to dress at parties / in formal situations;
- how to make appointments and when to be punctual;
- how to use body language (gestures, facial expression, physical contact…);
- language (polite / informal phrases used, e.g. when one asks permission to smoke)
- what not to do in a specific situation, e.g. talk with one's hands in one's pockets, rest one's feet on the furniture, backslapping.

Possible answers:
- It is customary to shake hands on meeting and saying goodbye to s.o.
- Respect titles (Doktor) and never automatically use s.o.'s first name when you are introduced unless you are asked to do so. Strangers normally use the formal 'Sie'. The use of the more intimate 'du' and s.o.'s first name, should best be mutually agreed on, except among young people or in informal situations where everyone is using 'du'.
- Appointments must be made in advance; if s.o. cannot keep an appointment, he / she cancels or postpones it by phone.
- An invitation to a German home is a special privilege and punctuality is essential. A man should bring flowers, which he unwraps before presenting them to the hostess. Avoid red roses, as they have romantic connotations, and never give 13 or an even number of flowers.

b) *Serious mistakes* (if not discussed in Task a) above):
- Never use s.o.'s first name until they ask you to do so.
- Never arrive at a meeting before the appointed time…

c) The Middle East, Japan, China…

■ **Guess meaning from the context**
Überprüfung von Bedeutung und Aussprache mit Hilfe eines einsprachigen Wörterbuchs.

Over to you!

■ **Write a diary entry / a parallel text / a love story**
Sketch: Siehe "Write a sketch…" TB S. 93.
Diary: Mindestens drei Tageseinträge. Beschreibung und Kommentierung der Tageserlebnisse (Gefühle, Gedanken, Erwartungen). Sprache: informell, unvollständige Sätze.
Parallel texts: Typisches Sprachmaterial für Ratschläge aus den Modelltexten herausziehen und ergänzen:
1. Textwortschatz: You are expected to… – Remember to… – … is frowned upon – …
2. Ergänzend: It is advisable to… – You are strongly advised not / never to… – To be on the safe side you should… – I would recommend that you…
Story: Siehe *Password to Skyline Plus Workbook* (ISBN 3-12-510462-9), S. 34–35 ("How to write a 'plot' story", "How to write a 'slice-of-life' story") oder *Password to Skyline Plus* (ISBN 3-12-510460-2), S. 117.

Meet the media

Dances with Wolves – Culture clash on film: Sehr gut geeignet für unterrichtsbegleitendes eigenständiges Arbeiten einzeln oder in einer Gruppe: schriftliches Produkt wie Facharbeit / Essay (Siehe Skills file, "Essays", SB S. 187, "Term papers", S. 189) oder mündliche, mediengestützte Präsentation (siehe "Presentations", SB S. 182–183, "Film scene analysis", SB S. 184–185). Vgl. auch Kernwortschatz (TB S. 101).

Working abroad SB S. 110–113

Siehe auch Zusatzmaterialien "On the phone" (TB S. 113) und "The world of work" (TB S. 114).

Test: Why Germans love the British TB S. 109

Klausur für den Leistungskurs
Textformat: newspaper article, 608 words
Vorschlag / Klausurtyp NRW: Tasks 1–3, A2
Bezugstexte des Kapitels: "The Germans throw in the towel"; "Auf wiedersehen, with great respect"
Eine mögliche Aufbereitung finden Sie auf TB S. 109.

Comprehension
1 Exemplified primarily by his German friend but also based on his experiences, Toby Helm portrays the Germans as being:
- mostly educated, cultured and well-travelled (ll. 17–18);
- enthusiastic Anglophiles (ll. 4–5, 11–18);
- proud of German achievements and how things are run in Germany (high level of investment in public services, high taxes, generous health care and old-age pensions, low crime rate) (ll. 20–23);
- not patriotic, politically correct (ll. 39–40, 47–48);
- the older generation: mostly friendly, open, humorous distance themselves from World War II (ll. 60–67).

Analysis
2 Features of the writer's journalistic style:
Structure: Ideas are developed step-by-step; paragraphs form thematic units (often with a topic sentence at the beginning); transitions are smooth; clear, easy-to-follow train of thought.
Language: easily understandable, medium level vocabulary with few exceptions (cf. "traumatized … paranoid about projecting itself as a nation" as an example of a pseudo-psychological register); clear, straightforward syntax with traces of spoken English, e.g. an incomplete sentence (l. 16); conversational, laid-back tone which switches between factual, serious assessments and humorous comments.
Other features:
- gives an **example** of one educated German (Andreas);
- extensive use of **quotations** as direct speech (ll. 4–5, 31–32, 65–66) or reported speech (ll. 45–46, 57–59);
- personal experiences / single examples serve as a basis for **generalizations** (ll. 26–29);
- **hyperbole** (e.g. ll. 11–13, 59), **jokes** (ll. 15–18, 65–67);
- **rhyming phrase** "lean and mean" (l. 23);
- **anecdotes** (ll. 30–32, 55–58);
- **quotations** frame the text (cf. first and last paragraphs);
- **allusion** to a historical event (the Blitz in London, l. 67).

The writer: journalist / probably foreign correspondent for the *Daily Telegraph* (British broadsheet); married; he lived with his wife in Berlin for some time; self-proclaimed expert on German culture.

Re-creation of a text
3 Features of the text format 'newspaper comment':
- structure: headline, paragraphs, clear train of thought;
- content: references to Toby Helm's statements, Andreas's national self-image;
- journalistic style: cf. Task 2, "Analysis" above.

Barriers and bridges

Test: Germans – the new Americans? TB S. 110

Klausur für den Grundkurs
Textformate: extract from a travelogue (337 words); cartoon
Vorschlag / Klausurtyp NRW: Tasks 1–3, B1 (Sachtext in Kombination mit Cartoon); alternatives to Task 3: A1 or A2
Zentrale Bezugstexte des Kapitels: "Pictures in our heads"; "The Germans throw in the towel"; "Auf wiedersehen, with great respect"; "Making fun of it all"
Eine mögliche Aufbereitung zu diesem Test finden Sie auf einer Kopiervorlage auf S. 110.

Comprehension
1 Changes between 1970 and start of the 1990s:
Germany: rubble in Hamburg → everything is new, cities are "rich, elegant, handsome"
Germans:
- fat → good-looking (healthy, tanned, fit)
- bad table manners → adequate table manners, health-conscious
- arrogant → quietly confident (friendly, happy, relaxed)

Constant features: clever, hard-working, prosperous

Analysis
2 *Setting:* Mediterranean holiday resort (Spain) controlled by the British and the Germans (see flags); early in the morning, sunrise is an allusion to old conflicts revived in a different context.
Four images of the Germans:
- single figure on the right, dressed in Bavarian style, slightly overweight, quick to reserve a sunbed, patriotic (towel in national colours) → the (Bavarian) German on holiday;
- (modern-day) single figure in the foreground (central image) – huge, muscular; threatening / intimidating / challenging body language (corresponds to the newspaper headlines: aggressive, bullying) → the rude German:
- historical reference associated with the figure on the left: older German, slim, ascetic body, detached, surveys the scene, wears a monocle, in control – strategic planner → the Nazi German;
- in the background a group of Germans goose-steps towards the water: orderly, disciplined – connotations of both a military combat formation and the modern work ethic → the efficient German.

Effect: The cartoon might reinforce readers' prejudices / ring a note of truth / remind them of similar experiences they had abroad; make them laugh because it plays on stereotypes…

Comment / re-creation of text
3 a) Include typical features of the text format 'formal letter';
- Comment on selected statements from the extract.
- Refer to the Griffin cartoon.

b) Comment on the German features summarized in Bill Bryson's statement, e.g. rich, ambitious, hard-working, health-conscious, confident of their place in the world.
- Point out recent trends in German society: growing confidence, strong focus on the EU, alienation from the American way of life…
- Refer to cartoon stereotypes plus other media images discussed in class, e.g. *Fawlty Towers* episode "The Germans" (SB pp. 105–107).

Test: Germans 'take too many holidays' TB S. 112

Mündliche Prüfung
Textformat: newspaper article, 276 words
Vorschlag / Aufgabenart NRW: Tasks 1–3, B1 (Text und Visualie) (A1 / A2)
Bezugstexte des Kapitels: "Pictures in our heads", "The Germans throw in the towel", "Auf wiedersehen, with great respect"
Eine mögliche Aufbereitung finden Sie auf TB S. 112.

Comprehension
1 *Text:* weak economy (ll. 12–14), low growth rate (ll. 14–15), fewer working hours compared to other European countries (ll. 6–8), high unemployment rate (ll. 15–16), country is facing a recession (ll. 34–35), a need for reforms (ll. 30–31).
Cartoon: Germany is portrayed as being economically strong and powerful / proud of its high-quality products and hi-tech companies. Its economic strength seems to be frightening / unstoppable / overwhelming.

Analysis
2 *Text:* More than ten years after reunification, Germany finds itself on the brink of a recession. Economic and social crises make reforms necessary, e.g. a renewal of the health and pension systems / a revival of the "made in Germany" trademark / technical innovation / reductions in labour costs / more flexibility in all parts of society / a more efficient education system / more competition.
Cartoon: In 1990, Germany's economic superiority was still internationally recognized and feared. Reunification was expected to lead to a boom in the economy with huge growth rates and greater political influence in Europe.

Comment / (re-)creation of text
3 a) Personal comment
b) clear structure – arguments from the text – references to recent trends – examples of social reforms – criticize Mr Clement's position as "a step in the wrong direction" / dismiss his statements as political rhetoric, which is unlikely to be translated into effective reforms – use rhetorical devices, e.g. address the audience directly ('you'), use personal pronouns ('we', 'I'), rhetorical questions, anaphora, similes.

Mündliche Abschlussprüfung zu "Barriers and bridges" TB S. 111

Gruppenprüfung mit drei Teilnehmern in Form einer Talkshow. Die Rolle des Moderators wird vom Prüfer übernommen. Die Gäste ergeben sich aus den im Unterricht bearbeiteten Texten. Eine halbstündige Vorbereitungszeit auf die Übernahme der zugewiesenen Rolle ist empfehlenswert. Eine Auswahl möglicher Rollenkarten befindet sich auf einer Kopiervorlage auf S. 111.

Einstiegsfragen für alle
- How necessary are intercultural experiences?
- Why is intercultural learning important?
- What is Germany's image in the world, and what challenges does the country face?

Barriers and bridges

Adjectives for characterization

Across

2 able to talk easily to other people
5 believing that certain things bring good or bad luck
6 dependable
9 not interested in serious or important things
10 good at producing new ideas, creative
12 able to move from one job or class to another
15 proud of your country
17 unwilling to stay in one place, always wanting new experiences
18 always doing what you are told
19 caring only about yourself
20 efficient, systematic
21 talking too proudly about yourself

Down

1 honest, not hiding anything
3 not proud, does not talk about his/her achievements
4 using unnecessary and complicated official rules
7 friendly to visitors
8 behaving in a polite and sensible way
11 having a strong desire to be successful
13 only interested in your own country and way of life
14 willing to give money or time to help other people
15 rich, wealthy
16 sure that you have the ability to do things well

Kernwortschatz

Images
a controversial/vague/inaccurate image
a popular/(un)flattering/justified image
a restricted/blurred/distorted perception of s.th.
a general idea/notion/assumption
to view/label/perceive s.o. as being …
s.o. is labelled/characterized as being …
to paint a picture
mutual images

Stereotypes
prejudice = previous judgement/preconceived idea/
 biased attitude
stereotype = a fixed, oversimplified image/
 prejudice that many people know and repeat,
 usu. in a catchphrase, e.g. "the efficient Germans"
auto-stereotypes = self-images which a group
 of people hold about themselves
favourite targets of stereotyping: minority groups
 and nations
national/racial/sexual stereotypes
Stereotypes…
– are easy explanations/survival tools
– help us to orientate ourselves
– help us to cope in a world which puts
 many demands on our attention
– are not genetically determined but
 gradually learned
– usu. contain some truth
to fit/a stereotype
to create/perpetuate a stereotype
to debunk/to break down a stereotype
to have a strong/deep-seated bias
to be prejudiced/biased against s.o.
to make a sweeping statement
to develop a critical attitude to stereotyping
to become aware of unfair generalizations

Cultures
to experience a culture clash/shock
to meet the challenges of a foreign culture
to adjust to new customs and habits
to adapt to unexpected circumstances
to be aware of/to accept differences
to tolerate otherness
to respect rules
to communicate successfully with s.o.
to develop an understanding for s.o.
to broaden one's horizons
to act with tolerance
to show empathy
to overcome difficulties
to acquire knowledge about an unknown country
cross-cultural contacts and encounters

Humour
is the quality of being entertaining or amusing.
It may be created through various devices and
nations/people may differ in their sense of humour.
to appreciate/share s.o.'s sense of humour
situational/verbal humour
deadpan humour
dry (sense of) humour
subtle humour
infectious humour
to amuse/entertain the audience
to make fun of s.o./to ridicule s.o./
 to laugh at, about s.th.
to have/produce/create/achieve
 a humorous/comic effect
to provoke/induce laughter

Devices
Devices which create humour include:
– **Stock characters** embody/personify
 a particular idea and lack the roundness
 of a real person (compare: flat/round
 characters in fiction); stock characters are based on
 stereotypes, i.e. fixed and generally
 accepted ideas of what a particular
 type of person is like (e.g. sexual, ethnic
 or professional stereotypes)
– **Verbal devices:**
 • black humour = relates to situations/
 jokes which try to amuse by making fun
 of the unpleasant things in life, e.g. murder, death.
 • euphemism = a gentle expression used
 instead of the more usual one to express
 unpleasant, frightening or embarrassing facts
 (e.g. comfort station in AE for public toilet)
 • hyperbole = a statement which is exaggerated
 • irony = saying one thing but meaning the opposite
 • pun = a play on words: a word has two different
 meanings so that the sentence it is in can be
 understood in two different ways
 • sarcasm = irony which is cutting and meant
 to hurt
 • understatement = opposite of hyperbole:
 s.th. is represented as being less important
 than it really is
– **Physical devices:**
 • slapstick = a phrase which refers to the use of
 exaggerated physical action, e.g. hitting, kicking,
 throwing things at one another and
 falling down to amuse the audience
 • parody = copying or imitating s.th. or s.o.
 in an exaggerated way

Barriers and bridges

Role cards for the ambassadors' game (SB S. 96–97)

You are the ambassador for **Botslavia**. In your country it is considered polite not to look directly at the person you are talking to. Fix your attention on a point just above his or her shoulder.
Remember to be as polite and respectful as possible in your tone and the selection of your topics.

You are the ambassador for **Gothland**. In your country it is considered polite to stand fairly close to the person you are speaking to, without actually touching. If they move away from you, you should move closer to maintain the distance.
Remember to be as polite and respectful as possible in your tone and the selection of your topics.

You are the ambassador for **Rana**. In your country it is considered polite to repeat the last thing your partner said.
Remember to be as polite and respectful as possible in your tone and the selection of your topics.

You are the ambassador for **Toko**. In your country it is considered polite to pay as many compliments to the person you are talking to as possible, e.g. regarding his or her good looks/excellent command of English/smart clothes.
Remember to be as polite and respectful as possible in your tone and the selection of your topics.

You are the ambassador for **Montuvia**. In your country it is considered polite to remain silent and nod for about ten seconds before answering a question.
Remember to be as polite and respectful as possible in your tone and the selection of your topics.

You are the ambassador for **Manocco**. In your country it is considered polite to welcome your partner with a long, low bow, after which you stand roughly 1.50 metres from them. Keep this distance at all times.
Remember to be as polite and respectful as possible in your tone and the selection of your topics.

You are the ambassador for **Herin**. In your country it is considered polite to give an initial welcoming bow and then to place both hands together throughout the conversation, as if you were praying.
Remember to be as polite and respectful as possible in your tone and the selection of your topics.

You are the ambassador for **New Westland**. In your country it is considered polite to give your partner a firm handshake and use their Christian name during a conversation.
Remember to be as polite and respectful as possible in your tone and the selection of your topics.

You are the ambassador for **Translavia**. In your country it is considered polite to welcome your partner with a kiss on both cheeks and to move on only after a final handshake.
Remember to be as polite and respectful as possible in your tone and the selection of your topics.

You are the ambassador for **Patemala**. In your country it is considered polite to greet and say goodbye to your partner with a handshake using both hands, and a bow. Inquire about the well-being of at least four family members.
Remember to be as polite and respectful as possible in your tone and the selection of your topics.

You are the ambassador for **Arragua**. In your country it is considered impolite to directly face a person who is talking to you. Try to stand at a right angle to him or her when you are listening. Then turn and face him or her when it is your turn to speak.
Remember to be as polite and respectful as possible in your tone and the selection of your topics.

You are the ambassador for **Kirkmenistan**. In your country it is considered polite to applaud each time the person you are talking to asks a question or makes a statement that you think is interesting.
Remember to be as polite and respectful as possible in your tone and the selection of your topics.

You are the ambassador for **Fania**. In your country it is considered polite to keep constant eye contact when someone is talking to you. (Try not to blink!) When it is your turn to talk, it is considered respectful to look at the other person's feet.
Remember to be as polite and respectful as possible in your tone and the selection of your topics.

You are the ambassador for **Bekin**. In your country it is considered polite to welcome your partner with a big hug and an inquiry about his or her health. Invite him or her to your country several times.
Remember to be as polite and respectful as possible in your tone and the selection of your topics.

You are the ambassador for **Cono**. In your country it is considered polite to touch the person you are talking to on the arm while he or she is speaking.
Remember to be as polite and respectful as possible in your tone and the selection of your topics.

Barriers and bridges

Planning a chat show / panel discussion

TOPIC OF THE SHOW: _____

STEPS

1 Group work (focus on one guest or the moderator)

2 Rehearsals in 'chat show groups'
   (end with a random selection of the performing group)

3 **The chat show / panel discussion** (audience take notes as 'critical viewers')

4 Evaluation (consider ability to act in role, entertainment value, quality of language, etc.)

GROUP WORK TASKS

Guests
1 Briefly share ideas about the character you are going to play.
2 Prepare a **reduced role card** to be passed to the moderator group as quickly as possible.
3 Prepare a **survival role card** to help you during the show.

Moderator
1 Prepare your **moderator role card.**
2 Use the **reduced role cards** to familiarize yourself with the guests.
3 Agree on the seating arrangement and prepare it.

HOMEWORK

Write a viewer's comment for a TV guide. Mention the topic and guests, and comment on the moderator's performance.

Barriers and bridges

Survival role card for a guest

NAME:_____

▶ **My interest** in the topic:

▶ **Opinion** on the topic (short and sweet):

▶ My main **character traits** (they might become obvious in a chat show):

▶ **Questions** I would enjoy being asked by the **moderator**:

▶ **Questions** I would like to ask other **guests**:

▶ My **introductory statement** (written in full):

▶ **Further ideas** for the discussion in note form:

▶ **Discussion phrases** I might need when being interrupted/pointing out a misunderstanding/ responding to what someone else has said:

Barriers and bridges

Moderator role card

NAME: _____

▶ Name of **my show**:

▶ **Question time:** When questions may be asked: _____

How long it will last: _____

Number of questions permitted: _____

▶ Statements **to start the show / introduce the topic**:

▶ **Provocative statements / questions to:**

– everybody:

– guest 1:

– guest 2:

– guest 3:

– guest 4:

– guest 5:

▶ **Useful phrases**, e.g. to interrupt someone, change the subject:

Barriers and bridges

Reduced role card: guest

– basic information for the moderator –

1. Name:

2. My interest in the topic:

3. Opinion on the topic (short and sweet):

4. My main character traits (they might become obvious in a chat show…):

5. Questions I would enjoy being asked:

6. My introductory statement will focus on:

Reduced role card: guest

– basic information for the moderator –

1. Name:

2. My interest in the topic:

3. Opinion on the topic (short and sweet):

4. My main character traits (they might become obvious in a chat show…):

5. Questions I would enjoy being asked:

6. My introductory statement will focus on:

Reduced role card: guest

– basic information for the moderator –

1. Name:

2. My interest in the topic:

3. Opinion on the topic (short and sweet):

4. My main character traits (they might become obvious in a chat show…):

5. Questions I would enjoy being asked:

6. My introductory statement will focus on:

Reduced role card: guest

– basic information for the moderator –

1. Name:

2. My interest in the topic:

3. Opinion on the topic (short and sweet):

4. My main character traits (they might become obvious in a chat show…):

5. Questions I would enjoy being asked:

6. My introductory statement will focus on:

Barriers and bridges

Evaluation sheet for adverts / commercials

Product				
Target group				
Advertising strategies • printed advert • radio advert • TV commercial				
Formal aspects (printed ad) **Layout** • visuals • colours • body copy **Language** • diction • syntax • tone • rhetorical devices **The body copy as a persuasive text**				
Presentation structure, organization, moderation media management, entertainment value eye contact with audience, address audience ("You…") …				

Klettbuch 510471 – *Skyline, Advanced Level: C*
© Ernst Klett Verlag GmbH, Stuttgart, 2004.

Barriers and bridges

Useful vocabulary to evaluate a presentation

General phrases
I was impressed/positively surprised by… • It was fun/a good idea to… • I really enjoyed… • What I especially liked about … was… • The most interesting aspect of your presentation was…

Positive adjectives
useful • informative • easy to understand • systematic • well-organized • carefully structured • entertaining • almost professional • perfect • convincing • creative • effective…

Personal impressions
I don't fully understand why… • I didn't find … useful • I had the impression that… • To be honest, I was not happy about… • At some points I found it hard to… • I am not sure if it was really necessary to…

Polite suggestions
Next time you might consider…/it might be a good idea to… • What about (using)…? • You could easily improve your presentation if you paid more attention to…

voice	(body) language	structure	content	media
• reduce/increase/adjust **speed** • little **variation** • put more **emphasis** on key words • avoid unnecessary **pauses** • speak **fluently**/clearly/as freely as possible • a distinct **pronunciation** • vary the tone and **volume** of your voice • talk in a friendly way	• **facial expression**: calm; establish and keep **eye contact** • face the audience at all times • maintain an erect, confident **posture** • stand firmly but relax • moderate but supportive use of **gestures** • show/signal **self-confidence** • smile • behave naturally • **language**: use short, clear sentences; familiar vocabulary	**Introduction** • greet the audience • state the topic/aim of your presentation • inform about… • catch and hold the audience's attention with/by… **Transitions** • should be clearly structured, easy-to-follow • divide the presentation into units with clear transitions • link the sections • signal a new idea • make short pauses **Conclusion** • repeat and emphasize ideas • finish with a conclusion/summary/an appeal • finish politely: thank your audience for listening/their attention	• provide **information**: facts and figures • express an opinion • present arguments and reasons • give examples • draw conclusions • demonstrate a good knowledge of the topic, be well-prepared	• coordinate media management • make use of **prompt cards** • attract attention • explain a point • use a legible print size/large print • manage the **overhead projector** • place a transparency on the projector • give people enough time to read

Group presentations…

involve all group members • take advantage of special talents • necessitate the co-ordination of the different contributions • include a moderator to link the parts of the presentation and make a concluding statement • should be carefully rehearsed • are more successful if only group members who are playing an active part are 'on stage' at one time.

Test: Why Germans love the British

Andreas, a cultured and well-travelled German lawyer who became a good friend in Berlin is such an Anglophile that sometimes I feel he needs restraining.

"It's just so beauuuuuutiful," he says of almost every corner of the British Isles he has visited.

When the conversation turns to London, where his wife, a diplomat, was posted for several years, he goes misty eyed.

The fact that German diplomats tend to be housed just off Hyde Park may slightly colour his judgment.

But Andreas's pro-British feelings run so deep that he could have been billeted in Deptford and still had the same passion for the place.

He goes shopping in England, although he now lives in Berlin, and loves Glyndebourne and English tea. His Anglophilia may be extreme, but the milder form of this condition is widespread among educated Germans, and that means most of them.

It is not that they believe that the British run the country better than they run their own. Far from it. Most Germans will strongly defend the German way of doing things, for example high investment in public services and high taxes to pay for them, over lean and mean Britain.

In Britain, they are convinced, all trains are dirty and late, crime is high and pensioners are poor.

Germans like paying huge sums for their health care and pensions because they love going to the doctor and living to a ripe old age in a society that protects them wonderfully to the last.

Once I had a mild cold in Berlin and a German friend said in all seriousness: "You must go to the doctor. You must not take risks with your health." In Britain, I told him, we only go to the doctor when we break a leg.

Andreas's Anglophilia, I think, has more to do with the past. Today's Germany, still traumatised by its role in two world wars, is a society paranoid about projecting itself as a nation or looking to anything in its past with pride.

Nearly 60 years after the Second World War, many of its people, even the young, are still reluctant to say they are proud of their country.

I shall never forget an interview with Chancellor Gerhard Schröder in which I tried to get him to say he was proud to be German.

He would not for fear that he might give the wrong signals. He was proud, he said, of many German achievements but not of being German.

It is against the background of extreme political correctness that Germans find British openness, humour and tradition so appealing. They have a need to let go, and to feel patriotic, but feel they cannot do so at home.

Hence their fascination with the monarchy and prime events on our social calendar such as the *Last Night of the Proms*. The Queen's Golden Jubilee was a truly great event in Germany, a source of intense fascination.

When *Der Spiegel* wrote a peculiarly warped and misjudged attack on the monarchy to coincide with the Jubilee, a former ambassador to London told me over dinner that the article was a great embarrassment to his country. It was a source of national shame.

Occasionally, particularly in Berlin, some older Germans withdraw when they hear English voices. But most are friendly and surprisingly open.

As we were packing up to leave Berlin a neighbour, now well into his 80s, came to pick apples from our trees. We got chatting about Britain. My wife asked him: "Have you ever been to London?"

"No," he said with a smile and laugh, "just over it."

(608 words)

By Toby Helm, *Daily Telegraph*, September 25, 2002.

---

12 **to be billeted somewhere** to be provided with somewhere to live – **Deptford** [detfəd] socially disadvantaged area in south-east London –
15 **Glyndebourne** ['glaɪndbɔːn] *(GB)* opera house situated in a town of the same name south of London – 52 **Last Night of the Proms** final event in a series of concerts entitled the Henry Wood Promenade Concerts; they are held in the Albert Hall, London

Tasks

1 What picture of the Germans does the writer convey in the article?

2 Examine the journalistic style Toby Helm uses to make his article accessible to and readable for his target group. What information does the article give about the writer himself?

3 In response to the article, Andreas (cf. ll. 1–3) replies critically in the form of a comment. Write this comment, which is to be published in the *Daily Telegraph* two days after the publication of the above article.

Barriers and bridges

Test: Germans – the new Americans?

It was getting on for midday and people were sitting out in the sunny plazas having lunch or eating ice-creams. Almost without exception they looked healthy and prosperous and often were strikingly good-looking. I remember German cities from twenty years before being full of businessmen who looked just as Germans were supposed to look – fat and arrogant. You would see them gorging themselves on piles of sausages and potatoes […] at all hours of the day, but now they seemed to be picking delicately at salads and fish, and looking fit and tanned – and, more than that, friendly and happy. […]

At all events, this relaxed and genial air was something that I hadn't associated with Germans before, at least not those aged over twenty-five. There was no whiff of arrogance here, just a quiet confidence, which was clearly justified by the material wealth around them. All those little doubts we've all had about the wisdom of letting the Germans become the masters of Europe evaporated in the Hamburg sunshine. Forty-five years ago Hamburg was rubble. Virtually everything around me was new, even when it didn't look it. The people had made their city, and even themselves, rich and elegant and handsome through their cleverness and hard work, and they had every right to be arrogant about it, but they were not, and I admired them for that.

I don't think I can ever altogether forgive the Germans their past, not as long as I can wonder if that friendly old waiter who brings me my coffee might have spent his youth bayonetting babies or herding Jews into gas ovens. Some things are so monstrous as to be unpardonable. But I don't see how anyone could go to Germany now and believe for a moment that that could ever happen again. Germans, it struck me, are becoming the new Americans – rich, ambitious, hard-working, health-conscious, sure of their place in the world. Seeing Hamburg now, I was happy to hand them my destiny.

(337 words)

From *The Lost Continent & Neither Here Nor There: Two Of The Funniest Travel Books Ever Written* by Bill Bryson, London: Secker and Warburg, 1992, pp. 356–357.

"Vell Englander, answer ze kvestion! Vy do you not like us?"

Cartoon: Front-page headline: GERMANS – AGGRESSIVE, BULLYING, SENTIMENTAL, ANXIOUS TO BE LIKED, MINORITY COMPLEX

Tasks

1 How does Bill Bryson view Germany and the Germans?

2 Analyse in detail the various images of the Germans visualized in the above cartoon. The cartoon was originally published in the *Daily Mail*. What effect do you expect the cartoon had on British readers?

3 Do **one** of the following:
a) Write a letter (dated back to the year 1992) to Bill Bryson responding to the extract from his travelogue. Include references to the above cartoon which you came across two years before on a summer holiday in Britain.
or

b) Taking recent trends in German society into consideration, comment on Bill Bryson's statement: "Germans […] are becoming the new Americans." (l. 33). In your comment, refer to the traditional German stereotypes presented in the cartoon and also in other media.

Mündliche Abschlussprüfung zu "Barriers and bridges"

Thema: Across cultures – overcoming barriers and building bridges

Guest 1
As a psychologist specializing in stereotypes, you know how national stereotypes work. Explain how the images, which nations have of one another, come into existence and suggest how to cope effectively with stereotypes.

Guest 2
You are a cartoonist/journalist for a British tabloid and regularly contribute cartoons/articles dealing with incidents which seem to confirm the traditional images of Germans which are popular in Britain.

Guest 3
You are a foreign correspondent for a British quality paper who has been living in, and reporting from, Germany for many years.

Guest 4
You are the former British foreign secretary Robin Cook. You still hold the same views on Britain's role in Europe as you did in 2001.

Guest 5
You are a well-known German politician, who strongly feels that Germany needs social, economic and educational reforms in order to cope with the challenge of globalization.

Guest 6
As a senior manager for a major German TV channel, you have to decide whether to buy the right to broadcast "The Germans" episode of *Fawlty Towers* in Germany, or not.

Guest 7
After leaving school, you travelled around the world. Now you are the editor of a series of guide books which aims to promote intercultural understanding by preparing travellers for culture shocks.

Guest 8
As the manager of a German company which operates worldwide, you point out the benefits of working abroad as early as possible in one's professional career.

Guest 9
Feel free to be yourself! Bring in your own intercultural experiences and views.

Barriers and bridges

Test: Germans 'take too many holidays'

"LAZY Germans" might seem like an oxymoron, but not to Germany's economics minister, who said yesterday his compatriots take too many holidays and are damaging the country's prospects.

5   Wolfgang Clement called for an increase in working hours and a cut in the number of holidays, saying Germans take an embarrassing number compared with other European workers.

"With regards to holidays, public days off and working
10 hours we have without a doubt reached our limit," he said. "Anyone who compares our holiday calendar with that of other countries can really start to worry." Germany's economy is one of the worst performing of all industrial countries and it has the lowest growth rate in
15 Europe. Unemployment, at 10.4 per cent, is at the highest level since German reunification, and Germany tops the table for *freizeit*, or free time.

The nation with a reputation for hard work has on average 43 days off a year – 13 public holidays, the rest
20 annual leave. It is followed by Austria and Spain which each have 37.

Britain comes fourth in a survey of 10 countries by the German Employers' Association, with 33.5 days, nine of them public holidays.

25 Mr Clement's remarks were partly directed at steel workers in eastern Germany who are striking for a shorter, 35-hour working week. Unemployment is at 18.3 per cent. "This amounts to a conflict at the wrong time in a totally wrong place," he said.

30 The Social Democrat, impatiently trying to push through economic reform against strong opposition, not least in his own party, has gained support from economics experts who say a cut in holidays or a one-hour increase in the working week could boost the economy, now close to
35 recession, by 1.6 per cent.

Economic analysts have predicted increased growth of 5 per cent next year, when several public holidays are due at weekends, said Mr Clement.   (275 words)

By Kate Connolly, *Electronic Telegraph*, June 19, 2003.

ILLUSTRATION: PHILIP ARGENT

Tasks

1 Compare the text and cartoon in terms of the images they convey of Germany's economic performance.

2 Explain the difference(s) between the two texts by placing them in a historical context. In your answer, refer to the traditional German image abroad.

3 Do **one** of the following tasks:
   a) In your experience, how do young Germans today feel about work and careers in the face of recent social and economic change at both national and international levels? Write a comment.
   or:
   b) Write a speech for a political opponent who takes up Mr Clement's criticism, but also calls for social reform at all levels and a new political role for Germany.

Barriers and bridges

On the phone

International telephone alphabet

A [eɪ] = Alfa	B [biː] = Bravo	C [siː] = Charlie	D [diː] = Delta
E [iː] = Echo	F [ef] = Foxtrot	G [dʒiː] = Golf	H [eɪtʃ] = Hotel
I [aɪ] = India	J [dʒeɪ] = Juliet	K [keɪ] = Kilo	L [el] = Lima
M [em] = Mike	N [en] = November	O [əʊ] = Oscar	P [piː] = Papa
Q [kjuː] = Quebec	R [ɑːr] = Romeo	S [es] = Sierra	T [tiː] = Tango
U [juː] = Uniform	V [viː] = Victor	W [ˈdʌbljuː] = Whisky	X [eks] = X-ray
Y [waɪ] = Yankee	Z [zed] = Zulu		

Note: Say "B as in Bravo" or "B for Bravo" not "B like ..."

Making a phone call

This is ... speaking
I'm calling from...
I'd like to speak to .../the person in charge of ...
... leave a message for...
I'm calling about... / The reason I'm calling is...
I'm returning your call.
I'm calling in reply to your ...

Receiving a phone call

Just a moment, please.
I'll put you through.
Sorry, the line's engaged *(BE)* / busy *(AE)*.
Would you like to hold?
Would you like to speak to s.o. else?
Would you like to call back later?
Would you like to try X's direct line later?

Note: When answering the phone in a private residence, English people often just say "Hello?" This is not impolite, just the beginning of a conversation. The caller should then identify him- or herself "This is ...".
When answering the phone in a business environment, English people usually give the name of the company/department and their own name, e.g. Short Systems/Personnel Department, Jane Brown speaking. Can I help you?

Tasks

Act out the following telephone calls in pairs (or in groups of three for the last task). Try to use the information above.

Partner A has read about vacancies for trainees at Short Systems for the summer. You would like to speak to someone who can give you more information. Ring up the company.

Partner B is the receptionist at Short Systems. You make a note of any enquiries about traineeships and take down callers' names, addresses, telephone/mobile numbers and e-mail addresses. You promise that someone will get back to them as soon as possible.

Partner A has applied for a position as a trainee at Short Systems and received an invitation to arrange an interview with a Mr Jones in the personnel department. Ring up the company.

Partner B is the receptionist at Short Systems. Brian Jones is a busy man and it is sometimes difficult to get through to him.

Partner A did an interview for a traineeship at Short Systems a week ago but has heard nothing since. Ring up the company and try to speak to the personnel manager Brian Jones as he conducted the interview.

Partner B is Brian Jones's secretary. He has gone to a trade fair in Cologne and will not be back until next week. You make a note of all callers' names, their reasons for calling and contact numbers so that Brian Jones can deal with them on his return.

Partner A has been offered a summer traineeship in the sales department at Short Systems. You have to contact Janet Murphy to get more details about when you should start. Ring up Short Systems.

Partner B is the receptionist at Short Systems. You know that Janet Murphy is ill but her colleague Miranda White is covering for her.

Partner C is Janet's colleague, Miranda White. Unfortunately, Janet is ill but you have all of the details about the new trainee.

Barriers and bridges

The world of work

Job application
to write a CV / résumé
to gain work experience
education / additional qualifications and courses
academic years
to apply for a position as …
to make an appointment
to take an aptitude test
to be available for an interview …/
    for work from (date) / immediately

Letter of application
enc. (= enclosure)
to make an inquiry / to enquire about …
long-range goal, long-term prospects
to volunteer, to do voluntary work
prospective employer
to make a recommendation
to provide a list of referees /
    references from a former employer
ref. = reference number
to make a request
to meet the requirements in the advert
to do a traineeship / an apprenticeship as a(n) …
to be an intern / to do an internship *(AE)*
to have a job placement for X weeks

Character traits
to be courteous / polite / efficient
    honest / responsible / versatile
    sincere / genuine / reliable
    ambitious / competitive / innovative
    to have good time-keeping skills
to enjoy a challenge when confronted
    with problems
to get hands-on experience
to use one's initiative in order to
    solve / tackle problems

The workplace
workforce / staff / personnel
job title
assistant manager / trainee manager
junior / senior manager
superior / employer
colleague / co-worker / fellow employee
to have a desk in an open-plan office
to share an office with … people
to do administrative work / clerical work

to work in a department such as …
    public relations / PR
    (the) purchasing (department)
    sales
    advertising
    accounts
    distribution
    personnel
the employers' association
trade union member
chairman, to chair the board of directors
managing director
to work in an area such as
    wholesaleing / retailing / trade
    banking
    telecommunications
    catering
    engineering
    computers
    product development
to attend trade fairs / exhibitions
to go on business trips (to…)
to travel a lot for work
to spend a lot of time on the road
to work in a branch (office) of …
factory / on the shop floor
corporate world / corporation
to have dealings with X company /
    international partners

Working conditions
core time
to do overtime
to work part-time, full-time, freelance
to have long working hours
flexible working hours / flexitime
to do seasonal work
to have a summer job
to be on sick leave
to cover for s.o. who is …
    ill / on sick leave / on maternity leave
    on holiday / on a business trip
to negotiate with an employer for …
salary, wages, pay
to have steady employment
a salaried worker
on a pay scale
sliding pay scale
pension scheme
bonus system
to suffer from stress
a work-related injury

Facing a global future

Didaktisches Inhaltsverzeichnis

	Titel	Textsorte (Wortzahl ca.)	Thema	Text- und Spracharbeit	Textproduktion (schriftlich/mündlich)
	Building a dream SB S. 114, TB S. 116	advert (188 words)	social, technological trends	describe a photo • interpret the content/layout of an advert • talk about advertising	write product information • speculate about the use of robots • write/act out a dialogue • write a mini-saga
📺	**Robots** SB S. 116, TB S. 117	documentary (607 words)	qualities/functions of modern robots	viewing comprehension	design a robot • discuss the use of machines
	Surefire predictions SB S. 116, TB S. 118	expository text (474 words)	history and future of technological advances	text analysis • describe tone	make predictions • assess impact of technological developments • write a criticism • hold a 'hot chair' discussion
	Professor Cyborg SB S. 118, TB S. 119	expository text (919 words)	computer implants in human beings	evaluate the benefits/dangers of computer chip implants in humans	discuss issues/present ideas
	Shopping for... SB S. 120, TB S. 120 📦 TB S. 132	expository text (774 words)	genetic engineering, designer babies, human cloning	assess ethical consequences of genetic engineering and cloning	brainstorm for ideas • talk about a cartoon • design a baby • hold a debate
	The brave new ... SB S. 122, TB S. 120	film review (726 words)	genetic engineering, societies in science fiction	comment on a still, character, a quote	compare film reviews with one's viewing experiences • analyse a scene • imagine/act out a dialogue
📺	**Forests for life** SB S. 124, TB S. 121	commercial (190 words)	deforestation, destruction of habitats	analyse and interpret a commercial (composition/message)	plan/present a commercial • devise campaign materials
	The view... SB S. 124, TB S. 122	expository text (551 words)	benefits of genetically modified plants	collect arguments • talk about a cartoon • discuss benefits of biotechnology	design an advert promoting GM foods
	What happens if ... SB S. 126, TB S. 123	advert (362 words)	negative economic effects of GM food	interpret the layout of an advert • analyse language and style	compare advert with a text • internet project
📺	**The challenge...** SB S. 127, TB S. 124	filmed speech (722 words)	speed of change in society and the resulting anxieties	viewing comprehension • understand and interpret political speeches	write a comment • discuss a quote
🔘	**Globalization ...** SB S. 127, TB S. 125 📦 TB S. 137	commentary (500 words)	the impact of globalization	discuss a quote • listen for gist/detail • complete a cloze test	write a comment • discuss an idea
	The other side... SB S. 128, TB S. 127 📦 TB S. 138, 139	non-fiction extract (1,060 words)	global work practices of multinationals	brainstorm ideas: 'global village' • assess global marketing strategies and work practices	do internet research about an international company
Over to you	**Globalization** SB S. 130, TB S. 127 📦 TB S. 136	expository text (654 words)	globalization, globality, culture	differentiate between concepts of globalization and culture	collect ideas in a table • give an opinion

Facing a global future

Einleitung

Das Kapitel "Facing a global future" behandelt zukunftsweisende Themen, die nicht nur Fortschritte im Bereich 'Science and Technology' als Ergebnis wissenschaftlicher Forschung aufgreifen, sondern den Menschen in den Mittelpunkt wissenschaftlichen Fortschritts stellen – als Nutznießer oder als potentielles Opfer seiner technischen Errungenschaften. Das 21. Jahrhundert wird die Menschen mit neuen Weltanschauungen, Lebensperspektiven und einer Weltordnung konfrontieren, deren Wertvorstellungen sich ständig im Wandel befinden werden. Der unaufhaltsame Prozess der Globalisierung und die spektakulären Entwicklungen im Bereich der Medizin (Genforschung) und Technik (Telekommunikation/Automatisierung) werden die Menschen in Zukunft ständig dazu auffordern, ihr Handeln vor dem Hintergrund gesellschaftlicher Verantwortung zu überprüfen. Da die Welt im 'global village' sich nicht mehr auf den unmittelbaren Wirkungskreis einzelner Individuen begrenzen lässt, müssen Menschen als 'global citizens' diese Verantwortung bezüglich moralischer und ethischer Vorstellungen auch auf globaler Ebene tragen. Die Komplexität dieser Themen wird durch die ebenso komplexen Inhalte dieses Kapitels aufgegriffen. Die S sollen sich nicht nur mit anspruchsvollen Texten und Medien auseinandersetzen, um ihre mündliche und schriftliche Sprachkompetenz zu verbessern, sondern müssen sich kritischen Themen stellen, die ihnen sowohl privat als auch beruflich (in der Medizin, in der Wissenschaft, der Wirtschaft und dem Handel) in ihrem späteren Leben begegnen werden – und auf globaler Ebene werden diese Auseinandersetzungen über soziale Verantwortung zunehmend, wenn nicht ausschließlich, in englischer Sprache erfolgen. Die Auswahl der Textsorten und Medien ist in diesem Kapitel bewusst auf die Entfaltung eigenständiger Meinungsbildung ausgerichtet: Die S sollen lernen, eigene Meinungen zu entwickeln und diese auch begründet zu vertreten, ihre Positionen jedoch auch in Debatten, Diskussionen, Rollenspielen und Vorträgen kritisch zu hinterfragen. Um der Entwicklung kritischer Meinungsbildung gerecht zu werden, sollen die Texte nicht nur zur Ausbildung textanalytischer Sprachkompetenz beitragen, sondern die S auch dazu anleiten, kreativ und eigenständig mit den Themeninhalten umzugehen, z. B. bei dem Entwurf von Werbekampagnen, dem Ausarbeiten von Referaten mithilfe des Internets oder der Präsentation eines Firmenprofils von international tätigen Firmen und Großkonzernen. Da derartige (Sprach)Kompetenzen von den S in Studium und Beruf gefordert werden, ist ihnen große Bedeutung beizumessen. Selbstverständlich kann die Auswahl an Texten und Medien nur einen Ausschnitt dieses hochkomplexen Themengebiets offenbaren, doch thematische Aspekte wie die fortschreitende Automatisierung der Gesellschaft, die Entwicklungen im Bereich der Gen- und Klonforschung, die Errungenschaften der Telekommunikation, die wachsende Umweltzerstörung sowie die wachsende Kluft zwischen der industrialisierten Welt und den Entwicklungsländern sind gegenwarts- und zukunftsrelevante Themen, die auch das Leben der S beeinflussen und geeignete Ausgangspunkte für weitere Forschungsprojekte (z. B. für Facharbeiten) darstellen.

Kernwortschatz: Kopiervorlagen TB S. 132 und 133

Während der Lektüre der Texte können die S einen Kernwortschatz zum Thema 'genetic engineering' und 'globalization' in Form von 'word fields' zusammenstellen. Siehe Beispiele auf TB Seiten 132 und 133.

Building a dream   SB S.114

Looking and thinking

1 This is a typical family portrait. The family members (father, mother, son and daughter) are ordinary-looking and probably Americans. They are grouped in front of the family home and are smiling at the camera. Even the dog, possibly a golden retriever, is a typical family pet. The only 'odd' family member is Asimo, a robot built by Honda, which is standing at the centre of the photo and waving at the camera. The reader focuses immediately on the robot and its featureless 'face' in particular. The reader can only guess at what is behind the black, gleaming visor. Honda's advert seems to suggest that Asimo is a robotic friend, who is just as important and welcome as any other family member. He may be smaller than everyone else, but he seems to be the most important 'person' in the photo.

2 *Characteristics:* Asimo could be a robotic housemaid or nanny which performs household chores. For example, it could cook and serve food, read the paper to you, clean the house and watch the children. It could also function as a mobile personal computer or home office, and type letters or send e-mails which you dictate. A humanoid machine like Asimo would make life easier and more comfortable. It would never contradict you or let you down.

Exploring the text

1 Die S sollten:
– ihre Werbetexte mit dem Text der Anzeige vergleichen und feststellen, inwiefern sich der Aufbau ihres Textes von dem der Werbefachleute unterscheidet.
– erklären, worauf sie in ihrem Werbetext Wert gelegt haben und welche sprachlichen Mittel (Metaphern, Symbole, Alliterationen, Wortspiele usw.) sie verwendet haben.
– begründen, welche Funktionen ihre Werbeanzeige dem Roboter zuspricht und welchen Nutzen die Käufer von einem derartigen Roboter erwarten können.

2 According to Honda, Asimo was designed to "actually help people" (ll. 2–3). This suggests that a robot needs to have human abilities, such as being able to see, think and hear, and it has to master the complexities of movement. One day, Asimo is supposed to assist elderly people, for example, with their household chores. If s.o.'s body does not function properly anymore, Asimo can serve as a substitute "set of eyes, ears and legs" (ll. 15–16).

3 a) *Tagline:* We're building a dream, one robot at a time; slogan: Honda – The power of dreams
b) Both the tagline and slogan convey the idea that the future is happening right now at Honda. The progressive tense in the tagline emphasizes the idea that the development of future technologies is an ongoing process, and Honda is trying to make dreams come true. The word "dream", which is used in the tagline and the slogan, is a powerful, emotive word that people associate with desires waiting to be fulfilled. Who does not dream of a future in which one is comfortable, prosperous and healthy? Honda's dream of building a fully functional robot may not necessarily correspond to other people's dreams, but the word "dream" has one fundamental connotation: to achieve s.th. that was once beyond your power. As regards human beings, there is nothing we cannot do if we only want it to happen: we have the power to control the future by turning our dreams into reality.

A step further

■ **Speculate about the use of robots in the home**
Positive effects: Robots as mechanical servants help with household chores, drive the car, do the shopping, entertain and talk to you when you feel lonely, look after children and sick people, repair the car or household appliances…
Negative effects: When they develop a mind and memory of their own, they may become disobedient and 'too intelligent'; you may feel observed and controlled by the robot's presence in your home; it could malfunction and threaten you and your family instead of serving and protecting you…

■ **Write a mini-saga**
– Die S sollen ihre selbständig verfassten Dialoge vorspielen.
– *Beispiel:* Asimo sighed and spoke to Honda's Headquarters. "It's useless, I've tried hard, but once I've wired and electrified these humans, their fuses blow and their control units collapse. The parents die straight away, their kids go mad." – "Don't worry Asimo, just get rid of them and report to Mission Control."

Robots

SB S. 116

Transkript

Claire: Now you might think what you've just seen was a piece of video taken by someone walking down a corridor holding a camera. But it wasn't a human being at all. It was a robot.
Now robots aren't new. They've been used in industry for many years.
But scientists are working on new developments all the time and some of the most exciting new developments are happening right here. This is the computer science department at the University of York. This is Doctor Nick Pears. He's a computer scientist and an expert in robots. So Nick, what exactly is a robot?
Nick: Well a robot's a device that's equipped with some sensors that can take in information about the robot's outside world, process that information which allows the robot to do something useful in the real world. This particular robot has two main sensory systems. Round the rim here you can see a set of sensors. It uses the sound waves to work out where it is. On the top here is a video camera which works as the robot's eye. It takes in visual information from the outside world and processes that to work out where it is.
Claire: Some basic robots are already in use in everyday life. In this restaurant in London, for example, a robot goes around serving drinks. If someone gets in the way, the robot stops and lets them pass.
Many of the robots in use now are not really robots. They are automated machines. They don't have proper sensors and they can't learn, but some of them are very sophisticated. This robotic dog, for example, which was built by Sony, is called Ivo. It can move around. It can use different parts of its body and it can show emotions. For example, it wags its tail when it's happy. But is it really happy? And is this really an emotion?
Claire: Nick's robot is called Arnold. Arnold sends information about what he sees and hears to Nick at his computer. Nick can then send information or instructions back to Arnold.
Nick believes that in the future we will have robots at home and they will do many of the things people do now. For example, the washing up, the cleaning, the cooking and the shopping. Arnold can identify straight lines and moving objects. If he sees something in the way, he can stop or move around it. Eventually Arnold will be able to recognize people and understand language. So Nick, looking ahead do you think robots will make a big difference to our lives?
Nick: I think they will make a big difference to our lives in a number of different areas. For example, in factories we may have robots moving materials from one part of the factory to another without any human intervention. In hospitals we might have robots performing operations. Another area would be something like exploration. We could send robots to different planets to explore their surfaces. And another area might be all kinds of dangerous situations where there may be fires or explosions. In those situations it would make much more sense to send a robot in rather than risking a human's life.
Claire: And what about in the home?
Nick: I think robots will make a big difference to our day-to-day lives. They'll do basic tasks such as cleaning the house, do the shopping, do the cooking, work in the garden and so on.
Claire: So eventually robots will be exactly the same as human beings?
Nick: Well, not exactly.
Claire: Oh hello, Arnold. Um, Nick, are you there? Nick, could I have a cup of tea? Please? … Oh thanks, Arnold.

Before you watch

■ **Describe the difference between machines and robots**
A machine is an automated device or tool designed to perform tasks. According to this definition, a robot is a machine as well, but we often associate human abilities and characteristics with robots.

■ **Design a robot**
Qualities: It only obeys / is loyal to one owner, it has the same mental age as its owner, it can speak English / French / Spanish so its owner can practise his / her language skills…

Facing a global future

Functions: It can help with homework, do its master's chores and keep his/her room tidy/clothes clean and ironed; it can negotiate with parents on behalf of its teenage owner…

While you watch

1 Several robots are shown in the sequence: they manufacture watches, make sushi and serve drinks. Ivo, the robotic dog can imitate a dog's movements and behaviour.
2 Dr Pear's robot is equipped with a sensory system which allows it to determine its position. The sensors use soundwaves and are located on the upper rim of the robot. There is a videocamera on top of the robot which functions as the robot's eye and processes visual information from the outside world. The camera and sensors are connected to Dr Pear's computer, from which he controls the robot.
3 a) They are simply automated machines. They do not have the senses that humans do.
b) Sony's robot Ivo is a robotic toy that can move around. It can move parts of its body and wag its tail. It is supposed to imitate a dog's behaviour as authentically as possible.
4 Robots can do household chores such as the washing up, the cleaning or the cooking. Robots are used, or will be used, to move materials without human intervention. They may perform operations in hospitals and they could be used in the exploration of outer space or in situations which are too dangerous for ordinary human beings.

A step further

■ Discuss the use of machines

Machines	Things you would miss…
home entertainment equipment such as personal computers/video game consoles	– entertainment value and excitement; – internet access to help with homework and e-mail friends
mobile phones/mobiles	– getting text messages and being easy to reach
answering machines	– being able to pick up phone messages
personal stereos, CD and DVD players, TVs and VCRs	– entertainment value, access to music and information
household appliances, e.g. washing machines, tumble dryers, vacuum cleaners, microwave ovens, fridges, freezers	– the convenience of having one's clothes washed and dried without any effort, having instant hot food, not having to plan meals…

Surefire predictions   SB S. 116–117

Before you read

■ Make predictions

Mankind will be better off: better healthcare due to progress in medical research, increased longevity, or improved quality of life for the old and sick because organs and limbs can be replaced as they wear out; people will work less and enjoy more free time because machines and computers will do the work; we can travel to the stars and live on distant planets; natural resources like oil and coal will be replaced by inexhaustible supplies of chemical substitutes or by sustainable energy sources; engines will run on water or oxygen, environmental pollution will be reduced by environmentally-friendly machines and factories, etc.
Mankind will be worse off: Progress in artificial intelligence may lead to the creation of machines that are superior to human beings; mankind may be dominated by powerful robots; computer devices and surveillance equipment may be used to monitor and even control whole populations; progress in genetic engineering may see the advent of human clones that will replace ordinary humans and cloned armies will be sent to war; designer babies will be created; people will no longer take an interest in the preservation of animal species threatened by extinction as they can be reproduced through genetic engineering…

■ Assess the impact of technological developments

Medicine: open-heart surgery, organ transplants, life-support machines, disinfectants, X-ray machines and CAT scans, antibiotics and anaesthetics…
Manufacturing: the invention of all kinds of machines, the steam engine, the power loom, the combustion engine, automated machines, the assembly line, computers, robots…
Telecommunications: the invention of the telephone and the radio, satellite communication systems, TVs, camera and cinema technologies, personal computer communication systems like the internet and e-mail, photocopiers, fax machines, mobile phones…

Background information

Julian L. Simon (1932–1998) was a professor of business administration at the University of Maryland. He wrote many books and articles about economics.

Exploring the text

1 Current technologies are based on inventions made during the industrial revolution (ll. 15–16). In the text, the term "industrial revolution" (l. 2) is written in inverted commas. Either the writer wants to emphasize its importance, or he wants to stress that this is not a precisely defined era in human history: the industrial revolution is an ongoing process that "is only part of the [technological] upheaval" which humans are faced with (ll. 4–5).
2 Due to developments in medicine people are healthier and have a longer life expectancy (ll. 12–14). In the past, people could not take it for granted that specialists and drugs would be available when they were sick. Healthcare and medicines, which only the rich could afford in the past, are now available to greater numbers of people in developed countries. Health and life expectancy are also closely related to economic factors: only healthy workers can contribute to economic growth, early deaths and disease will negatively affect the workforce and reduce productivity.
3 The high standard of living in rich countries attracts migrants from poor and developing countries. There is a growing demand for young workers in industrialized countries where the workforce is ageing rapidly. Indeed, usually it is young people who decide to migrate in search of work.
4 There is a limit to our physical abilities: we cannot live forever unless we undergo genetic change. Communication

Facing a global future

and transport facilities cannot speed up any further. Extraordinary discoveries in technology would be necessary to change our lives even further.

5 If there are no economic shortages any more, people might reconsider the importance of human values. They might rediscover things which are usually very important to human beings, such as love and mutual understanding, the ability to communicate with one another and the desire to take care of others, perhaps on a global scale. Of course, taking current trends into account, the writer is not too convinced that this re-examination of human values will happen, which is why he wishes mankind luck.

6 a)/b) *Tone/Feelings:* The writer seems to be resigned: Whatever is supposed to happen will do so eventually. Mankind does not seem to be able to control its fate. Change – be it fast or slow – is unstoppable and resistance is futile. Some passages of the text appear slightly cynical, for example, the reference to a possible holocaust (ll. 7–8) that might delay change and progress, but would not stop it. The process of migration is referred to as a drama because it triggers off a cycle which repeats itself again and again. The fact that the writer wishes mankind luck underlines his lack of optimism about the future.

A step further

■ **Write a criticism**

Mögliche Ideen: Predictions which may not happen:
- "within a century or two ... the rest of humanity is almost sure to attain the amenities of modern living standards" (ll. 6–7). Many developing countries have been unable to improve their economic situation in the last centuries and it is unlikely that their situation will improve, considering the level of national debt many of them face, natural disasters and wars can reverse the progress made in a country by a hundred years;
- "the spreading of a high level of living will be speeded by ... increased migration from poor to rich countries" (ll. 20–21): migrants often do menial, poorly paid jobs, which barely support themselves and their families back home (siehe "Mexico is memory" SB S. 10–11 und "Being illegal in the US", Begleit-Video/-DVD, Ausschnitt 1.

■ **Hold a 'hot chair' discussion**
Siehe Skills files "Discussions", SB S. 193.

Professor Cyborg   SB S. 118–119

Zusätzliche Aufgabe: Before you read

■ Nowadays people and animals can have computer chips implanted under their skin. Discuss the advantages and disadvantages of this procedure.
Advantages: Famous people are always in fear of being kidnapped. They could easily be tracked down with the help of surveillance systems;
Parents can keep track of their children's whereabouts.
Disadvantages: People will assume that they are constantly being spied upon as in an Orwellian society.
Carriers will no longer feel independent. Surveillance technology may also give them a false feeling of security: they may think that s.o. will rush to help whenever they are in danger.
Lost pets can be found very quickly.
The whereabouts of criminals and prisoners on parole could be monitored by the police.

Exploring the text

1 Kevin Warwick wanted to find out whether his behaviour would be affected in any way when his brain was linked to a computer by the transponders. This was shown to be the case as he noticed that he felt closer to the computer after a time (ll. 24–25). The experiment also showed that Prof Warwick could control his surroundings: his computer booted when he entered the building, lights went on and doors opened automatically for him. The transponders also allowed him to be located in the university building.

2 Professor Warwick dismisses the idea that the implant turned him into a helpless victim of total surveillance, typical of an Orwellian society (ll. 16–17). Indeed, he benefited from what the transponders allowed him to do. However, he admits that the positive experiences and feelings of power that such devices produce could blind people to their negative features (ll. 19–20).

3 a) *Benefits:* Electrical impulses sent from his brain may be able to operate computers without Professor Warwick having to use keyboards or a computer mouse (ll. 38–40). He may be able to re-experience his own nervous signals by "playing back" the recorded data (ll. 43–44)

4 *Disadvantages:* Human beings may not be entirely human anymore when computer implants provide them with additional sensory information: they may turn into "superhumans" or "computer-controlled human slaves" (ll. 58–59). Dangers of this kind outweigh the positive aspects of Prof Warwick's system. However, he himself firmly believes that intelligent machines will surpass human abilities in the years to come (ll. 64–66).

b) Die S sollen abwägen, ob diese Technologie für den Menschen eher Nachteile als Vorteile bietet.

Background information: further developments

The experiment described in the text was taken a step further on March 14th, 2002, when a microelectrode array was implanted onto the median nerve in Professor Warwick's wrist. The array had direct connections to his nerve fibres and was linked to a novel radio transmitter/receiver. This in turn was linked to a computer. The aim of the project was to generate medical benefits especially for those with spinal injuries and to improve human capabilities when joined to a machine.

Source: http://www.world-information.org/wio/program/amsterdam/events/.

A step further

■ **Discuss issues / present ideas**

a) *Indicate location:* Famous/rich people who are potential kidnap victims or pets could receive computer implants and be located with GPS. The same goes for convicted criminals such as paedophiles or murderers who are released from prison on probation. The police can check their whereabouts at all times and ensure that they do not re-offend.

Facing a global future

Influence surroundings: The disabled, and especially wheelchair users, would benefit from implants which allow them to open doors or switch appliances on and off, simply by thinking about it;
S.o. could operate machines from a distance in dangerous situations, e.g. to destroy explosives;
People could get housework done with no physical effort simply by using their brains to operate household appliances.
Justification: Implants can be justified when they benefit the disabled, give people more free time or make society more secure. It could be argued though that they also make people lazy as they no longer have to do boring housework. Implants would pose a threat to mankind as soon as they were used as mind-controlling devices, especially if they could be programmed to influence large numbers of people at the same time. People under the influence of such devices would risk losing their privacy and independence.
b) Die S sollen auf S-pages "Presentations", SB S. 182–183 hingewiesen werden.

Shopping for humans   SB S. 120–121

Before you read

■ **Brainstorming**
Siehe "Kernwortschatz", TB S. 132 für Ideen.

■ **Talk about the cartoon**
Which one am I going to pick? – Are they all the same price? – Are they all alike? – Are they any good? – What if I decide I don't like the baby I choose? – Is there a money-back guarantee? – Perhaps I had better look in a shop specializing in babies and not just in a supermarket.

Exploring the text

1 There is nothing natural about cloning human beings: the "gift of life" (ll. 2–3), which has always been considered to be something unpredictable and uncontrollable yet wonderful, will gradually lose its significance if all people need to do is to pre-select the desired characteristics of their offspring. Parents will not create a human being, but a customized product in the "ultimate shopping experience" (l. 4). The clone will be expected to satisfy its parents' desire for perfection and beauty.
2 We often associate technical aspects of engineering with the term "production". Something is produced to a certain predetermined standard and quality. The final product can then be checked to see if it meets all the necessary requirements. "Creation" is the opposite of "production". The natural creation of a human being cannot be mapped out according to a predetermined pattern, it remains unique and unpredictable. Cloning enables us to produce a human being whose 'quality', 'function' and 'design' are as predictable and reliable as those of any industrial product.
3 a) The *Book of Genesis* describes the creation of mankind as a God-given creation. Mankind was created in God's image. The "second genesis" of mankind that Jeremy Rifkin refers to in l. 15 is man-made and artificial. Anyone can "become a private god" (l. 16) and produce babies in his or her personal image.

b) Jeremy Rifkin concedes that certain hereditary diseases, which are carried in one or other of the parents' genes, could be eliminated when you clone children. Naturally, no one wants to pass on a genetic disposition for certain diseases, so it seems acceptable to produce designer babies under such circumstances. However, Jeremy Rifkin is concerned about where to draw the line. If anything is possible in the future, parents will want to benefit from these methods. Cloning could also enable us to create a new form of "immortality" (l. 37) as certain favourable genetic traits are perpetuated in future generations time and again.
4 Jeremy Rifkin is most concerned about the children who are "ordinary" or "uncloned" or born either physically or mentally disabled in a world based on the notion of perfection. He fears that they will not be treated with empathy or tolerance. Once s.o. deviates from the genetic norms and appears defective in some way or carries an error in their genetic code, they might be ostracized by a society whose members have lost the human capacity to feel sympathy for each other. Once the communal spirit of charity is lost, it cannot be revived again.

A step further

■ **Design a baby**
a) E.g. He/she should have an above-average IQ, have specific physical traits (blonde hair, be over 1.80 metres tall, have green/… eyes…), have a physique which allows him/her to be good at sports, have excellent eyesight, hearing…
b) *Happier/successful:* The baby would be equipped to be successful both academically and in the sporting world; it would be impossible to equip the baby to deal with problems which stem from his/her surroundings, as these influence his/her character, too; it would also be impossible to prevent accidents later on which could impair his/her health…

■ **Hold a debate**
Pros: By cloning children and removing defective genes, one could give a child a healthy start in life and save on major medical costs both to the parents and the state; children often inherit their parents' traits as nature already carries out a pre-selection of genetic material so why cannot scientist imitate nature and just make sure that children do not pick up any negative traits?…
Cons: Cloning involves a lot of money so only the rich can afford to create the superhuman generation; no method is foolproof and s.th. could go wrong; no one has the knowledge to decide what a child should be like, not even its parents, and parents and scientists could harm a child by interfering with its genetic make-up…

The brave new world of "Gattaca"   SB S. 122–123

■ **Comment on a still**
Although the people in the still have different features, they all look the same. They all conform to a certain dress code (black jacket and white collar) and they are all sitting and working in rows. The figures are all looking anxiously in the same direction, perhaps they are waiting for s.th. unpleasant to happen. The room appears dark, oppressive and somewhat threatening, yet it also looks as stylish and perfect as the

office workers. As dark colours prevail in the still, the viewer might feel slightly uneasy when he/she looks at the people: the atmosphere is cold and there is no sign of movement in the office or the workers' faces, they might as well be robots waiting for orders.

Exploring the text

1 a) *Dreams and ambitions:* Vincent dreams of becoming a crew member on an expedition to one of the moons of Saturn.
b) *Society:* Vincent was born naturally into a world of genetically designed humans. As a "Godchild" he is prone to heart problems and other diseases, and is therefore not allowed to become a fully accepted member of Gattacan society. He is classified as an "In-Valid" and can only perform menial jobs. He challenges Gattacan society by pretending to be a 'valid' and he works just as hard or even harder than all the other 'perfect' human beings to become an astronaut. Vincent assumes the identity of a man who has the right genetic make-up and is prepared to provide him with samples of genetically perfect tissue.
2 Roger Ebert might mean that ordinary human beings are never flawless. We are never perfect and we make mistakes in order to learn from them. As soon as human beings try to be perfect, they resemble robots that do not make mistakes or show emotion.
Agree: –
3 "When parents can order … will they?" siehe "Shopping for humans", SB S. 121, Zeilen 41–42, "Researchers at fertility clinics say that they are already besieged by requests to clone".
– "Would you take your chances… the make and model you wanted" individual answers, e.g. It is impossible to protect a child completely; How can you decide what your child should be like?
– How many people … of all available cars? The answer might seem to be "none" but very often people's choice of car is affected by how much they can pay or how much they know about cars.

Meet the media

■ Societies in science fiction

a)/b) There is usually a mixture of "ideas" and "aliens" in successful science-fiction films. The less human the alien creatures and robots are (as, for example, in the *Alien* saga by Ridley Scott) the more heroic human beings appear when, weak and mortal as they are, they defeat the virtually indestructible, alien life forms. The more human the robots appear (as, for example, in the *Terminator* series, where the humanoid robot transforms from a killing machine into the saviour of mankind), the less heroic ordinary human beings are because they are unable to control their own lives. We are often fascinated by human societies depicted in films and TV series such as *Star Wars* and *Star Trek* because the characters live on distant planets and rebuild our imperfect world from scratch. They provide us with a vision of a future which is not yet within our grasp, and may never be. The most important aspect is that we, as human beings, can relate to the societies portrayed in such films. We can only relate to and identify with humans as robots and automatons do not reflect our fears or ambitions. The societies can be either utopian or dystopian. The more perfect such societies try to be, the more dystopian they are.

Facing a global future

■ Analyse a scene / imagine, act out a dialogue

1 a) The setting does not remind the viewer of a typical hospital or what one might imagine a fertility clinic to be like. The characters seem to be in a stylish laboratory or a manager's office. The geneticist and Vincent's parents discuss the 'creation' of their second child, but the nature of their conversation may strike viewers as being rather unusual because they are not discussing a happy event or the result of mutual love. The child's creation is referred to as a kind of technological achievement, and the sterility of the surroundings reflects the sterility of the creation of a genetically engineered child.
b) The geneticist's language reveals that he is in control of the situation and the discussion. He appears omniscient and shows his expertise by using formal language, and technical and scientific terms associated with genetic engineering. He is not talking about babies. Indeed, he refers to one of the pre-selected, fertilized eggs as "the most compatible candidate" for a successful life as if he was talking about a job applicant.
2 The parents are left more or less speechless. Although they feel uneasy they do not protest because they lack any plausible arguments. They have to accept the geneticist's opinion that life has to be perfectly designed before birth as it already has enough in-built imperfections. They can either choose a child conceived and born the ordinary way or get the perfect child with no imperfections. As the scientist says, "you may conceive naturally a thousand times and never get such a result". Again the world "result" gives the impression that the geneticist is talking about the outcome of a scientific experiment rather than the birth of a human being.
3 Conversation –

Forests for life   SB S. 124

Transkript

Voice-over 1: The white shark has a body language all of its own which we are only beginning to recognize. This inquisitive shark uses it … It's suppertime…
Voice-over 2: Scary isn't it having your home destroyed around you? But your home can be rebuilt. Ours has taken 5 thousands of years to grow. Without our forest home, we apes will become extinct in your lifetime and it's not just us, thousands of species will also disppear. An area of ancient forest the size of a football field is destroyed every two seconds, 24 hours a day, seven days a week – that's bigger than France 10 and Spain – in the last ten years. Rainforest timber like this is used on building sites, sometimes only once and then thrown away. These doors were trees in Africa our forest home, much of it chopped down illegally by international logging companies. Thousand-year-old trees in Canada are destroyed just 15 for stuff like this. Why destroy ancient forests for wood and paper when it could all come from responsibly logged timber.
Voiceover 3: He doesn't have a voice but you do. Tell your government to clean up the timber trade and ban illegally logged timber.   20

Before you watch

■ Plan a commercial

Message: Air pollution and global warming will increase as a result of deforestation. Plant and animal species will be

Facing a global future

threatened with extinction. Humans will suffer because the ecological balance will also be affected.
Target audience: There is no exclusive target audience for such campaigns, but many adverts often address young people because advertisers and environmental activists believe that they are easier to influence. Young people are more open and less indifferent to warnings concerning the future because they believe that they can still change things.
Film material: typical shocking images, e.g. dying animals, vast wastelands, smog-filled cities; a more modern approach: children sitting in sterile rooms learning about nature (and its destruction) from ancient history books, maybe yearning for a swim in the sea or a walk in a forest, which is not provided by virtual reality technology…
Presentation: a collage, transparencies, act out commercials…

Watching and thinking

Step 1: *Mögliche Eindrücke:* The stark contrast between the different parts of the commercial: the unrealistic destruction of the family's home contrasts with the apparently peaceful tranquillity of the gorilla's jungle home; the gloomy atmosphere at the end of the commercial: a gorilla walks around a warehouse which stocks endless supplies of wood products and rolls of toilet paper. One cannot see the animal: all that is visible is its ghostlike shadow cast on the doors and toilet paper towering above it.
Step 2: There are three main sense units: the first part shows a family sitting at home watching an animal documentary when suddenly their house is demolished by bulldozers and men wielding chainsaws, the second part shows the animals in their natural surroundings and the effects of deforestation on nature and the third part shows the gorilla walking around the warehouse.
Step 3: *Function of cuts, speed, montage and field sizes:* There is an extremely quick succession of cuts in the first part of the commercial. The director uses eyelevel shots to show the people's faces. These shots give an impression of authenticity. At first, everything appears normal. The family is watching a documentary about white sharks looking for prey. When the documentary voice-over excitedly announces that "it's suppertime" for the white shark, the family is suddenly attacked as well. Then the camera focuses on the bulldozers wrecking the walls and the chainsaws cutting through the family photos. The terrified family behaves like helpless animals as they try to find shelter from the people who are destroying their home. Only the father tries to fend off the intruders.
The second part appears more peaceful. The camera focuses directly on the monkeys' faces, particularly their sad eyes (detail shots, close-ups). One monkey starts screaming when a chainsaw is switched on and then overhead shots show us an aerial view of vast areas of deforestation.
In the third part, the camera zooms in on the endless amounts of timber, wooden doors and toilet paper. The long aisles remind us of a maze. The gorilla is caught in the maze, from which there is no escape. The "dead rainforest timber" used to be part of the gorilla's habitat. Now, it appears to be dying, too: The shots of the gorilla's shadow might imply that it is becoming invisible. It is helpless and powerless and as it cannot be seen and it does not have a lobby to fight for its interests.
Voice-over: The function of the voice-over is to warn people of the dangers of illegally logged rainforest timber. The voice-over speaks from a monkey's perspective. It warns that its extinction is imminent should deforestation not be stopped. The monkey accuses consumers around the world of destroying their habitats by wasting precious wood for trivial things like toilet paper, which is often made from illegally logged timber. In the end, the voice addresses the audience directly when it says "Why destroy ancient rain forests when wood supplies could come from responsibly logged timber?" The final voice-over by Richard Attenborough (b. 1923), British actor and director of animal documentaries, reminds the audience that the gorillas do not have a voice and it is up to ordinary people to put pressure on governments to ban illegally logged timber.
Taglines: First sense unit: Have you ever been driven out of your habitat? – Second sense unit: Nature is priceless – until man comes along. – Third sense unit: Look at all of that toilet paper. Ever wondered where it comes from?
Step 4: S sollen ihre Ergebnisse ggf. mithilfe von Plakaten oder Folien präsentieren.

A step further

■ **Devise a campaign / set up a Greenpeace Group**
Anregungen an S: Visit www.greenpeace.org and use 'illegally logged timber' and 'deforestation' as key words in a web search. Gather statistics about deforestation. You could also order written material on deforestation. Decide on the layout of a photo campaign and determine what texts should be included in a brochure or leaflet to be distributed in your school or community.
Damit S ausreichend Zeit haben um Texte zu schreiben, Informationen zu sammeln, eine Fragebogenaktion / Interviews durchzuführen, könnte dieses Projekt im Rahmen einer Projektwoche durchgeführt werden.

The view from Ghana SB S. 124–125

Before you read

■ **Think of arguments**
Arguments for GM food:
– Crops can be modified to grow in very hot and dry, or very cold climates.
– GM crops can be made resistant to pests.
– The endless supply of GM crops can save starving people's lives and make famines a thing of the past.
– GM food is of a predictable and uniform quality.
– GM food keeps fresh longer / is not as perishable as non-GM food.
– GM food can be enriched with valuable nutrients.
Arguments against GM food:
– GM crops might destroy natural plants.
– GM food might have adverse effects on our health.
– The long-term effects have not been researched yet.

■ **Talk about a cartoon: Nothing's labelled…**
a) If fresh produce is not sufficiently labelled, consumers will not know that fruit and vegetables have been genetically modified. This issue is very important for consumers because it is impossible to detect the difference between ordinary and GM food, judging by appearance alone. However, people expect GM products to be bigger and fresher, and to look and

Facing a global future

taste better. Funnily enough, in the cartoon the shopper does not realize that the giant apple has been genetically modified.
b) *Personal view:* underinformed, do not see any cause for concern, worried that food is not being labelled properly…

Exploring the text

1 *Hinweis:* Die Ursache von 'Vitamin A deficiency' müsste 'emphasis on starchy food' heißen und nicht 'childhood blindness' (siehe SB S. 125).

Problems	Causes	Biotechnological solutions
vitamin A deficiency	emphasis on starchy food	"golden rice" fortified with betacarotene
food storage problems, tons of food rot	lack of refrigeration	GM crops ripen slowly, so there is more time to get them to market
loss of food before it is harvested	viruses and pests	pest-resistant crops
hunger, as crops cannot grow	poor soil, extreme heat, drought	heat-resistant crops
death from diseases like cholera and hepatitis B	vaccines are too expensive / people have no access to them / insufficient refrigeration to preserve them	vaccines grown in fruit and vegetables

2 Americans do not necessarily depend on the benefits of GM food. Consumers already have access to tasty, healthy foods. Farmers may profit from the use of insect-resistant crops, but these are benefits they can do without because they already grow enough crops and produce more food than is needed. For Africans, however, access to sufficient quantities of fresh food can make the difference between health and illness, or life and death.

A step further

■ Design an advert –

What happens if you drink GM coffee
SB S. 127

Looking and thinking

1 The photo is supposed to shock the reader. The family are obviously poor and have to beg for money. They are not wearing proper clothes, but are wrapped in blankets that conceal their faces. Their posture shows their despair. Only the younger child seems to stare intently at the reader. The mother and the older child remain anonymous and faceless, which reminds us of photos of poor people in developing countries.
What is different, though, is that the mother and children do not appear to be in a poor country or desert village plagued by drought and famines, but on the pavement of a street similar to those in the West. The tagline, written in bold print, implies that we are responsible for the woman's plight because of our consumption of GM coffee. If you only read the tagline, without looking at the photo, you would expect a different photo, perhaps one showing the adverse side effects of GM coffee on us the readers. The first four lines of the advert copy meet this expectation as well. The reader feels addressed by what seems to be a medical warning (ll. 1–4), according to which up to 60 million people might be affected by the serious side effects of drinking GM coffee. As we are normally told that genetically modified crops prevent famines in poverty-stricken countries, and it is only the consumer who might suffer from negative side effects, we are intrigued to read on.

2 Ordinary coffee beans cannot be harvested by machines as they do not all ripen at the same time. The beans are often grown by smallholder farmers in developing countries and picked by hand, thus providing farm workers with a livelihood. As genetically modified coffee beans ripen at the same time, they can be harvested by machines in great quantities. A large workforce would no longer be needed to pick beans on large plantations and farmers would be unable to compete with the big coffee growers. Thus, many people would have to move to the cities in search of work. They would be "plunged into conditions of appalling health, squalor and the inescapable unemployment of the urban developing world" (ll. 26–28), just as the photo in the advert shows us.

3 Cf. the answer to question 1. *Weitere Ideen:* The advertiser has a particularly difficult task in attracting the reader's attention because he/she is not trying to sell a product. Instead, the advertiser is appealing to the reader's emotions and sense of responsibility towards people in developing countries. The advertiser's message is straightforward and easy to comprehend. He/she addresses the reader directly by asking him what he/she can personally do, apart from showing disapproval. The advertiser emphasizes the fact that it is up to the reader to decide whether he/she wants to buy GM coffee or not: In the long run, supermarkets will not stock GM coffee if customers do not buy it anymore. The advertiser also uses imperatives to address the reader ("Use it", "Call us…", "Return the coupon.") because he/she wants the reader to get involved in ActionAid's fight against poverty in developing countries. The telephone hotline as well as the information coupon and the organization's internet address at the bottom of the page provide the reader with various means of taking immediate action.

A step further

■ **Compare advert with a text**
George Acquaah's tone: Positive, upbeat, constructive (i.e. the problems can be solved in a constructive way by planting GM crops), hopeful…
George Acquaah welcomes the advent of genetically modified crops as they can make a difference between life and death in developing countries. He claims that more food can be grown to reduce hunger and poverty, and to prevent diseases caused by malnutrition. GM crops open up new opportunities for food storage. GM crops can also serve as edible vaccines when their chemical components are part of the crops.
Tone of the advert: negative, accusing, down-to-earth, pessimistic, despairing, appealing… ActionAid is convinced that GM coffee only has adverse effects on people in developing countries: They will lose their livelihoods and become even poorer than they are now.

Facing a global future

Internet project

Folgende Hinweise sollten beachtet werden, bevor die S ein Thema bearbeiten:
- Es gibt eine Vielzahl von Webseiten, die sich mit dem Thema Gentechnik auseinander setzen. Wie das Thema sind auch sie ständig im Wandel. Häufig sind die Betrachtungsweisen sehr einseitig, daher sollte eine gewisse Anzahl von Webseiten im Vorhinein sondiert und den S einige "Startseiten" angeboten werden, die meistens auch wieder durch Links auf themenähnliche Seiten verweisen (siehe auch SB, S. 127).
- Es sollte sichergestellt werden, dass nicht alle S ähnliche Themenaspekte behandeln. Sinnvoll wäre eine grobe Einteilung in die Themen 'human cloning, animal cloning, therapeutic cloning, genetically modified crops'. Die S sollten unterschiedliche Textformate bearbeiten, z.B. könnte eine Gruppe (jeweils maximal 3–4 S) Cartoons zu dem entsprechenden Thema behandeln, andere könnten einen aktuellen Zeitungsartikel vorstellen, wiederum andere könnten die Inhalte einer Webseite oder einer Organisation (Aktivitäten, Zielsetzungen) präsentieren und kritisch hinterfragen.
- Wenn die zeitliche Planung es zulässt, sollten die S ihre Ergebnisse nicht nur anhand von Thesenpapieren, Folien oder Powerpoint Präsentationen vortragen, sondern aktiv die Unterrichtsstunde gestalten. Dazu gehört, dass sie die Lehrerrolle übernehmen und somit Fragen entwickeln, den übrigen S Zeit zur Bearbeitung gewähren und natürlich so ausführlich vorbereitet sind, dass sie auf eventuelle Fragen der S zu ihrem Referatsthema eingehen können. Eventuell können Sie die Texte bzw. Cartoons als HA zur nächsten Stunde in Vorbereitung geben, damit die S sich nicht nur intensiv auf ihre eigenen Referatsthemen vorbereiten, sondern damit auch mehr Interesse für die Themen anderer Gruppen geweckt wird. Im Allgemeinen sollten die individuellen Vorträge nicht länger als fünf bis sieben Minuten dauern, damit die Referatsreihe nicht zu viele Unterrichtsstunden einnimmt. Die Referate sollten nicht mehr als drei bis vier Unterrichtsstunden einnehmen, es sei denn, die S gestalten den Unterricht selbstständig. Wenn die S die Themen in zwei bis drei Unterrichtsstunden vorbereiten, sollten die Ergebnisse auf Diskette bzw. Memorystick gesichert werden, damit die S sie zu Hause vervollständigen und auch in eine präsentable Form für das Referat umarbeiten können. Diese Ergebnisse können die S auch an ihre private E-Mail Adresse versenden, so dass sie zu Hause ebenfalls Zugriff auf ihre Daten haben.

The challenge of change SB S. 127

Transkript

My friends I believe that we are living through an era of global change that is one of the most dramatic and unpredictable in the history of our world. Hardly a month passes us by without some breathtaking development in science or in technology. You know that in 1990 two American futurologists published a book entitled *Megatrends 2000*. They did not need to look too far – a mere 10 years. Yet one word does not appear in that book, the word 'internet', the phenomenon that is transforming all our lives today. So our world is moving at breakneck speed and continuous change is among the hardest things for human beings to hear. Small wonder that ours has been called an age of anxiety, or, in the title of Francis Fukuyama's latest book, *The Great Disruption*. Very appropriate, I thought. *(interruption by protests from the audience; Blair asks the protestors to sit down and says he will answer their questions later.)*

So I believe it is no exaggeration to say we are in the middle of the greatest economic, technological and social upheaval the world has seen since the industrial revolution began over two centuries ago.

Globalization, however, is not merely an economic phenomenon. And that is why our response cannot simply be an economic response. During most of the twentieth century, scarred as it was by ideological conflict, such a concept would have been unthinkable. In that sense you could say that globalization started here in Germany with the fall of the Berlin Wall and the end of the Cold War. Last night I walked with Chancellor Schroeder over the Glienecker Bridge, where once spies between East and West were swapped. Those exchanges were going on not much more than a decade ago. The Berlin Wall – it seems strange to say now – fell just 11 years ago. And it was only once those ideological barriers came down all over the world that the choice became not the state or the market but how we develop a dynamic market, an intelligent state, an active civil society.

Earlier this week I participated in an event to launch the first draft of the book of life, – the human genome project. The power that this information puts at our disposal almost defies our comprehension, does it not? Only future generations will be able fully to evaluate its significance. And we react with wonder to it but also with some sense of foreboding. Wonder at the frontiers that science has created, foreboding at what lies beyond at what this means for us, for our destinies, for what we understand to be the natural order of things.

So globalization, it's brought economic progress, yes, material well-being, certainly, but also fear and change. Children who could be offered drugs in the school playground; who grow up sexually at a speed I for one find frightening; parents who struggle in the daily grind of earning a living, raising a family, often with both parents working, looking after elderly relatives; a world where one in three marriages ends in divorce, where jobs can come and go because of a decision in a boardroom thousands of miles away, where ties of family, locality, country, seem under constant pressure and threat. Yet a world where our living standards rise, and our opportunity to travel, to communicate with one another our grandparents could never have dreamt of.

This global world is a world with a paradox at the heart of it: greater individual freedom, but greater interdependence. We can do more as individuals, yet the very nature of globalization means that what we do affects others more. We buy and consume more as a matter of personal choice, yet the opportunities we have and our quality of life depend ever more on choices we make together: good schools, environmental pollution *(interruption by protests, Blair repeats that he will answer questions later, provided they are asked in English)*, safe streets, or at an international level, world trade agreements, nuclear weapon control.

So, this global change is fast, it is fierce and the issue is this: Do we shape globalization or does globalization shape us? That is the sole key to politics in a modern world: how to manage change. Resist change: futile. Let it happen: dangerous. So, the third way, if you like, manage it.

Facing a global future

Before you watch

Associate key words with globalization

Hinweis: All of the key words in the box can be associated with globalization.
Mögliche Quellen/Ideen: Prosperity, trade expansion, access to markets, trade agreement... Television coverage of world trade summits often address these issues in the context of the gap between rich and poor countries and unfair trade relations as well as the social and military conflicts that result from economic discrepancies.

- E-commerce, communication technology: Advances in communication systems, such as the advent of internet and mobile phones, have greatly improved communication worldwide in recent years.
- International investment: Multinational corporations, e.g. McDonald's and Nike, produce and sell their products in countries around the world.

Hinweis: Das Thema Globalisierung wird in den Oberstufencurricula vieler Unterrichtsfächer behandelt. Die S sollten Beispiele aus Fächern wie Erdkunde, Sozialwissenschaften oder Geschichte anführen können.

While viewing

1 According to Tony Blair, we are witnessing "an era of global change" because we are surrounded by breathtaking developments in science and technology. He gives an example to show that our era is indeed quite unpredictable: a book entitled *Megatrends 2000*, published in 1990, did not even mention the internet, a phenomenon that has transformed and shaped our lives in recent years. Tony Blair also emphasizes the fact that the ongoing process of globalization has helped us to overcome social, political and even ideological barriers and conflicts, e.g. the Cold War, in a way that people would have considered impossible only a decade ago.

2 a) Tony Blair finds 'ordinary' social issues particularly frightening: the sale of drugs in school playgrounds, children who grow up sexually at an early age, the fear of unemployment, high divorce rates, overworked parents who cannot look after their children properly, the difficulties families face when caring for elderly people, etc.
b) These problems are not only related to globalization, in fact, they have little to do with it. However, Tony Blair knows that these problems and changes are quite common in industrialized societies around the world, and he tries to address issues that his audience can relate to or identify with. By using a common denominator, he succeeds in arousing the audience's interest in his speech as many of his listeners probably share his fears.

3 a) According to Tony Blair, the globalized, interconnected world is full of paradoxes: We are offered greater individual freedom, yet at the same time our personal choices affect people around the world. Globalization forces us to think about issues such as education, world trade agreements, nuclear weapons control and pollution at an international level. Tony Blair asks his audience to "manage change" rather than resist it or "simply let it happen".
b) Die S sollten darüber diskutieren, inwiefern der Mensch als Individuum mit den Veränderungen seiner Lebenswelt umgehen kann. Hat er überhaupt einen Einfluss auf die Veränderungen, die um ihn herum geschehen?
Tony Blair advises his listeners to "manage change". This may sound easy, but the actual process involves active participation by all members of society. Considering the "breakneck speed" at which globalization evolves, people will find it increasingly difficult to control. Even in an interconnected world, where everything appears to be mobile, changeable and dispensable, human beings are still restricted to the countries or areas they live and work in. The driving forces behind globalization, however, have an impact on countries around the world, and not just on individual countries.

A step further

Write a comment

Mögliche Ideen: People in industrialized countries have certain responsibilities when they "enjoy individual freedom", that is to say the freedom to live and work where they want, to consume commodities at the lowest price possible, to be protected by the laws of democratic societies, to be entitled to (free) education and health care and to have a social welfare system to fall back on. These benefits cannot be taken for granted. Often, people in developing countries do not enjoy these benefits despite working for international corporations. Not only do we have an economic interest in helping developing countries, we also have a moral and ethical responsibility towards them. We should try to stop child labour and prostitution, exploitation, poverty and pollution, not only at a national, but also at an international level.

Discuss a quote

Our present age is indeed an "age of anxiety" because people feel unable to comprehend, let alone control, the changes which are taking place. Young people, in particular, may feel overwhelmed by the changes around them. The welfare state is no longer able to support the huge number of unemployed and there is no guarantee of employment anymore. People find it increasingly difficult to plan ahead and organize their lives as they often do not know what will happen in the next few years or even months. Hardly a week passes by in which the media do not report on military conflicts and terrorist attacks, outbreaks of potentially lethal diseases, economic slumps and environmental disasters.

Globalization – the key issues SB S. 127

Eine mögliche Aufbereitung finden Sie im TB auf Seite 137. Die Trackpunkte geben den Anfang des Abschnitts auf der Begleit-CD *Additional Texts for Listening Comprehension and Selected Texts* (ISBN 3-12-510472-6) an.

Transkript

23 We live in a world of quite dramatic change. Some thinkers believe that the world is changing as fundamentally today as happened with the early development of industrial society in the late eighteenth century. I think there is a good deal of truth in this view. There are three major sets of changes happening in contemporary societies and it is the task of sociology to analyse what they mean for our lives today. They are the following.
First, the impact of globalization. 'Globalization' refers to our increasing interdependence. Our lives are more closely tied than ever before to events and happenings many miles away, sometimes even on the other side of the world. The influence

Facing a global future

of globalization is everywhere, including in the poorest countries in the world. Its most obvious expression is to be found in the role of financial markets, whose fluctuations affect each and every one of us. But globalization isn't just economic: it refers also to the increasing intensity of communication, and to greater cultural and political integration. The past few years have seen a revolution in communications, linked to the connection of satellite technology to computers. We can communicate with anyone, at any point in the earth, and at any time in an instantaneous way. Instantaneous communication changes many aspects of how we live. Cultural globalization is evident in the spread of the English language around the world and in the films and TV programmes that are sometimes seen by hundreds of millions of people in different countries. Politically, the world is more interconnected than it ever was before: most governments now recognise that there are many decisions which can't be tackled simply on a national level – an example is ecological issues, which truly need to be confronted globally as well as locally.

24 The second big influence is that of technological change. Information technology is altering many of the ways in which we work and in which we live. The nature of the jobs people do, for example, has been transformed. There are far fewer people working today making manufactured goods than once was the case. Many such jobs have become automated, as a result of the introduction of information technology.

25 The third fundamental set of changes is in our everyday lives. Our lives are structured less by the past than by our anticipated future. Habit, custom and tradition play less of a role for us than they did for previous generations, especially in the industrialised areas of the world. A good example here is the changing role of women. Women's role in society used to be largely fixed by tradition: it consisted mainly of a home-centred life, involving learning for children. Today, however, women want increasingly to live more autonomous lives; and in Western countries large numbers of women now are in the paid labour force.

Sociology has a crucial part to play in working out both why these trends have become so important and what their likely consequences will be.

Background information

Anthony Giddens (b. 1938) Director of the London School of Economics. He has written 34 books and numerous reviews and articles. His most recent role has been as an advisor to British Prime Minister Tony Blair. In this capacity he has helped to popularize the ideas of a left-of-centre politics, "The Third Way".

Before you listen

■ Discuss a quote

In the late eighteenth century, industrial societies witnessed a revolution in science and technology that is indeed comparable to that of our era. The invention of the telephone finally enabled people to communicate with each other across great distances. The advent of electricity, the invention of the steam engine, and later on of other machines, reduced the amount of manual and menial work people had to do. The speed at which means of transport developed (trains, cars, etc.) led to an increase in national and international travel and thus greater intercultural exchange and communication.

Listen for gist

1 Anthony Giddens mentions three different sets of changes: The impact of globalization – The influence of technological change – Changes in our everyday lives.

2 *The impact of globalization:* increasing interdependence – fluctuations in financial markets affect countries worldwide – increasing intensity in communication – greater political and cultural integration – instantaneous communication – cultural globalization – the spread of English as a world language – a politically interconnected world where many issues are tackled on a global scale.

The influence of technological change: the impact of information technology – the nature of jobs is changing, work is becoming increasingly automated.

Changes in our everyday lives: habits, traditions and customs are becoming less significant – women's roles are no longer fixed by tradition – women's lives are no longer home-centred, but instead are increasingly autonomous.

Listening for detail

1 Globalization is not just an economic phenomenon as it involves greater political as well as cultural and technological integration. The revolution in communication technology in recent years, which came about as computers were linked to satellites, is at the centre of the globalization phenomenon. There is a greater degree of intercultural identity as the same films and TV programmes are watched by millions of people around the world. Political issues, such as pollution, need to be addressed by governments at an international level.

2 a) … to our increasing interdependence.
b) … is everywhere, including in the poorest countries of the world.
c) … changes many aspects of how we live.
d) … more interconnected than it ever was before.

3 a) technological change; b) altering; c) nature; d) transformed; e) manufactured; f) automated; g) fundamental; h) everyday; i) anticipated future; j) custom; k) previous; l) changing role; m) largely; n) home-centred; o) autonomous; p) paid labour.

A step further

■ Write a comment

Customs and traditions give people a feeling of security in a world that is changing fast and inexorably. Of course, nowadays people have to be tolerant and open-minded towards change and unexpected situations in their lives. However, when people forget their traditions, cultural experience gets lost. In the future, people may yearn for the return of certain traditions, e.g. the 'functional family' or the guarantee of a 'lifelong job'. Such traditions may make life appear slightly monotonous, but they also provide a degree of stability.

■ Prepare a short speech

New job opportunities have opened up for women across the globe. In the Western world, women can nowadays perform the same tasks and do the same jobs as men. However, it is still often up to women to organize their lives as full working members of society and mothers at the same time. A woman's decision to work after having children is nowadays widely accepted in most societies, whereas only a generation ago working mothers were often belittled or referred to as "bad" or "neglectful" mothers. The fact that many women are no longer dependent on their husbands to provide for them has had a dramatic impact on society. It is debatable whether this development is favourable or disadvantageous to women and society in general.

It is also debatable whether women in developing countries have benefited from social changes. Many women in Asia may have switched from hard manual labour in the fields to factory work. Yet, this change has not brought about financial independence and fulfilment. Instead the women work for a subsistence wage which barely keeps them and their families alive. Female workers often do unskilled work in sweatshops and are exploited by corporations because their labour is cheap and they are easy to replace. These women are the real victims of globalization, as they work in poor and often dangerous conditions, while the world does not appear to notice.

The other side of the global village

SB S. 128–129

Before you read

■ **Global village**

The term 'global village' is actually a contradiction in terms. A 'village' refers to a small community where only a small number of people live. The inhabitants usually know each other and communicate easily because there are no major distances involved. The term 'global village' reduces all the countries in the world to the size of one village because nowadays countries are linked by means of modern communication technologies. All kinds of information can be retrieved from the internet, and geographical distances have virtually disappeared because people can communicate no matter where they are.

Background information: Naomi Klein

> **Naomi Klein** (b. Montreal, 1970) is a journalist and author of the bestseller, *No Logo: Taking Aim at the Brand Bullies* (2001). In her book, she examines the growing economic and cultural influence of multinationals.

Exploring the text

1 a) The workers wanted to improve working conditions. They demanded payment at the legal rate for working overtime. Up to then, they had been forced to work overtime without any extra pay.

b) Jakarta's labour legislation favours the employers' and factory owners' needs and interests. The compromise which the employers reached is only a "mock solution" to the problems of the badly paid factory workers. The workers who were thought to be behind the strike were fired because there are no laws to protect their rights. For the remaining workers, overtime will no longer be compulsory, but the payment for doing it will nevertheless remain "illegally low" (l. 16).

2 The workers cannot relate to the garments they produce because they do not need them in hot climates. Many workers who produce computers often lack the skills to operate them. Indeed, they usually cannot afford the products made for Western countries because they are out of their price range.

3 Marketing strategists want us to believe that the global village is an incredibly exciting and interesting place where global citizens engage in global communication and enjoy a "world-wide style culture". There are no boundaries in the global village and anything is possible if you have computer access. The world has become a "logo-linked globe" because we can all relate to the most prominent and universally known trademarks and brand names.

4 According to the writer, there is a growing gap between rich and poor nations. Third World countries do not necessarily benefit from globalization as major companies exploit workers and fail to create additional jobs. Whereas multinationals make "unimaginable profits" (l. 75), their workers may not even have a full-time, permanent contract. Communication technologies may span the globe, but the workers who produce the hardware often do not know how to use it.

A step further

■ **International company**

Draw up a company profile of an international company: Siehe Kopiervorlagen im TB Seiten 138–139.

Globalization SB S. 130–131

1 The term 'globalization' has become a modern buzzword or catchphrase that is widely used but difficult to define as it covers a great number of ideas. People often associate it with the rise of a consumer culture that has its origins in the US. This culture expresses itself in the global availability of American consumer goods, such as Coke, McDonald's fast food, etc. According to the text, the process of globalization has resulted in an increase in international trade and financial investment. Constant access to modern information technologies, such as the internet, gives the impression that there are hardly any boundaries anymore (ll. 13–15). People now live in an interdependent, interconnected world (l. 16).

'Culture' is just as difficult to define: it not only refers to the commonly accepted and tolerated traditions and beliefs passed down from one generation to the next, but also to constant change as individuals and groups evolve and form new sets of ideas.

'Globality' also alludes to the network of 'cultures' that prefer to blend and mix with each other rather than confront each other as they did in the past.

2 Norman Klein refers to a phenomenon that goes hand in hand with the forces of a global market: Although there are strong influences on youth culture, food choices, entertainment, fashion and even moral and ethical concepts, no single culture will accept a customised, ready-made package of ideals, tastes and beliefs. As soon as new products are launched, they are assimilated by local people who process the information with reference to their own cultural tastes, preferences and expectations. In this way, even a product that is marketed, purchased, and indeed recognized on a global scale, becomes "localized". In other words, it is adapted to local tastes, thus increasing its acceptance. This explains the rise of bhangra pop in India (cf. ll. 24–28), or the astonishment felt by tourists when they rediscover products abroad that they thought originated from their home countries. It may sound paradoxical that the US, as an amalgam of virtually all world cultures, is accused of being the driving force

Facing a global future

behind cultural imperialism. Often perceived as a monolithic one-size-fits-all culture, America is the epitome of a multicultural society. As far as political and economic processes of globalization are concerned students might mention aspects of the world of work on a global scale: Multinational companies set up firms in different parts of the world and thus foster the domestic markets in these countries. Although the company's production sites can easily be established on foreign territory, it is the local people who conduct business and thus reshape the international image of the company.

3 The "pervasiveness" of American culture and its dominance of the fashion and entertainment industries: American films and music appeal to people worldwide; English is used widely in the entertainment industry and in modern information technologies, such as the internet, which in itself has become a medium to reach people on a global level.

Other factors include:
- the popularity of US brands;
- American dominance of the second half of the twentieth century and references to the American Century;
- the concept of the American Dream (here: the pursuit of happiness and material prosperity). This dominance is contradicted by the multicultural character of the US. The US is often criticized for focusing on its nationalist or patriotic ideals and keeping a distance from the rest of the world. In fact it is the prime example of a multicultural society: elements of myriad immigrant cultures are assimilated and, later on, accepted as part of American society.

A step further

■ **Discuss Westernization and Americanization**
The term 'Westernization' often refers to the introduction of successful social, political and economic standards in developing countries. These standards are supposed to reduce poverty and raise living standards.
'Americanization': American culture and beliefs have an overwhelming influence on countries around the world (and also on their economies and cultures). 'Americanization' is often considered to be patronizing and is sometimes referred to as 'cultural imperialism'.

■ **Give an opinion**
Steps that need to be taken so that all members of the global community enjoy the benefits of globalization: Rich countries should work with poor ones to promote mutual interests; developing countries should be given access to scientific developments and information technologies to help their economies to grow; an international body should give greater powers to developing countries to control the process of globalization; investment in developing countries will create jobs, improve infrastructure, medical services and education facilities; the resulting increase in living standards will give rise to new markets for companies in developed countries…

Kopiervorlage: Work practices in developing countries, TB S. 140

> Die S können im Anschluss an die Bearbeitung der Cartoons und Texte auf Seite 140 (siehe mögliche Lösungen oben rechts) ein Projekt zum Thema 'Work practices in developing countries' durchnehmen.

Before you look

1 Students will probably refer to the labels sewn into their sportswear. Most of the clothes and shoes they wear are produced in countries like Taiwan, Korea, China, Indonesia, and Malaysia. They are not likely to know much about these countries, let alone about working conditions there and will probably assume that workers are not paid very much and have to work very hard.

2 *Arguments:* Sportswear is overpriced in general, but many people are willing to pay a lot of money because it is fashionable; people often buy sportswear, not to do sport but because they consider them to be fashion items, or they like the brand, or they want to look the same as or different from other people. They are often prepared to pay more for quality products. Clothes and brands often tell others something about a person's character or way of life. You do not *have* to be a successful athlete to buy expensive equipment, but other people may think that you are athletic, successful and full of energy if you do. When people buy Nike shoes or sportswear, they often believe that they have bought a truly American product: Nike is an American company and it represents the "American sports culture", which is admired and copied by young people around the world. What they do not see is that most products are manufactured in countries with low labour and production costs which do not justify the high prices the products are sold at.

Looking and thinking

1 One cartoon shows young Asian girls working on an assembly line in a Nike shoe factory. They look exhausted but they are wearing fake smiles: someone has taped stickers over their mouths which bear the famous Nike logo. In this case the logo could be mistaken for a smile. In the background, you can see a large poster of an athlete who seems to be shouting the company's world-famous slogan: "Just do it".
The other cartoon shows a very young boy sitting on the ground sewing footballs together. The boy's clothes are torn. Next to him you can see large boxes that contain an endless supply of leather patches waiting to be sewn together. In the background, there are hundreds of finished footballs. We can read the boy's mind: A thought bubble shows us that he is dreaming about a football match in which he can play, have fun and score goals himself.
Both cartoons have the same theme in common in that they show how sportswear manufacturers exploit children and young women in the Far East.

2 The cartoonist wants to stress that sportswear and sports equipment manufacturers must not be allowed to make a profit at the expense of child labourers and low-paid workers in the sweatshops in Asia. Workers are subjected to gruelling working conditions, which they are not permitted to talk about as illustrated by their taped mouths. The unhappy little boy does not even have a mouth. Workers do not have a voice to attract the public's attention, and as nobody knows of their plight, their suffering will continue. In the West, we often do not seem to care where products come from, and when a label says that something was handmade we usually think that a highly skilled worker was trained to produce it. The cartoons show that this is not necessarily the case.

3 The cartoons reinforce the comments. The workers explain that they have no rights and are forced to work overtime in double shifts with hardly any breaks. They are not allowed

Facing a global future

to complain about conditions and receive low pay for their hard work. The price of a pair of fashionable trainers easily exceeds their average monthly wage of $50. Employers even deduct money for registration fees. Young women are often abused by managers.
Reactions: e.g. shocked at the harsh conditions in which labourers work; slightly guilty for buying sportswear produced in such conditions and thus contributing to the exploitation of the workers; helplessness as individuals can hardly influence companies responsible for such work practices.

A step further

■ Do research / write an essay

Die S sollten bei dieser Aufgabe das Internet nutzen und können auf die Adressen zurückgreifen, die auch im TB S. 138 zu dem Thema "child exploitation and child labour" aufgeführt sind:
Diese Seiten können als Ausgangsbasis für eine intensivere Recherche dienen und sollen dem S die Möglichkeit geben, Informationen zu sammeln, zu strukturieren und in einem eigenen Essay wieder zu verwerten. Die Leitfragen sollen den S einen Rahmen vermitteln, der viele Beispiele und Argumente aufzeigt und mit dessen Hilfe konkrete Informationen gesucht werden können. Die S sollten unterschiedliche Beispiele von Kinderarbeit bzw. von Ausbeutung von Kindern nennen (Kinderarbeit in der Teppich-, Farben- und Textilfärbungsindustrie, in der Textilverarbeitungsindustrie, in Steinbrüchen und in der Landarbeit, Kinder als Prostituierte, als Opfer des Sextourismus).
Natürlich kann diese Aufgabe den S auch dazu dienen, ein mündliches Referat vorzubereiten.

Test: (You)² – You Again   TB S. 134

Klausur für den Grundkurs
Textformat: magazine article, 423 words
Vorschlag / Klausurtyp NRW: Tasks 1–3, B1
Zentrale Bezugstexte des Kapitels: "Shopping for humans" (SB S. 120), "The brave new world of 'Gattaca'" (SB S. 122). Eine mögliche Aufbereitung zu diesem Test finden Sie auf einer Kopiervorlage auf S. 134.

Comprehension

1 For ordinary people around the world, human cloning is a bewildering and perplexing issue. They have nightmarish fantasies about the future of human cloning and its adverse consequences for mankind. However, people's ideas about human cloning are probably incorrect and exaggerated and the "ethical hand-wringing" Brian Alexander talks about may be irrelevant when other "biotech dilemmas" are considered. People still focus on the question whether human beings should be cloned or not. According to Brian Alexander, it is pointless asking this question: Human cloning cannot be prevented: it may happen today, tomorrow or it may have happened yesterday. The idea of human cloning is fraught with fears and feelings of insecurity about the impact of cloning on our lives in the not-too-distant future. The arrival of Dolly, the first cloned sheep, received worldwide media coverage. This event terrified many people as they saw the advent of hitherto unknown reproductive technologies. However, scientific research in human and animal cloning is nothing new. Animal cloning experiments were proposed as early as 1938. Since then, people have worried about the potential dangers of cloning. Now that the first animals have been successfully cloned, people assume that the next step will be "designer children", "organ farms", "human replicants" or "subhuman clone armies".

Analysis

2 a) Brian Alexander seems to suggest that no matter how much we discuss the issue of human and animal cloning we will not get satisfactory answers to our questions as nobody can predict the future. According to the writer, it is futile to resist change: Cloning is inevitable and we will not be able to judge its effect on humanity until it becomes a reality. People always feel uncomfortable with advances in science and technology, but they have to adapt to them, no matter how overwhelming they are. Brian Alexander seems to mock politicians and members of the clergy for engaging in scaremongering, but he knows that there may be some truth behind their fears. People believe that cloning will eradicate people's individuality.
b) In this context, Steen Willadsen's comment is quite remarkable: Cloning is retrograde and therefore superfluous because we have already turned into a homogenized mass which acts and thinks, dresses and talks the same way. We would rather conform to the ideals of the crowd than stand out and defend our individuality. Mr Willadsen's statement itself, of course, is exaggerated.

Recreation of text

3 Die S sollen hier eine ausführliche Diskussion entwickeln, die die unterschiedlichen Standpunkte der einzelnen Interessenvertreter plausibel widerspiegelt. Dazu gehört, dass sie die Inhalte der Texte und Diskussionen aufarbeiten, die während der Unterrichtsreihe behandelt wurden. Die Meinungen des Kirchenvertreters müssen ethisch-religiöse und moralische Fragen zum Thema Gentechnik aufwerfen. Wissenschaftler sollten die unterschiedlichen Vor- bzw. Nachteile ihrer wissenschaftlichen Erkenntnisse und Errungenschaften einbringen (genetisch veränderte Lebensmittel, therapeutisches Klonen, Stammzellentherapie, Fortpflanzungstechnologien, etc.). Die Äußerungen der Politiker / Soziologen sollten auf die Auswirkungen der Gentechnik auf gesamtgesellschaftliche Entwicklungen eingehen (wirtschaftliche Kosten und Nutzen). Die Diskussion muss logisch strukturiert sein und zeigen, dass der S den Kernwortschatz 'Genetic Engineering' (TB S. 132) beherrscht und idiomatisch korrekt anwenden kann.

Test: How would we feel if blind women claimed the right to a blind baby?   TB S. 135

Klausur für den Leistungskurs
Textformat: newspaper article, 762 words
Vorschlag / Klausurtyp NRW: Tasks 1–3, B1
Zentrale Bezugstexte des Kapitels: "Shopping for humans" (SB S. 120), "The brave new world of 'Gattaca'", (SB S. 122) Eine mögliche Aufbereitung zu diesem Test finden Sie auf einer Kopiervorlage auf S. 135.

Facing a global future

Comprehension

1 Modern antenatal technology makes it possible to detect potential birth defects and genetic diseases in unborn babies. It may appear paradoxical and morally unacceptable to use such technology to produce children with disabilities just because the parents would like their offspring to be disabled. If nature decides that unborn children should have certain disabilities, there is little we can do and the disabled children must be given all the support they need. However, prospective parents should not impose "pre-selected" disabilities on their unborn children just because they believe that disabilities are cultural differences or character traits that make children special or more likeable. In fact, by imposing disabilities on their children, they often restrict their lives to a great extent. As Jeanette Winterson says, no matter how much we try to provide support for people with different physical capacities, "we cannot change the simple fact that it is better to have five senses than four" (ll. 61–63). Our healthcare systems should not support parents who willingly choose to give their child a handicap even before it is conceived. The child's life will always be defined by the disability, and that will rob them of the ability to decide what to do with their future. Children with "designer disabilities" may find it difficult to cope with the fact that it was not nature's unpredictability that made them disabled, but their parents' wish to force a handicap upon them.

Analysis

2 Jeanette Winterson is contemptuous of the idea that people might create designer babies with disabilities. She strongly criticizes parents who think that is ethically acceptable to conceive children they would like to 'endow' with disabilities, a concept which she refers to as "genetic imperialism". In the writer's opinion, these people are selfish and egoistic because they believe they can control their children's lives and make them depend on their parents. Throughout the text, she mocks the two deaf, lesbian women who have succeeded in having deaf babies with the help of a deaf sperm donor. She refers to them as the "Deaf Lesbians", written in capital letters, uses exaggeration ("had they adopted one such child, or 20, we would all be praising their goodness, ll. 10–11) or farfetched and funny comparisons ("we can't be committed at birth to spending the rest of our lives as circus performers or bank clerks or missionaries", ll. 16–18). She also uses rhetorical questions to convince readers that she is right ("surely this is a blessing, not a bore? Must we control everything?", "should the medical system support parents who want their children to suffer a serious handicap?"). Her examples evoke sympathy among readers for those children fated to be born with "designer disabilities".

Recreation of text

3 Die S sollten zunächst Jeremy Rifkins Ausgangszitat interpretieren, indem sie erklären, was die Ausdrücke "architects of our own evolution" und "humanity" bedeuten. Sie sollten erklären, dass sich die Menschheit nicht mehr auf eine höhere Gewalt oder auf die Natur als ausführende Kraft im Evolutionsprozess verlässt, sondern selbst die Evolution gestalten will. Die Evolution unterliegt keiner natürlichen Entwicklung mehr, sondern entwickelt sich zu einem "Baukastensystem", dem jeder Architekt neue Elemente nach Belieben zuordnen kann, um den Evolutionsprozess eigenmächtig zu verändern. Die Menschlichkeit mag bei diesem Prozess verloren gehen (und auch die Menschheit mag dabei untergehen). Die S sollten dann die unterschiedlichen Standpunkte der einzelnen Interessenvertreter des kontroversen Themas "Genetic Engineering" darlegen. Dazu gehört, dass die S die Inhalte der Texte und Diskussionen aufarbeiten, die während der Unterrichtsreihe behandelt wurden.
– Die Meinungen von Kirchenvertretern müssen ethisch-religiöse und moralische Fragen zum Thema Gentechnik aufwerfen.
– Die Wissenschaftler sollten die Vor- bzw. Nachteile ihrer wissenschaftlichen Erkenntnisse und Errungenschaften einbringen (genetisch veränderte Lebensmittel und Pflanzen, therapeutisches Klonen, Stammzellentherapie, Fortpflanzungstechnologien, usw.).
– Die Standpunkte von Politikern können aufgegriffen werden (Auswirkungen der Gentechnik auf gesamtgesellschaftliche Entwicklungen, wirtschaftliche Kosten und Nutzen).

Der Vortrag muss logisch strukturiert sein und zeigen, dass der S den Kernwortschatz "Genetic Engineering" (TB S. 132) beherrscht und idiomatisch korrekt anwenden kann.

Test: The ever-growing presence of the US culture industry TB S. 136

Mündliche Prüfung
Textformat: newspaper article, 320 words
Vorschlag / Klausurtyp NRW: Tasks 1–3, B1
Zentraler Bezugstext des Kapitels: "Globalization" (SB S. 130)
Eine mögliche Aufbereitung zu diesem Test finden Sie auf einer Kopiervorlage auf S. 136.

Comprehension

1 In developing countries, people regard the mere presence of American brands and products as 'progress': if they buy American products or go to theme parks such as Disneyworld, they feel like Americanized global citizens. America symbolizes prosperity, modernity and liberty. The availability of American products and services "signals the rise of a worldly middle class" (ll. 6–7). People feel that their quality of life is enhanced when they have access to an American lifestyle. At the same time, local and domestic producers are encouraged to improve their own products and services as American ideals set international standards. This in turn also benefits customers.

On the other hand, the omnipresence and omnipotence of American products may have a negative impact on other countries' traditions and sense of identity. There is a risk of American culture imposing itself on foreign cultures. In the prosperous, industrialized West, it is usually the intellectuals who lament Americanization, but in developing countries cultural imperialism is seen as a key to obtaining and controlling political domination.

When other countries are forcibly subjected to the American lifestyle and culture, terrorists and fundamentalists may feel the time has come to show America that the world does not necessarily want to be Americanized.

The human race is fascinating in its cultural and ethnic diversity and should not be homogenized. Weber says that you do not have to harbour fundamentalist or terrorist ideas to believe that not every corner of the globe should look like a Californian shopping mall.

Analysis

2 Jonathan Weber only refers to American examples of cultural imperialism. He strongly opposes "American globalization" and uses graphic phrases to show that he considers Americanization to be undesirable. He mentions:
- "the pervasiveness of Americana" (= a neologism; symbolizes American beliefs, traditions and culture in general) (l. 3);
- "the popularity of US brands ... pose a threat" (ll. 11–12);
- "to lament Americanization" (ll. 14–15);
- positive terms, e.g. diversity, human race, fascinating, creativity are contrasted with negative ones, e.g. damage, destroy, homogenized, least-common-denominator, urgency, concerns, alarming, a deserved comeuppance, arrogant, out-of-control superpower, America is imposing its lifestyle, mass murder;
- images/metaphors, e.g. "cultural Chernobyl" (ll. 17–18) and "handmaiden of political domination" (ll. 19–20).

Comment

3 *Advantages:*
- An increase in global, inter-racial and inter-ethnic understanding;
- Promotion of mutual interests;
- Different cultures become globally interlinked;
- Fast access to information via the internet;
- Widespread use of and access to the latest communication technologies;
- Travel opportunities at a global level;
- Global trade and job markets are created;
- Effective international authorities/laws are needed to regulate globalization, for example, the IMF and the WTO;
- International investment in developing countries leads to job creation and improvements in infrastructure, medical services and educational facilities.

Disadvantages:
- An ever-growing gap between affluent and less wealthy countries;
- Developing countries may be controlled by wealthier ones;
- Global players resulting from mergers such as Daimler and Chrysler influence world markets and have a negative impact on smaller companies;
- Poor people hardly ever have access to the internet or other communication technologies, and are thus excluded from the global economy;
- Globalization may create jobs, but many companies and multinationals also streamline production, lay off staff and move production from the West to countries where labour costs are lower;
- Poor nations often cannot afford many of the luxury products sold in the West. Chevrolet and McDonald's are symbols of American freedom and choice, but these companies cannot introduce these values into societies in developing countries;
- Economies are becoming increasingly interdependent. An economic crisis in one country will inevitably affect financial markets around the globe.

Americanization/globalization: Many of the mechanisms which have created globalization are American in origin. The internet, many multinationals and the dominance of the English language in business, science and computing originate from the US. Americanization is often considered to be a somewhat aggressive form of globalization. Opponents of Americanization believe that the US impose their culture and way of life on other countries and thus undermine, or even destroy, the culture and traditions there.

Facing a global future

Kernwortschatz: Genetic engineering

General terms
scientific research
advances in medicine/medical research/
  biotechnology
scientist/researcher
the potential opportunities/
  dangers of uncontrolled scientific research
to do research in s.th.
a research project/a study
to make progress
to invent/to discover
an outstanding discovery

Reproductive cloning
to alter/to modify a genetic code/DNA
to insert a gene into s.o.'s DNA
to inject new genetic material into a cell
to alter chromosomes
to create designer babies and designer pets
to replace deceased family members
to allow infertile couples to have children
to give people the opportunity
  to reproduce themselves
to create/clone a genetically engineered child
to create/to preserve the elite in society
to choose a baby's looks,
  outward appearance,
  character traits,
  level of intelligence
to enhance human attributes
to substitute/replace unwanted character
  traits, genes

Therapeutic cloning
to eradicate inherited/genetic diseases
  such as cystic fibrosis, haemophilia …
to be free of hereditary diseases
to provide a sibling/relative
  with blood/bone marrow/organs
to suffer from a terminal disease
to have a rare blood disease
to develop drugs/vaccines
  to treat autoimmune deficiencies
to stop the ageing process in human beings
to make s.o. immortal
to be terminally ill
to suffer from a potentially fatal disease
donor organs, a donor
to donate organs, eggs, sperm,
  human tissue, cells
to screen/test pregnant women
  for hereditary diseases
to avoid birth defects/disabilities
to become pregnant through/
  by IVF (in vitro fertilization)
to reduce human suffering

Moral implications, ethical issues
s.th. is morally and ethically acceptable,
  unacceptable,
  highly objectionable,
  intolerable,
  offensive
to tamper with nature/human life
to play God
to interfere with nature,
  with God's creation
to respect the integrity/the dignity of life
to treat people as individuals
to have an ethical responsibility
  towards future generations
to jeopardize the welfare of
  future societies
to endanger the well-being of
  particular groups in society
nature is beyond human control
  and has its own laws
to affect s.th. adversely
to have consequences for s.th.
to have a strong impact on s.th.
to make irrevocable mistakes
s.th. has irreversible effects
to influence s.o./s.th. to a great extent
to object to (doing) s.th.
to reject the idea of doing s.th.
to oppose s.th.
to outlaw cloning

Genetically modified food, GM food
to increase the world's food supply
to combat world hunger
to help famine-hit countries
to use fewer pesticides/
  insecticides
plants may become resistant to pesticides
to create crops with added
  vitamins/nutrients
to create plants that survive
  in hot and dry climates
to make plants heat-resistant/
  herbicide-resistant
to pose serious health risks
organic food versus GM food
to destroy the ecological
  balance (of s.th.)

Kernwortschatz: Globalization

Globalization and economic relations
the World Bank
the World Trade Organisation (WTO)
the International Monetary Fund (IMF)
economic growth/an economic boom
international investment and growth
to expand trade
trade agreements
the New Economy
start-up companies
e-commerce
a global market
a global economy
the creation of a global job market
to do/conduct business
   in several countries
to open up new markets abroad
to have access to foreign markets
to market products on a global scale
to found/establish/set up companies
a company's subsidiary
to negotiate/to enter (trade) negotiations
favourable conditions foster/promote/
   encourage entrepreneurship
multinational firms/corporations/companies
global player
mergers and joint ventures
to merge with another company
to employ local staff/
   to employ staff locally
to find/to seek employment with a company
to be employed by…
to be made redundant/
   to be(come) unemployed
to fire/to lay off/to dismiss workers/staff
a hiring-and-firing mentality
to streamline operations
   (e.g. Companies streamline operations
   by laying off staff.)
to subsidise/to grant subsidies
to increase/to contribute to
   material prosperity/wealth
economies are no longer self-sufficient,
   but become more interrelated/
   interdependent/
   interlinked/
   intertwined
an increase in capital flow contributes
   to trade expansion
an important driving force for the
   global economy
to raise living standards/standards of living
the economic situation has improved
economic conditions have deteriorated
s.th. offers restricted or unlimited prospects
   for prosperity
a financial crisis/several financial crises
economies are affected by financial crises

Globalization: controversial issues
proponents/advocates/supporters
   of globalization
opponents of globalization, anti-globalists
anti-globalization campaigners
economic and cultural globalization
economic and cultural hegemony/dominance
a loss of cultural identity/lack of diversity
a growing/an ever-widening gap between
   rich and poor countries
poverty-stricken countries
to be controlled/to be patronized by
   economically more powerful countries
to become economically dependent on
   industrialised countries
the fiercely competitive world market
to compete with other companies
rivals/competitors
companies profit from cheap labour
employees work in sweatshops
to lower the minimum wage
to neglect safety in the workplace
developing countries/Third World countries
to benefit from/to profit from
   the advantages of globalization
globalization enriches/impoverishes countries
wages do not cover ordinary living expenses
to bridge the global divide
growing disparities between Western/
   non-Western countries
to be a victim/a beneficiary of globalization
globalization may evoke/breed
   fundamentalist ideas/terrorism
ethnic and religious fundamentalism could prove
   a serious threat to democracy/world peace
to live in abject poverty
to suffer exploitation
to protect the interests of the poorer countries
to combat poverty and technological backwardness
the survival of the fittest
globalization may aggravate conflicts
   between the rich and the poor
child labour, enforced labour

Advantages of globalization
an increase in global, inter-racial,
   inter-ethnic understanding
promotion of mutual interests
different cultures become globally interlinked
fast access to information on
   a global scale via the internet
widespread use of and access to
   the latest communication technologies
global travelling opportunities
international investment in developing countries:
   creation of jobs,
   improvements in its infrastructure/
   medical services/educational facilities

Facing a global future

Test: (You)² – You Again

Human cloning has become inevitable. "It will be done by someone, somewhere," Columbia's Sauer asserts. And when it's done, say experts, we'll be in for a major shock. Not because human cloning will be as terrible and dis-
5 ruptive as widely assumed. But because we will realize that most of our ideas about it were wrong, that the cloning fostered by our imaginations and nightmares doesn't really exist. We'll also see that the ethical hand-wringing over the issue is anachronistic compared with
10 other biotech dilemmas waiting just around the bend.

But that's in the future. In the present, the persistent question remains: When will it happen? Nobody knows, but it could be tomorrow. Or it could have been yesterday. Michael Bishop, president of Infigen, is convinced – going
15 only on rumor and what his gut tells him – that a human has already been cloned, we just don't know about it. "It is being done," he insists. "I have no doubt. It would be stupid and naïve to think it's not." […]

The idea of human cloning was not born with Dolly,
20 though it may have seemed so at the time. We've been building up to it for the better part of a century. Animal-cloning experiments were proposed as early as 1938 and carried out in the 1950s. An alarm about human cloning sounded back in 1971, when James Watson – who with Francis Crick and Maurice Wilkins won the 1962 Nobel
25 Prize for discovering the structure of DNA (and who now runs Cold Spring Harbor) wrote a prescient essay for the Atlantic Monthly called "Moving Toward Clonal Man". In it, he warned that human clones were coming and that society was woefully unprepared.
30
In 1984, Steen Willadsen cloned the first mammalian embryo, using a sheep. He was quickly followed by Neal First, a University of Wisconsin researcher who cloned a cow embryo. Dolly arrived 10 years later, and then Richard Seed announced he would try it with people.
35
The controversy surrounding Dolly and Richard Seed exploded so forcefully that it still reverberates. President Bill Clinton worried openly about human replicants. Dick Armey, the Republican majority leader in the House of Representatives, predicted the coming of "designer chil-
40 dren, organ farms, and a growing disregard of the sanctity of life. This is a brave new world we must not enter." […] The late Cardinal John O'Connor of New York evoked an apocalyptic vision of "subhuman" clone armies. "You could just keep producing and say, 'They are expendable.
45 Give 'em a gun and send 'em out!'"

(423 words)

By Brian Alexander, "(You)² – You Again", *Wired Magazine*, February 2001.

---

2 **Sauer, (Mark)** famous IVF (in vitro fertilisation) doctor at Columbia University in New York – 14 **Infigen** US company specialising in genetic engineering, especially in reproductive science – 27 **Cold Spring Harbor** a laboratory specialising in genetic engineering; it is located on Long Island near New York – **prescient** ['presɪənt] which foretells the future – 38 **replicant** *here:* human clone – 43 **the late Cardinal** i.e. he is not alive anymore – 45 **expendable** which you can do without

Tasks

1 Outline the key issues regarding human and animal cloning as presented in the extract.

2 a) In your opinion, what is the writer's attitude towards cloning? How does this attitude show in the extract?
b) In one of the other passages in the article, the writer quotes Steen Willadsen, who said, jokingly: "It is retrograde to clone. There are other ways of making people identical. We can put them through the same schools and subject them to eight hours of TV every day. That works a lot better."
Do you agree with this statement?

3 Michael Bishop, president of Infigen, invites you to join a panel discussion where leading scientists such as James Watson, Richard Seed and Mark Sauer as well as political and church representatives talk about the advantages and risks of genetic engineering. You have been elected to represent your school because you are particularly interested in the future of genetic engineering.
Imagine and write down the discussion.

Test: How would we feel if blind women claimed the right to a blind baby?

In the long argument over designer babies, did anyone imagine that parents might prefer a designer disability? While we were all worrying about the bionic offspring of the super-rich, two deaf lesbians in America were going
5 round sperm banks, trying to make a deaf baby.

It sounds like the start of a bad joke, except that they have now managed it twice, thanks to a friend with five generations of deafness in his family. They claim that they are especially well equipped to look after a deaf child,
10 which I am sure is true, and had they adopted one such child, or 20, we would all be praising their goodness.

The difference, of course, is that no child should be forced inside its parents' psychosis – whether they be from a hardline religious sect or Deaf Lesbians. The truth is that
15 all of us have to contend with our parents, for good or ill, but at least we can't be committed at birth to spending the rest of our lives as circus performers or bank clerks, or missionaries. We have free will, and the great thing about growing up is personal choice.

20 What choice is there if your parents have already decided that you are going to be deaf, and that deafness will be your defining identity, just as it has been theirs? This is not the beauty of compatibility, it is genetic imperialism.

25 Deaf people, they say, have heightened senses, and a relationship to the world not shared by the hearing population. Fine, I have no trouble with that. But identity is going to be a big issue for the kids of the Deaf Lesbians, because both women belong to a radical group that
30 defines deafness like blackness – not as a disability but as cultural difference.

My closest friend is black. She married a white man and their eldest child looks like an English rose – pale skin, blond hair, blue eyes. Nature does this kind of thing, and
35 it is a celebration of difference and sameness all mixed up together. Nobody knows what kind of baby any two people will produce – and surely this is a blessing, not a bore? Must we control everything? If the answer is yes, we are paranoid. If either of the Deaf Lesbians in the US had
40 been in a relationship with a man, deaf or hearing, and if they had decided to have a baby, there is absolutely no certainty that the baby would have been deaf. You take a chance with love; you take a chance with nature, but it is those chances and the unexpected possibilities they bring, that give life its beauty.

I am always on the side of risk, and always suspicious of control. The more controls we have, the less free we become. Parents usually try to control their children, and later their children hate them for it, while busily repeating
50 the damage themselves.

How would either of the lesbians have felt if their own parents had said that heterosexuality was such a beautiful thing that they had to screen out any potential gay gene in their children, just to make sure they had a good life?

55 How would any of us feel if the women had both been blind and claimed the right to a blind baby? Even if we transform the language of disability into a dialectic of alternative functioning, should the medical system support parents who want their child to suffer a serious handicap?

60 We can make our world as friendly as possible for people with different physical capacities, but we cannot change the simple fact that it is better to have five senses than four, however enhanced the loss of one allows the others to be.

65 I believe that hearing, like sight, is a blessing, and if we are prepared to use technology to breed children we have deliberately disabled, it is not only the language of disability that will have to be radically reworked, but our entire moral perspective.

70 What this case suggests is that we can do what we like to our children, even if the consequences of our actions are irreversible.

As lesbians, the two women should know something about choice and personal freedom. They both practise as
75 mental health specialists, so I hope they have a colleague who will be able to talk it through with two kids who turn up in 20 years, explaining that their mothers decided that they had to be deaf. (762 words)

By Jeanette Winterson, *The Guardian*, April 9, 2002.

13 **psychosis** a mental disorder which results in one losing contact with reality – 57 **dialectic** *here:* a logical argument

Tasks

1 Outline the arguments put forward in the article against having a baby with a "designer disability".

2 What is the tone of the article? Explain how Jeanette Winterson conveys her strong disagreement with what she calls "genetic imperialism" (ll. 23–24) throughout the text.

3 In 2001, Jeremy Rifkin, author of *The Biotech Century*, and president of The Foundation on Economic Trends in Washington DC, said, "In our desire to become the architects of our own evolution, we risk the very real possibility of losing our humanity."
In your debating club at school, you are asked to give a talk on the pros and cons of genetic engineering. Use the above quotation as an initial thesis for your talk.

Facing a global future

Test: The ever-growing presence of the US culture industry

For many countries, especially in the developing world, the ever-growing presence of the US culture industry is a mixed blessing. On the one hand, the pervasiveness of Americana can be seen as a sign of progress. US brands are symbols of wealth and modernity and freedom. Drinking coffee at Starbucks or taking the family to Disneyland signals the rise of a worldly middle class. On a more concrete level, Western companies often bring a measure of quality and service that are both a boon for local consumers and a prod for domestic firms to raise their standards.

At the same time, the enormous popularity of US brands overseas can pose a threat not only to a nation's domestic industries but to its cultural traditions and sense of identity. For decades now, intellectuals in Europe have lamented the Americanization of their societies. Euro Disney, now known as Disneyland Paris, was once famously denounced by the French theater director Ariane Mnouchkine as a "cultural Chernobyl". In the developing world, cultural imperialism has long been seen as the handmaiden of political domination, another way for strong countries to take advantage of the weak.

Even champions of globalization increasingly fret that it may damage or destroy the diversity that makes the human race so fascinating, leaving nothing but homogenized, least-common-denominator forms of creativity. In the wake of September 11, there is a new urgency to these concerns. The fury of the terrorists – and of the alarming number of people around the world who viewed the attacks as a deserved comeuppance for an arrogant, out-of-control superpower – is sparked in part by a sense that America is imposing its lifestyle on countries that don't want it. And one needn't condone mass murder to believe that a new world order that leaves every place on the globe looking like a California mall will make us all poorer. (313 words)

By Jonathan Weber, "The Ever-Expanding, Profit-Maximizing, Cultural-Imperialist, Wonderful World of Disney. The serious business of selling all-American fun" for *Wired Magazine*, February 2002.

6 **Starbucks** *(US)* coffee bar chain – 18 **Chernobyl** Ukrainian town; an explosion in a nuclear power plant there in 1986 caused the world's worst known nuclear reactor disaster

Tasks

1 According to Jonathan Weber, what are the consequences of what he calls "cultural imperialism" (l. 18)?

2 How does Jonathan Weber's language show what he thinks of global Americanization?

3 Discuss the advantages and disadvantages of cultural, economic and technological globalization. In doing so, explain whether you consider the terms 'globalization' and 'Americanization' to be identical, or not.

Globalization ‹over to you› SB S. 130–131

Exploring the text

1 a) Point out the key concepts that the writer associates with the terms 'globalization', 'globality' and 'culture'.
   b) Explain why it is difficult to find an exhaustive definition for these terms.
2 Analyse Norman Klein's statement in ll. 28–32: "As things get more global … they're actually becoming more localized."
   Is this view generally true or not when applied to economic, cultural and political globalization?
   Base your answer on your findings in the text and the work you have done on globalization in class.
3 Why is America often portrayed as the driving force behind globalization? What factors might contradict this view?

A step further

■ In groups, discuss whether you think the terms 'Westernization' and 'Americanization' are identical or not. Collect your ideas in a table and present them to the rest of the class.

■ In your opinion, what steps need to be taken to allow all members of the global community, and especially developing countries, to enjoy the benefits of globalization?

Facing a global future

Globalization – the key issues SB S. 127

Before you listen

■ In the commentary you are about to listen to, Anthony Giddens, social theorist and expert on globalization, claims that "some thinkers believe that the world is changing as fundamentally today as happened with the early development of industrial society in the late eighteenth century". Would you agree with this viewpoint, or not? Give reasons for your answer.

Listening for gist

According to Anthony Giddens, there are "three major sets of changes happening in contemporary societies".
a) Listen carefully to the commentary and try to identify these changes.
b) Try to collect as much information about each aspect as possible.

Listening for detail

1 According to Anthony Giddens, why is globalization not just an economic phenomenon?

2 Complete the following sentences based on what Anthony Giddens says in the commentary.

 a) Globalization refers _____

 b) The influence of globalization _____

 c) Instantaneous communication _____

 d) Politically, the world is _____

3 Listen carefully to the commentary again and fill in the gaps in the text below. Sometimes two words have to be added.

 The second big influence is that of (a) _____ . Information technology is (b) _____ many of the ways in which we work and in which we live. The (c) _____ of the jobs people do, for example, has been (d) _____ . There are far fewer people working today making (e) _____ goods than once was the case. Many such jobs have become (f) _____ , as a result of the introduction of information technology.

 The third (g) _____ set of changes is in our (h) _____ lives. Our lives are structured less by the past than by our (i) _____ future. Habit, (j) _____ and tradition play less of a role for us than they did for (k) _____ generations, especially in the industrialised areas of the world. A good example here is the (l) _____ of women. Women's role in society used to be (m) _____ fixed by tradition: it consisted mainly of a (n) _____ life, involving learning for children. Today, however, women want increasingly to live more (o) _____ lives; and in Western countries large numbers of women now are in the (p) _____ force.

A step further

■ Do traditions play less of a role in today's society than they did for previous generations? Write a short comment.
■ Consider the role women currently play in different societies around the globe. To what extent have women benefited from globalization? Prepare a short speech and present your ideas in class.

Facing a global future

Global research

In today's world it is important to understand the social, cultural, economic and political forces that influence our lives on a global scale. In an interconnected world these global forces have become compelling issues you may want to deal with in a classroom presentation or a term paper. The internet offers a huge range of websites to choose from, but it is becoming increasingly difficult to obtain balanced information. The following websites and ideas may help you to choose suitable texts, images and even videos.

Globalization

www.polity.co.uk/global The webpage "Global Transformations" is ideal if you want to look up definitions of the term 'globalization'. You can find new articles on different global issues and interviews and comments by social theorists. The best feature of the website is its section of "Globalization Links" (www.polity.co.uk/global/links.htm). You can find information from online news services around the world (newspapers, magazines, online news websites), statistics, reports about scientific developments and the environment, information about governmental and non-governmental organizations and reference services (encyclopaedias, digital maps, etc.)

www.aworldconnected.org "A World Connected – Celebrating global exchange, opportunity and human freedom" confronts visitors to the website with key questions on globalization. The site has got a section entitled "Stories" which shows globalization through the eyes of people who are directly affected by it. There is also a good section on "Links and Resources".

www.theglobalist.com "The Globalist's Guide to Globalization – For global citizens. By global citizens" has many up-to-date feature stories on globalization, as well as background information and texts on issues such as globalization and culture, children, companies and environment.

* * *

Global issues

If you want to do research on a specific global issue, check the following websites:

www.un.org/issues "Global Issues on the UN Agenda" contains a lot of information about topics such as children, climate change, decolonization, drugs and crime, education, human rights, least developed countries, refugees, science and technology, sustainable development and terrorism.

www.guardian.co.uk/specialreports/index The Guardian's online edition has an excellent A–Z section of "Special Reports", an archive of articles and comments on a range of contemporary issues, such as world inequality (globalization, famines, global population) and green issues (the global fishing crisis, renewable energy, waste and pollution, spreading deserts, etc.) and on many other issues.
(For environmental issues you may also refer to www.greenpeace.org or http://www.foei.org – Friends of the Earth International.)

* * *

Children

If you want to do research on issues concerning children (child trafficking, commercial sexual exploitation, child labour, child soldiers, children with HIV/AIDS and children's rights) refer to the following sites:
www.globalmarch.org (Global March Against Child Labour)
www.savethechildren.org.uk
www.endchildexploitation.org.uk
www.unicef.org and http://unicef.org/protection/index_childlabour.html
www.warchild.org
www.gmfc.org/index.html (Global Movement for Children)

Facing a global future

Presenting a company profile

Task: Present a company profile

Many so-called global players, multinational corporations that do business in countries around the world, have become icons of globalization. Draw up a company profile of a multinational corporation of your choice. Here are three possible companies and their websites:
- The Coca Cola Company: http://www2.coca-cola.com
- McDonald's: http://www.tommyhilfiger.com/info
- Tommy Hilfiger: http://www.mcdonalds.com/corp.html

Companies which operate globally often give detailed information about their history and corporate identity on their website.

- The **Coca Cola** Company writes about the "Coca Cola Promise", its marketplace, workplace, environmental and community beliefs, its ideas on active living and leadership, and its involvement in countries around the world.
- The **McDonald's** Corporation explains its company's values, social responsibility and care for the environment.
- **Tommy Hilfiger**, a textile company which produces fashionable designer clothes, informs consumers about its company's mission, history and global work practices. It also responds to negative publicity which the company has been confronted with in recent years.

Research

In your company profile, you should do the following:

▶ present the company's history;

▶ talk about its products and why they are famous around the world;

▶ refer to successful marketing or advertising campaigns;

▶ comment on the company's mission and ideals, and its corporate identity;

▶ describe the company's pay schemes and its global labour practices (if available);

▶ collect data on the company's sales/turnover and profits, if available (cf. "Annual Report");

▶ include photos as well as relevant and interesting statistics;

▶ collect articles and comments about the company's operations using an internet search engine. Try to find critical statements, cartoons, current reports or interviews with the company's employees or managing directors, etc.

Presentation

After completing your research, decide how you want to present your findings in class.
You may want to:

▶ refer to Skills file, "Presentations" on pages 182–183 of your book;

▶ prepare transparencies and handouts for your fellow students;

▶ bring along suitable material to illustrate your points and attract your listeners' attention (a product, an advert, photos, etc.);

▶ develop a company quiz (i.e. a multiple choice test checking on dates and figures, a true-false test, etc.) for your listeners to fill out during the presentation to make sure that they listen attentively;

▶ think of questions you could ask your listeners to think about (ask for their opinions on controversial issues);

▶ develop a power point presentation;

▶ present a video or a recorded interview which you downloaded from the internet (check your school's computer facilities before doing so).

Facing a global future

Globalization: Work practices in developing countries

Before you look

- Have you ever wondered where the sportswear and fashionable clothes in the high-street shops are produced? What do you know about the countries which produce these clothes and their work practices?
- How expensive are the clothes you buy? Why do you buy them? Do you think that the price you pay reflects the actual production costs?

Looking and thinking

1. Describe the two cartoons in detail. What do they have in common?
2. What message is the cartoonist trying to convey?
3. a) Read the following comments taken from interviews with Third World workers of major sportswear companies. Then compare the workers' comments with the cartoons. Explain in what way the comments reflect the message conveyed by the cartoons.
   b) How do you feel about the cartoons and comments?

> **Phan, 22, migrant worker in a Thai garment factory:**
> "Every day we work from 8am until noon, then break for lunch. After lunch we work again from 1pm until 5pm. We have to do overtime every day, starting from 5.30pm. We work until 2am or 3am during the peak season. We always have to work a double shift. Although we are very exhausted, we have no choice. We cannot refuse overtime work, because our standard wages are so low. Sometimes we want to rest, but our employer forces us to work. I earn around US$50 (£27) per month, but I pay $3 for electricity, water, and dormitory. I also pay $5 for rice. The employer also asks us to pay $7 per month for the workers' registration fee. So, I only have $35 left for all my other living expenses. In some months during the low season when I earn less, I only have 30 or 40 cents left that month. I would like to demand the improvement of working conditions. However, we do not feel we can demand higher wages, welfare, and legal status."
>
> **Indonesian factory worker:** "There is a lot of verbal abuse. The management calls us names throughout the time when we work. They call us 'stupid', 'lazy', 'useless', 'bastard's child' and other crass words. They say, 'You don't deserve any more than this.' Some girls start crying. Physical abuse happens too. Our ears are often pulled, and managers yell directly into our ears. Pretty girls in the factory are always harassed by the male managers."
>
> Source: http://news.bbc.co.uk/go/pr/fr/-/1/hi/business/3532325.stm: "Olympic Race: Tales of Workers' Woes", March 4, 2004.

A step further

- Find out about child labour around the world and write an argumentative essay entitled "Why the world needs to address the problem of child labour and child exploitation". Your essay should consider the following questions:
  - What countries still have not banned child labour?
  - What kind of conditions do children have to work in?
  - What does a child worker's daily routine look like?
  - What impact does labour have on the children's mental and physical development? Are there any long-term effects?
  - Do the children receive any kind of formal education?
  - What happens to children once they reach adulthood?
  - What can be done to abolish child labour and exploitation?

Shakespeare & love

Didaktisches Inhaltsverzeichnis

	Titel	Textsorte (Wortzahl ca.)	Thema	Text- und Spracharbeit	Textproduktion (schriftlich / mündlich)
🔘	Shakespeare's words SB S. 132, TB S. 143	quotations from plays (114 words)	love and life	recite quotes • discuss Shakespeare's language	paraphrase • express agreement • speculate
	Shakespeare and his times SB S. 133, TB S. 143	fact file (230 words)	Shakespeare's life, historical events	describe an impression • think of interview questions	mind map / fact file
📺	… early years SB S. 133, TB S. 144	documentary extract (381 words)	Shakespeare's childhood and youth	viewing comprehension	add details to a timeline
	Elizabethan England SB S. 134, TB S. 144	fact file (436 words)	Shakespeare's age	explain images	write a diary entry • monologue / sketch • web search / plot summary
	All the world's… SB S. 135, TB S. 145	fact file (440 words)	Shakespeare's theatre	make comparisons	work with *Shakespeare in love*
🔘	Sonnet 18 SB S. 136, TB S. 145 📖 TB S. 165	poem (114 words)	eternal love	summarise • talk about time • describe a line of argument • talk about a Shakespearean sonnet • talk about tone	apply a definition • translate • read / record an interpretation
🔘	Sonnet 116 SB S. 137, TB S. 146 📖 TB S. 166	poem (109 words)	define 'love'	talk about true love • listening comprehension • explain metaphors	suggest titles • compare attitudes • write an e-mail • hold a dramatic recital • write a sonnet
	The world's most… SB S. 138, TB S. 147	plot summary (415 words)	piece together the plot	identify logical connections	relate a film poster to the plot
	The Prologue SB S. 139, TB S. 147	play extract (108 words)	dramatic summary of the plot	recap the form of a sonnet • work with a fact file	present the plot in a different way • rewrite the prologue
	The first meeting… SB S. 139, TB S. 147	play extract (214 words)	love at first sight	describe reactions • examine rhetorical devices • explain imagery	dramatic reading in pairs
	The balcony scene SB S. 140, TB S. 148	play extract (266 words)	courtship	compare images • examine a line of argument	discuss the importance of names
	"Farewell,…" SB S. 141, TB S. 149	play extract (371 words)	separation	outline a scene • describe a mood • examine symbols, images	compare a photo and a poster
Using your skills	Projects: Romeo… SB S. 142, TB S. 150 📖 TB S. 188, 189	mini-performance • key scenes on film	act out scenes • transfer a scene to the screen	discuss language • setting and cast • cinematic devices	find key scenes / write script / perform play
	Shakespeare in love SB S. 143, TB S. 150	screenplay (790 words)	two men compete for one woman's love	write a plot summary • describe stills • talk about love • describe Shakespearean English	discuss comic elements / characterization • analyse stage directions • write a director's commentary • compare scenes to fact files
	Shakespeare, man of the Millennium SB S. 146, TB S. 152 📖 TB S. 103–105, 164, 188–189	newspaper article (694 words)	Shakespeare's relevance today	explain idioms, write a monologue • summarize reasons • discuss	write an article (tabloid) • hold a panel discussion • write a news item, choose visual material

Shakespeare & love

📺	Shakespeare – a great author SB S. 147, TB S. 153	documentary extract (323 words)	Shakespeare's relevance today	viewing comprehension: understand arguments	identify features of a documentary
Using your skills	Romeo and Juliet… SB S. 148, TB S. 154	feature film	selected scenes	describe settings • describe atmosphere, camerawork	keep a viewing log • write a film review
📺	The music of love SB S. 149, TB S. 154	music video clips (184 words) (334 words)	types of love	define types of love • compare images and lyrics • discuss mood • analyse features of a music video clip • discuss special effects	imagine video clips
💿	The poetry of modern love SB S. 150, TB S. 156	five poems (31, 55, 65, 119, 113 words)	modern love	listening comprehension • talk about tone • … the speaker • explain images	express an opinion • illustrate poems with photos • write a mini-saga
📺	Lessons in love SB S. 152, TB S. 157 TB S. 167	TV sketch (255 words)	how to behave on a first date	speculate about a still • explain comic effects • describe appearance and body language	evaluate the sketch
	The four stages… SB S. 152, TB S. 157 TB S. 164	newspaper article (855 words)	relationships within a lifetime	collect collocations • describe stereotypes • think of questions for a survey • discuss language • revise if-clauses	give an oral summary • write a news item • hold a 'hot chair' interview • write a parallel article, a lonely hearts advert • hold a phone conversation • stage a talk show
	The way of… SB S. 155, TB S. 158 TB S. 103–106	non-fiction extract (1,130 words)	customs which define relationships in other cultures	read and discuss the text in groups	conduct a panel discussion • write an essay
Using your skills	Love story… SB S. 158, TB S. 159	text type: screenplay	creative activity: develop a short film	develop a storyline based on a photo, text, short story	write a dialogue • sum up a storyline • create a character profile

Einleitung

Das Kapitel "Shakespeare and love" setzt sich aus zwei im Wesentlichen eigenständigen Sequenzen zusammen. Es enthält zum einen eine Einführung zur historischen Person Shakespeares und seinem Werk (im Sinne eines 'taster course') und zum anderen eine Textauswahl zum Thema Liebe. Da auch die Beispieltexte zu Shakespeare das Thema Liebe behandeln, wurden beide Sequenzen in einem Kapitel zusammengefasst. Für weitere Kombinationsmöglichkeiten der Texte siehe S. 143.

Nach einer Eröffnung des Kapitels durch klassische Zitate zum Thema Liebe ("Shakespeare's words", SB S. 132), folgen drei Info-Bausteine zu seiner Biographie (SB S. 133), der Epoche, in der er lebte (SB S. 134), und der Rolle des Theaters zu dieser Zeit (SB S. 135). Diese Bausteine werden durch zwei 'documentary extracts' auf dem Begleitvideo bzw. der -DVD ergänzt. Das Kontextwissen liefert eine Grundlage für die darauf folgenden Shakespeare Texte. Die Auswahlkriterien für die Sonette (SB S. 136–137) und Dramenauszüge (SB S. 139–142) waren neben dem thematischen Bezug die Repräsentativität der Texte für das Werk Shakespeares, ihre thematische Aktualität sowie die sprachliche Zugänglichkeit. Der Aufgabenapparat fördert neben dem inhaltlichen Verständnis vor allem die Fähigkeit zur Analyse der Bildersprache. Des Weiteren knüpfen die zu den beiden Sonetten hinführenden Aufgaben an die Lebenswelt der S an, während die "A step further" Aufgaben anwendungs- und produktionsorientierte Übungen anbieten.

Auf der Grundlage eines Plotpuzzles zu *Romeo and Juliet* und des Posters der Luhrmann-Verfilmung (SB S. 138) werden zentrale Auszüge dieser klassischen Liebesgeschichte schrittweise erarbeitet. Dadurch ergibt sich eine Weiterführung des thematischen Leitmotivs Liebe und die Wiederaufnahme der Form des Sonetts im dramatischen Kontext. Zentral ist für den Aufgabenapparat die Ergänzung analytischer Fragen auch durch Methoden, die den Text als "Aufführungstext" interpretieren. Im Anschluss an die eher lehrergesteuerte Texterschließung bieten sich als schüleraktivierende Aufgabenformen die "mini-performance", die filmische Umsetzung der Schlüsselszenen (vgl. die Mini-Projekte auf SB S. 142.) oder auch der Einsatz der Luhrmann-Verfilmung von *Romeo and Juliet* an (vgl. das "Using your skills" im SB S. 148). Eine weitere Möglichkeit ist der Einsatz des Films *Shakespeare in love* im Anschluss an die Bearbeitung des Drehbuchauszugs (vgl. SB S. 143ff). Der Sachtext "Shakespeare – man of the Millennium" (SB S. 146–147) thematisiert abschließend die heutige Stellung dieses Genies. Die Aktivitäten Podiums-

Shakespeare & love

diskussion und Fernsehbericht ermöglichen es den S, den Kapitelinhalt zu rekapitulieren und in ein anderes Medium umzusetzen.

Anhand einer breiten Auswahl an Texttypen wie z.B audiovisuelle Textformate, Sketch, Lyrik und Sachtext wird das Thema Liebe weiter in aktuellen Facetten vertieft. Die audiovisuellen Textformate bestehen aus zwei 'music video clips' (cf. "The music of love", SB S. 149ff) und einem Sketch (Rowan Atkinson "Lessons in love", SB S. 152) auf dem Begleitvideo bzw. der -DVD. Die sich anschließende Zusammenstellung von Texten bietet die Möglichkeit, das Thema Liebe in ausgewählten aktuellen Facetten vertiefend zu behandeln. Mit Hilfe des Begleitvideos bzw. -DVDs können als audiovisuelle Textformate exemplarisch zwei Videoclips ("The music of love", S. 149ff) und der Rowan Atkinson Sketch "Lessons in love" behandelt werden. Die weiteren Texte ermöglichen die vergleichende Analyse moderner Liebesgedichte ("The poetry of modern love", SB S. 150f), die Diskussion einer zeitgenössischen Liebes-Biographie ("The four stages of love", SB S. 152ff) oder auch das kooperative Erarbeiten eines Sachtextes über die Geschlechterbeziehungen eines afrikanischen Stammes ("The way of the Wodaabe", SB S. 155ff). Der Perspektivenwechsel in diesem letzten Text ermöglicht im Sinne interkulturellen Lernens die Auseinandersetzung mit anderen Formen des Zusammenlebens.

Das abschließende Schreibrezept für ein Drehbuch ("Love story: writing a twenty-minute script", SB S. 158–159) kann folgendermaßen eingesetzt werden:
– als längerfristige unterrichtsbegleitende HA;
– als Projekt, bei den Schülergruppen in einem Wettbewerb miteinander zu konkurrieren;
– als Hilfestellung für eine Facharbeit.

Obwohl die Abfolge der Texte im Kapitel einer bestimmten Logik folgt, bleiben die Einzeltexte auf vielfältige Weise kombinierbar. Beispielsweise ließe sich die chronologische Struktur (Liebe in Shakespeares Werk bis heute) auch umdrehen durch eine Einführung ins Thema Liebe anhand von aktuellen Texten (Sketch, Musik-Videoclip, usw.) und eine anschließende Historisierung am Beispiel Shakespeares. Ferner bietet sich an:
– die Sammlung moderner Gedichte zur Vorbereitung der Shakespeare-Sonette zu nutzen;
– mit dem Drehbuchauszug aus *Shakespeare in love* über ausgewählte Filmszenen zu *Romeo and Juliet* überzuleiten;
– die entsprechenden Textauszüge aus *Shakespeare in love* und *Romeo and Juliet* als Sprungbrett zur Behandlung eines ganzen Films oder Dramas einzusetzen.

So bietet das Kapitel eine Fülle von Möglichkeiten, das Thema Shakespeare und sein Werk inhaltlich interessant und methodisch motivierend zu erschließen.

Kopiervorlage: Kernwortschatz, TB S. 162–163

Während der Bearbeitung der Texte können die S einen Kernwortschatz zum jeweiligen Thema, z. B. 'poetry', 'drama', usw. in der Form von 'word fields' zusammenstellen. Eine Auflistung der wichtigsten Begriffe finden Sie auf S. 162–163 dieses Heftes.

Shakespeare's words SB S. 132

Methodischer Tipp

Die SB-Seiten 132–135 können schülerorientiert in einem Stationenlauf erarbeitet werden. (Einzelkopien für jede Station, Bearbeitung ohne Buch). Bei den Aufgaben sollte hierfür ggf. eine Reduktion oder auch eine Differenzierung zwischen 'obligatory task' und 'additional task' vorgenommen werden (Zeit: 2 Unterrichtsstunden).
Station 1: "Shakespeare's words", Task 1, die ersten drei Spiegelstriche;
Station 2: "Shakespeare and his times", Tasks 1, 2;
Station 3: "Elizabethan England", Tasks 1a, b (b is extra);
Station 4: "All the world's a stage", Tasks 1, 2 (2 is extra).
Als vertiefende HA eignen sich alternativ die schriftlichen Textproduktionen 'diary entry' und 'monologue' ("Elizabethan England", SB S. 134, Tasks 2, 3).

Looking and thinking

1

Explanations	Speakers, situations
1. Love makes one do silly things / is often linked to a lack of judgement or responsibility.	Experienced, older person looks back on mistakes of youth.
2. Youth is transitory, so let's make the most of it: 'carpe diem' attitude.	Young lover speaks to beloved.
3. Men are unreliable, untrustworthy.	Bitter, disappointed, possibly older woman speaks to female friends.
4. Love is an emotionally intense experience, usu. with a risk of suffering and a temporary inability to think straight.	Mature, educated person, experienced in love and familiar with poetic language, expresses thoughts, possibly in a soliloquy.
5. Life is transitory and meaningless.	Frustrated person sums up experiences, possibly in view of his / her own death.
6. Lovers often fail to see the truth; they do unreasonable things.	Detached, experienced person explains the behaviour of people in love by means of a generalization.

2 Sensible remarks about universal topics expressed in a language which is poetic, concise and memorable.

Shakespeare and his times SB S. 133

Exploring the text

1 *Life:* born into a high-ranking, prosperous family (privileged, access to education); marries early, a woman eight years his senior, whom he leaves with three children three years later (flight from responsibilities, a failed marriage or the law); succeeds in London in many artistic fields (man of

Shakespeare & love

many talents: successful both professionally and financially, a clever businessman, good reputation, prominent figure of his age); lives in London for a long time (his career is his main priority, prefers the busy life in the city); buys a large house in Stratford (to provide for his family or as a status symbol).
Age: period of peace, political stability, blossoming culture, poor standards in health and medicine (the plague as a constant threat)…

2 Questions are likely to refer to gaps in the biography, e.g. the lost years, or actions which may be viewed from different perspectives. If the students could travel back in time, they could ask Shakespeare's father, Anne Hathaway, his children, actors in the King's Men, the queen, theatre-goers… Experts on Shakespeare today could be a professor of literature, an actor / actress in a Shakespearean play…

Shakespeare's early years

The documentary extract focuses on Shakespeare's childhood and youth. *Possible additions to the timeline:*
1564 William Shakespeare is born in Stratford-upon-Avon, the first son of a prominent and prosperous businessman who was mayor of Stratford at one time. Over 29,000 people die during the plague in London, while in Stratford the deadly disease passes over the Shakespeares' home.
From 1572 Shakespeare attended the local grammar school where he studied the classics, learned to speak Latin, and was taught rhetoric and logic.

Transkript

Voice-over: The eldest son of John Shakespeare and his wife Mary remains an enigma to this day for despite the quantity of his great literary works, almost nothing remains of his private writings.
So shrouded in doubt are the events of his life that even the date of his birth in Stratford-upon-Avon, April 23, 1564, is a scholarly assumption.
He was lucky to stay alive. In Elizabethan Stratford, where red crosses daubed on the house doors showed the deadly path of the bubonic plague, the Shakespeares' house and their infant son's life was spared. William's parents were well respected – his father at one time became mayor of Stratford – and were financially prosperous.
Though unproven, it is safe to assume that the young William would have enjoyed the benefits of their position by attending the local grammar school, the King's New School. Attendance was free to any child residing in Stratford who had reached the age of seven years and could read.
Prof. Stanley Wells, The Shakespeare Institute, Stratford-upon-Avon: Shakespeare's father was a prominent townsman in Stratford – he was mayor when Shakespeare was four years old. This sort of position – of the father – would enable the son to have free entry to the grammar school, the King's New School of Stratford. It was a good school, a well respected school. We have no records of the school at all, we have no names of any of the pupils who went there so we can't absolutely say for certain that Shakespeare attended school. On the other hand, it's 99.9% certain that he did because it was there and he was here. The school gave a grammar school education which means a literary-based education as virtually all education was in Shakespeare's time. That means that from the age of about eight onwards he would have had to speak in Latin at the school that was the required language for teaching. He would have studied the classics, the classical writers, that would have been the main item on the curriculum. He would have studied writers such as Ovid, Cicero – Virgil as he got older. He would have had a very good education in rhetoric, in logic, in the standard literary subjects that were taught. In other words he would have had just the sort of education to prepare him for being a writer.

A step further

■ **Start a mind map / fact file**
Transfer the facts from the timeline to a mind map / fact file. Further categories are provided by the following pages: 'Elizabethan Age', 'theatre' and 'the sonnets'. Other categories, e.g. 'Shakespeare today' or 'his works' might be explored in individual research. (Cf. *Discovering Shakespeare,* ISBN 3-12-576350 and *The Story of Macbeth,* ISBN 3-12-576218, Internet, CD-ROMs, e.g. *Shakespeare on CD-ROM,* ISBN 3-12-576218).

Elizabethan England   SB S. 134

Working with the fact file

1 a) *Extract from* Richard II: England is a powerful monarchy; an island which is difficult to conquer; it has a privileged geographical position; it is a place of outstanding, natural beauty with a happy population.
Main text: close links between politics and the Church (the national denomination depends on the ruler; religious intolerance); acceptance of a God-given hierarchical order in life and society; different forms of entertainment, which range from plays to public executions; marriages were often arranged; strict moral standards were applied; a father's authority was unquestioned…
b) "sceptered isle" (l. 1): royal island or monarchy; a sceptre is a stick carried by a king or queen;
– "seat of Mars" (l. 2): military power; Mars was the Roman god of war;
– "Eden, demi-paradise" (l. 3): prosperous, happy place;
– "fortress" (l. 4): secure, able to defend itself;
– "precious stone" (l. 7): stability, of high value;
– "silver sea, which…" (ll. 7–10): protection.
2 *Ideas:* Comment on the new monarch, give personal experiences (pastimes, family situation).
3 Observations may refer to changes in politics (e.g. democracies are more common than monarchies), the family (e.g. the different types of family structures), the role of the Church (e.g. its decreasing influence), social structures (e.g. the large middle class) and different forms of entertainment (e.g. less violent, more media-dominated), etc.
4 The following plot summary of *Hamlet* may be used as a model of how to reduce a plot to its main elements:
The Danish Prince Hamlet is in mourning for his dead father. He resents his mother Gertrude's hasty marriage to his uncle Claudius, who is the new king. The dead king's ghost appears to Hamlet, tells him that he was murdered by Claudius and demands revenge. Hamlet broods constantly until he confirms his uncle's guilt. Hamlet kills Polonius, the king's adviser, by accident, and is exiled to England. He returns secretly to find that his former love, Ophelia, Polonius's daughter, has gone insane and drowned herself, and her

Shakespeare & love

brother Laertes is seeking revenge. The play ends with the deaths of Hamlet, Claudius, Gertrude and Laertes.
Hinweise: The plot puzzle of *Romeo and Juliet* on SB page 138 may also be shortened to the length of the model text.
Task: Compare the plot summaries in class. They should include the main characters and what happens and why. They should not include unnecessary details, opinions or quotes (approx. 100 words).

Additional task

■ Learn the key terms for the Elizabethan Age. The terms below refer to events in the time period from 1485 to 1625. Match the terms with the correct definition / explanation in a) to e). 1. Renaissance – 2. Reformation – 3. Age of Exploration – 4. Age of Discovery – 5. Elizabethan era.
a) It began when King Henry VIII (father of Elizabeth I) split from the Pope and the Catholic Church in Rome and founded the Protestant Church of England.
b) It refers to a time of major scientific progress with the invention of the telescope, the discovery of the circulatory system, and the definition of decimal fractions and the laws of planetary motion.
c) It signifies the English Renaissance at its height in Queen Elizabeth I's reign. She was a great patron of the arts, and the theatre in particular.
d) It means 'rebirth' and describes an incredible flowering of art, learning and literature. This movement began in Italy and crossed the Channel to England in the last two decades of the fifteenth century.
e) It highlights major sea expeditions to new territories and the expansion of trade and commerce.
Lösung: 1 d), 2 a), 3 e), 4 b), 5 c)

All the world's a stage – Shakespeare's theatre   SB S. 135

Working with the fact file

1 Themes were topical / related to the audience's experiences, spectators were close to the stage, performances were open to everybody and affordable (especially if you were prepared to stand as the groundlings did), lively, communicative atmosphere the audience expressed approval or disapproval immediately, extra comfort in covered galleries, attractive costumes...
2 *Theatre today:* seats only, few open-air theatres, the audience usu. remain quiet during a performance, spontaneous responses are rare, usu. elaborate scenery and artificial lighting, theatre-going tends to be more exclusive...
3 *Shakespeare in Love:* performances at court, box offices, the Globe theatre, brothels and taverns, criminals, run-down areas, afternoon performances, theatres were noisy places, the audience's reaction was conveyed immediately, groundlings, wealthier spectators in covered galleries, no female actors...

Additional task: A short presentation

■ In groups of five to six, prepare an introduction to the topic 'Shakespeare and his age'. Keep within a time limit, e.g. 30 minutes. First agree on a sequence of contributions, and then divide the work among group members. Your presentation could be between six and eight minutes long. You could use the quotations on p. 132. For further tips cf. SB, Skills files pp. 182–183.

Shakespeare's love poetry   SB S. 136–137

Background information: The sonnets

Shakespeare's sonnets were first mentioned in 1598 by a Cambridge schoolmaster. The full sequence of 154 sonnets was first published in 1609. Today, it is generally agreed that Shakespeare wrote the sonnets between 1590 and 1594. Some people claim that they are purely fictitious and that Shakespeare was using his imagination and poetic skills to deal with fairly traditional themes. Others argue that the sonnets record events in Shakespeare's life and reflect his true thoughts and feelings.
If we read the sonnets in the given order, they tell the following story: Sonnets 1–126 are written to a young man; Sonnets 127–154 concern a woman, who has come to be known as "the dark lady". The speaker in the poems becomes increasingly friendly with the young man, who is of a high social rank. At first, the speaker simply urges the young man to marry and have children. However, as his feelings become more intense, he expresses the desire to immortalize his friend in verse. The dark lady causes the speaker some emotional pain. She is his mistress, but is unfaithful to him, both with the young man and others. The sonnets criticize both her looks and morals.

Before you read

■ **Summarise the sonnet / describe an impression**
a) A declaration of love, a description of a beautiful loved one...
b) *Reasons for fame:* love is a timeless theme, poetic language, memorable rhymes, enthusiastic tone...

Kopiervorlage TB S. 165

■ Put the lines of Sonnet 18 into the correct order. (Siehe TB page 165). Cf. definition of a Shakespearean sonnet, SB S. 136 for help.

Additional task: Photo SB S. 136

■ Look at the photo on SB page 136. What ideas do you associate with the landscape? Z.B. nature in full bloom, summer – the most enjoyable season of the year, warm sunny days, holidays, time to relax...

Exploring the text

1 a) The speaker claims that the loved one's beauty surpasses that of a summer's day. He supports this claim by describing the brevity of summer, the fact that it can be too hot or cloudy and that everything that is beautiful will inevitably decay. In order to protect his loved one from this danger, the speaker offers to make the beloved one immortal in his sonnet. His belief that poetry can defeat mortality is reinforced by his promise that the loved one's beauty will live on in his verse as long as humanity itself.

Shakespeare & love

Additional task (before 1b)

■ Find the noun forms of the first four adjectives in the "Talking about time" box. Collect collocations and sample sentences. You could use a monolingual dictionary.

b) At the beginning (ll. 1–2), the speaker asks a *rhetorical question* which introduces the theme of the sonnet, i.e. a comparison of the beauty of summer and his beloved. The *answer* he provides is clear: his beloved's beauty and character are far superior. The following lines give *examples / arguments:* the summer can be stormy, short, too hot and cloudy; it is a short-lived season during which the weather can be changeable. In fact, change and time are the natural enemies of beauty. This *generalization* (ll. 7–8) poses a *problem* for the speaker: how can he ensure that the addressee's perfection, unlike the beauty of the summer, will be permanent and eternal? The speaker makes a *promise* to preserve his loved one's perfection (ll. 9–10). His timeless poetry provides an escape from the power of death (ll. 11–12): he claims immortality both for the poem (and himself) and the loved one as long as humanity survives (ll. 12–14). Mortality will be overcome by the existence of the sonnet. The speaker's confidence in this solution is forcefully expressed in the concluding couplet.

2 "thy eternal summer" = his loved one is unchanging, even immortal;
– "summer" = beauty / perfection / warmth / pleasantness; although the speaker focuses on the shortcomings of this season, summer is usually regarded as the best season in the year or as a symbol of the prime of life;
– "his shade" = death's power; physical decline and death are inevitable / inescapable / unavoidable; "death" is personified as a powerful and boastful figure which is proud of its control over human lives (l. 11).

3 The poem exemplifies the features of a Shakespearean sonnet: 14 lines / iambic pentameter (in the recording, the speaker breaks with this pattern to avoid monotony) / three quatrains / concluding couplet / a clear line of argument.
Note: It may be argued that the outward form and internal reasoning are not fully consistent: "But" in line 9 indicates a turn in the argument and possibly a more logical arrangement of the lines into 8 + 4 + 2. The rhyme scheme, with cross rhymes (abab) in the quatrains and a pair rhyme (gg) in the final couplet, suggests an arrangement of 4 + 4 + 4 + 2.

4 E.g. *So lange Menschen atmen und Augen sehen (hier), So lang lebt dies, und dies gibt Leben dir.*

5 a) / b) –

Additional task: extended version of task 5

■ In groups of five to seven, stage an entertaining introduction to Sonnet 18 as follows:
Part 1, First encounter: While waiting in a London underground station, two or three students see a poster with the full text of the sonnet and try to make sense of it.
Part 2, Interview: A sonnet expert explains the main ideas of the sonnet / (Or two experts give different interpretations in a dialogue.)
Part 3, Dramatic presentation: Experiment with different reading techniques, e.g.
– share the reading or different speakers say lines in different ways;
– use repetition, echoes and vary the length of pauses;
– include sound effects, music;
– include mime or a freeze frame in a scene.
A moderator links the different parts.

Before you read

■ **Describe 'true love'**
Characteristics: lifelong, absolute faithfulness, etc…
What should not happen: One partner is unfaithful, controls / restricts the freedom of the other, leaves him / her alone in times of need / in a crisis…
Photo: an old couple sitting on a bench holding hands…
Simile / Metaphor: True love is (like) a ghost (everyone talks about ghosts but few have seen one); … (like) heaven on earth…

■ **Listen to the recording**
True love is eternal / unchanging / timeless. *Beim zweiten Vorspielen könnten die S key phrases identifizieren:* "ever-fixed mark", "never shaken", "not time's fool"…

Exploring the text

1 a) "impediments" = obstacles / problems, i.e. different kinds of changes (l. 3; modern examples of impediments are getting older, losing one's physical attractiveness, children leaving home) or the disappearance of love from a relationship (l. 4). Cf. also "tempests" (l. 6), i.e. difficult times, arguments, conflicts.
b) –

2 Love is…
– "a marriage of true minds" (l. 1) = a union of faithful partners;
– "an ever-fixed mark" (l. 5); as stable as a lighthouse or the North Star) = unchanging, constant, everlasting;
– "the star to … unknown" (ll. 7–8) = a landmark in life, s.th. of unestimable value.

3 Die S sollten ihre Wahl begründen. 'Difficult' lines, e.g.
– ll. 1–2: the allusion to the Christian marriage service;
– l. 4: ambiguity of the term the "remover": an unfaithful person, s.o. who leaves a loving relationship, or Time itself which "removes", i.e. destroys, all things;
– ll. 9–10: beauty is transitory – personification of Time as the merciless reaper;
– l. 12: biblical reference to Doomsday (Judgement Day) as the absolute end of life.

A step further

■ **Suggest titles**
E.g. Eternal beauty (Sonnet 18), True love (Sonnet 116).

■ **Compare attitudes**
The speaker in Sonnet 18 admires the addressee's beauty (ll. 2, 9–10) and character. Love is not mentioned directly and it remains open if the 'strong affection' is mutual, or not. The speaker in Sonnet 116 gives a general definition of (true) love as an enduring power which triumphs over time and death / as a deep and permanent mutual attachment which goes beyond physical attraction and resists all changes.

Shakespeare & love

- **Write an e-mail**

E.g. Hi, secret admirer! I must admit I find the sonnet you sent very flattering although I am not sure if I fully understood its message. Did you mean…?

- **Hold a dramatic recital**

E.g. Student 1: Shall I compare thee to a summer's day? *(euphoric or thoughtful tone)*
Student 2: "Oh no, stop beating about the bush!" (down-to-earth, irritated) or "I've heard that one before… it must have been in one of those boring lessons by…" *(dismissive, bored)*

- **Write a sonnet**

Shall I compare school to hell?
Is it really a struggle, a war, a fight?
The first parallel I can think of is the bell
Which inexorably calls us inside…

Kopiervorlage, TB S. 166

Zur Vorbereitung auf eine Sonnet-Klausur siehe "Sonnet 116 – a model interpretation" mit einem entsprechenden Aufgabenapparat im TB S. 166.

Additional task

- What indications, if any, are given in Sonnet 18 that it is written to a young man?

The world's most famous love story – an introduction SB S. 138

Getting started

1 Correct order: 2, 6, 3, 7, 9, 1, 8, 5, 4.
2 a) Juliet stands on her balcony and confesses to being in love with Romeo (cf. Box 3);
– Romeo kills Tybalt in revenge for the fatal wounding of Mercutio (cf. Box 7);
– Romeo cries when he hears of Juliet's 'death' (cf. Box 8);
– Romeo and Juliet kiss on Juliet's balcony (cf. Box 9);
– The two portraits at the bottom of the poster do not seem to be linked to any specific scene, but they could be taken from the ball where the two main characters meet for the first time (cf. Box 6).
b) The lovers hope for a future together in spite of the family feud; their ill-fated love against all odds; Romeo takes vengeance / revenge for his friend's death; the tragedy of the lovers' deaths ends the conflict between their families.

The Prologue SB S. 139

Exploring the text

1 a) Ll. 1–4: the background to the tragic love story: the long-standing feud between two noble families in Verona continues;
– ll. 5–8: the tragic outcome of a love story between members of these two families – the suicides of the lovers end the bitter conflict;
– ll. 9–12: the play will show how the lovers' deaths lead to the reconciliation of the two families.

b) These and more questions about the details of the plot remain unanswered: Where and how do the lovers meet? How do the lovers hope to overcome the seemingly insurmountable distance between their families? In what way is their love "death-marked"? What tragic incidents lead to the lovers' deaths?

2 a) The poem takes the form of a Shakespearean sonnet (cf. SB p. 136): 14 lines, three quatrains and a concluding couplet; it has the typical rhyme scheme, iambic pentameter.
b) *Reasons:* create suspense and attract attention by revealing the essentials of the plot, and at the same time, raising questions about the precise details of the tragedy;
– present the main themes of the play, i.e. love and hate, conflict and reconciliation;
– give the audience a chance to settle down for the proper beginning of the action.

The sonnet acts as an introduction to / advertisement for the play; it outlines the structure of the play while indicating its main theme, i.e. love; the audience is likely to recognize this dramatic device.

3 a) Options for dramatizing the prologue: a single speaker = announcer (e.g. the director or William Shakespeare), two characters discuss the plot of the play, a narrator speaks from offstage, a song…
b) *Prose text:* The play is set in beautiful Verona, Italy. Two families of equal, noble rank have a long-standing conflict. The children of these mortal enemies are fated to fall in love; their tragic deaths end their parents' feud. The subjects of our two-hour play include the story of their fatal love-affair, their parents' quarrel and the way in which it could only be ended by the lovers' deaths. If you are patient and give us your attention, we will fill in the details you might have just missed by performing as well as we can.

4 *Methodische Hinweise an die S: Practise in groups of two to four students. Divide the lines among the speakers. Then, in a second step, think of where you should stand and move on stage. Also consider what information you can convey by body language. You will have to perform in front of the class. Afterwards, we will compare presentations in terms of dramatic effectiveness.

The first meeting of the lovers SB S. 139–140

Exploring the text

1 Juliet has a strong emotional effect on Romeo. He is deeply impressed / fascinated / overwhelmed / smitten / dazzled by her beauty – two exclamations and numerous images reveal his enthusiasm for this "rich jewel" (l. 3) and "snowy dove" (l. 5). It seems to be love at first sight (l. 9); his other experiences of love cannot compare with this truly unique encounter / fade to insignificance in view of her "true" beauty (ll. 9–10). However, in spite of being blinded by Juliet's beauty, Romeo still plans how he can approach her / introduce himself / make contact with her (ll. 7–8).

2 *Alliteration:* The double alliteration in l. 1 (teach … torches to; burn bright) introduces the idea of brightness in relation to how Romeo perceives Juliet in this situation. From his perspective, Juliet is a source of light which surpasses the brightness of the torches / outshines the crowd and thus absorbs his full attention / radiates qualities which set her apart from the other guests.

Shakespeare & love

Metaphors: Two complex sets of metaphors underline the contrast between Juliet's brightness (i.e. attractiveness) and the comparative darkness of her surroundings:
- ll. 2–4: Juliet = "a rich jewel" (= glitters brightly; seems invaluable, priceless) which hangs upon the Ethiop's ear (= expression here is used loosely to mean any African); "cheek of night" (the dark background);
- ll. 5–6: Juliet = "snowy dove" (= white, graceful) surrounded by "crows" (= black birds known for their harsh cries).

Also note the following *rhetorical devices*:
- rhetorical question (= a question to which the answer is obvious) in l. 9 emphasizes Romeo's emotional response;
- personification of "sight" (l. 9): Romeo asks his eyes if they have seen his true love up to now – the question implies that he has not;
- chiasmus (= words used in the first half of a sentence are reversed in the second half) in line 4: "Beauty too rich for use, for earth too dear". This stylistic device reinforces Juliet's attractiveness;
- hyperbole (= exaggerated language) of line 1.

Übergang zum zweiten Auszug, SB. S 140

In GA, arbeitsteilige Bearbeitung nach Wahl:
- Romeo loves Juliet from the first moment he sees her. Do you believe in 'love at first sight'? What, do you think, happens in the moment when two people fall head over heels in love?
- Write an interior monologue in modern English, which Romeo might have spoken on seeing Juliet. Think of images to express his emotions and end the monologue with "I have never seen true beauty till this night".
- Suggest effective 'chat-up lines' for Romeo.

Einführung von *key words* von L

- *Pilgrims*, to show their *faith*, made long journeys to the *shrines* of the Holy Land. They brought back *palm leaves* as proof of their visits, and so were known as *'palmers'*. The word *palm* has a second meaning – it refers to the flat part on the inside of your hand.

3 a) The central image, i.e. of a pilgrim worshipping at a shrine, underlines the depth / purity / sincerity of Romeo's love. The images / religious words used are as follows:
- "to profane" (l. 1) = to make s.th. dirty, to desecrate;
- Juliet's hand is compared to a "holy shrine" (l. 2) i.e. a sacred place of worship; an object of admiration / respect / veneration;
- Romeo's lips = "blushing pilgrims" (l. 3) who stand ready to give a respectful kiss, here: a first indication of Romeo's true intentions;
- Romeo = "pilgrim" (l. 5) i.e. a person who travels a long way to pay his / her respects to s.o. he / she admires;
- "devotion" (l. 6) = worship, veneration i.e. admiration from a respectful distance;
- Juliet = saint (l. 7) = s.o. who is worshipped;
- "palm to palm" (l. 8): Palmers would touch the hand of a holy statue with their own hand rather than kiss it;
- "prayer" (l. 10) = words you say when speaking to God;
- "faith" (l. 12) = strong religious belief.

b) The masked ball is an informal chance to flirt with s.o. Romeo and Juliet are not formally introduced and do not even know one another's names at the time of the exchange. Romeo takes advantage of the anonymity of the masked ball and chats up Juliet in a clever and somewhat cheeky way by both hiding and revealing his intentions in imagery. His flirtatious and rhetorically skilful approach is successful: in a playful conversation and battle of wits, Romeo and Juliet exchange loving and suggestive words, and then kiss. Juliet is flattered by Romeo's interest and scarcely disguises her positive response. Romeo quickly overcomes any shyness / hesitation / reluctance she might feel.

4 *Body language:* Romeo might bow or even kneel; he gradually reduces any initial physical distance by touching Juliet's hand with his own hand and possibly with his lips; later he holds her hand and increases eye contact.
Tone: playful / suggestive / joking…

5 In the first quatrain Romeo indicates his intentions and expresses his feelings clearly, whereas Juliet uses the second quatrain to phrase a positive, yet hesitant response. They share the third quatrain and the concluding couplet, thus revealing their mutual infatuation. The flirtatious exchange quickly leads to a first kiss.

Shakespeare uses the sonnet as the most suitable poetic form for the beginning of a love story. In Romeo and Juliet's first conversation, both form and content indicate their love and perfectly capture the awkwardness, yet irresistibility, of the moment.

The balcony scene   SB S. 140–141

Exploring the text

1 Catching sight of Juliet at a window, Romeo applies the following phrases to Juliet in a soliloquy (= speech in which a character speaks his or her thoughts aloud): "light" (l. 1), "sun" (ll. 2, 3), "fair" (ll. 3, 5), "my lady … my love" (l. 7), "bright angel" (l. 10), "glorious" (l. 11), "messenger of heaven" (l. 12). As when he first saw her at the masked ball, Romeo's description of Juliet focuses on images of light and brightness (Juliet = sun / angel) thus highlighting her as a positive influence and source of hope in his life.

2 The lovestruck Juliet is talking to herself about Romeo. But instead of using images to praise his qualities, she gets down to the practical matter of wondering why he has to be a Montague. The soliloquy shows that Juliet is fully conscious of the hatred that makes their families deadly enemies. While unaware that Romeo can overhear her (l. 21), she declares her love, and then considers the seemingly insurmountable problem she is facing.

Juliet's words follow a logical argument. She sees the problem as one of names. Her line of reasoning goes like this:
- The problem she faces: the man she loves is Romeo Montague, and his name makes him her enemy (l. 17).
- 1st solution: Romeo could refuse to be a Montague. Then he would no longer be her enemy (l. 18).
- 2nd solution: Juliet stops being a Capulet. Then she would no longer be his natural enemy (ll. 19–20).
- Identification of the name 'Montague' as the core of the problem: the character Romeo remains the same despite his name, the name is just a label (ll. 21–30).
- 1st solution repeated: appeal to Romeo to give up his name (l. 31).
- Result / benefit: he can have Juliet in return (ll. 32–33).

Shakespeare & love

Additional question

■ Discuss the following questions with a partner:
– Can you separate a name from a person?
– Can you change your name and become someone else?

3 People may change their names because they are teased about them (names with funny or negative connotations) or when they get married. Countries and institutions change their names in response to a new political situation (Soviet Union → Russia), or when taking on new responsibilities (EEC = European Economic Community → EU = European Union). The discussion could address the problem of hyphenated names (Leuthäuser-Schnarrenberger), the contrast between popular and rare names (Müller vs. Queda) and possible discrimination if one has a 'foreign' name.

Additional questions / activities

■ How does the photo on page 141 relate to the text of "the balcony scene"?
(Note: Shakespeare does not use the word 'balcony' and provides no such stage directions, but Romeo's comparison of Juliet to the sun and an angel suggests that he is looking upwards; in addition, the balcony allows the audience, and Romeo, to listen to Juliet's monologue – cf. line 10 – and also makes it plausible that she is not aware of his presence at the beginning of the scene.)
■ Use the internet to find out how the Italian city of Verona takes advantage of the popularity of the balcony scene, and the whole play, to promote the city to visitors.
(Note: Verona establishes a controversial link between the play and historic figures by advertising Juliet's house with its balcony and her tomb, and also Romeo's house, as major tourist attractions.)

Methodischer Hinweis

Übergang zum nächsten Auszug: Die S können sich mit Hilfe der *plot summary* (SB S. 138) die Ereignisse nach der Balkonszene in Erinnerung rufen.

"Farewell, farewell!" SB S. 141–142

Exploring the text

1 The lovers are at the bedroom window and both in turn try to put off the moment of their separation. At first Romeo, who is aware of the danger if he is discovered, feels he must leave for Mantua. Juliet begs him to stay. For a moment, he agrees to do so and face the consequences joyfully. However, his words alert Juliet to the danger of the situation, and she appeals to him to go. The Nurse's news that Lady Capulet is coming adds urgency to the lovers' parting.

2 Ll. 1–5: Juliet is still in a romantic mood, unwilling to accept the dawning day;
– ll. 6–11: Romeo is sober, composed and realistic;
– ll. 12–16: Juliet acknowledges her lover's inevitable departure but still argues calmly that he has plenty of time;
– ll. 17–25: Romeo deceives himself, is resigned, is prepared to live for the moment and face death;
– ll. 26–35: Juliet is suddenly apprehensive and regretful, sober and realistic; she becomes aware of the imminent danger for Romeo, fears for his safety and urges him to go;

– l. 36: Romeo is depressed and hopeless;
– l. 42: Juliet calmly draws the obvious conclusion, her pragmatic reaction shows her to be in control of her emotions;
– l. 43: Romeo sadly accepts the separation.

3 *Night*: Its romance and beauty are symbolized by the nightingale, which sings melodiously at night (ll. 2, 4); "night's candles" (l. 9) possibly refer to 'stars'.
Day: "some meteor" (= phenomenon associated with the night) as "a torch-bearer" for Romeo's journey to Mantua (ll. 14–15). Juliet compares the first light of day with a meteor in order to persuade Romeo that it is still night;
– the day is associated with separation and danger, its arrival is announced by the (unpleasant) song of the lark (ll. 6, 27–28);
– "envious streaks" (l. 7) of light in the east is an example of personification;
– "jocund day stands…" (ll. 9–10) = personification;
– "the morning's eye" (l. 19), i.e. the first light of day = personification;
– "More light and light, more dark and dark our woes" (l. 36); antithesis (= use of pairs of opposites for effect) indicates Romeo's mixed feelings about the new day;
– "let day in, and let life out" (l. 42) = antithesis.

Additional questions / activities

■ Relate the photo on p. 142 to one or two lines from the farewell scene.
■ Try speaking ll. 1–36 in different ways, e.g. Juliet is loving / impatient / bossy / sleepy; Romeo is loving / afraid / anxious to leave / irritable. Focus on key statements, e.g. l. 11.
■ Imagine Lady Capulet comes in just as Romeo speaks line 11. Improvise what would happen.
■ "He goeth down" (l. 43). How would you stage this part of the scene? Think of options with or without a balcony.
■ Turn the text into a film script – you will have to reduce the dialogue. Give reasons for your choices.

👁 **Talk about the photo** SB S. 142

Personal comments on different versions of the play based on impressions conveyed by the poster / photos may involve the casting of the main characters (To what extent is it possible to identify with the characters?), the (dis)advantages of traditional and modern performances, etc.

A step further

■ **Compare original scene and screenplay**

	Original scene	Screenplay
Parallels	Setting = Juliet's bedroom	Setting = Viola's bedroom
	Morning: Romeo and Juliet have spent the night together	Morning: Viola and Will have spent the night together
	The lovers are aware of the danger of discovery.	The lovers are aware of the danger of discovery.
	The nurse helps when s.o. threatens to discover them.	The nurse helps when s.o. threatens to discover them.

149

Shakespeare & love

	Original scene	Screenplay
Differences	They are standing at the window.	They are still in bed.
	They have been woken by birds.	They have been woken by a sunbeam.
	Juliet's marriage to Paris has not been arranged yet.	Viola's marriage has been arranged.
	Romeo and Juliet never see one another alive.	Viola and Will meet again.

Projects: Romeo and Juliet SB S. 142

■ Mini-performance

Der Input im SB sollte in einer Planungs- und Organisationsstunde durch Nachfragen der S konkretisiert werden. Der Absprache bedarf hier insbesondere:
- der Zeitrahmen: 1 Planungsstunde / 3–5 Stunden GA / 2–3 Stunden für die Gruppenpräsentationen mit ca. 15 Minuten pro Vorführung;
- die Leistungsbewertung (Aspekte könnten sein in der GA z. B. Eigenständigkeit, Kooperation, Engagement, Verwendung der Zielsprache, Sprachkompetenz; Kriterien einer gelungenen Gruppenpräsentation könnten sein z. B. Einbeziehung aller Gruppenmitglieder, sinnvolle Arbeitsteilung, klare Aufgabenzuordnung, transparente Strukturierung, effektive Koordination, situations- und rollengemäße Sprachverwendung, funktionaler Verwendung von Requisiten und anderen Hilfsmitteln, etc.)

Grundlage für ein 'peer assessment' direkt nach jeder Aufführung könnte ein gemäß den verabredeten Bewertungskriterien strukturiertes 'observation sheet' in Rasterform sein. Orientierung über die Feedbackregeln und Vorschläge zu deren angemessener Versprachlichung befinden sich auf Seiten 188–189.

■ Key scenes on film

Für eine Verfilmung sind in einem ersten Schritt mehrere Aspekte zu beachten:
- Language: eine sinnvolle Kürzung des Textes;
- Setting: Übernahme der örtlichen und zeitlichen Vorgaben (Verona, 15. / 16. Jahrhundert) oder geographisch-zeitliche Verschiebung z. B. im Sinne einer Aktualisierung des Stoffes);
- Cast of characters: vgl. Beispiel Leonardo di Caprio / Claire Danes (siehe Poster, SB S. 120); Findung und Begründung einer 'ideal cast' (money is no object!).

Die konkrete Arbeit an den Textausschnitten sollte dann arbeitsteilig erfolgen sowie – für den funktionalen Einsatz – das Vorschlagen von 'cinematic devices' wie camerawork, music, symbolic props, etc. und stage directions wie position and movements on stage, body language, use of voice, etc.

Shakespeare in love SB S. 143–145

Before you read

a) *Plot*: cf. www.us.imdb.com or www.suntimes.com/ebert/ebert_reviews/1998/12/122505.html.

Mit folgenden Stichwörtern können S den Anfang des Plots selber verfassen: life is a mess – short of money – writer's block – sham audition – in disguise – stately home – love at first sight – sudden inspiration – to be promised in marriage – the queen's approval – to risk s.o.'s wrath – secret affair.
Characters: William Shakespeare (Joseph Fiennes), Viola De Lesseps / Thomas Kent (Gwyneth Paltrow), Queen Elizabeth I (Judi Dench), Lord Wessex (Colin Firth).

b) *Still, SB p. 143*: Will Shakespeare and Viola de Lesseps at the beginning of their relationship; Will takes advantage of Elizabethan dance conventions to approach Viola at a ball.
Still, SB p. 145: Confidential exchange between Lord Wessex and Queen Elizabeth in which she approves his marriage plans, but also suggests that Viola has had sexual relations and not with Lord Wessex (cf. SB, ll. 83–84).

Exploring the text

1 Romantic / mutual love between Will and Viola, (ll. 1–4);
- ill-fated love refers to the tragic ending of *Romeo and Juliet* (ll. 7–9);
- courtly love of Elizabethan theatre (l. 44);
- unrequited love, possibly Lord Wessex has feelings for Viola (ll. 52–53);
- sexual love, true love in a play (l. 60);
- absence of love in a marriage which has been arranged for financial reasons (l. 68);
- sexuality, virginity, unfaithfulness are implied in the line "she has been plucked" (l. 84).

2 a) *Comic elements*:
- situational humour / comic moment (ll. 15–16);
- the queen's use of verbal humour: jokes at her guests' expense (ll. 55–56, 68, 70–71), witty comments ("I know who I am", l. 43), irony (ll. 80–81);
- contrast between the superiority of the queen and the exaggerated reverence of the guests (ll. 55–57).

Characterization:
- the pompous and self-important Lord Wessex as a comic figure ("lordly fool" in ll. 14, 67–69, 73–74, 82–83);
- Will Shakespeare as the naive outsider who is unfamiliar with the etiquette demanded by the situation (ll. 49–50);
- Viola facing the queen: insecure, intimidated, somewhat naïve, nervous.

b) Further cinematic options to emphasize comic aspects: close-ups of faces highlight emotions / reactions; exaggerated body language of the actors…

3 ll. 7–9: Insurmountable problems will lead to an unhappy ending;
- ll. 76 –78: The bet on a play which reveals "the very truth and nature of love", with the queen as a judge, foreshadows the performance of Will's play and the queen's verdict on it.
- l. 83: In view of Viola and Will's relationship, the queen's support for Viola's marriage to Lord Wessex indicates further complications.

Close-up: language

The suitability of the language for the screen is based on:
- the non-redundant dialogue (quick exchange of carefully-phrased remarks, simple syntax, understandable diction; the language is skilfully reduced to a minimum, but has a maximum effect);

Shakespeare & love

- rhetorical devices such as imagery (metaphors: "broad river" in l. 8, "stolen season" in l. 10, "plucked" in l. 84) and Wessex's antithetical phrase in ll. 65–66, "young … wise");
- the queen's direct, epigrammatic (= short, clever, amusing) way of speaking hint at Shakespeare's use of language.

A step further

■ **Viewing the film scenes**

a) **Viola's bedroom (DVD: chapter 16, from 00:55:19)**
Camerawork: Only three shots, all of them static; the first and third are medium shots of the couple in bed, the second is a full shot of the room, in which attention is drawn to a picture of the queen beside the window (i.e. she is omnipresent in both public and private life); fairly long shots, no music, no camera movement: slow-paced action, emphasis on dialogue.
Actors/actresses: In contrast to the screenplay, Will is already awake and staring at the ceiling; the actors' tone is sober, sad and realistic as Will talks about his play ("a broad river divides my lovers", l. 8) and Viola about their relationship ("This is a stolen season", l. 10).
Anmerkung: Die durch […] gekennzeichneten Kürzungen betreffen im ersten Fall (SB S. 143, Z. 16) zwei kurze Zwischenszenen (Der erzürnte Lord Wessex fordert Violas Nurse auf, schleunigst ihre Herrin zu holen, und Viola begründet Will noch einmal die Unvermeidbarkeit der bevorstehenden Zweckhochzeit.), die in erster Linie die schon bekannten unterschiedlichen Interessenlagen der Beteiligten erneut verdeutlichen und somit den Konflikt der beiden abgedruckten Kernszenen nur kurz unterbrechen.
Die zweite Kürzung (SB S. 144, Z. 27) weist auf Wills Anwesenheit während der folgenden Szene hin (vgl. Z. 72).
Im dritten Fall (SB S. 144, Z. 32) handelt es sich um ein zehnzeiliges Zwischengespräch zwischen Lord Wessex und Will während der Audienz bei der Königin, in dem Lord Wessex seinen Verdacht hinsichtlich eines ihm noch unbekannten Mitbewerbers um Violas Gunst zur Sprache bringt.

Greenwich Palace (DVD: chapter 17, from 00:58:06)
Note: In the scene Will is disguised as Viola's "country cousin Miss Wilhelmina" so that he can accompany Viola and Lord Wessex to their audience with the queen.
Camerawork: A perfectly symmetrical establishing shot shows Greenwich Palace from the entrance gate; the following long shot of the queen on her throne links this scene with the preceding one; the dialogue between the queen and Viola is shown in static, medium, reverse-angle shots; their difference in status is conveyed by the low-angle shots of the queen and high-angle shots of Viola; shots of the audience and close-ups of Lord Wessex and Will highlight their reactions to the dialogue; after the queen's exchange with Lord Wessex, a close-up of his face and some threatening music reveal his angry, vengeful mood.
Actors/actresses: In the moments before the audience, Will's disguise and attempts at using a female voice attract a lot of attention as he contrasts sharply with the pomp of the royal court. He also informs Lord Wessex, incorrectly, of the identity of his rival for Viola's affections (dramatic irony!). The second contrast is between Viola's shy, submissive behaviour (in spite of her contradiction in l. 61) and the queen's authoritative voice and tongue-in-cheek humour, which is used at the expense of both Viola and Wessex.

b) Speaking in the first person ('I'), the director is likely to comment on the action, characters and cinematic devices in the two scenes. In the original commentary (DVD: Bonus Materials_More_John Madden commentary track), John Madden focuses on the following aspects:
The first scene: nearly cut from the final version – characters' awareness of the difference between fiction and reality – calmness of the scene in contrast to the accelerating speed and "darker musical colour" of the following argument between the lovers because of Wessex's arrival.
The second scene: real location of the scene, Hatfield House, not Greenwich Palace, which no longer exists – funny moment when Will forgets to curtsey and Viola reprimands him – courtiers' clothing and elaborate make-up – the queen as a key figure in Elizabethan life – importance of the scene in paving the way for further developments and the ending.

■ **Watch selected scenes**

The film visualizes a lot of facts about Elizabethan times, which are also covered in the fact files on pp. 133–135, e.g.
- "Shakespeare and his times" (SB p. 133): Theatres were closed because of the plague.
- "Elizabethan England" (SB p. 134): the dominant political role of Queen Elizabeth I; the hierarchical structure of society with the queen and nobility at the top and the lower classes at the bottom; the god-given order which made crossing class barriers, e.g. by marriage to s.o. from another class, almost impossible; the theatre and pubs, as well as fighting and rioting, were the main forms of entertainment; marriage in the upper classes was based on wealth and status.
- "Shakespeare's theatre" (SB p. 135): the theatre was round, partly open to the sky, had a high stage and a canopy overhead, supported by pillars (cf. photo, SB p. 135); the theatre was situated in a run-down area with brothels/taverns and a lot of criminal and trading activities in the streets roundabout; spectators came from all classes; noisy performances; ban on female actors, etc.

The character of Will Shakespeare also reveals clear parallels to the historical figure (cf. fact file: "Shakespeare and his times", SB p. 133), e.g. his time as an established actor, playwright and poet in the London theatre world.
However, Shakespeare's case of writer's block, his reputation as a womanizer, and the love affair with Viola de Lesseps and the link to the writing of *Romeo and Juliet* are pure fiction.

Additional viewing task

■ View the film for references to the sonnets and the play *Romeo and Juliet*.
Lösung: Will declares his love to one character in a sonnet (the most popular form of poetry in his time). He overcomes his writer's block when he sees Viola, to whom he devotes Sonnet 18 (cf. SB p. 118).

■ What parallels do you notice between *Shakespeare in Love* and *Romeo and Juliet*? (Cf. table below.)

Shakespeare in Love	Romeo and Juliet
– competition between theatre companies	– feud between families (cf. SB p. 139, "Prologue")
– Will's frustration: he has writer's block.	– Romeo's general dissatisfaction with life
– Rosalind as Will's muse (= inspiration)	– Romeo's relationship with Rosalind

Shakespeare & love

Shakespeare in Love	Romeo and Juliet
– Masked ball at the De Lesseps's house: case of false identity (Will as Marlowe), Wessex's rage, Will meets Viola.	– Masked ball at the Capulet's house: case of false identity, Tybalt's rage, Romeo meets Juliet (cf. SB pp. 139–140, "The first …").
– Balcony scene: nurse helps Viola (SB p. 143, l. 13)	– Balcony scene: nurse helps Juliet (SB pp. 141–142)
– Marriage to Wessex means Viola will go abroad.	– The killing of Tybalt causes Romeo's banishment.
– Queen approves Viola's marriage (cf. SB p. 145, l. 82).	– Prince's command
– Viola's shock (believing Will is dead); she realizes that she loves him.	– Juliet's shock at Romeo's identity; she realizes that she loves him.
– night spent together	– night spent together
– Parents arrange Viola's marriage.	– Parents arrange Juliet's marriage.
– Everything ends well: theatre companies are reconciled, the queen has the last word.	– Tragic ending: the lovers' deaths reconcile the two families, the Prince has the last word.

Additional viewing task

■ Watch the performance of *Romeo and Juliet* in the film *Shakespeare in Love* (when Viola plays Juliet) for:
– the stutterer's perfect delivery of the first eight lines of the Prologue (SB S. 139): "Two households…";
– key excerpts from the play.

Shakespeare, man of the Millennium SB S. 146–147

Before you read

■ **Nominate a German Personality**
E.g. Goethe, Gutenberg, Einstein….
Qualities: inventive, creative, dedicated to helping others…

■ **Explain idioms**
a) *Note:* Idioms are usu. listed under the **first main word**.
– **green**-eyed jealousy, cf. green with envy = very jealous;
– to **knit** your brows = to frown as a sign of concentration or anger;
– to make a **virtue** of necessity = to use a task one has to do to one's advantage;
– not to sleep a **wink** = not to be able to sleep at all;
– to give / get **short** shrift = to give / get little attention;
– cold **comfort** = a piece of good news about a bad situation that does not make you feel better.

Additional task

■ Think of German equivalents for the English idioms.
Lösungen: grün vor Eifersucht / Neid, die Augenbrauen zusammenziehen / die Stirn runzeln, aus der Not eine Tugend machen, kein Auge zutun, jemanden kurz abfertigen, schwacher Trost

b) *Topics:* crisis in a relationship – monologue by a lover / husband who feels betrayed by an unfaithful partner…

Exploring the text

1 *Reasons:* His works … "enriched the English language" (ll. 3, 17–19, 44); provide employment / an income for actors (l. 15); have been translated into many languages (ll. 16–17); are compulsory in British schools (l. 21); are performed on all continents (ll. 21–22); became accessible worldwide as the British Empire brought English to the four corners of the globe (ll. 28–29); have set an example for national poets as to how they can create a national identity (ll. 30–31); have been constantly re-interpreted (ll. 32–35, 41); have been frequently turned into successful films (ll. 36–38); present conflicts without answers, continue to fascinate audiences (ll. 39–41); can be adapted to other formats, e.g. ballet (ll. 45–47); have replaced the classics (ll. 49–50); reveal Shakespeare as a "humane" and "religious writer" (l. 54).

Additional task

■ Group the reasons given in task 1 above under headings, e.g. influence, status, fame, topicality, flexibility…

2 a) Sir Winston Churchill (British Prime Minister, who led Britain successfully during World War II); William Caxton (brought printing to England); Charles Darwin (defined human evolution as a selection process, i.e. the "survival of the fittest"); Isaac Newton (mathematical and scientific genius); Oliver Cromwell (possible web search activity: he fought the monarchy and rose through civil war and revolution to the highest office in the state; he united the three nations within the British Isles and, under him, England acquired its first colonies).
The comparison could point out the areas in which the nominees reached prominence, e.g. in politics and science, and the long-term effects of their achievements.
b) *Further ideas:* universal topics, stories of timeless appeal, fascinating characters, suspense-filled plots…
3 Mögliches Tafelbild siehe Seite 153 oben:
Die Vorgabe des 'indirect speech' könnte zu einer grammatischen Wiederholung in Beispielsätzen genutzt werden: He / She said that … had voted… / … is / was known…
Evtl. Wortvorgabe (short article: 200–300 words)
4 –

A step further

■ **Hold a panel discussion**
– Vorstellung des Unterrichtsvorhabens über Folie (Kopiervorlage "Planning a … panel discussion", TB S. 103);
– Vorbereitung der Diskussion "Should Shakespeare be nominated 'International Personality of the Millennium'?" in arbeitsteiliger GA (1 Gast – eine Gruppe von 3–5 S);
– Erstellung einer "Reduced role card: guest" als Information für den Moderator / die Moderatorengruppe (siehe TB S. 106);
– Auswahl des Gruppenrepräsentanten in der Diskussion am Ende der Vorbereitung nach Zufallsprinzip, Hinweis auf 'prompt cards', die von den S selbst erstellt werden sollen (siehe "Survival role card for a guest", TB S. 104).
Variation: Statt L als Moderator bereitet sich eine Gruppe von 3–5 S auf die Moderatorenrolle vor (auch als Tandemmoderation möglich), mit Input Kopiervorlage "Discussion:

Shakespeare & love

Category	Popular paper (tabloid)	Quality paper (broadsheet)
Main aim	entertainment	information
Presentation	visually attractive Events are: – dramatized by exaggeration, sensationalism, speculation – personalized by highlighting individual experiences, feelings and perspectives (focus on "human interest")	verbally challenging Events are described / presented: – objectively (facts and figures) – comprehensively, i.e. placed in a context, using a balanced, detached reporting style and include a variety of observations / comments
Tone	emotional	sober, down-to-earth
Language	everyday, colloquial, informal: – emotive diction to stir up feelings – easily accessible imagery describes events graphically – simple syntax: short, often incomplete sentences, use of phrasal verbs (e.g. 'to put off' instead of 'to delay')	difficult, complex, abstract, formal: – neutral diction, more sophisticated and specific vocabulary (e.g. to deteriorate) – emotions not expressed directly, little imagery – complex syntax: longer sentences with varying structures and subordinate clauses
Structure / layout	– text plus pictures – large print, different print sizes – short paragraphs (often only one sentence) – sub-headings	– focus on text – small print, with little variation in size – long paragraphs (usu. two or more sentences) – no sub-headings

moderation rules" (siehe TB Seite 188) und Kopiervorlage "Moderator role card" (siehe TB S. 105);
- Vorgehensweise: Zur Vorbereitung können auch neu gemischte Gruppen mit je einem Vertreter aus jeder Gäste-/Moderatorengruppe parallel im Klassenraum ein 'rehearsal' durchführen. Eine Gruppe wird dann für die Präsentation ausgewählt. Die Zuschauer machen sich hierbei Notizen zum kommunikativen Verhalten;
- Feedback: Dies wird vom L moderiert. Die Kopiervorlage "Discussion: feedback rules" (siehe TB S. 189) liefert hierbei sprachliche und strategische Hilfestellung.

Meet the media

■ **Write a news item, choose visual material**
A TV news item is part of a news programme.
Mögliche Konkretisierungsideen:
- Let's check the text for phrases / sentences the newsreader might use in his script (e.g. ll, 1–9, 16–18, 32–38, 48–50).
- Two interviews refer to the expert statements in the text.
- A picture of Shakespeare (SB, page 132) might be used as a background for the newsreader.
- The newsreader should know his / her text by heart, or be supported by a teleprompter-style text support.

Anschließend Evaluation: e.g. the newsreader's text and diction, the coordination between the different parts, etc.

Shakespeare – a great author   SB S. 147

Transkript

Professor Stanley Wells: The greatness of the writing means that it goes on having the power to move people, to enchant people, to express people's opinions for them, I suppose. I think this is one of the things we value from Shakespeare, he
5 encapsulates ideas which we still want to go on expressing in words which are totally memorable so that the English language has become permeated with quotations from Shakespeare.
Robert Smallwood: The fullness of range is what's extra-
10 ordinary for me. And people laughing, crying, loving, people in pain, people at war, people in every conceivable human situation are given language which expresses precisely and exactly the feelings that one is being required to understand and share.
Brian Blessed: The earth has had its author as I've said so 15 many times – it would be very greedy to want another. Chekov is wonderful, Schiller is wonderful, Goethe, we have many many authors but Shakespeare is it. God has smiled on this human being and he's been given to this blue planet, the earth, this great author, and I don't think we've begun to 20 really find Shakespeare yet. I don't think we've dug in remotely. I think it's amazing how little we've achieved and I think to a certain extent 90% of the time we do him a disservice because we fear him and we shouldn't.
Voice-over: "If you prick us do we not bleed. If you tickle us 25 do we not laugh. If you poison us, do we not die and if you wrong us, shall we not revenge."
"All the world's a stage and all the men and women merely players, they have their exits and their entrances and one man in his time plays many parts. His acts being seven ages." 30
"Out, out, brief candle! Life's but a walking shadow, a poor player that struts and frets his hour upon the stage and then is heard no more, it is a tale told by an idiot, full of sound and fury, signifying nothing."
As Hamlet poignantly says "The rest is silence". 35

1 *The arguments in the documentary:*
- Professor Stanley Wells, Director of the Shakespeare Institute: great works which move people and express topical ideas in memorable words.
- Robert Smallwood, Deputy Director of the Shakespeare Centre, Stratford-Upon-Avon: wide range of human situations and accessible language.
- Brian Blessed: unique position in literature, only partly researched and understood.
- Voice-over: choice of famous quotations of timeless truth.

2 Features of a (historical) documentary as shown by the two Shakespeare sequences "Shakespeare's early years" and "Shakespeare – a great author":
- historical pictures of Shakespeare and his handwritten works;

Shakespeare & love

- period music in the background;
- information and links provided by a voice-over;
- dramatised scenes (e.g. the plague, a pub) and characters (Shakespeare);
- footage (of the school today and inside a church);
- analysis / comments by experts.

Effects: creates the impression of authenticity; recreates the Elizabethan Age; sets Shakespeare in a historical context…

Romeo and Juliet on film   SB S. 148
Viewing log

Siehe "Viewing log assessment", TB S. 187.

Focus on: The Prologue

1 *Format:* A news item in a newscast, a documentary film…
Purpose: E.g. Element of surprise, attracts viewers' attention as they probably expect a more conventional Shakespearean production; it makes upcoming events seem more authentic / plausible; it allows the director to give a preview of events to come without giving away the plot…

2 *Verona Beach:* modern city; urban skyline is dominated by skyscrapers, which bear the names of their owners, Capulet and Montague. A statue of Jesus Christ seems to be caught between them, possibly implying that Christian teachings have been suppressed by the corporate owners.

3 *Flashforwards:* Many of the characters seem to be involved in violent scenes, thus implying that the film is very violent. There is no mention of a love story, which is what the audience would expect of a trailer from *Romeo and Juliet*.

Focus on: The encounter…

1 a) *Atmosphere:* lively, carefree, upbeat; characters are in a holiday / reckless mood; this impression is conveyed by their brightly coloured shirts and the open-top car.
b) The atmosphere changes when the Capulets pull into the petrol station. One signal is the change in the soundtrack, which has overtones of a Western. A further signal is the close-up of a black cowboy boot stamping out a lighted match.

2 Fast cuts add to the tension created by the characters and the situation. The effect is increased by the staccato way the actors deliver their lines.

3 *Close-ups:* licence plates, Mon 005, Cap 005: serve as coats of arms for the houses and indicate their power;
- Tybalt's face, and especially his eyes: he is determined to cause a fight; he obviously hates the Montagues;
- oil company slogan, "Add more fuel to your fire": has a double meaning: it points to the explosive situation between the two families and implies that the fights make the feuding worse;
- Tybalt's black, high-heeled boots with silver, metal mountings: remind us of a gunman in a Western;
- name of the gun "Sword 9mm": reminder of the swords used in the original play.

4 *Elements:* soundtrack, e.g. steel-guitar, gun-shots, especially the shot which ricochets off of the metal sign; shootout situation where characters wait for the first person to draw; characters take cover behind their cars as cowboys would behind water troughs and wagons.

5 Tybalt threatens Benvolio, even though the latter wants to prevent a fight, "Turn thee Benvolio and look upon thy death"; he is portrayed as an unforgiving, vengeful character – the close-ups of his face and boot convey this impression effectively as do his lines in the scene: "What, draw and talk of peace? I hate the word as I hate hell, all Montagues and thee." His body language is tense at all times as shown by his precise and purposeful way of moving. He shows his weapons provocatively to Benvolio and later kisses his gun. His devil-like appearance characterizes him as 'the bad guy'.

A step further

■ Write a film review –

The music of love   SB S. 149
Before you watch

■ **Define types of love**
- Romantic love is when s.o. feels a strong, often idealistic, emotion for s.o. else;
- Unrequited love is when s.o.'s feelings are not returned by the loved one;
- Ill-fated love is when a love affair ends in misfortune for those involved;
- Puppy love is a strong, but usu. temporary, feeling of love among young people;
- Undying love is a strong emotion which lasts forever.

■ **Think of video clips** –

Transkript: Love is a stranger

Love is a stranger in an open car
To tempt you in and drive you far away
And I want you
And I want you
And I want you – so it's an obsession   5

Love is a danger of a different kind
To take you away and leave you far behind
And love love love is a dangerous drug
You have to receive it and you still can't get enough of the stuff

It's savage and it's cruel and it shines like destruction   10
Comes in like the flood and it seems like religion
It's noble and it's brutal, It distorts and deranges
And it wrenches you up and you're left like a zombie

And I want you
And I want you   15
And I want you so it's an obsession

It's gilt edged, glamorous and sleek by design
You know it's jealous by nature, false and unkind
It's hard and restrained and it's totally cool
It touches and it teases as you stumble in the debris   20

And I want you
And I want you
And I want you so it's an obsession.

Musik und Text: Annie Lennox / David Stewart.
(c) Astwood Music / Logo Songs Ltd., für D: Musik-Edition Discoton GmbH (BMG Music Publishing Germany), München / Rudolf Slezak Musikverlage, Tegernsee.

Shakespeare & love

Before you watch

a) "Love is a stranger…" (l. 1): s.th. unknown, dangerous, unpredictable, it could take you anywhere but it will be fun ("open car")…
"Love is a danger…" (l. 3): it is not a physical danger, it is more emotionally risky and can have an untold effect on your feelings / mind…
b) –
c) *Mood:* carefree, haunting, threatening, reckless…

Watching and thinking

1 *Mood:* begins innocently and positively; it becomes more threatening, painful and confusing as love becomes "an obsession"…
2 *Role of the lead singer:* varies in each shot as the singer had different costumes, hairstyles and make-up; in most of the scenes, except for the footage of the band, the singer is playing a role of some kind;
Male characters: play a secondary role as the female singer dominates most of the scenes, e.g. in one shot, the singer embraces a man in an over-the-shoulder shot, but we do not see his face; the singer also dresses as a man and at the end of the clip, projects a heartless, almost zombified image;
Settings / costumes: vary constantly, yet are often familiar as they seem to be taken from films, e.g. a cabaret scene from a thirties film and a rescue scene from a fire, and even a Duane Hanson sculpture (two shoppers with a trolley); some of the settings are surreal, e.g. where one of the singers (Dave Stewart) is dressed as a king;
Links: Ideas mentioned in the lyrics are used as props, e.g. "stranger in an open car" / singer is driven in a car, "flood" (l. 11) / the sea, or are conveyed by the singers in some way, e.g. "danger" (l. 6) / one singer simulates a heart attack, repetition of "I want you" is accompanied by a threatening hand gesture in the last verse; "obsession" is symbolised by the fire in the rescue scene and also the singer's zombie-like movements in the last scene of the clip;
Plot vs. chain of associations: The images in the clip reflect types and aspects of love rather than giving a complete storyline (cf. "All Woman").

Transkript: All Woman

He's home again from another day
She smiles at him as he walks through the door
She wonders if it will be okay
It's hard for her when he doesn't respond

5 He says babe you look a mess
You look dowdy in that dress
It's just not like it used to be
Then she says…

I may not be a lady
10 But I'm All Woman
From Monday to Sunday I work harder than you know
I'm no classy lady
But I'm All Woman
And the woman needs a little love to make her strong
15 You're not the only one

She stands there and lets the tears flow
Tears that she's been holding back so long
She wonders where did all the loving go
The love they used to share when they were strong

She says yes I look a mess   20
But I don't love you any less
I thought you always thought enough of me
To always be impressed

I may not be a lady
But I'm All Woman   25
From Monday to Sunday I work my fingers to the bone
I'm no classy lady
But I'm All Woman
This woman needs a little love to make her strong
You're not the only one   30

He holds her and hangs his head in shame
He doesn't see her like he used to do
He's too wrapped up in working for his pay
He hasn't seen the pain he's put her through

Attention that he paid   35
Just vanished in the haze
He remembers how it used to be
When he used to say

You'll always be a lady
Cause You're All Woman   40
From Monday to Sunday I love you much more than you know
You're a classy lady
Cause You're All Woman
This woman needs a loving man to keep her warm

You're the only one   45
You're a classy lady
Cause You're All Woman

So sweet the love that used to be
So sweet the love that used to be

We can be sweet again   50

Musik und Text: Lisa Stansfield / Andy Morris / Ian Devaney (c) Big Life Music Ltd.
für D: Musik-Edition Discoton GmbH (BMG Music Publishing Germany),
München.

Before you watch

■ **Explain one side of the story**
E.g. *Man:* After being together for so many years, I feel that she doesn't make an effort to look pretty anymore. It's as if she doesn't care what I think or doesn't think it worthwhile doing s.th. about her appearance…
Woman: We have been married for years and somehow we have slipped into roles. He goes out to work and I take care of the housework. I don't see a need to get all dressed up just to clean the floors and he is so taken up by his work that he probably doesn't even notice me anyway…

■ **Write a storyline** –

Shakespeare & love

Watching and thinking

1 a) The couple seem to be on bad terms; he seems to be angry with her for some reason and she pleads with him before becoming angry, too; she seems to be very upset; it becomes clear that the relationship seems to be missing the romance and carefree feelings that the couple once shared.

b) *Special effects:* Images are superimposed on one another so that the clip portrays a number of different couples. This seems to imply that relationships can lose their meaning no matter what age, colour, etc. those involved are. The singer is present in the scenes, yet seems to be invisible. In this way, she / the song provides voice-over narration which explains / comments on the relationships and expresses the characters' feelings for them. The flashbacks at the end of the video seem to reflect the thoughts of each partner and finally create a more positive mood.

2 The repetition of the simple, straightforward lyrics brings across the message of the song in a haunting, effective way. The images support the message but probably would not be clear without the lyrics.

3 The couples embrace at the end of the clip and seem to have found some feelings for one another. The song also appears to end on an upbeat, relatively hopeful note, "We can be sweet again".

A step further

■ Work out differences between clips –

The poetry of modern love SB S. 150–151

Before you read

■ Listen to recordings, describe tone (Siehe unten.)

Poem	a) Type / phase of love	b) Tone
"Unfortunate …"	pretending to love s.o.	warning, admonishing, detached
"Coat"	memories of a lost love that is looked back to with a feeling of regret	nostalgic, regretful, sad
"Symptoms…"	the agony of being in love	sober, at the end: encouraging
"Sonnet XLII"	sadness of a loveless existence after many love affairs	matter-of-fact, melancholy, almost depressed
"After …"	falling in love	thoughtful, reflective, quietly cheerful

Exploring the texts

1 "Unfortunate…": is experienced in matters of love, knows that intense passion will not last; speaker = female friend, older adult
- "Coat": has found that love can be oppressive, values his / her freedom, regrets having given up a relationship and – in retrospect – appreciates its intimacy / warmth; speaker = teenager or young adult of either gender
- "Symptoms…": the speaker is experienced in matters of love; aware of the loss of reason and the intensive feelings involved; is sympathetic towards people who suffer for love: speaker = older adult, possibly male
- "Sonnet XLII": fleeting romances instead of stable, loving relationships / speaker seems unable to maintain relationships, now leads a lonely, loveless life awaiting death; speaker = older woman
- "After…": the speaker admits to having just fallen in love, refuses to listen to the voice of reason; speaker = teenager or young adult, probably female

2 "Unfortunate coincidence": –
- "Coat": "throw you off like a heavy coat" (ll. 2–3) implies a desire to break off a relationship which is perceived as a burden and loss of freedom (a weight on the speaker's shoulders)
- "Symptoms…": "Love is a universal migraine" (l. 1) with clear "symptoms"; it is a well-known, common, uncontrollable state which is not logical and can easily be recognized by certain signs
- "Sonnet XLII": "winter" (l. 9) of life and "summer sang in me" (l. 13) imply that the last phase in life / death is near, the prime of life is over
- "After…": "the juke-box inside me is playing a song" (l. 7), "juke-box" = heart / emotions, overwhelmed by feelings of joy

3 a) Rank poems according to:
- tone (most to least positive): After… – Symptoms… – Unfortunate… – Coat – Sonnet XLII
- language (most to least complex): Symptoms… – Sonnet XLII – After … – Unfortunate… – Coat
- most effective use of poetic devices: for an assessment of the quality of the images cf. Task 2.

b) –

A step further

■ **Illustrate poems with photos**

E.g. Unfortunate… – couple in an intimate embrace, but one of them is looking away; Coat – middle-aged man / woman sits on a park bench and looks into space, he / she is hunched with the cold (leafless trees indicate winter); Symptoms… – older woman / man sits at an old-fashioned desk, writes a letter of advice; Sonnet XLII – older woman sits in a rocking chair in a candle-lit room, listening to the rain outside (visible through a window in the background); After … – wet, windy day on Waterloo Bridge, two people move in opposite directions, both of them are carrying red umbrellas.

■ **Write a mini-saga**

A mini-saga is a prose text of exactly fifty words, neither more nor less, excluding the title (According to guidelines from the *Daily Telegraph*, the title should not be more than 15 words long).

Beispiel: Target of Affection

She left without saying where she was going. It wasn't the first time. Her husband followed her, parking some distance from where she met her lover. The husband's rifle failed to hit its target. He hurried home. On her return the wife innocently shouted, "Missed me?" – "Yes," seethed the husband.

Shakespeare & love

Lessons in love

SB S. 152

Transkript

Good evening and welcome to the Boston University Huntington Theatre for this the second part of our course in "Elementary courting for men". May I say how pleased I am with tonight's turnout – some 800 people, which is very
5 gratifying.
Tonight we look at the first date. Obviously taking out a girl for the first time is a very complex issue. The first crucial step is, having arranged to pick up your date, not to look like a complete idiot when she opens the door…
10 It's best to look as though your attention has been momentarily distracted …
But when you do notice her it is vital to say how pretty she is looking straight away … but don't overdo it …
If at this point you are introduced to her parents, attitude is all
15 important. You can be too casual … you can be too keen …
When you've said goodbye to the parents, again don't overdo it, lead her to your car and remember to open the door. [Fade out]
Before long you will arrive at the restaurant, get out of the car
20 and escort her to your table. Then tuck her into her seat yourself and attract the waiter's attention.
Selecting from the wine list is important. Complete ignorance is not good. When the bottle arrives, there's much to be made in the tasting of it but don't be too professional.
25 With eating, again, moderation is the order of the day. Again, don't eat too fast … But don't eat too slowly.

Before you watch

■ **Describe a still**
Mögliche Ideen: A man is kneeling on the floor / is down on his knees; his eyes are cast upwards in a reverent way; he seems to be admiring or praising s.o. or he could even be begging s.o. to do s.th. …

Watching and thinking I

Humorous parts: –
Basic comic effects:
– combination of situational humour (Rowan Atkinson acts out / dramatizes the speaker's advice) and verbal humour (the speaker suggests moderation and warns against extreme behaviour; the speaker uses surprisingly informal phrases for a formal talk, e.g. "complete idiot"; he uses understatement, e.g. "Complete ignorance is not good"; he also uses hyperbole, e.g. "… taking out a girl … is a very complex issue");
– contrast between the stereotypical characters / situations (the speaker's dry, theoretical lecture vs. the somewhat inexperienced lover's 'greenhorn' mistakes), or the speaker's elevated language compared to the banality of the topic;
– Rowan Atkinson's use of slapstick, i.e. exaggerated physical action;
– dramatization of extreme behaviour / opposites.

Watching and thinking II

■ **Note-taking in a grid**

Situations	Speaker's advice
picking her up	"Don't look like an idiot when she opens the door. Look as if your attention has been momentarily distracted. Say how pretty she looks."
meeting her parents	"Don't be too casual or too keen."
arriving at the restaurant	"Escort her to your table, tuck her into her seat and attract the waiter's attention."
selecting from the wine list	"Don't be too professional in the tasting."
eating your meal	"Show moderation in your speed."

■ **Speaker's appearance**
Appearance and body language: formally dressed in a suit, white shirt and tie; serious expression, erect posture, refers to notes, seeks eye-contact, speaks with emphasis, uses pauses for effect, varies his intonation – the speaker comes across as an expert / educated professional.

■ **Rowan Atkinson's body language**
Elaborate and varied body language relating to facial expression, gestures and movements. Prepare this task using the Copymaster "Body language", TB page 167.

A step further

■ **Evaluate the sketch**

Additional task

■ Think of further situations on a first date that the speaker might offer advice on. Write a script for his part. Then act out the talk and its dramatization.

■ In groups, write the script for another speech on a topic related to love. Then rehearse and perform the speech (and an accompanying sketch) in the classroom.

The four stages of love

SB S. 152–153

Before you read

■ **Collect collocations**
E.g. to have / to establish / to maintain / to improve / to break off a ~ with s.o.
a ~ between … and … / a father-son ~ / interpersonal ~s
a close / friendly / intimate / warm / steady / long-lasting / stormy ~
a superficial / casual / strained / hostile ~

■ **Describe stereotypes**
a) Wiederaufnahme der Kollokationen zuvor, z. B.
– A womanizer prefers short, casual, superficial relationships
– A lonely heart longs for a steady, close, long-lasting relationship…

Shakespeare & love

b) Brainstorm locations, e.g. a pub, club, supermarket... Then collect characteristic chat-up lines for the character who is most likely to take the initiative.

Additional task: Discuss the improvisations.

> A chat-up line may be: poor / ineffective / conventional / unimaginative; clever / probably successful / original / unusual...
> The other person's reaction may be: enthusiastic / friendly / polite / neutral / hesitant / cold / cool / unresponsive...
> Advances could be ignored / rejected / met with a favourable response.
> to make advances towards s.o. / ... a pass at s.o. *(informal)*

■ **Ask questions**
E.g. Which of the terms in the box would you use to describe yourself? (cf. box, S. 152) – If none of them apply, how would you describe your attitude to love? – What main characteristics should an ideal partner have?

Exploring the text

1 Überprüfung des Leseverständnisses durch Reduktion auf den informativen Kern: At 50, men are biologically programmed to undergo a revival of their emotional lives. This revival is the fourth stage in a genetically determined pattern: first: teenage love, second: a serious relationship leading to marriage, then, sexual exploration (within or outside marriage) and falling in love again (possibly with one's own wife).
Talk at a press conference: cf. Skills file "Presentations", SB pages 182–183.
News item: one paragraph which includes the most important information only.
2 a) The writer's biography fully corresponds with the first three stages of the "programme" (cf. ll. 7–21). The fourth stage is more complex and varies greatly (ll. 24–25). There is no guarantee that a mature person will choose more wisely (ll. 26–29) / there is the danger that the person will give up after having frustrating experiences (ll. 30–34) / you need to be lucky to find a suitable partner (here: a lonely hearts column) (ll. 35–44) / an increased awareness of, and sensitivity to, the qualities necessary for a good relationship (ll. 47–54).
b) The writer is honest and direct; he finds the psychological study partly enlightening but also doubts – and even feels threatened by – the theory that his emotional life follows a pre-determined pattern (ll. 59–66).
3 Light-hearted, not very serious, conversational tone with interjections (cf. ll. 28, 35–36, 47, 50), witty phrases / idioms (ll. 31, 38, 51) and enumerations used for emphasis (ll. 22–23, 32–33); informal phrases (e.g. ll. 13, 35, 66) mixed with literary phrases ("palls" (l. 22); a humorous simile: "a row of butterflies ... back" (ll. 65–66) and a formal / scientific register (ll. 14, 65); clear, straightforward syntax. The writer relates the study honestly and openly to his own biography, skilfully integrating quotes in his personal examination of the study. The text is fluent, thought-provoking and entertaining.

Close-up: if-clauses

a) Zuerst Beispiele im Unterrichtsgespräch sammeln und die entsprechenden Regeln wiederholen (hier: 'if-clauses types II and III'). Dann in PA Fragen sammeln und anschließend in 4-er Gruppen auf grammatische Richtigkeit überprüfen lassen ('peer assessment').
b) *Variante:* 3 S teilen sich die Rolle des Autors im 'hot chair' und beantworten abwechselnd die Fragen bzw. ergänzen sich gegenseitig.

A step further

■ **Write a parallel text**
Geeignet als HA. Perspektivenwechsel zur weiblichen Reaktion auf die Phasentheorie und deren Überprüfung anhand der eigenen Erfahrungen. Gruppen von 4 bis 5 S lesen und kommentieren wechselseitig (im Kreis weiterreichen!) ihre Texte: Rufzeichen und Unterschlängeln bei gelungenen Formulierungen, sowie Fragezeichen und Bleistiftkennzeichnung möglicher Fehler mit Korrekturvorschlägen. Abschließend Auswahl des besten Textes für die Präsentation im Kurs.

■ **Write a lonely hearts advert, dialogue**
Lonely hearts advert: Die folgenden Beispiele zeigen als Modelle Stil und Inhalt dieses Textformats; sie sollten darauf überprüft werden, ob sie zum Autor passen würden:
– Lonely, slim male seeks female under 40 to put some fun back into life, non-smoker.
– Honest male, 39, would like to meet lady 36–46 for friendship and possible romance, financially independent.
– Clint Eastwood look-alike, seeks attractive, cuddly female under 40 for a relationship and fun: pubs, clubs, dancing.
Phone conversation:
– Decide who phones who.
– Collect some phrases to get the conversation started, e.g. Greeting: Hello, this is ... I am ...
Response: It's great to hear from you...

Meet the media: Television show "This is your life"

Reason to invite John Robert: well-known journalist for the *Telegraph* / his life as a test case for the study by the Institute of Psychology in Rome. Possible surprise guests could add information about John Robert's biography: the girl he fell in love with at university and to whom he returned after the failure of his marriage / his first wife / a male friend from his bachelor years / as a climax his present wife. Rollenzuweisung, inhaltliche Abstimmung, Proben in Gruppen. Siehe "Participating in a talk show", TB S. 164 für nützliche Vokabeln. 1–2 Gruppen sollten Gelegenheit erhalten, die Show zu präsentieren. Die vier Vorschläge für die Beobachter sollten mit den S abgesprochen und ggf. konkretisiert werden. Beispiel 'language observers': differenzierte Beobachtungsschwerpunkte wie 'pronunciation', 'asking questions', 'vocabulary'. Eine Reflektionsphase könnte sich anschließen mit Stellungnahmen zum Ablauf der Show und zum Erfolg dieser Methode; Beiträge der S in dieser Reihenfolge: der Moderator – die Gäste – Fragesteller – die Journalisten – die Programmplaner – die Sprachbeobachter (Letzteres kann in die Folgestunde verschoben werden).

The way of the Wodaabe   SB S. 155–157

Reading in groups

Die Methode ist inspiriert von Reinhild Fliethmanns Aufsatz "Literature Study Groups im Fremdsprachenunterricht" (*Neusprachliche Mitteilungen* 3/2002, S. 155–162). Der Vorschlag stellt dar, wie diese Methode im Unterricht amerikanischer Schulen gehandhabt wird und macht anschließend Vorschläge zur Übertragung dieses Ansatzes auf den deutschen Fremdsprachenunterricht ab Klasse 10. Zentrales Ziel ist im Sinne eines "Over to you" die innerhalb einer GA weitgehend eigenständige und arbeitsteilige Bearbeitung eines Textes. Das Konzept wurde von R. Fliethmann für Langtexte und längere kooperative Arbeitsphasen adaptiert. Es eignet sich aber auch für einen längeren komplexen Sachtext wie den vorliegenden.

Zeitlich ideal ist eine Schulstunde für:
- die erste Besprechung der Methode (stilles Lesen des Input-Textes im SB S. 155 – Nachfragen – Gegenüberstellung der Vor- und Nachteile der Methode – ggf. Modifizierung wie z. B. die Zusammenlegung der Rollen bei weniger als 6 Teilnehmern);
- das Scannen des Textes in EA;
- die Zusammenstellung der Gruppen ('random groups', evtl. gesteuert durch gleichmäßige Verteilung der lernstärksten/-schwächsten S);
- die Rollenzuweisung (nach Absprache eigenständig in jeder Gruppe).

Auf der Grundlage der Bearbeitung des Textes gemäß der zugewiesenen Rolle erfolgt dann in einer weiteren Doppelstunde die Gruppendiskussion des Textes und die anschließende Bearbeitung ausgewählter Aspekte/Textstellen im Klassengespräch.

Sample questions/statements:
- the chairperson: How did you feel when reading...? – What was surprising/interesting/strange? – What questions did you have after reading the text? – Can we learn anything from the Wodaabe?
- the passage master: I would like to read ... – I would like to share this section with you because I found it shocking/informative/controversial/thought-provoking/well written/confusing/... – How do you feel about it?

Der 'investigator' sollte u.a. Zugang zum Internet haben. Ein zentrales Thema für das vertiefende Klassengespräch sollte sein: 'the pros and cons of an arranged marriage', i.e. parents choose a husband or wife for their child.

A step further

■ Conduct a panel discussion

Vorbereitung der 'panel discussion' durch Zusammenstellung der Gästeliste im Plenum (Kriterien für die Auswahl transparent machen!), dann Ausgestaltung der Rollen in arbeitsteiliger GA (je Gast – eine Gruppe von 3–5 S).

Zur transparenten Information und zur Steuerung des komplexen Arbeitsprozesses ist eine Verlaufsübersicht hilfreich, die vom L nach der Festlegung des Themas und der Gäste per Folie den S vorgestellt wird (vgl. Kopiervorlage TB S. 103).

In der GA Erarbeitung einer "Survival role card for a guest" (Kopiervorlage TB S. 104) bzw. einer "Moderator role card" (Kopiervorlage TB S. 105); zur Optimierung der Koordination zwischen Moderator und Gast reichen die Gäste-Gruppen möglichst bald eine "Reduced role card: guest" (siehe Kopiervorlage TB S. 106) zur Information an die Moderatorengruppe weiter.

Auswahl des Gruppenrepräsentanten in der Diskussion am Ende der Vorbereitung nach Zufallsprinzip.

Zur Moderatorenrolle: mögliche Variationen: ein S oder der L als Moderator oder Tandemmoderation durch zwei S;

sprachlich-strategische Hilfestellung durch Kopiervorlage "Discussion: moderation rules" (vgl. TB S. 188).

Erprobung der Show: zur Vorbereitung führen neu gemischte Gruppen mit je einem Vertreter aus jeder Gäste/Moderatorengruppe parallel im Klassenraum ein 'rehearsal' durch. Eine Gruppe wird dann für die 'öffentliche' Präsentation ausgewählt. Bei Zeitmangel: Ohne rehearsal Auswahl des Gruppenrepräsentanten in der öffentlichen Diskussion am Ende der Vorbereitung nach Zufallsprinzip.

Während der Show machen sich die Zuschauer Notizen:
- zu den Argumenten und Positionen/zum kommunikativen Verhalten einzelner Gäste;
- zum Moderationsgeschick des Moderators.

Der L notiert auf je einer kleinen 'hot card' pro S höchstens drei auffällige Fehler, diese werden am Ende der Stunde dem betreffenden S mitgegeben (die Fehler könnten auch ggf. zu Beginn der Folgestunde von ihnen vor der Klasse reflektiert werden).

Evaluation: Mögliche Bausteine der lehrermoderierten Auswertungsphase:
- Statements der Teilnehmer: How did you feel...? – How did you cope with the role?
- Rückmeldung der Gäste für die Teilnehmer liefert hierbei sprachliche und strategische Hilfestellung (siehe auch "Discussion: feedback rules", TB S. 189).
- Rückmeldung zur Methode an den L: What was effective? – What can be improved?

Vereinbarungen für die nächste 'chat show' bzw. 'panel discussion' schriftlich auf Poster fixieren.

■ Write an essay

Verweis auf Skills file "Essays" im SB S. 187.

Love story: writing a twenty-minute script SB S. 158

Using your skills

Before you start

Durch diese Übung soll S bewusst werden, dass der Dialog auf das Wesentliche begrenzt sein sollte und möglichst viele Informationen visuell vermittelt werden sollten.

Ergänzende Hilfe: Start with a general introduction. Include details about:
- the setting, i.e. time and location of the action;
- the two characters, e.g. name, job, age...;
- the situation at the beginning of the scene, e.g. the position and appearance of the characters.

Ggf. Funktionen von Regieanweisungen (= stage directions) wiederholen, e.g. information about entrances and exits, setting, body language, movements, silences, pauses and the tone used. Regieanweisungen werden kursiv geschrieben und in Klammern gesetzt (handschriftliche Alternative: zweite Farbe).

Step 1 Finding an idea

Die Szenen der Übung "Before you start" können hier weiterbearbeitet werden.

Hinweis: How to sum up a plot: Briefly describe the setting and the characters. Then say what happens and how events are logically connected. Use the present tense. Avoid direct speech. Keep it short and sweet.

Shakespeare & love

Step 2 Creating character profiles
Profile der Charaktere arbeitsteilig in den zuvor etablierten Gruppen erstellen, dann präsentieren und ergänzen. Auf die Box zu 'flat / round characters' (SB S. 159) verweisen.

Step 3 Preparing a plot outline
Computerversierter Protokollant erstellt in HA Reinschrift der Notizen des Unterrichts. Die Datei könnte allen Gruppenmitgliedern zugesendet werden. Die weiteren Arbeitsschritte (vgl. Steps 4–6) sollten von Gruppenmitgliedern in HA (am Computer) ergänzt und allen zugesendet werden.

Step 4 Writing a dialogue
Hinweis 1: Begrenzung des Dialogs auf das Wesentliche, Vermeidung von Redundanz und überlangen Statements. Hinweis auf die Möglichkeit 'voice-over narration' (= a voice speaking offscreen which gives background information, fills in gaps in the story, or reveals a character's thoughts) einzusetzen.

Step 5 Choosing cinematic devices
Vgl. auch die "special effects" Box im SB S. 87.

Step 6 Writing the screenplay
Die Umwandlung der Rasterplanung in das Screenplay-Format ist der abschließende Arbeitsschritt.

Ergänzende Aufgabe

Act out your script in a stage performance or turn it into a film. Vgl. hierzu *Password to Skyline Plus* (ISBN 3-12-510460), Strategy page 123 "Acting out a dramatic text").

Test: All the World's in Love With Shakespeare I   TB S. 168

Klausur für den Grundkurs
Textformat: newspaper article, 524 words
Vorschlag / Klausurtyp NRW: Tasks 1–3a/b, A1/A2
Bezugstexte des Kapitels: "Romeo and Juliet on film" (SB S. 148), "Shakespeare in love" (SB S. 143), "Shakespeare – man of the Millennium" (SB S. 146).
Den Klausur und die entsprechenden Fragen finden Sie auf einer Kopiervorlage auf Seite 168.

Comprehension
1 Special position in international literature / outstanding historical figure: popular all over the world (world genius with a cross-cultural appeal).
One simple explanation is financial, i.e. the cheap brand name. The most important one is the enduring quality of Shakespeare's work, due to the richness of the language, the quality of the characters and the convincing plots which can be reinvented in all ages.

Analysis
2 ll. 1–8: starting point, i.e. Shakespeare's declining position at US universities;
ll. 9–28: examples of Shakespeare's continuing worldwide recognition balance the US trend;
ll. 29–40: two attempts at explaining Shakespeare's success (cheap brand name, latent power of his work);
ll. 41–49: presentation of the usual arguments, which are found to be sufficiently convincing;
ll. 50–62: a provocative new theory.

Comment / (re-)creation of text
3 a) In general, students are likely to speak in favour of the writer's arguments. They are expected to comment in detail on the evidence of Shakespeare's popularity as outlined in the article, e.g. most-produced playwright in America; voted "Briton of the millennium" in England; numerous films are based on his works, etc.
b) Letter type: formal letter
Example:
Sir,
In your article of 20th March, 1999, Michiko Kakutani claims that … [individual arguments are presented clearly and politely] …
Yours sincerely,
[signature]

Test: Sonnet 73   TB S. 169

Klausur für den Leistungskurs
Textformat: sonnet, 121 words
Vorschlag / Klausurtyp NRW: Tasks 1–3a/b, A1/A2
Bezugstexte des Kapitels: "Sonnet 18" (S. 136), "Sonnet 116" (S. 137), "The Prologue" (S. 139), "Sonnet XLII" (S. 151).
Den Klausur und die entsprechenden Fragen finden Sie auf einer Kopiervorlage auf Seite 169.

Comprehension
1 *Age:* past his prime, beginnings of physical decay / decline and old age ('in the autumn of life', cf. "yellow leaves, or none, or few do hang", l. 2), sophisticated descriptions / images imply that the speaker's mental capacities are unaffected by physical decline;
Mood: calm, composed, thoughtful;
View of life: realistic (the good times are over), reflects on the transience of his life;
Experiences with love: the poem is addressed to a beloved person; the speaker feels loved by the addressee, with whom he seems to have a long-term relationship.

Analysis
2 The images related to the speaker are "yellow leaves" on a "bough" i.e. a tree in autumn; "twilight of a day (l. 5); the dying "ashes" of a fire. They reflect the speaker's advanced age, physical decline and imminent death. A further image is "black night" (l. 7) which symbolizes (the coming of) death.
Form / language: 14 lines in iambic pentameter, 3 quatrains as units, 1 indented concluding couplet, carefully ordered sequence of ideas / train of thought, rhyme scheme: cross rhymes (abab) and a final pair rhyme (aa), examples of old English.
Themes: transitory nature of life versus permanence of love, true love in the sense of a close, trusting relationship, continuity and mutual commitment.
Conclusion: formally / thematically a typical Shakespearean sonnet.

Comment / (re-)creation of text
3 a) Personal comment: –
b) Possible beginning: My dear, we've been together for a long time now – we have experienced good times and bad. You used to be…

Shakespeare & love

Test: All the World's in Love With Shakespeare II TB S. 169

Klausur-Variante für den Grund- oder Leistungskurs
Textformate: newspaper article (292 words), documentary extract
Vorschlag / Klausurtyp NRW: Tasks 1–3a / b, B2 (A1 / A2)
Quelle: Michiko Kakutani, *The New York Times*, March 20, 1999; "Shakespeare – a great author" (siehe Begleitvideo und -DVD *Skyline, Advanced Level: Media literacy*, Sequenz 9)
Bezugstexte des Kapitels: "Shakespeare's early years" documentary extract (SB S. 133 und Begleitvideo und -DVD, Sequenz 8, hier ergänzend 'documentary features' aufzeigen zur Vorbereitung auf Frage 2), "Romeo and Juliet on film" (SB S. 148), "Shakespeare in love" (SB S. 143), "Shakespeare – man of the Millennium" (SB S. 146).
Den Klausur und die entsprechenden Fragen finden Sie auf einer Kopiervorlage auf Seite 169.

Comprehension

1 *The writer's view:* Siehe suggested answers zum Test: "All The World's..." im TB S. 160.
Arguments in the documentary:
– Professor Stanley Wells, Director of the Shakespeare Institute: great works which move people and express topical ideas in memorable words.
– Robert Smallwood, Deputy Director of the Shakespeare Centre, Stratford-Upon-Avon: wide range of human situations and accessible language.
– Brian Blessed: unique position in literature, only partly researched and understood.
– Voice-over: choice of famous quotations of timeless truth.

Analysis

2 Features of a (historical) documentary as shown by the two Shakespeare sequences "Shakespeare's early years" and "Shakespeare – a great author":

– historical pictures of Shakespeare and his handwritten works;
– period music in the background;
– information and links provided by a voice-over;
– dramatised scenes (e.g. the plague, a pub) and characters (Shakespeare);
– footage (of the school today and inside a church);
– analysis / comments by experts.

Effects: e.g. creates the impression of authenticity; recreates the Elizabethan Age; sets Shakespeare in a historical context.

Comment / (re-)creation of text

3 a) In general, students are likely to speak in favour of the writer's arguments. They are expected to comment in detail on the evidence of Shakespeare's popularity as outlined in the article and the documentary (see above).
b) Letter type, formal letter: Siehe suggested answers zum Test: "All The World's..." im TB S. 160.

Mündliche Prüfung: How important are Shakespeare's works at the beginning of the new millennium? TB S. 164

Format: Gruppenprüfung mit drei Teilnehmern in Form einer Talkshow. Die Rolle des Moderators wird vom Prüfer übernommen. Die Gäste ergeben sich aus den im Unterricht bearbeiteten Texten.
Thema: How important are Shakespeare's works at the beginning of the new millennium?
Die entsprechenden Rollenkarten befinden sich auf Seite 164.

Shakespeare and love

Kernwortschatz

Shakespeare

outstanding literary figure
literary genius
man for all ages
universal acclaim

Love

to fall (head over heels) in love with s.o.
to be madly in love (with s.o.)
to be infatuated with s.o.
to declare/express one's love for s.o.
a deep/sincere/true/romantic/
  undying/inrequited love
love at first sight
a passionate love affair
a loveless relationship
love against the odds

***

Poetry

A poem
- consists of/is divided into/
  is made up of …
  … lines/stanzas/sections
- follows a clear rhyme scheme:…
- has an introductory/middle/
  concluding stanza/section
- is marked/characterized by a … tone
- conveys a certain message

A sonnet
14-line poem in iambic pentameter
three quatrains (four lines of verse),
  concluding couplet (two lines)

The speaker
- makes use of complex images/
  highly poetic language
- reveals his attitude towards…
- conveys his feelings about…
- poses the question: if…
- appeals to the reader to…
- argues that…
- describes…
- aims to convince the reader of s.th.
- arouses compassion with/
  sympathy for…

An image
- may be a simile/a metaphor for
  s.th./a symbol of s.th.
- represents/stands for/symbolizes…
- arouses certain associations
- is appropriate/original/conventional or
  far-fetched/obscure/exaggerated

- has a deeper meaning in so far
  as … is concerned
- describes s.th. vividly
- explains s.th. graphically
- expresses/suggests an idea
  in a memorable/indirect way
- evokes particular emotions/
  responses/reactions
- has certain connotations

The tone reveals/reflects the speaker's
  feelings. It may be…
- matter-of-fact/detached
- melancholy/sad
- cheerful/enthusiastic
- humorous/joking/playful
- emotional/harsh/accusing
- ironic/sarcastic
or it:
- signals resignation/frustration
- suggests/indicates
  disappointment/anger

The language
- includes diction
  (= the way words are pronounced),
  vocabulary,
  syntax (= arrangement of words
  in a sentence)
- is informal/colloquial/concrete/
  emotive/or
- is formal/abstract/high-flown/
  poetic/figurative…

Shakespeare and love

Drama
Elements of drama
theme, action
setting (= place and time of action)
plot (and subplots) (= logical connection of
  events, i.e. what happens and why)
characters
language, atmosphere

A play
tragedy, comedy
author/playwright/dramatist
a play is set in (a city, a country) and
– appeals to the audience's emotions
– delights and instructs the spectators
– arouses pity/evokes fear
– deals with a theme/topical issue…

Tragedy
a play in which the sequence
  of events leads to a catastrophe
s.o.'s downfall is caused by
  a character flaw or error
  of judgement
the events arouse pity and fear
  in the audience
a tragedy deals with characters
  of high rank/lower-class characters
it presents a conflict/a disaster
it has a tragic ending/ends in disaster
a tragic hero enjoys prosperity
  and has a high standing/
  good reputation; he usually…
– makes a fatal error
– makes the wrong decision(s)
– sets off a train of events which
  goes out of control
– causes his own downfall/
  misery/destruction
– awakens our pity by his suffering
– creates fear when we recognize
  similar shortcomings in ourselves
– has a tragic outcome/ending

The action
the plot is the result of interaction
  between characters
the action …
– takes place in a single setting
– rises/moves to a crisis
– reaches a turning-point
– indicates further developments
– foreshadows an unhappy ending
a complex plot is based on discovery,
  intrigue, misunderstanding, deception

Structure
script: acts, scenes
prologue, exposition (= background information)
rising action introduces
  obstacles and setbacks
conflict, crisis
climax (= point of maximum suspense)
turning-point
falling action (hero's fortune in decline)
catastrophe (brings about the
  hero's death)
resolution/denouement (= final outcome)
discovery, new balance

Language
monologue, dialogue, aside
written in prose/in verse
lines/passages of lively dialogue
the language…
– reveals certain characteristics
– drives the plot
– determines the tone of the play

Characters
main and minor characters
hero, heroine
protagonist, antagonist
to be in conflict with opponents/fate
an event brings about the
  hero's downfall
a character has a high social status/rank
to deliver a monologue
to whisper an aside
to address another character
to overhear a conversation
to enter into a dialogue with…

Performance
to stage/perform a play
stage directions provide information about
  entrances/exits/the setting/
  body language/moods/silences/pauses
the curtain rises and falls
props, scenery, costumes
the (Shakespearean) stage projects
  into the seating area
the director
the actors/actresses/members of the cast …
– play a major/minor part/role in a play
– enter/leave the stage
– make an entrance from the left/right
– rehearse a play
– wear costumes and make-up
the audience/the spectators
  applaud/boo a performance

Shakespeare and love

Participating in a talk show

What the presenter might say

… when starting the show and talking to the audience:
Thank you for the warm welcome / that very warm round of applause…
Welcome to a new edition of (name of TV show)!
My special guest tonight is … / hardly needs any introduction… / I'm sure you all know my special guest tonight, it's…
He / she is famous for… / well-known for… / is extremely popular with…
A big round of applause please for…

… when talking to a new guest:
It's great that you could come along today / this evening…
Please, take a seat. Make yourself comfortable. Let's talk about … first.
How did you feel / react when…? / What was it like when…?
Looking back, would you have done anything differently?
What would you have done if …. had happened?
If you had the chance to meet X again, how would you feel about it? / Well, now you have the opportunity! Let me welcome … / It's great having you on the show.

… when ending the show:
I'm sorry to say that our time is up.
Thank you for joining me today.
I hope you've enjoyed the show.
Tune in again next week for another edition of "This is your life". / Until then goodnight.

What a guest might say

… when he / she comes on stage:
Thank you for the invitation. I've always dreamed of being your guest. I've never been on TV before.

… when remembering the "good old days" / the past:
I still remember the first time I saw / met … It was the year…
I must admit that at the time I was…..

… when he / she talks about the star guest:
To be quite honest… / I don't want to lie here…
We were pretty close for a time.
What I admired about him at the time was his …
What I was not happy about was the way he tried to…
In fact I have bad / pleasant memories of a situation where…
After some time I saw … in a different light. I realized that…
But then we went different ways / lost sight of each other…
I always planned to contact him again / give him a ring / get in touch with him again but somehow I never got round to it.

… when talking about what happened after they lost sight of each other:
I studied at university / became a… / went on a trip around the world… / married and raised … kids / never married / remained single / lived with my boyfriend / girlfriend…
My career as a … didn't last long. When I was offered a job as … That was the highlight of my career. Later I made a career change. I started a career as… And was quickly promoted to… Professionally I was very successful: I…

✂--

Test: "Shakespeare and love"

Thema: How important are Shakespeare's works at the beginning of the new millennium?

Role cards

✂--

Guest 1 As a historian specializing in Shakespeare and the Elizabethan Age, you argue that his works can only be understood if one has a background knowledge of Shakespeare's life and times.

Guest 2 You are a professor of literature who has just published a book entitled *Shakespeare and love*, which includes selected sonnets and play extracts. You strongly recommend this anthology as a class reader for advanced students of English.

Guest 3 You are Sandra Barwick from *The Telegraph*, the writer of the article "Shakespeare, man of the Millennium". Feel free to present views from your article.

Guest 4 You are a student of English at a German high school who argues that Shakespeare should not be a compulsory part of the school curriculum for German pupils.

Guest 5 You are a surprise guest who has a very special relationship to, and opinion on, Shakespeare and his works.

Guest 6 Feel free to be yourself! Bring in your own experiences with Shakespeare at school.

Shakespeare and love

Shall I compare thee…?

Put the following lines of Sonnet 18 into the correct order with the help of the definition of a "Shakespearean sonnet" on the right. Copy your solution onto a sheet and compare it with the original on page 136 of your book. The first two lines have been given to you.

Shakespearean sonnet A sonnet is a fourteen-line poem written in iambic pentameter, i.e. an unstressed syllable is followed by a stressed syllable five times. The Shakespearean sonnet is usually made up of three quatrains (four lines of verse) and a concluding couplet of two lines, sometimes written 4 + 4 + 4 + 2, which form clear units in a line of argument and rhyme abab cdcd efef gg.

---

[1] Shall I compare thee to a summer's day?

[2] Thou art more lovely and more temperate:

[ ] Sometime too hot the eye of heaven shines,

[ ] And summer's lease hath all too short a date;

[ ] But thy eternal summer shall not fade,

[ ] Rough winds do shake the darling buds of May,

[ ] Nor shall Death brag thou wander'st in his shade,

[ ] So long as men can breathe or eyes can see,

[ ] And every fair from fair sometime declines,

[ ] When in eternal lines to time thou grow'st.

[ ] By chance, or nature's changing course untrimmed:

[ ] And often is his gold complexion dimmed;

[ ] So long lives this, and this gives life to thee.

[ ] Nor lose possession of that fair thou ow'st,

---

temperate mild – **eye of heaven** *(fig.)* sun – **lease** *(legal)* the right to use s.th. for a certain time – **date** *here:* duration – **darling buds** lovely, young flowers – **to brag** to speak proudly – **to time thou grow'st** you and time become one, i.e. eternal – **eternal lines** immortal verses – **complexion** *here:* appearance – **course** *here:* state – **untrimmed** uncontrolled – **to owe** *(old)* to possess

Shakespeare and love

Sonnet 116 – a model interpretation

Sonnet 116 has the straightforward structure of almost all Shakespearean sonnets. It consists of three quatrains, which rhyme abab, and a concluding couplet. The line of thought conforms to this pattern and is equally simple. After an opening statement, it consists of definitions of what love is and what it is not. Some variation in structure is introduced by means of three cases of run-on line (ll. 2–3; 5–6; 9–10). The pace of the sonnet is, for the most part, one of steady iambics. The vocabulary used is also mainly simple and everyday, and the only image which might present some difficulty to the modern reader is in line 8. The whole poem gives an impression of effortless mastery as much as calm conviction.

In the opening statement the speaker addresses himself using the word "impediment". This calls to mind the following part of the marriage service in *The Book of Common Prayer*: "If any of you know cause, or just impediment, why these two persons should not be joined in holy matrimony, ye are to declare it now, or remain silent forever". The most important phrase in the quatrain, however, on which all else depends, is "the marriage of true minds" (l. 1). In such an ideal "marriage" or union, all physical considerations are of secondary importance. It is the mental harmony that matters. The word "true" is not just meant to be understood as 'faithful' and 'honest' in the everyday sense, but also as "truly meant for each other". Thus, the two minds in the relationship find a complement in one another. The speaker believes that this union of minds in the relationship between himself and his friend happens rarely, and should make the relationship strong enough to overcome all obstacles.

Two impediments are mentioned in lines 3–4 of the sonnet, although only in abstract terms. The first impediment is an "alteration" in the beloved, whether in appearance (cf. also l. 9 onwards) or behaviour. The second definition of what love is not (l. 4) says that real love will not change its course or attitude ("bends") because the loved one does so. By such a change we may understand that the loved one is unfaithful, though it could also be taken to mean no more than disinterest or neglect.

In the next quatrain love is compared to a sea-mark or beacon (a light-house would be the modern equivalent) which faces and withstands the force of the storm. True love should withstand the most violent, emotional stress. The beacon is also a guiding light, but this idea is now transferred to "the star" by which the sailor in his ship ("bark", l. 7) may set his course, i.e. the speaker leads his life. A further connotation might be that with such a permanent anchor, the "wandering" (l. 7) lover / beloved may feel free to pursue new interests and experiences.

According to the speaker, love is not the "fool" of personified time, i.e. love is not to be mocked and deceived by time. While love sees the physical damage brought about by time, true love is based on other values. In line 10 we have the conventional image of time using the curved sickle to destroy everything within its reach, including physical beauty: Rosy lips and cheeks are signs of youth and fade with increasing age. Love, however, is not affected by the passage of time. Indeed, love is eternal whereas time / life can be reduced to "brief hours and weeks" (l. 11). The worst that Time can do is to bring death and this will be faced and endured by love to the last moment (i.e. "the edge of doom", l. 12). This climactic line closes the third quatrain on a note of calm defiance. With its confident tone, the concluding statement in the final couplet is a fitting end to the poem. (648 words)

Tasks

Study the model analysis of Sonnet 116 and complete the tasks.

1. What aspects of the sonnet are dealt with in each paragraph?
2. Highlight the connectives used in the interpretation to link ideas. Think of possible alternatives.
3. How does the text include quotations and text references?
4. Which phrases could you use to analyse any poem?
5. Which ideas go beyond what you have discussed in class? Do you find these statements convincing, or not?
6. Which phrases or sentences do you find high-flown? Try to re-phrase them simply in your own words.
7. Write a comparative analysis of Sonnets 18 and 116 (cf. pages 136 and 137 of your book).

Shakespeare and love

Body language

Use your dictionary to make a vocabulary map on body language. Here are some words and phrases to start you off in each category:

> to twist one's mouth • a handshake • to crawl • to shrug one's shoulders • to pull a face • to have clenched fists • to fold one's arms • to stand stiffly • to stroke s.o. • an upright posture • to embrace s.o. • to frown • to cross one's legs • to stick out one's tongue • a wrinkled forehead • …

Note: Some words fit into more than one category.

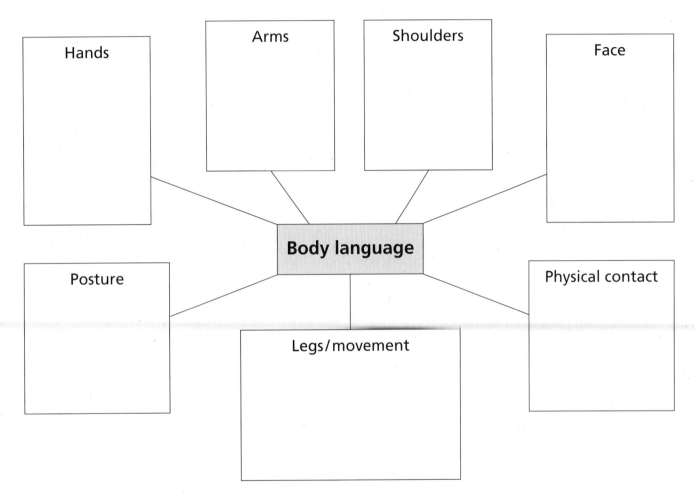

- Use the vocabulary you have found to describe the body language of the people in the photos below.

- In pairs or small groups, try to visualize a relationship or situation in a freeze frame (= standing as if one is frozen in the middle of an action). The other students describe and comment on your ideas.

Shakespeare and love

Test: All the World's in Love with Shakespeare I

Only two years ago, a report that two-thirds of America's leading universities had dropped the Shakespeare requirement for English majors in favor of courses on popular culture and gender studies prompted worries that the playwright – regarded by many leftist ideologues as the quintessential Dead White Male – was becoming a has-been, a victim of the commissars of political correctness and watered-down curriculums.

Today, happily, it is clear that such reports of Shakespeare's demise were vastly exaggerated. He is still the most produced playwright in 1990s America, and in England he was recently voted in one BBC poll "the Briton of the millennium."

There are replicas of the Globe Theater in London and Tokyo, and in Germany his birthday prompts an annual celebration. As the scholar Jonathan Bate, author of *The Genius of Shakespeare*, points out, the Bard has become "a world genius" with a "crosscultural appeal" that defies both the debunking of academic radicals and the stuffy canonization of traditionalists.

Shakespeare in Love – a witty movie that works an improvisation on the playwright's life – was nominated for 13 Academy Awards and shares a nomination for Best Picture with *Elizabeth,* another film set against the backdrop of Elizabethan England.

These pictures are only the tip of the Shakespeare iceberg. Coming soon are a slew of movies based on his plays …

Certainly the fact that Shakespeare is a brand name, one who neither demands royalties nor contests rewrites, has something to do with this. But there is a latent power to his work that has allowed successive generations of directors, critics and actors to continually reinvent him in their own image and to find new ways (some profound, some forced, some silly) of pointing up his relevance. Restoration critics emphasized his role as a dramatic playwright who addressed public and political issues. Romantics portrayed him, romantically, as the poet of melancholy and love. And modernists have stressed the difficulty of his work, its layered, contradictory meanings.

Just what is it about Shakespeare's work that accounts for his enduring ability to engage the popular imagination, his accessibility to so many eras and cultures? The usual reason offered for his greatness – the richness of his language, the range and depth of his characterizations, the fecundity of his imagination – do not explain why he – rather than, say, Dante or Chaucer – has remained a household name. Nor do paeans to his storytelling gifts; after all, he lifted most of his plots from existing works.

In his controversial book, *Reinventing Shakespeare*, Gary Taylor, an editor of an Oxford University Press edition of the playwright's works, suggested that the Bard owed much of his success to happy accidents of history. "If France had won its wars against England, if England like other countries had been culturally transformed by the upheavals of the late 18th century," he wrote, "then Shakespeare would almost certainly not have achieved or retained the dominance he now enjoys."

Shakespeare's current international reputation, in Taylor's view, was at least in part "the fruit not of his genius but of the virility of British imperialism, which propagated the English language on every continent." (517 words)

By Michiko Kakutani, *The New York Times*, March 20 1999.
Copyright © 2004 by The New York Times Co.
Reprinted with permission.

---

3 **English major** *(AE)* a student studying English as a main subject – 7 **commissar** *here:* s.o. in a position of power who ensures that rules are followed – 19 **debunking** showing that s.o.'s good reputation is false – 23 **Academy Awards** Oscars (for outstanding films) – 30 **to contest** [-'-] *here:* to oppose – 36 **Restoration** refers to a period in British history around 1660 when the monarchy was re-established – 47 **Dante, Chaucer** 16th century European writers – 48 **paean** ['pi:ən] *(formal)* song of praise – 61 **virility** *here:* energy

Tasks

1 How does the writer rate Shakespeare's current international reputation? What explanations does he offer for his assessment?

2 Analyse how the writer structures his ideas.

3 Do **one** of the following:
  a) How convincing are the writer's arguments that the world is indeed in love with Shakespeare?
  or:
  b) Write a letter to the editor of *The New York Times* in response to the article. Describe the attitudes of advanced students of English in Germany towards Shakespeare and say what role his works should play at German schools.

Shakespeare and love

Test: Sonnet 73

That time of year thou mayst in me behold
When yellow leaves, or none, or few, do hang
Upon those boughs which shake against the cold,
Bare ruined choirs, where late the sweet birds sang.
5 In me thou seest the twilight of such day
As after sunset fadeth in the west,
Which by and by black night doth take away,
Death's second self, that seals up all in rest.
In me thou seest the glowing of such fire
10 That on the ashes of his youth doth lie,
As the death-bed whereon it must expire,
Consumed with that which it was nourished by.
   This thou perceive'st, which makes thy love more strong,
   To love that well which thou must leave ere long.

1 **behold** *(old)* see – 3 **bough** [baʊ] branch – 10 **his** *here:* its – 12 **consumed** *here:* destroyed – 13 **perceive'st** see – 14 **ere** before

Tasks

1 What do you learn about the speaker? Consider age, mood and his attitude towards life and love.
2 Analyse the imagery in the sonnet in detail. Is this a Shakespearean sonnet, or not? Give reasons for your answer.
3 Do **one** of the following:
   a) As a young person, how appealing do you find the sonnet, compared with other sonnets you have read in class?
   or
   b) Imagine the person who is being addressed in "Sonnet 73" ("thou", ll. 1, 5, 9, etc.) replies to the speaker's comments in a letter. Write this letter.

Test: All the World's in Love with Shakespeare II

Only two years ago, a report that two-thirds of America's leading universities had dropped the Shakespeare requirement for English majors in favor of courses on popular culture and gender studies prompted worries
5 that the playwright – regarded by many leftist ideologues as the quintessential Dead White Male – was becoming a has-been, a victim of the commissars of political correctness and watered-down curriculums.
   Today, happily, it is clear that such reports of
10 Shakespeare's demise were vastly exaggerated. He is still the most produced playwright in 1990s America, and in England he was recently voted in one BBC poll "the Briton of the millennium."
   There are replicas of the Globe Theater in London and
15 Tokyo, and in Germany his birthday prompts an annual celebration. As the scholar Jonathan Bate, author of *The Genius of Shakespeare*, points out, the Bard has become "a world genius" with a "crosscultural appeal" that defies both the debunking of academic radicals and the stuffy canonization of traditionalists. 20

Shakespeare in Love – a witty movie that works an improvisation on the playwright's life – was nominated for 13 Academy Awards and shares a nomination for Best Picture with *Elizabeth*, another film set against the backdrop of Elizabethan England. 25

These pictures are only the tip of the Shakespeare iceberg. Coming soon are a slew of movies based on his plays…

Certainly the fact that Shakespeare is a brand name, one who neither demands royalties nor contests rewrites, has something to do with this. But there is a latent power to his 30 work that has allowed successive generations of directors, critics and actors to continually reinvent him in their own image and to find new ways (some profound, some forced, some silly) of pointing up his relevance. (284 words)

By Michiko Kakutani, *The New York Times,* March 20 1999.
Copyright © 2004 by The New York Times Co. Reprinted with permission.

3 **English major** *(AE)* a student studying English as a main subject – 7 **commissar** *here:* s.o. in a position of power who ensures that rules are followed – 19 **debunking** showing that s.o.'s good reputation is false – 23 **Academy Awards** Oscars (for outstanding films) – 29 **to contest** [-ˈ-] *here:* to oppose

Tasks

1. How does the writer rate Shakespeare's current international reputation? What arguments put forward in the documentary show that Shakespeare is a major historic personality?
2. What features of a documentary does the extract reveal, and what is their effect?
3. Do **one** of the following:
   a) How convincing are the arguments from the article and the documentary that Shakespeare is a historic figure of lasting popularity?

or:

b) Write a letter to the editor of the *New York Times* in response to the newspaper article. Describe the attitudes of advanced students of English in Germany towards Shakespeare and say what role his works should play at German schools.

City lights

Didaktisches Inhaltsverzeichnis

	Titel	Textsorte (Wortzahl ca.)	Thema	Text- und Spracharbeit	Textproduktion (schriftlich / mündlich)
	Aspects of the city SB S. 160, TB S. 171	collage	city life	associate ideas with photos	collect ideas in a mind map
◎	Out in the city SB S. 161, TB S. 171	poem (179 words)	praise of city life	describe characters • comment on the form of the poem • describe the tone	discuss poem's appeal to the senses
◎	New York SB S. 161, TB S. 171	song (297 words)	impressions of New York City	analyse associations • listening comprehension • explain images	compare singer's attitude with other songs • write a song / diary entry • find poems
	It's London… SB S. 162, TB S. 172 TB S. 183	newspaper article (783 words)	role of London in the UK	fact file: analyse text / compare it with a cartoon • explain phrases, metaphors • talk about trends	web search: present a city
Using your skills	Project: a trip to London SB S. 164, TB S. 173	activity	plan a trip to London		find out about accommodation and sights • write a letter
◎	Can you hear me… SB S. 165, TB S. 173	extract from a play (1,048 words)	mistakes made in town planning	denotative and connotative meanings • rhetorical devices	speculate about social problems in blocks of flats • analyse a statement • write an essay
Using your skills	Project: A talk… SB S. 167, TB S. 174	activity	give a talk on improving your town	–	record ideas • plan a talk • make cue cards • develop materials for a presentation
	The Language of the Streets SB S. 168, TB S. 174	essay (1,181 words)	urban vs. country experience • the African-American experience in the city	find examples of modes of presentation • analyse criticism	apply criticism in text to today • compare development of US and German cities • compare photo with the text
	The Cabbie from Calcutta SB S. 170, TB S. 175	short play (2,382 words)	encounter between an immigrant from India and an American	outline plot • discuss characterization / satire • examine stage directions • analyse humour • find features: 'short play' • correct mistakes	speculate about readership of a journal, problems immigrants have, the title of the play • write a letter
Using your skills	Projects SB S. 175, TB S. 177	activities	write a radio play • compare two short plays		act out and record the radio play • compare "The Cabbie…" with "Los Vendidos", SB pp. 22–29
	Power to the cities SB S. 176, TB S. 177	magazine article (918 words)	the development of megacities	surviving without a dictionary • analyse text / draw conclusions • explain phrases	draw up a foreign policy for a city • analyse transport problems • apply 'small-is-beautiful' concept / plan an ideal city
	Los Angeles… SB S. 178, TB S. 178	newspaper article (780 words)	controversial growth of residential areas in Los Angeles	describe s.th. • discuss arguments for / against • analyse a problem • explain phrases / find antonyms	collect ideas in a mind map: Los Angeles
	Why I live… SB S. 180, TB S. 179	essay (884 words)	living in the prairies	describe / compare / respond to an attitude • describe tone	pair work: discussion • write an essay • imagine a conversation

City lights

Einleitung

Ziel dieses Kapitels ist es eher, einen Einblick in den Themenbereich 'Cities' zu geben, als einen umfassenden Überblick zu verschaffen. Dabei wurde versucht, der Forderung nach einer Mischung von fiktionalen und nicht-fiktionalen Texten Rechnung zu tragen und die Interessenlage der S einzubeziehen. Auch eine angemessene Berücksichtigung der verschiedenen englischsprachigen Räume wurde angestrebt, z. B. New York in einem Lied mit demselben Titel auf SB S. 161 und dem Kommentar "The Language of the Streets" (SB S. 168), Los Angeles in dem Zeitungsartikel "Los Angeles sprawl bumps angry neighbour" (SB S. 178) und die britische Perspektive in dem Zeitungsartikel "It's London vs. Britain" (SB S. 162) und im Bühnenstück "Can you hear me at the back?" (SB S. 165). Maßgeblich für die Textauswahl im Kapitel war weiterhin, dass die Problemstellungen nicht nur ausschließlich heute akut sind, sondern ein länger währendes Interesse gewährleisten sollen. Die Texte haben vielfach Appellcharakter, weil sie sich durch (von L oder von S auszuwählende) weitere Texte ergänzen und in ihrer Thematik weiterverfolgen lassen.

Kernwortschatz: Kopiervorlage, TB S. 182

Während der Lektüre der Texte können die S einen Kernwortschatz zum Thema 'City life' in Form von 'word fields' zusammenstellen, z. B. town planning, housing, transportation, cultural life, usw. Ein Kernwortschatz befindet sich auf einer Kopiervorlage auf Seite 182.

Aspects of the city   SB S. 160

Looking and thinking

■ **Collect ideas in a mind map**

a) *Aspects:* cultural appeal of the city; environmental problems caused in particular by heavy traffic and pollution; hustle and bustle of crowded streets…

Hinweis: Die Fotos können entweder über OHP oder Beamer präsentiert werden oder als Vorlage im SB. Ergänzende oder kontrastierende Fotos oder andere bildliche Darstellungen, auch Cartoons sollten hinzugezogen werden. Es ist ratsam, einen detaillierten Wortschatz zur Beschreibung der Fotos einzuführen (oder von S sammeln zu lassen.). Hierzu gehört u. a.

Foto oben links: billboard, illumination, skyscrapers, neon signs
Foto oben rechts: congested traffic, exhaust fumes, smog, air pollution, cause of pollution, high-rise buildings
Foto unten: visual / acoustic impact, melee, faces are blurred, camera techniques, telephoto lens, wide-angle lens
Mögliche Suchaufgabe: Beschaffung von Bildern, die ebenfalls Aspekte des Stadtlebens darstellen, beispielsweise über Internet, Reisebüro, usw. mit Präsentation im Unterricht s. u.

Additional activity: A brochure of a city

■ Make a collage showing aspects of cities like London or New York. Arrange your photos / pictures / slogans / texts on a poster. You may also include song lyrics/acoustic material, e.g. Frank Sinatra: "New York", Ralph Mc Tell: "Streets of London", The Beatles: "Penny Lane".

b) *Beispiel einer Mind map:*

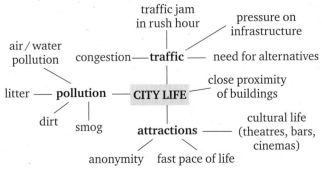

Out in the city   SB S. 161

Exploring the text

1 The characters seem to be in a street, at an open-air market and on a bus. Harry sings a greeting to Winston and his brother Leroy; Billy Brisket (brisket = usu. a particular cut of meat) is selling meat and fish; Maltese Tony is smoking and watching the amusement arcade. The impression conveyed is of a lively street scene and that everybody is busy doing s.th. different, i.e. the hustle and bustle of a market in the city.
2 *Hints:* Tripe, cows' heels, live eels suggest a busy market street with stalls, possibly in a poor area. The live eels would imply that the city is near the sea. Double-decker buses are a typical feature of English towns and of London in particular. Also the mixture of cooking smells (Indian, Greek, Chinese) imply a multi-ethnic city like London.
3 *Form:* The poem is divided into stanzas: The first four and the second last stanzas have an equal number of lines and a similar rhythm, the fifth stanza is much longer, as is the last stanza.
Poetic devices: Regular rhythm, except for ll. 22–29 and the last stanza; mixture of description, e.g. ll. 30–33, narration (= the speaker recounts an incident), e.g. ll. 9–12, 17–20, direct speech, e.g. ll. 10, 22–29 and personal address ll. 1–8; the use of rhetorical/stylistic elements such as parallelism (ll. 5, 7) and repetition to emphasize ideas (cf. box SB, S. 19).
4 *Tone:* light-hearted, personal, enthusiastic.
5 The poem appeals to several senses at the same time:
– vision: "Blood-stained rabbits … live eels" (ll. 15–16) and "neon lights" (l. 30);
– sense of hearing: "bouncy city rhythm" (l. 3), "snare drum" (l. 6), "everybody's talking" (l. 21);
– sense of smell: "take-aways" (l. 7), "the smoky breeze smells of Indian cooking Greek and Cantonese" (ll. 35–37);
– sense of touch: "mind your backs" (l. 26).

New York   SB S. 161

Eine mögliche Aufbereitung zu diesem Hörverstehenstext finden Sie auf einer Kopiervorlage auf Seite 183. Der Trackpunkt gibt den Anfang des Liedes auf der Begleit-CD (ISBN 3-12-510472-6) an.

City lights

Transkript

10 New York

In New York freedom looks like too many choices
In New York I found a friend to drown out the other voices
Voices on the cell phone
Voices from home
5 Voices of the hard sell
Voices down the stairwell
In New York, just got a place in New York.

In New York summers get hot, well into the hundreds
You can't walk around the block without a change of clothing
10 Hot as a hairdryer in your face
Hot as a handbag and a can of mace
In New York, I just got a place in New York
New York, New York.

In New York you can forget, forget how to sit still
15 Tell yourself you will stay in
But it's down to Alphaville

New York, New York, New York
New York, New York, New York

The Irish have been coming here for years
20 Feel like they own the place
They got the airport, city hall, concrete, asphalt, they even got the police
Irish, Italian, Jews and Hispanics
Religious nuts, political fanatics in the stew,
25 Living happily not like me and you
That's where I lost you … New York

New York, New York
New York, New York

In New York I lost it all to you and your vices
30 Still I'm staying on to figure out my midlife crisis
I hit an iceberg in my life
But you know I'm still afloat
You lose your balance, lose your wife
In the queue for the lifeboat

35 You got to put the women and children first
But you've got an unquenchable thirst for New York

New York, New York
New York, New York

In the stillness of the evening
40 When the sun has had its day
I heard your voice a-whispering
Come away child

New York, New York

Musik und Text: Paul Hewson / Dave Evans / Larry Mullen / Adam Clayton
© 2000 Blue Mountain Music Ltd.
Used by Permission of Music Sales Ltd.
All Rights Reserved. International Copyright Secured.

Listening for gist

1 Verse 1: voices from all sides; 2. the climate / unbearable heat; 3. restlessness; 4. multi-ethnic city / land of immigrants; 5. the singer's personal life and experiences; 6. his dilemma: to stay or go.

2 The speaker points out both the advantages and dangers of life in New York. The city seems to be stimulating on one hand and stifling on the other. At a personal level, it has, in some way, led to the breakdown of his relationship ("living happily not like me and you", l. 25 and "lose your wife", l. 33). This has, of course, had an upsetting effect on him ("lose your balance", l. 33).

Listening for detail

1 *Voices:* to drown out the other voices (–); on the cell phone (+/–); from home (+); hard sell (–); down the stairwell (+/–), possibly the voices belong to people who are arguing or being noisy.
Life: midlife crisis (–); hit an iceberg in my life (–); the lifeboat (+/–)

2 "Alphaville" (l. 16) = alpha stands for the beginning, and for leadership and excellence
– "in the stew" (l. 24) = melting pot an image which refers to immigrant society in the US
– "the iceberg" (l. 31) = trouble, hidden danger (possible allusion to the sinking of the *Titanic;* this idea is referred to again later in the line "in the queue for the lifeboat", l. 34)
– "I'm still afloat" (l. 32) = he has coped with the problems (unlike a boat which hits an iceberg)
– "an unquenchable thirst for New York" (l. 36) = he cannot get enough of it, he cannot be satisfied

3 *Positive aspects:* different nationalities / ethnic groups live there in harmony; it is a stimulating city; it is satisfying and demanding at the same time
Negative aspects: too many choices; people try to sell you things; summers are too hot; it makes you restless

4 Dies ist eine Aufgabe zur ästhetischen Perzeption. Reaktionen können kaum vorhergesagt und Wahrnehmungen der S nicht antizipiert werden. Es bleibt eine 'Risiko' Aufgabe, im Rahmen von ästhetischer Erziehung (vgl. Lehrplan).

A step further

■ **Compare attitude and other songs** –

■ **Write a song / diary entry** –

It's London vs. Britain SB S.162–164

Before you read

Methodischer Tipp

"Two countries in one land" könnte als Zusatz- oder Einführungstext (möglicherweise gesondert vom SB präsentiert) vorweg eingeführt werden.
Mögliche Arbeitsformen: arbeitsteilige oder arbeitsgleiche Arbeit in Kleingruppen mit Reflexion der Ergebnisse. Der Cartoon wird danach hinzugezogen.
Alternative: Beginn mit alleiniger Vorlage und Behandlung des Cartoons.

City lights

■ **Analyse fact file / compare with a cartoon**

a) *Impression*: Its economic output is enormous; the service industry and financial sector are more important than manufacturing; there is a lot of poverty in some areas; central London contains various ethnic communities; property is expensive; the Government spends a lot on subsidies for public transport.

b) A number of areas in London are among the poorest in Britain; there may be ethnic tensions in central London due to the presence of a number of minorities; the cost of living is high there…

c) The couple in the cartoon obviously want to buy a house in London but they have not got enough money for a property there (cf. ll. 10–13).

While you read

Die S sollen diese Aufgabe während des gemeinsamen Leseprozesses vollziehen; es bietet sich eine Unterbrechung nach jeweils 3–4 Abschnitten an. Die Ergebnisse der S sollten zu einem Summary weiterverarbeitet werden.

Exploring the text

1 a) London's house prices are twice the national average; economic output in London is £2,000 higher than in the rest of the country (ll. 16–17); the GDP per person and salary levels are significantly higher (ll. 17–18); there is a much higher density of ethnic minorities in London than in the rest of the country (ll. 31–34); more immigrants go to London than to any other area in the UK (l. 35); London has a younger population: 40% are between 20 and 44 years of age compared to 36% in the rest of the country (ll. 53–54); the city is becoming more attractive than the country and people are moving back there (ll. 46–47); the people of London seem to be more liberal (ll. 55–56).

b) M25 is the motorway dividing London from the country and it also seems to be a type of border which separates and makes London different from the rest of the country.
Empfehlung: Veranschaulichung durch Landkarte / Autokarte

2 "Level of subsidy" = amount of financial support given to poorer areas;
– "fiscal transfers" = *here*: movement of money / financial support from London to poor regions;
– "work down the phone lines" = to live and work in the country, communicate with the workplace and customers over the telephone;
– "urban chic" = the attractive side of a city;
– "an Agatha Christie Britain" = a romantic, Victorian concept of Britain. Agatha Christie (1890–1976) wrote crime novels set among the upper classes and in the country houses of England.

3 The capital's economy is doing very well and it has to provide subsidies for poorer parts of the country (ll. 21–23). The GDP generated per person in London has risen to six times the level of fifteen years ago. Pay levels are almost a third higher than in the rest of the country (ll. 18–19). Job opportunities are not based on old-fashioned manufacturing industries but on modern service industries and financial services (ll. 20–21, fact file ll. 4–6). London has a large, young working population (ll. 53–54).

4 a) "to drive…" = increase the gap, sharpen the conflict; "mushrooming…" = coffee bars are becoming more widespread, i.e. growing out of the ground like mushrooms

b) *Further metaphors*: "cash machine" (ll. 25–26) = s.th. which provides money; "world's melting pot" (l. 37) = the phrase usu. refers to America and its ethnic communities; "Manhattan-upon-Thames" (ll. 37–38) = Manhattan is the better-off area of New York; "a magnet" (l. 39) = London attracts people.

Close up: vocabulary

to fall behind – to overtake (l. 9); *to decrease by six times* – to increase sixfold (l. 18); *to plummet* – to soar (l. 20); *to go into a recession* – to boom (l. 21); *a decline* – (economic) growth (l. 38); *going downhill* – on the rise (l. 47)

A step further

■ **Carry out a web search, present a city**
Siehe folgende Webseiten:
http://www.manchester.gov.uk/
http://www.leeds.gov.uk/
http://www.london.gov.uk/

Project: A trip to London   Using your skills   SB S. 164

Das Projekt eignet sich u.U. auch als längerfristige, außerunterrichtliche Aufgabe und könnte im Rahmen von Projekttagen bearbeitet werden. Es ist insbesondere sinnvoll als langfristige Vorbereitung einer Studienfahrt nach England.
Siehe folgende Webseiten:
Unterkunft (Youth Hostel Association): www.yha.org.uk/
Informationen für einen Aufenthalt in London:
www.timeout.com/london/accom/14.html
www.hostellondon.com/cityinfo/city.php
Als Alternative bietet sich eine Reise nach New York an. Siehe Kopiervorlage im TB Seite 183.

Can you hear me at the back?   SB S.165–167

Before you read

■ **Buildings**
a) / b) *Improvements*: They could be knocked down and the architects could start again; recreational facilities e.g. lawns, flowers, a fountain would improve the area around the building; it could be painted in bright, contrasting colours; a mural would make the building more unusual / attractive…

👁 **Talking about the photo**   SB S. 165
Description: eight-storey building, each flat has a communal balcony; there is no real green area outside the house just some bushes; the building looks very sterile and anonymous with no personal touches such as flowers on the balconies…
Social problems: Residents lack in privacy which can lead to tension or conflicts with one's neighbours; children have nowhere to play safely outside the building so they have to play indoors…

👁 **Talking about the photo**   SB S. 166
E.g. The building dominates the whole area. The colour of the stone is not attractive and its forbidding facade does not

City lights

invite one to go inside. It seems to have been built to impress and probably took a lot of money and effort.

Background information
Brian Clark (b. 1932 Bournemouth, England) is a playwright and writer of television screenplays.

Exploring the text

1 a)/b) *Criticisms:* High-rise buildings are not suitable for people to live in (ll. 16–18); the city centre should not be dominated by office blocks (ll. 25–26); towns are built to look like groups of blocks (ll. 35–36); planners do not ask residents what they want ("We make a whole town *for* you, not *with* you", l. 64).

2 *Denotation:* a child's toy; small, plastic blocks which can be used to build things.
Connotation: technical or semi-technical constructions, buildings and landscapes are created using blocks.
In Philip's view Legoland symbolizes uniformity and restricted creativity. The box-like buildings were based on what planners thought was attractive at the time (cf. "plonked", l. 69).

3 Philip uses the following rhetorical devices to persuade his audience to accept his ideas and criticism.

Rhetorical devices	Effect
hyperbole: "what price Art … your body, your soul, your past, your future" (ll. 52–53)	– emphasis to show how serious the situation is – to shock his audience
enumeration/connectives: "Firstly", "Let's look at some buildings", "Which brings us to this twentieth century shrine…"	– structures the talk so that the audience knows what to expect
alliteration: "brown study of boring boxes" (l. 36)	– emphasizes a point
irony: "The town centre. I'm very proud of that" (l. 35); "this twentieth-century shrine" (l. 47)	– shows how ridiculous s.th. is
sarcasm: "planners may say … We don't!" (ll. 18–20); "You can do all sorts … need the therapy." (ll. 43–45)	– ridicules the planners – makes the audience think
repetition: "a box" (ll. 53–54); "we" (ll. 61–65)	emphasizes a point
use of personal pronouns: e.g. we, you	– attracts the audience's attention – strikes up a rapport
appeal to the audience: "Don't let them do it" (l. 74)	– wins audience's support – concludes the talk effectively

A step further

■ Analyse statements

He criticizes the planning processes of architects and town planners. He implies that it would be more appropriate to allow residents to participate in planning projects.

■ Write an essay

Methodischer Hinweis: Rollen-/Planspiel
Das Thema 'Flughafenbau' könnte ausgeweitet und die Ergebnisse der Essays zur Grundlage für ein Planspiel/Rollenspiel gemacht werden: Podiumsdiskussion (mit vorbereiteten Argumentationsschienen) zwischen einzelnen Interessenvertretern wie: Anwohner, Naturschützer, Vertreter des Flughafens, Vertreter einer Aufsicht führenden Behörde, Kommunalpolitiker usw.
Zur Vorbereitung, insbesondere was die Präsentation von Argumenten betrifft, empfiehlt sich:
– "Presenting an argument", SB S. 193;
– "Presentations", SB S. 182–183.

Project: A talk on improving your town: — Using your skills SB S. 167

The Language of the Streets SB S. 168–169

Before you read

■ Ethnic minorities

a) *Problems:* language problems which make communication difficult and lead to isolation; the formation of ghettos (with further negative consequences) creates prejudice and racial tension…

b) *Solutions:* take steps to overcome language barriers; consciously take steps to integrate minorities in the community, provide mentors who help newcomers to find their feet, instruct them in customs in the host country and help them to improve their language skills…

Methodischer Hinweis
Als Hinführung zum Text könnte eine Diskussion (eventuell auch als 'Pyramid discussion' – siehe TB S. 90 "Before you look") durchgeführt werden mit folgender Aufgabenstellung:
■ In small groups, agree on definitions of 'racism', 'nationalism', 'discrimination' and 'integration'. Compare your results with other group's and with dictionary entries for these terms. Vgl. "Panel discussion", SB S. 157.

Background information
James Baldwin (1924–1987) American writer, noted for his novels on personal and sexual identity, and his essays on the civil-rights struggle in the US. Born in Harlem into great poverty, James Baldwin lost his father at a young age. His reports on the civil rights activities of the 1960s made him a special target of the FBI.

Exploring the text

1 James Baldwin uses two examples to explain why he is fascinated with silence.
– He refers to an incident in the country when he was greeted by a woman. He thought the encounter and the woman's reaction were odd because he had "become

City lights

accustomed to the incredible silence" (ll. 11–12) of the city. This silence seems to separate the city from the country.
- He refers to New York in the snow when its citizens behave like children at a fair and talk to one another. The communication disappears again however as the snow does. (Cf. ll. 15–19.)

2 a) / b) There are clear differences: In the country, you have a sense of self and what you are doing. The ground you walk on is real. The sky is visible and it signals what kind of day you are going to have. The sun often determines the course of one's activities and duties.

In contrast, every day in the city means a separation from reality. One's vision is obstructed by skyscrapers and walls, and one must make an effort to see the sky. Both the noise and claustrophobic effect of the city separate people from reality and one another, so that they have no way back to reality.

3 The predominant mode in the second half of the text is argumentation (= mode of writing to prove a point or persuade the reader to accept a proposal), description (= the picturing in words of people, places, etc.) and narration (= the telling of incidents) are more important in the first half.
The introduction (ll. 1–3) is an argumentative outline of James Baldwin's plan for the essay.
In ll. 4–19, he mixes narration and description to illustrate differences between city and country life.
The argumentation is carried on from ll. 20–25 and is then supported by the description of a typical day spent in the country (ll. 26–34).
From ll. 35–46 we are presented with a description of the city which serves both as an illustration of life there and a more general criticism of the American city.
In ll. 47–62 James Baldwin uses narration to illustrate how the African-American population were treated.
The last section from l. 63 to the end is argumentation, in which the writer evaluates and discusses the consequences of the European immigrants' wish to be regarded as being white and how they have been trying to escape from the areas populated by African-Americans.

4 Americans have to 'rediscover' the idea that in a democracy people depend on, and cannot live without, each other (ll. 41–46).
- Americans should own up to holding African-Americans "captive" (l. 56) and to the reasons why the black population came to America in the first place ("part of the hidden thing … and confront", ll. 58–59).
- No-go areas such as the South Bronx were created when the whites left (ll. 75–77). White America is on the run from the black population (ll. 77–79).

A step further

■ Apply views and criticisms today
Mögliche Fragen / Ideen zur Gültigkeit von James Baldwin's Ausführungen:
- Role / influence of Latino population on American society as a result of the influx of Spanish-speaking immigrants from Central and South America: this population brings its language and culture with it and does not become 'white'.
- The African-American population has got increasingly positive publicity through their prominence in the worlds of television, film, sport and music.

Querverweise: Texte im SB wie "An Amazing Journey", SB S. 7 und "Mexico is memory", SB S. 10.

■ Compare with German cities
- Trends in the US are towards anonymity, ghettoisation and 'white flight'.
- Trends in Berlin: influx of Turkish people and immigrants from Eastern countries such as Poland, the Czech Republic and Croatia have led to the formation of ghettos and the growth of nationalism.
- Other German cities are experiencing a growth in the influence of Islamic cultures, cf. the building of mosques.
- The different federal German states have different attitudes towards further integration.
- Developments in the fight against terrorism may alienate some foreign nationals as terrorism is used as a reason or excuse to cut back on the number of immigrants entering the country.

■ Talking about the Harlem billboard SB S. 169

Issues: James Baldwin describes the problem of surviving in the poor areas of New York such as the Bronx and Harlem and how difficult it is to make a life there when you are black. The billboard is more precise about what makes survival difficult as it lists the problems facing young, black males in Harlem: drug addiction, criminality, unemployment and a lack of self-confidence.

The Cabbie from Calcutta SB S. 170–175

Before you read

■ Speculate about readership
E.g. well-educated; able to deal with complex texts with few photos and a high frequency of charts and graphs; business people such as managers and executives who are interested in the economy and politics…

■ Speculate about the problems of immigrants
E.g. understanding and speaking the language of the host country, getting used to the customs, habits and attitudes there, being accepted by the native population…

■ Speculate about the title
Meaning / function of the term 'cabbie' (more AE term, not so widespread in Britain) *informal form of* 'cabdriver'; it indicates a certain social class or profession. The reference to Calcutta / India implies a British context, e.g. London, where one often sees Indian nationals. The play seems to be about an immigrant who drives a taxi cab.
Mögliche Anbindung an die Erfahrungen vom jungen Inder in "England was a peculiar-tasting smoked fish", SB S. 44–47.
Hinweis: In diesem Zusammenhang kann auch auf Einflüsse durch Literatur hingewiesen werden: In den letzten Jahren ist eine Zunahme von aus dem indischen Raum stammenden Schriftstellern / Schriftstellerinnen zu verzeichnen. Es sei verwiesen auf Namen wie: Salman Rushdie, Vikram Seth, Zadie Smith u.a. Anbindungsmöglichkeit an das Kapitel "Cultural mix and clash – UK" im SB.

Exploring the text

1 The play is set in New York. Mrs Hartford, a rich, white, upper-class American takes a taxi to Wall Street. The driver is

City lights

Raggi, an immigrant from Calcutta, who is still having problems adapting to the American way of life and culture. During the journey, Mrs Hartford learns about Raggi's Indian background, his understanding of America and his aspirations. She invariably tries to question or rectify his expectations by contrasting them with her own view of America and the American way of life. In this way, Mrs Hartford is portrayed as s.o. who is suspicious of foreigners as she feels they are taking over the country. Raggi's views and opinions call her own attitude into question until she finally realizes that she loves America "in her own way". The encounter between the rich widow and the poor cabdriver finishes and she gives him a small tip of a quarter, which has a different value for each of the two characters.

2

	Raggi	**Mrs Hartford**
language (creates cultural and linguistic misunderstandings)	– confident (only pretends to be insecure) – uses a mixture of politeness ("dear lady", l. 30) and attempts to be informal ("You can call me Fred", l. 34)	– confident, becomes less secure, – condescending, haughty, bored – corrects Raggi's language mistakes – lack of understanding / interest ("Yes, yes. How nice … Another alien", ll. 36–37)
appearance	wears jeans, Bruce Springsteen T-shirt; accessories: *Wall Street Journal*	wears gown, diamonds, jewels; accessories: a lot of make-up, a wig
actions	– reads *Wall Street Journal*; – reflective, talks to himself; – contrasts Indian home with the American way of life	– gets into the cab (demanding, direct) – somewhat standoffish, conservative – shows signs of hesitation, disagrees with Raggi, is impatient

3 *Production notes* (= short, precise information about characters and length of the play). This kind of information is particularly relevant in catalogues / lists of plays which are used when people select a play for performance or study purposes.
Other production notes refer to costumes (ll. 4–6), props (l. 7) and sound effects (ll. 9–10). The notes which refer to the costumes also tell us more about the characters.
Stage directions given in the play:
- describe the characters' actions (e.g. ll. 28, 30, 51);
- convey sound effects (ll. 85–86, 125);
- indicate the character's tone of voice or s.th. about him / her (ll. 36, 82–83, 162).

4 Bei der Lösung dieser Aufgabe können die S die Box "Talking about humour", SB S. 107 zu Hilfe nehmen.
Humour is created **verbally** by means of:
- *puns* e.g. "hick" or "hack" (ll. 20, 202–205); "black and write" / "black and white" (l. 48); Raggi / Ragoo, (ll. 104–105); "buttock" / "butt" (ll. 113–117);
- *exaggeration*, e.g. "Very dangerous walking in the Indian jungle at night for a container of milk, huh?" – "No. Very dangerous milking a sleeping water buffalo" (ll. 149–151); "soon I'll be raking in the big shmucks" (l. 214).

Humour is also based on **incongruity** i.e. inappropriate language or actions which lead to misunderstandings. *Examples:*
- "Cabbie is your middle name?" (ll. 30–32) Mrs Hartford assumes that Raggi is serious;
- the two characters have different concepts of the term 'alien', cf. ll. 36–37 and l. 54 for Mrs Hartford's attitude and ll. 40–41 for Raggi's more positive opinion;
- "fast food" means 'convenience food' to Mrs Hartford (l. 77) and 's.th. which you have to move quickly to catch' to Raggi (cf. ll. 78, 80–81);
- the two characters' perceptions of "walking distance" diverge greatly, cf. ll. 134–141;
- Raggi understands "dog eat dog" more literally than Mrs Hartford in ll. 165–166.

5 All of the features mentioned in the box are applicable:
- short in length: six pages;
- one setting: a New York taxicab for the length of a taxi ride;
- no subplots: the characters are driving to Wall Street and nothing much happens outside this;
- situation is more important than plot: the meeting between the two characters from different backgrounds is more significant than the plot;
- concentration on critical situations: Mrs Hartford gets into the cab, they drive along, they almost hit s.th., they arrive and she gets out again.
- few characters: Mrs Hartford and Raggi;
- characters reduced to most important characteristics: Mrs Hartford is condescending and very confident, Raggi is subservient and talkative;
- short dialogues: the dialogues are mainly one or two lines long with only a few exceptions.

A step further

■ **Suggest corrections**

Raggi's mistakes	**Corrections**
in black and write (l. 48)	in black and white, i.e. one writes with black ink on white paper
pepper mine (l. 107)	salt mine *(fig.)* = place where one has to work hard
pain in the buttock (l. 113)	*short form* 'butt' is actually used in the idiom
hit the dock (l. 128)	hit the deck = go down onto the floor quickly
telling me about flit (l. 144)	telling me about it
hold your haunches (l. 146)	hold your horses = do not go so quickly
real boomer (l. 146)	real bummer = bad situation
a gypsy = s.o. who travels around (l. 179)	in a jiffy = very quickly
a hick = *(informal)* simple country person (l. 201)	a hack = type of taxi
two butts = *(slang)* part of the body one sits on, l. 234	two bits = 12 and a half cents

■ **Satire on aspects of American society**
Hinweis: Die S sollten die Box "Satire", SB S. 69 einbeziehen.
- the exaggerated importance of middle names (ll. 30–31) (cf. George W. Bush);

City lights

- the importance of corporations in every day life (IBM, Polaroid, ll. 50–52) as well as brand names, fast food (McDonald's, Kentucky Fried Chicken, ll. 70–76) and microwave TV dinners (l. 63);
- the tendency to sue for compensation (l. 225).

Generally speaking, Mrs Hartford represents and caricatures American ignorance of other nations, living conditions and habits abroad.

Hinweis: Diese Aspekte könnten weiter verfolgt werden mit Hilfe von Auszügen aus Veröffentlichungen wie *Downsize This* (Michael Moore, Pan: London, 2002) oder *Made in America* (Bill Bryson, Minerva: London, 1995) sowie *The World We're In* (Will Hutton, Abacus: London, 2002).

■ Letter –

Projects   Using your skills   SB S. 175

■ Radio play –

■ Two short plays

Diese Task eignet sich als Thema zur Bearbeitung innerhalb einer Facharbeit. Vgl. Hinweise zu "Term paper" im SB S. 189.

Power to the cities   SB S. 176–177

Surviving without a dictionary

Folgende Worte dürften Schwierigkeiten bereiten und sollten erklärt werden: 2 **to levy taxes** to collect – 10 **to urge** to advise strongly – 13 **allocation** to give a certain amount to s.o. – 17 **incubator** *here:* office which supports businesses when they are first established – 24 **peril** danger – 46 **monochrome** which has only one colour – 54 **replica** an exact copy – 59 **congestion** heavy, slow-moving traffic.

Hierzu gehört auch das Vokabular, das in "Close-up: vocabulary" behandelt wird.

Before you read

■ **Rank factors**

a)/b)/c) Die hier vorgeschlagene Aufgabe dient der Einstimmung in den thematischen Rahmen 'living conditions' bzw. 'town vs country'. Die S sollen zur Reflexion des persönlichen Konzepts ihres Lebensraums, ihres eigenen späteren Wohnorts angeregt werden. Dadurch werden unter Umständen bereits mögliche Problemkonstellationen ('urban problems') deutlich, die zu einem späteren Zeitpunkt mit dem Text verknüpft werden können.

Exploring the text

1 *Evidence:* Some US cities already have the power to collect their own taxes and allocate funds. These functions used to be the responsibility of the state (ll. 5–7).
- Cities are reducing national authority: Some cities have put pressure on the EU and as a result more funding has gone to city areas (ll. 12–13).
- Trade alliances between cities are becoming more significant (ll. 16–17), cf. examples of Helsinki and Barcelona.

2 *Lessons:* Growth leads to problems such as overcrowding and the appearance of slums. The challenges of growth must be met, and, if possible, planned for in advance. Possible solutions include mentoring systems: some Eastern European cities are mentored by Western cities, cf. ll. 35–36; sharing problems when cities are close to one another (ll. 36–38).

Mögliche Fragestellungen / Aufgaben

Hinweis: In diesem Kontext könnten Ideen in Verbindung mit 'twin towns' untersucht und beleuchtet werden.
■ Do you know any towns that are linked in a partnership with another European town?
Why did these two towns form a partnership?
What advantages does the partnership have for both parties?

3 Growth was controlled in Curitiba from the start. The following decisions were made:
- Curitiba would not imitate America's love of skyscrapers and bigness or turn into a town of boring, concrete highrises. Instead, the emphasis was put on an elegant combination of "nature and architecture" (l. 47).
- The city would not be dug up to build a subway system. Instead, a metro bus system was introduced to transport huge numbers of passengers (ll. 51–52).
- Old buildings would not be knocked down to make way for more cars and traffic. Instead, the focus was placed on pedestrians' needs and on the preservation of a natural environment (ll. 57–59) (cf. Task 4 "small is beautiful", which is closely linked to these ideas).
- Manufacturing would be restricted to the satellite towns (ll. 59–61) and production within the city would be limited to workshops (l. 61).

4 a) The concept implies that cities do not need gigantic solutions to problems or developments such as skyscrapers. Simple, appropriate solutions are better than complex, highly technical ones.

Background information

The "small-is-beautiful-philosophy" goes back to a concept in the 1970s, which was propagated in particular by E.F. Schumacher in his book, *Small is beautiful: Economics as if People Mattered* (Harper & Row, 1973). In it he set out his ideas about problems of increasing production and about the greatest resource, education. He expressed doubts about nuclear energy, the development of the Third World, and the organization and ownership of capital (in other words: a criticism of modern capitalism).
Indeed, many ideas about the human factor in cities and the concepts of minimalism go back to, or were taken up in, the small-is-beautiful school of thought; cf. minimalist architecture or tendencies in Feng Shui, an attitude/concept of the world in line with Asian concepts of the connection between man, nature, and the environment (partly Buddhist, partly Shinto-Japanese, or Chinese).

b) This kind of policy would focus more attention on the needs of the individual. Planners would first consider what (negative) effects developments could have on the community and those who live and work there, and then adjust their plans accordingly.

City lights

Close-up: vocabulary

province = area of responsibility; **infrastructure responsibilities** = duties related to the provision of basic facilities, such as transport, buildings, water and energy supplies; **proximity** = being near to s.th.; **to mimic** = to imitate / copy; **to gut** = to dig up

A step further

■ Draw up a foreign policy for a city

a) *Implications*: Cities could use their contacts with cities in other countries to put pressure on governments whose policies they do not agree with; richer cities could grant development aid directly to poorer cities in order to improve the infrastructure there or to reduce environmental damage…
b) *Aims*: e.g. to reduce pollution caused by traffic and industry, to achieve acceptable safety standards, to provide drinking water, to fund educational programmes…
How to achieve this: include businesses in development projects – give tax reductions if businesses cooperate; provide advisers and technical support to cities in developing countries; share technical and business know-how by means of exchange programmes…

■ Analyse transport problems

Der Problemkreis 'traffic in cities' ist ein gesonderter Rahmen. In diesem Zusammenhang können Fragestellungen wie 'tolls' und 'road tax' untersucht und erörtert werden. Hier dürfte insbesondere die vor einiger Zeit eingeführte ("congestion charge") in London von Interesse sein. Siehe Aufgabe unten.

Web search

> ■ Find information in the internet about the congestion charge in London (cf. http://observer.guardian.co.uk/).
> ■ Find out about the urban growth of cities like Atlanta, Boston, New York, Washington D.C., San Diego or San Francisco. Use the web to find out about urban problems in these cities and attempted solutions. Report your findings to your class.

■ Apply the 'small-is-beautiful' concept –

Los Angeles sprawl bumps angry neighbor
SB S. 178–179

Before you read

■ Collect ideas in a mind map

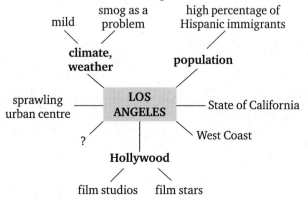

Exploring the text

1 The Newhall Ranch project is a large housing project, which involves the construction of over 20,000 houses in the next 20 years. The project is planned for an area of countryside on the outskirts of Los Angeles. As a result the project has become a bone of contention there.

2 *Pros:*
- It will provide housing for 70,000 people in the LA area (l. 6).
- It is a "sensitively planned community" (l. 11);
- It is organized by "a responsible developer" (l. 12);
- The developer has experience in realizing large projects with affordable housing (ll. 12–13).

Cons:
- Newhall Ranch embodies all of the mistakes that have been made in the development of California's urban areas over the past decades (ll. 8–9);
- The project is regarded as yet another badly planned suburb (ll. 9–10);
- The development is insufficient to solve housing problems in Los Angeles (ll. 14–16).
- The open countryside will be encroached upon (ll. 58–59).

3 The population of California is expected to grow by 18 million people over the next 25 years and that of the Los Angeles region is to increase by 6 million. Town planners have come to the conclusion that housing needs of this proportion can only be met by providing taller buildings and by building on the outskirts of cities. This type of planning, however, is difficult to realize in a region where residents set great store by the idea of living in a house with a garden and a pool (as part of the American Dream).

Close-up: vocabulary

1 last frontier = an area which is natural and untouched / unexplored by man;
- battle zone = a development about which there is much controversy;
- affordable slices of the American Dream = everybody wants to be able to buy his or her own share of the American Dream (here a house with a garden and pool);
- a Holiday Inn-like existence = allusion to the standardization of facilities in this hotel chain;
- to vaporize your open space = to diminish open areas by spreading buildings all over them.

2 *Antonyms*: well-planned – ill-considered (l. 10); to support – to block (l. 8), to oppose (l. 30); trivial – serious (l. 49); in a planned way – indiscriminately (l. 58); supporters – critics (l. 7); rejected – approved (l. 56); to deny – to acknowledge (l. 36); unreliable – responsible (l. 12)

Zusätzliche Aufgabe / Film Tipp

> ■ Write a text promoting the area where you live. Try to include some of the ideas voiced in the article and the new words / phrases you have learned in the chapter.
> ■ Im Zusammenhang mit der Thematik "Power to the cities" und in Verbindung mit dem Text "Los Angeles sprawl bumps angry neighbour" empfiehlt sich der Einsatz des Films *Falling Down* mit Michael Douglas, Regie Joel Schumacher, USA 1996 (DVD ISBN 7 321921 126482).

Why I live where I live SB S. 180–181

Before you read

- **Read a text / discuss preferences**

a) Die Aufgabe kann entweder mündlich oder schriftlich gelöst werden.
Ideen: people are less anonymous than in the city, time has no meaning in the country, once it gets dark you have to go home, it is a realistic place…
b) In Abänderung der PA könnte der Informationsaustausch über ein 'Kugellager' erfolgen: die S stehen einander in einem Innenkreis und einem Aussenkreis gegenüber; jeweils ein gegenüberstehendes Paar befragt sich (und hält die Information fest; dann bewegen sich Innenkreis und Außenkreis gegeneinander um 2 Positionen, und das neue Paar tauscht die Informationen aus.

Alternative Texteinführung

- Read the article carefully and then visualize the train of thought in the form of a flow chart or mind map.

Background information: Sandra Birdsell

Sandra Birdsell (b. 1942, Hamiota, Manitoba, Canada) novelist and short-story writer. Her upbringing on the Prairies, its people and landscape have much to do with her writing.

Exploring the text

1 *Vancouver:* It has crazy people, who are nice to meet but not all of the time (ll. 13–16); the city blocks out the mountains, distances her from nature (ll. 16–17).
Toronto: The people of Toronto are also crazy, but in an artificial way (ll. 12–13). She sometimes likes to see the skyscrapers there (ll. 56–57).
Montreal: She likes to party there (l. 57).
All three cities have features which the writer needs now and again.
2 She likes nature and the fact that the days melt into one another "even last Friday … lose track of tomorrow" (ll. 40–41); she feels close to the people who lived there before her, they are very present to her (ll. 43–47).
3 She is self-sufficient ("All I want to do is find a quiet place, huddle down in the sand and stare at the ocean", ll. 17–18) and complacent as shown by her offhand attitude towards the tourists ("this is something … of my place", ll. 48–50). She also seems to be close to the forces of nature which damage her house and make food go off (ll. 32–37). She is independent of time, and thus has a timeless existence (cf. references to "Dracula" in ll. 21–22 and "ancestors" in ll. 43–47).
In contrast, the tourists are restless (cf. ll. 52–53, "you'll see them … in search of a hill") and superficial ("this is something tourists can never discover … with their blink-and-you'll-miss-it view of my place", ll. 48–50). They also seem to be estranged from nature, which they regard as a kind of facility, cf. "tourists skimming across the valley in their boats or trolling with empty hooks" (ll. 6–7).
The writer's use of an ironic or negative lexis when referring to the tourists ("roar across the valley"; "churning up the water"; "a brave one") implies that they are arrogant and do not fit in in the countryside.
4 Definition of tone = the writer's attitude towards the subject matter and his/her audience. The tone may be characterized as personal, familiar, intimate (report of personal experiences and attitudes) and direct ("You can just say to hell with tomorrow", l. 42). At times the tone is also casual (use of abbreviated forms as in "I've contemplated", "It's", "I'll"), or even chatty, e.g. the writer asks and answers questions in ll. 7–10.
Phrases such as "true", "now", "I'll admit" and "you know the type" indicate the writer's attitude, and her attempts to persuade the reader and draw him/her into the narrative.

A step further

- **The writer's attitude**

Unusual: People do not usually feel as close to their ancestors as the writer obviously does, unless it is part of their culture, e.g. the Aborigines, cf. fact file "Aboriginal beliefs", SB p. 51. The first nations, the native population of Canada, who would have lived on the prairies, also had a strong belief in the presence of ancestors in this world.

- **Opinion about city / country life**

Zusatzaufgabe: Creative writing

- a) Write a text or design an advert promoting the area you live in. Consider the points of view discussed in "Before you read" and arguments given in the text.
- b) You could use your text as a basis for a brochure featuring your home town / area. Find interesting pictures or photos. You could look at the tasks you completed at the beginning of this chapter for ideas.

- **Write an essay –**

- **Imagine a conversation –** SB S. 181

Test: Why my plan for London will work TB S. 184

Klausur für den Grundkurs
Textformat: commentary, 559 words
Vorschlag / Klausurtyp NRW: Tasks 1–3, A2
Bezugstext des Kapitels: "It's London vs Britain" (SB S. 162).
Der Klausurtext und die entsprechende Aufbereitung finden Sie auf einer Kopiervorlage auf Seite 184.

Comprehension

1 London's growth started in 1983 and increased tremendously from 1989 onwards. This increase was caused by a high rate of natural population growth and the arrival of large numbers of visitors and incomers from abroad.
Consequences: increased demand for (affordable) accommodation, a high rate of homeless households, damage to public services and private firms as potential employees cannot find accommodation in London and do not take up employment there.

City lights

2 He deals with David Rose's views first by welcoming him and *The Observer* to the debate; he then criticizes Mr Rose for not mentioning the reasons why he, Ken Livingstone, is committed to increasing the number of affordable homes. Finally, he criticizes Mr Rose again for suggesting that population trends are actually in reverse and also implying that Ken Livingstone's own forecasts are incorrect.

3 *Language:* The syntax is relatively simple as the writer uses few complex sentences; there is a predominance of simple and compound sentences, i.e. basically paratactic structure; elements of the argumentative text type: logical arrangement; use of connectives; problem-solution sequences; use of examples and statistics; inclusion of comparisons; the writer makes mainly simple lexical choices and prefers common-core, familiar vocabulary with relatively few difficult words; the text is precise in places and includes few abstract terms; occasional colloquialisms (e.g. "rubbish").

Style: modern Standard English, rather more spoken than written (cf. length of sentences, use of connectives, non-specialist vocabulary), some degree of informality (simple lexical choices and syntax).

All features contribute to a fluent and, in places, elegant presentation of the arguments. On the whole, the text conveys the impression of a speech (cf. rhetorical devices such as enumeration of points, repetition of key words, exaggeration, e.g. "baleful inheritance", (ll. 29–30).

4 Cf. SB page 111, "Using your skills" for an example of a formal letter.

Test: Big City Glissando   TB S. 185

Klausur für den Leistungskurs / Mündliche Prüfung
Textformat: poem, 128 words
Vorschlag / Klausurtyp NRW: Tasks 1–3, A2
Bezugstexte des Kapitels: "Out in the City" (SB S. 161), "New York" (SB S. 161). Andererseits könnte als Voraussetzung die Behandlung von "Can you hear me at the back" (SB S. 165–167) bzw. "The Language of the Streets" (SB S. 168–169) zugrunde gelegt werden. Der Text ist gleichzeitig aufbereitet für eine mündliche Prüfung (siehe TB S. 185).

Comprehension
1 The speaker is obviously standing on a balcony high over Manhattan. He is surrounded by lights, music and a crowd of people, when he is approached by a slender lady dressed in white, who remarks on how she experiences that particular moment. The events seem to take place in the fall / autumn as signalled by the heat and winds. After the lady's mysterious / ambiguous comments on the view / atmosphere / situation, and her disappearance, the speaker is handed a note with an equally mysterious comment.

2 Some of the images make the characters and events seem unreal, e.g "a waist that could fit through a bracelet" is characteristic of the lady.

- "A dove bursting out of the other (eye)" indicates a desire for peace and quiet.
- "Black pitchers of tequila": possibly indicates the quiet, stifling atmosphere and turns everything into black isolation
- Manhattan traffic is a "mix of silver and yellow snakes", thus creating the impression of constant movement.
- "Winds trapped in white altitudes" signals the noise of air movements high above the streets,
- "heavy river and its evening jewels" implies the slow movement of the boats / lights on the river.
- "Lost stars" might denote the futility of unfulfilled dreams.
- A man who "directs actors who paint words on their faces": suggests that the world is a stage of the unreal / make-believe.
- The human beings are exposed to the sun, which "melts all of us as if we had wings", i.e. human beings try to fly like Icarus in an attempt to become like the gods.

All of the images seem to imply that man, despite his achievements, is still surrounded by natural forces, and the conflict between the real and the artificial is never-ending.

Analysis
3 The title fits the poem to the extent that some of the events take place on a balcony high over Manhattan with the traffic in the background ("a mix of silver and yellow snakes"). The musical reference in the title also seems to reflect the feeling of longing and the melancholy mood expressed in the poem ("sallow women", "she complains of the heat", "winds trapped in white altitudes", "up there the sun melts all of us"). The title is a mixture of familiar and unfamiliar terms. "Big City" has become a standard term, as opposed to 'small town'; it does not obviously refer to NYC (which would be "The Big Apple"). "Glissando" refers to a quick succession of notes, which may imply speed or a series of fast-moving impressions and transitoriness. This is in keeping with the last two lines of the poem.

Re-creation of text
4 Students are expected to turn their view of the poem into a report / comment / note which may be part of a diary. The entry could also be extended into a piece of creative writing, i.e. students might add / elicit / express ideas or impressions that go beyond an interpretation of the poem.

Oral tasks
1 / 2 / 3 Erwartungshorizonte: siehe suggested answers 1, 2, 3.

A bad dream   SB S. 183

Transkript
Beginning
Good morning, err, ladies and gentlemen. Erm pity, pity to … that we're stuck in here on erm such a sunny day, erm, yea, but … but I've been asked err to give this talk on effective presentations because as most of you are probably aware, I've 5
recently been on a training course and err err the boss, the boss thought it would be a good idea if I were to come here and pass on to you what I've learnt so that you will be able to make better presentations. Err, now, it shouldn't take too long and hopefully, hopefully you won't find it err too boring. 10
Right, well, I'd like to start, if I may, with a, with a brief outline of my talk … Erm, I've got it here somewhere …, hold on erm, just a second … … ah, yea … here it is, right, sorry about that. Yea, right, now, the first point I'd like to make is that you have to prepare properly. Now, as you can see, I have 15
got all of my notes prepared here so err we shouldn't have a problem with that.

City lights

So, first lesson, preparation is the key. Now, erm …
– Excuse me, can I ask a question?
Sorry, sorry, can you possibly keep questions to the end, otherwise I'm simply never gonna get … through all this, all right?

Language
Nevertheless, the attention span of a typical audience is 15 to 20 minutes. In addition, the research, which incidentally was carried out in Europe and North America and thus makes no claims for other cultures, clearly demonstrates the primacy and recency effect. Consequently, one is obliged to conclude that most of what is said in the middle of a presentation is not retained by the audience. The conclusion one draws therefore is that to ensure the audience's retention of material, one should reiterate one's main points frequently. There are, however, other variables which should be taken into account at this juncture. A major, err … a major impalement? No, err … a major impatience. No, err, it must be a major impediment, yes, sorry, yes, that's it, a major impediment to effective communication is the…

Visual aids and body language
Err, right, now erm, I've got some interesting statistics on this overhead transparency, erm, so I'll, err…
Err, right. Doesn't seem to be working. Err, always check it's plugged in. Ah, right, there we are, right, now, what these stat … err, sorry, erm, happens to the best of us, erm, oh no, hang on, erm, ah, there we are. Right, I'll just try and refocus it.
Sorry about this, I should've checked this before. Right, good, there we are. Now, these statistics are from a survey. Now, what they basically show is…
– Sorry, but I can't see it.
Sorry, what you can't read it at the back?
Erm, right, well, I'll try and make it a bit bigger … erm, err, erm, right, well, I'll, I'll read it out for you then. All right?
Erm, right, now this is a survey of the worst fears of 3000 U.S. inhabitants. Err, speaking before a group, 40%, bugs and spiders, 10%, heights…

Voice
I'd now like to turn to cross-cultural presentations. In other words, what issues should you consider when presenting to people from another country. Perhaps, the most important issue here, being British, is that of humour. When we look at other cultures, we see that humour, during a presentation, is not so universally appreciated as we may have thought. In many cultures humour, in a working environment is perceived as 'frivolous', not serious. So it may be counterproductive to use too much humour. The key is to get to know as much as possible about the other culture before your presentation and if you can't …

Ending
So, a clear message is important, especially for the end, or the 'conclusion'. Right, well, err, that's about it, I think I've just about covered everything I've learnt about, err, presentations. Erm, I'll just check my notes, hold on, oh, yea, yea, sorry, yea, there is just one thing I haven't covered, erm, the language you use. Err, try not to use formal words because formality does not help us to communicate effectively. Good, it's finished. I'm glad I remembered to say that and now I have definitely finished, a bit late, I'm sorry you all had to miss your lunch hour, still, well, err, thanks very much.

Questions
– Umm, excuse me.
Oh, sorry, yes, you had a question?
– Yes, I have two in fact. What surprises me, or one thing that surprised me in your presentation today was the amount of time you say is necessary for the preparation of a good presentation.
Uh huh.
– This seems to me to be totally unrealistic in that, for the majority of us here, we just don't have that sort of time at our disposal. And I'd also like to know something about electronic presentations.
Yea, well, I think that electronic presentations in today's marketplace are a necessity. Good, right, any more questions? No, right, well, thanks very much.
– You didn't answer my first question.
What was it again? What was it again? What was it again? What was it again? What was it again?

Viewing tasks SB p. 183

Die Aufgabe bezieht sich auf Video Sequenz 13 auf dem Begleitvideo "Skyline Media Literacy" (ISBN 3-12-510473-4) und auf der Begleit DVD (ISBN 3-12-510474-2).
Für eine Strukturierungsvorlage vgl. Kopiervorlage "A bad dream – viewing notes" im TB S. 186. – Mögliche Notizen:
a) *Beginning*
– wears an ill-fitting, unfashionable jacket (tie and jacket do not match)
– throws his bag on the floor
– tells ineffective jokes / laughs artificially
– gives long-winded explanations
– excuses himself for being there
– claims to be well prepared but is obviously disorganised
Language
– haltingly reads out a written script
– tries to impress by using high flown phrases and complex syntactic constructions
– cannot read what he has written
– turns away from his audience / does not keep eye contact with them
Visual aids and body language
– discovers that the overhead projector does not work
– does not know how to place a transparency on the OHP
– uses an illegible transparency (the print is too small, the layout is unattractive)
– turns his back to his audience
– reads from the transparency
Voice
– speaks in a monotonous voice
– yawns
– seems to be bored / disinterested / unmotivated…
Ending
– checks his notes and finds things he has forgotten
– expresses his relief to have survived the talk
– wants to leave as quickly as possible
Questions
– does not offer to take questions
– does not really listen to questions
– forgets questions
– does not answer the questions he is asked – just makes generalizations
b) Die Verbesserungsvorschläge in der rechten Spalte der Kopiervorlage ergeben sich weitestgehend aus der vorgenannten Kritik. Für detailliertere Hinweise vgl. Skills files "Presentations", SB S. 182–183.

City lights

Kernwortschatz

Housing
house prices
to be on a modest salary
affordable accommodation
soaring prices
high-rise buildings vs. detached houses
to stack flats on top of each other
council estate
condo(minium)
block of flats
ghetto
infrastructure
single family home
to provide homes
urban/suburban area

Transportation
to use/be dependent on
  public transport
to commute into (name of town)
  every day
to rely on one's own transport
traffic jams/congestion
congestion charge (e.g. in London)

Town planning
to exploit brown-field sites
to invest in/provide an infrastructure
to address urban issues
satellite town
suburbia
demolition of buildings, to demolish
loss of open spaces
to make way for development
to encroach on the countryside/
  greenbelt areas

Cultural life
recreational facilities
a lively pub scene
shopping malls
proximity to s.th. (e.g. theatres)
ethnic diversity
to promote the city

Countryside/nature
rural/rustic area
in the heart of the country
village/settlement/residential area
a thatched cottage
a beauty spot
wildflowers
grasshopper/cricket
boulder/granite
lake/river/stream
land/soil/ground
rolling hills
to retreat to the countryside
to plant a tree

Tourism/travel
to sightsee/to go on a day trip
to travel abroad
to make a journey/go on a (bus)tour
en route to somewhere
to be on the move
to travel overland
to hitchhike/to hitch (a ride)
to do … miles per hour (mph).

Socio-economic development
(economic) growth
output
Gross Domestic product (GDP)
to increase/to decrease
  – significantly
  – drastically
  – slightly
  – noticeably
to levy taxes
fiscal policy
urban issues
economic trend
to provide venture capital to start
  a business
to grow weary of s.th
to reclaim land
homogenization
a gap (between)
national average
to rank (below/above)
to provide working and living space
nimbyism (acronym for
  'not in my back yard')
green party
ancestor
tradition
change of paradigm

Town/city
town centre
city centre/inner city
capital
city-dweller
metropolis
a hip place to live
standard trappings
suburb/outskirts
urban/civic/municipal
resident
neighbourhood
downtown/uptown *(AE)*

City lights

New York SB S. 161

Vocabulary

2 **to drown out** to cover up a noise by making noise o.s. – 3 **cell phone** *(AE)* mobile phone *(BE)* – 5 **hard sell** *(informal)* sales strategy where one uses pressure to make s.o. buy – 6 **stairwell** part of a building where the stairs is located – 8 **well into the hundreds** over a hundred degrees Fahrenheit, i.e. more than 37°C – 11 **mace** chemical which burns when in contact with the skin – 16 **Alphaville** store/gallery in New York – 24 **stew** meat and vegetables cooked in a liquid; *here:* a mixture of nationalities – 29 **vice** fault in one's character – 36 **unquenchable** *here:* never-ending

Listening for gist

1 What ideas does the singer associate with New York? Try to define one idea for each verse of the song.
2 How would you describe the singer's attitude to New York? Would you say that he is happy living there, or not?

Listening for detail

1 The singer repeats the following words: voices – hot – life. Make a note of the contexts in which he uses the words and decide whether they have positive or negative connotations.
2 What images does the singer use? Try to explain them in your own words.
3 Point out the positive and negative aspects of the city as presented in the song.
4 Listen to the soundtrack. In what way does the music fit the lyrics?

A step further

1 Compare the attitude expressed in "New York" with presentations of cities in other songs, e.g. "New York, New York" (Frank Sinatra). You will find the lyrics of songs about cities in the World Wide Web.
2 Imagine the speaker's wife replies to the sentiments in the song and gives her side of the story. You may keep the format of the song or choose another format such as a diary entry.
3 Find poems about New York, e.g in the internet or poetry anthologies in your school library. Collect your findings in your personal folder and write comments about each piece.

Project: A week in New York City

Task
You have decided to go on a seven-day trip to New York with some friends. Working in small groups, prepare the trip. Collect the information in a file as your personal travel guide "A week in New York City". You could present your work in class or during an open day at school.

Discuss and decide: how many people are going on the trip – when you want to travel – how you want to fly – where you want to stay (hotel, hostel, other) – what you want to see and do in New York

Collect the following information: flight connections (including conditions and costs) – accommodation (including booking/reservation conditions) – sights and cultural attractions – special events taking place at the time of your visit

Work out: transportation costs (flight, local transport) – accommodation costs – the approximate cost of living per day (food, refreshments) – other costs (entrance fees, excursions, tours)

Find information: in guide books – at a travel agent's – at tourist information centres – on airline websites – in the web (see below)

Useful websites
www.nyctourist.com
www.thingstodo-newyork.com
www.the-hotels-new-york.com
www.virtualtourist.com
www.NYCvisit.com
www.newyork.com
www.transitio.de (key word: New York)
www.travel.yahoo.com
www.mustseenewyork.com
www.redhotchilli.co.uk (key word: New York)
www.home.nyc.gov (portal)
www.frommers.com (destinations – New York)

City lights

Test: Why my plan for London will work

In the following text London's mayor Ken Livingstone outlines the reasons why the London Plan is necessary. This document, which was put forward in 2002, plans the construction of 459,000 new homes for 700,000 people in London by 2016.

London's population is expanding at an unprecedented rate. The upward trend began in 1983, but took off in 1989. Since then London has already grown by 600,000 people – a city the size of Sheffield. London's growth is based on deep-rooted trends: a high rate of natural population growth – London accounts for a massive 72 per cent of the UK's increase in population – and large numbers of visitors and incomers from abroad.

Planning to accommodate this growth is the biggest regional issue facing the UK. It is critical not just for Londoners, but for the prosperity of the whole country. Increasingly, London is the engine of the UK economy. London can attract jobs in businesses and financial services companies that would not locate in other British cities but generate wealth and spin-off benefits across the UK. If they went elsewhere it would be to Paris, Frankfurt or New York.

Building more homes for London's growing population is one of the biggest challenges London faces. So I welcome David Rose and *The Observer* joining in a debate which is becoming increasingly important for government, London's businesses, councils and ordinary Londoners. My 'State of London' poll this year found that shortages of affordable homes came top of Londoners' concerns about the city.

Like many of London's other problems, these shortages are the legacy of past failures to invest in the capital and its infrastructure and the abolition of city government and strategic London-wide planning. They are London's baleful inheritance from Mrs Thatcher.

David Rose's article (*Focus*, last week) strangely failed to mention the reasons why the Government, the boroughs and I are so committed to increasing the supply of homes – especially affordable homes. First, there are the 54,000 London homeless households forced to live in temporary accommodation – the highest for a decade. They and their children deserve better.

Then there are the growing number of Londoners on moderate incomes unable to afford to buy or rent on the open market with the average London house price now more than £200,000. One estate agent estimates this might be as many as 800,000 households.

These shortages are damaging London's public services, which cannot recruit the nurses, teachers, and other key workers who make London a good and safe place for us all to live. And they are damaging private firms who face the same recruitment problems and cost pressures. That puts at risk London's prosperity and economic competitiveness.

No mayor of London can ignore the best expert predictions about London's likely population growth and the forecasts in my draft London Plan are deliberately conservative. Mr Rose is wrong to suggest these trends may be going into reverse. Latest Government figures support my projections – in fact they are slightly higher. Last week, Cambridge Econometrics produced independent forecasts of population growing by 860,000 to 8.37 million in 2016 compared with my forecast of a rise of 700,000 to 8.15m. [...]

Burying our heads in the sand and ignoring the facts about London's population growth would inevitably lead to repeating the mistakes of the Thatcherites. Good strategic planning to co-ordinate the huge public and private investment London needs is the social democratic solution to improving Londoners' quality of life. It is the course that the Government and I are both set on – in the national interest as well as London's. (559 words)

By Ken Livingstone, *The Observer*, August 25, 2002.
observer.guardian.co.uk

---

1 **unprecedented** unexpected – 30 **Mrs Thatcher** Margaret Thatcher, British Prime Minister from 1979 to 1990 – 55 **Cambridge Econometrics** an industrial and economic forecasting group

Tasks

1 How does Ken Livingstone explain the reasons for London's growth and its consequences?

2 How does Ken Livingstone react to David Rose's views?

3 Point out in what ways the language and style support Ken Livingstone's arguments.

4 Write a letter to the editor of *The Observer* suggesting ways in which the mayor could tackle housing problems in London.

City lights

Test: Big City Glissando

A crowded balcony and she
In white, with a waist
That could fit through a bracelet,
Whispers, "Three dreams in one eye,
5 A dove bursting out of the other…"
Black pitchers of tequila,
Quick music from a corner,
Sallow women and raincoats
Slung over the railing,
10 Manhattan below, a mix
Of silver and yellow snakes.
Later she complains of the heat,
The winds trapped in white altitudes,
Of the heavy river and its evening jewels,
15 "Lost stars," she mumbles,
And disappears…
In a far room the leaning man
Blows dust off his sleeve,
Directs actors who paint
20 Words on their faces,
Slips me a note from her,
Yellow ink, an unsure hand:
"Up there the sun melts all of us
As if we had wings…"   (125 words)

Nicholas Christopher, Repr. In: *New York Poems*,
ed. Howard Moss, New York, Avon Books 1980.

glissando rapid ascending or descending accord (on a piano or harp) – 8 **sallow** yellowish, unhealthy-looking

Tasks

1 Outline what happens in the poem as regards the situation, events and characters involved.
2 In what way do the images used support the ideas expressed in the poem?
3 Explain the title and discuss to what extent it fits the poem.
4 The speaker writes a diary entry reporting on the events in the poem and reflecting on the encounter with the woman. Write down this entry.

Oral tasks

1 Briefly explain what happens in the poem.
2 Pick out and explain some of the images used in the poem.
3 Explain the title and to what extent you think it fits the poem.

City lights

A bad dream

	The mistakes the speaker makes	The advice you would give him / he gives himself
Beginning		
Language		
Visual aids and body language		
Voice		
Ending		
Questions		

City lights

Viewing log assessment

Student's name: _____

Formale Aspekte	• cover • table of contents • structure • layout / visual appeal • legibility • deadline observed	

Inhalt	[Classroom material / results]
	
	Viewing notes:
	
	1. basic comprehension:
	  • plot
	  • characters
	  • relationships
	  • quotes
	
	2. further analytic focuses:
	  • reorganisation of observations:
	    – additional narrative
	    – thematic or cinematic features / items / chapters
	
	3. additional ideas	

Filmkritik	**Communicative performance**
	
	• structure – sequence of paragraphs:
	  – layout
	  – sense units
	
	• contents
	  – introductory paragraph
	  – range of information
	  – critical assessment
	
	Linguistic performance
	
	• correctness
	• fluency
	• style	

City lights

Discussion: moderation rules

Preparation

Content	Methods
■ Make sure you are familiar with the main aspects of the topic and the vocabulary necessary to discuss it. ■ Prepare a brief introduction to get the discussion started. You should: – greet participants – explain the topic of the discussion – make a provocative/controversial statement about the topic, or – show a poster, photo, etc. about the topic.	■ Prepare prompt cards with key words on important aspects of the topic. These are useful: – as a memory aid – as a way of structuring the discussion. ■ Have pen and paper ready to make notes on: – aspects you might need to sum up – aspects that need to be referred to again – the order of the speakers.

Leading a discussion

Structuring the discussion	Moderating the discussion
■ Make sure the topic being dealt with is clear to everyone: *We are now dealing with... – We might discuss... – The problem in question is... – Have we covered all aspects of...?* ■ Make sure there are not too many digressions from the point and/or repetitions. *Can we stay with...?* ■ Sum up main results and introduce a new aspect. *We have found out that... – We might now turn to...* ■ Make sure that the discussion does not come to an inconclusive end. You could: – sum up the main results, or – ask the speakers to make final statements.	■ Always remember: Your role is to moderate the discussion, not to express your own opinion or judge opinions expressed by others. ■ Include everyone. You may have to invite quieter participants to join in the discussion. *What is your opinion of...? – How do you feel about ...? – Would you like to share your views on...?* ■ Cut people short if necessary. Be polite. *I have a number of people on my list waiting to say something... – Would someone else like to reply to this? – If I can just stop you there, X wants to come in there.* ■ Prevent people rambling from the main point. *Could you specify what you want to say concerning...?* If necessary: *Would you please come to the point?* ■ Make sure speakers are not constantly interrupted. *I have your name on the list – You'll have your turn right away.* If necessary: *Would you please let ... finish his/her statement? – Would you please listen to...?* ■ Make sure participants do not talk at the same time. *Let us first discuss ..., and then we will turn to... – Can we hear ... first, and then you can give your opinion.* ■ Keep the discussion going: – by making a controversial statement/drawing a controversial conclusion on the basis of what has been said, *Does that mean that ...? – Would you all agree then that...?* – or, by introducing a new aspect if the discussion has come to a standstill. ■ Avoid questions which 'kill' the discussion, e.g. – rhetorical questions (*Do you really think that...?*) – suggestive questions (*You don't really believe that...? – Wouldn't you agree that...?*) – questions which only require a yes/no answer.

City lights

Discussion: feedback rules

When you have listened to a talk or presentation and are making notes about your reactions, keep the following purpose of feedback in mind.

> **Feedback…**
> - provides a fair response to someone's work
> - boosts a speaker's confidence through justified praise
> - points out areas which could be improved by giving constructive criticism

When it comes to giving constructive criticism – or taking it as is the case with the speaker(s) – try to follow these guidelines.

A. Giving feedback

1. a) If possible, start with a positive comment.
   What I especially liked was… • It was fun / a good idea to… • The most interesting aspect of your presentation was… • I really enjoyed…

   b) Try to use positive adjectives.
   useful • informative • easy to understand • systematic • well-organized • structured • varied • skilful • entertaining • thought-provoking • professional • impressive…

2. Talk about your personal impression.
   I don't understand why… • I didn't find … useful • I had the impression that…

3. Express your criticism politely.
   To be honest, I was not happy about… • At some points I found it hard to… • I am not sure if it was really necessary to…

4. Conclude with a concrete suggestion for improvement.
   Next time it might be a good idea to… • What about…? • You could easily improve your presentation if you paid more attention to…

B. Receiving feedback

1. Listen carefully and try to understand how the criticism / comments are intended.

2. Accept the feedback.
   I see what you mean… • Thank you. • That's definitely something to think about.

3. If necessary, ask questions to avoid misunderstandings.
   So your suggestion is to…? • Have I understood you correctly that…?

4. When responding to comments or criticism do not defend or justify yourself. Simply accept any praise:
   It feels good to… • I am glad you…
   … or focus on the suggestion for improvement:
   I will think about… • It may indeed be a good idea to… • That is a useful tip.

Klettbuch 510471 – *Skyline, Advanced Level: C*
© Ernst Klett Verlag GmbH, Stuttgart, 2004.

Acknowledgements

The editors wish to thank all authors, publishers and literary agencies who have given permission to use copyright material. Sources are given next to the texts. The following list acknowledges copyright holders who are not identical with the publishers quoted and also gives specifications requested by copyright holders. Every effort has been made to locate owners of copyright material, but in a few cases this has not proved possible and repeated enquiries have remained unanswered. The publishers would be glad to hear from any further copyright owners of material reproduced in this book.

P. 8: Bread and Roses (Ken Loach, 2000) © Road Sales GmbH. Auszug mit freundlicher Genehmigung; p. 25: Copyright 2002 U.S. News & World Report, L.P. Reprinted with permission; p. 26: © **1999, Newsweek. Reprinted with permission.**; p. 27: From THE TORTILLA CURTAIN by T. Coraghessan Boyle, copyright © 1995 by T. Coraghessan Boyle. Used by permission of Viking Penguin, a division of Penguin Group (USA) Inc.; p. 42: Benjamin Zephaniah, Propa Propaganda (Bloodaxe Books, 1996); p. 47: Reprinted with the permission of A. P. Watt on behalf of Caryl Phillips; pp. 63–64: USA – The sound of the Navajos in Arizona, Folge 6 (Peter Prestel) © Peter Prestel; p. 86: © GUARDIAN; p. 91: "If only we all played cricket…" (Andreas Missler-Morell, 1995). © Foreign and Commonwealth Office, London. Mit freundlicher Genehmigung des London Television Service.; p. 109: © Telegraph Group Limited, 2002; p. 112: © Telegraph Group Limited, 2003; p. 117: Robots (5B), aus: English for the Future Video (Andrew Bampfield, Andrew Littlejohn, Diana Hicks, 2001), © Cambridge University Press. Reproduced with permission; p. 121: Save the forests (2002). © Greenpeace UK/BBC/Nitrate Films UK. Mit freundlicher Genehmigung der GREENPEACE MEDIA GMBH; p. 124: Tony Blair "Erste Weltethos-Rede" (Speech to the Global Ethics Foundation), gehalten an der Universität Tübingen 30.06.2002. Mit freundlicher Genehmigung von Tony Blair und der Universität Tübingen; pp. 144, 153: The Life of William Shakespeare (Jeremy Freeston, 1995). Extracts © MXCIXV Eagle Productions Limited. All rights reserved; p. 157: Elementary Dating, aus: *Rowan Atkinson Live* (Thomas Schlamme, 1992 TV). © RTL TELEVISION GMBH. Mit freundlicher Genehmigung; p. 180: A Bad Dream (4B), aus: "Professional Presentations" (Malcolm Goodale, 1998), © Cambridge University Press. Reproduced with permission.

Picture credits

Cover photos: top left, bottom left: MEV Augsburg, bottom right, Getty Images; p. 110: Bulls Press, Frankfurt; p. 112: Atlantic Syndication, London; p. 140: Seppo Leinonen, Orivesi; p. 167: MEV, Augsburg.